THOMAS LODGE AND OTHER ELIZABETHANS

The Manor House of Rolleston

THOMAS LODGE AND OTHER ELIZABETHANS

EDITED BY

CHARLES J. SISSON

1966

OCTAGON BOOKS, INC.

New York

Reprinted 1966
by special arrangement with Harvard University Press

OCTAGON BOOKS, INC.
175 FIFTH AVENUE
NEW YORK, N.Y. 10010

LIBRARY OF CONGRESS CATALOG CARD NUMBER: 66-18029

Printed in U.S.A. by
NOBLE OFFSET PRINTERS, INC.
NEW YORK 3, N. Y.

PREFACE

IT IS well to realise that the great Dictionary of English Biography, in respect of most Elizabethans, has no more than traced the outlines of biographies yet to be written. The plain fact is that we are still only at the beginnings of our study of the Elizabethans, a fact which would be more fully realised were it not for the preponderating attention given for many generations to Shakespearian research. And of all single groups of documents that still await the searcher, the most copious, and most neglected, is the records of the great Prerogative Courts of Law, which have yielded so much information to the present writers. The intention of this book is to show to what purpose these records may be used as a source of biographical material.

Its foundations were laid in the winter of 1928–29 by two groups of students, one at Harvard and one at Radcliffe. The starting point was a series of original documents, bearing upon Elizabethan biography, which I had discovered in the Public Record Office in London. I took photostats of these documents to serve as material for a seminar, and distributed them among my students. With the help of the admirable resources of the Widener Library at Harvard, enthusiasm, let loose upon sometimes slender documentary novelty, wrought miracles of exegesis. Work was thus begun upon additions to our knowledge of the lives of a group of interesting Elizabethans, including Barnabe Barnes, Ulpian Fulwell, Gabriel Harvey, Lodowick Bryskett, John Lyly, Michael Drayton, Simon Stafford, Simon Forman, Edmond Tyllney, and Sir George Buc. Some part of this work was subsequently continued and completed in England by two pilgrims. Miss Deborah Jones took charge of the preliminary material bearing upon Bryskett and Lyly, and Mr. Mark Eccles of that upon Barnes and Buc. At the end of a year or more spent in ransacking all available sources of further information, in which the original clue was found to ramify almost beyond power of control, a series of four biographical sketches was completed, to which I have added a similar study of material towards a life of Thomas Lodge.

Such is the amazing wealth and completeness of the records of our ancient and stable civilisation, that it is possible, at an interval of three centuries and more, for Elizabethan men and their surroundings to be reconstructed and brought to life again with the detail and vividness almost of contemporary life. And with this rebirth of men and their affairs — interesting enough in itself to the historical imagination — the immortal part of those among them who are men of letters, their written work, grows more significant and more comprehensible.

The systematic study of records underlying the several parts of this book was carried on in a spirit of mutual helpfulness, and the knowledge gained was pooled, so that each writer owes much to the others. In the account of Lodge, for instance, my personal contribution to the volume, I owe more than one valuable reference to Mr. Eccles. In return, I was able to suggest to Mr. Eccles the first hint of the Border feuds lurking behind the story of Barnes. All of us stand indebted to the endless courtesy and good will of the authorities of the Public Record Office, the British Museum, Somerset House, and the London Guildhall. Considering the restricted means at their disposal, and the volume of work carried on by them on behalf of international scholarship, especially the first two, the facilities they offer are the admiration of the student

who profits by them. I owe gratitude also to the Rev.
E. S. Longhurst, M.A., Vicar of Rolleston, for help and
hospitality, and for permission to reproduce the Memorial
Tablet in Rolleston Church; to Mr. E. H. S. Longhurst,
B. A., who kindly photographed it for me, and who also
lent the block of the Rolleston Manor House; to Mr.
T. A. Matterson, of Derby, who allowed me to reproduce
the sketch of the Manor House in his possession; and to
the Librarian of the Public Libraries of West Ham, Mr.
Sydney A. Hatcher.

My personal thanks are due to my two groups of fellow-
students at Cambridge, to my collaborators, who have
borne in friendly fashion with their editor, to the Harvard
University Press for its long-suffering skill in the presentation of intractable material and its patience with delays,
finally to Harvard and Radcliffe Colleges for the grant of
fellowships to Miss Jones and Mr. Eccles for the purposes
of this volume.

CHARLES J. SISSON

UNIVERSITY COLLEGE, LONDON
        October, 1931

CONTENTS

CONTENTS

LIST OF ILLUSTRATIONS

THOMAS LODGE AND HIS FAMILY

By CHARLES J. SISSON

CONTENTS

THOMAS LODGE AND HIS FAMILY

INTRODUCTORY

IN LODGE'S excellent novel of *Rosalynde* the hero Rosader, falling on occasion into a passionate humour,
asked a rhetorical question that was curiously pertinent to
Lodge's own career: 'Should the honour of the father
shine in the actions of the son?' Rosader goes on to recall
his father's exhortations unto concord among brethren, and
after a struggle with himself decides to save Saladyne from
the lion, rejecting the base philosophy of the proverb *non
sapit qui non sibi sapit.*

Setting aside Lodge's literary activities, as his family
would fain have set them aside, the web of his life is spun
mainly of these two threads, Lodge's refusal to fall in with
the ideals of life which guided the respectable and wealthy
City clan into which he was born, and his unhappy relations with his elder brother William and to a less degree
with his younger brother Nicholas. An embarrassing mass
and variety of documents bear upon these two points
mainly, and bring us nearer to the compilation of the material necessary for a full biography of Lodge.

Edmund Gosse wrote in 1883, as preface to the Hunterian Society's edition of Lodge's works, what still remains the standard account of his life.[1] Gosse wrote with
grace, and his manner was charming and kindly towards
the great men who sat to him for their portraits. Lodge
emerges from the ordeal without a stain upon his char-

---

[1] *Thomas Lodge*, by Professor N. B. Paradise (1931), appeared after this book
had gone to press, too late for me to avail myself of it. A general monograph upon Lodge and his work, it does not, however, touch this essay at
many points.

acter, and Gosse absolves his writings of any autobiographical significance when it might appear to be unfavourable to the writer. Further information, however, gives
point to Lodge's own outburst in the preface to his translation of Josephus. 'Would God the Historiographer did
not affect flattery!' There is much that bears closely upon
certain episodes in his life in a number of his writings. This
holds true not only of his play *A Looking Glass for London
and England*, and of certain miscellaneous works, but even
of his famous novel, from which Shakespeare took the story
of *As You Like It*. In a measure Orlando himself is the
young man Thomas Lodge, as Lodge saw himself, though
hardly as Lodge was in fact. And the new information to
be presented here may help to interpret Lodge's works and
the reflections they offer of the facts of his life.

My purpose is therefore, in the first place, to state such
facts as have come to my notice concerning Lodge and his
family, and, secondly, to relate the facts of his life to his
printed works, as far as possible, and to attempt a description and estimate of his character as it appears with
what seems to me unmistakable clarity.

Gosse, lamenting the want of material, suggested that if
we had adequate information for a full and continuous
biography of Lodge, pictures of all the principal conditions
of his life, the spectacle would be a noble one, including, as
he states it, the stately civic life of London, Oxford in its
first glow of humanism and liberal thought, the dawn of
professional literature in London, the life of a soldier
against Spain and the adventures of a free-booting sailor
on the high seas, the poetry and the science of London, the
London stage, the anatomical lecture-room at Avignon,
the humdrum existence of a country practitioner in medicine, and the perilous intrigues of sympathizers with
Catholicism. These, however, are not my themes. Such

new information as bears upon these romantic matters tends to disqualify them in a measure for their place in the general nobility of the spectacle, and Lodge's share in sea-adventure, for example, sinks to a less ideal level. Oxford was, moreover, long past its first glow of humanism; scholarship was mostly thought of as a means to an end, and young scholars like Lodge and many another looked upon it as the golden key to a career. We must not idealize our Elizabethans.

It may, therefore, serve some useful purpose to insist upon certain aspects of life which are not mentioned in Gosse's admirable summary of the outstanding features of Lodge's career and of the age he lived in, those unromantic aspects which were, and still are, daily unfolded in Courts of Law. Thomas Lodge was a lawyer himself, a member of Lincoln's Inn, and so describes himself with some pride. He was not a good lawyer, but he was a great patron and benefactor of the legal profession after his fashion. For he was a frequent and most persistent litigant, and so, incidentally, himself ensured to future generations some measure of intimate knowledge of the facts of his life from boyhood to old age.

Nor was he alone in his litigiousness, for both elder generations and contemporaries of his family appear frequently in law records and add to the mass of information upon the history of that section of London society of which he was so recalcitrant a member. It is, in general, important for the full understanding of Lodge's career and character to have some knowledge of his family circle, which broadens out, in the light of these documents, into a numerous and homogeneous group of London tradesmen and merchants of high distinction, inter-allied by marriage, and with the common link of membership of the great Grocers' Company.

Thomas Lodge was, as is well known, the second son of Sir Thomas Lodge, a notable Grocer, and Lady Anne Lodge. The date of his birth can now be fixed with the help of an affidavit cited in Star Chamber and a deposition in the Court of Requests. In the former [1] he gives his age as thirty-six on 23 April 1594, in the latter [2] as forty-six on 8 May 1604. In a third piece of evidence, a deposition in Star Chamber,[3] his age is not given. It is clear that Lodge was born between 9 May 1557 and 23 April 1558. During the first half of this period the town house of the Lodges was situated in St. Michael's and during the second in St. Peter's, Cornhill. There is no record of his birth in the Register of either of these parishes, and we may take it that he was born at his father's country house at West Ham, of which we hear a great deal in a series of lawsuits.

1 *Star Chamber Proceedings* 5, L 44/4.
2 *Requests* 11, Bundle 436.
3 *Star Ch. Pro.* 5, L 6/3.

I. SIR THOMAS LODGE

THE full story of the life of Sir Thomas Lodge would, I think, prove to be extraordinarily interesting, and the study of Lodge's family may well be opened with some chapters from the career and the activities of this Elizabethan Lord Mayor of London. The business affairs of a great Elizabethan Grocer were by no means confined to shopkeeping or to dealing in any one kind of commodity. There was no limit to the variety of financial adventures open to an enterprising speculator like Sir Thomas, one of the creators and distributors of the money that made possible the vast developments of English trade in the sixteenth century. Of three depositions in the Court of Chancery, one gives us his age as fifty-two on 11 October 1562,[1] the second as fifty-seven on 23 January 1565,[2] and the third as sixty on 16 March 1572,[3] data which would fix his birth at some time between 24 January 1507 and 16 March 1512. The variations are unusually wide, and we are perhaps justified in preferring the estimate of Lodge's earliest deposition, made before his troubles came upon him, when his memory was perhaps more accurate. It is also midway between the two other estimates. We may, therefore, accept the dates 12 October 1509 to 11 October 1510 as giving the probable margin.

I know nothing for certain of Lodge's parentage or origin. An account of the family is given with circumstantial detail in the 1623 *Visitation of Shropshire*.[4] Sir Thomas is there stated to be the second son of William Littleton, alias

[1] C 24/55, Beame *v*. Buckland.
[2] C 24/72, Chomley *v*. Constable.
[3] C 24/103, Grocers *v*. Wanton.
[4] Harl. Soc., *Visitation of Shropshire, 1623*, II, 284 (from MS. Harl. 1396, f. 222).

Lodge, of Le Lodge in Cresset, Shropshire, and the grandson of Sir William Littleton, of Frankley, Worcestershire.
Six brothers and sisters are named, including two Edwards (who both married), Anthonicus, Jocosa, Elizabeth
and Anne. The family is elsewhere derived[1] from Odard de
Logis, Baron of Wigton in Cumberland, which is obviously
inconsistent with the derivation given of the name of
Lodge, replacing that of Littleton, 'ratione habitatione in
le Lodge' (sic). Richard Lodge, of whom we shall hear
later, is not named. No mention is made of the first marriage of Sir Thomas to the sister of Stephen Vaughan. But
a second marriage is recorded, after that with Anne, described as daughter of Sir William Laxton. Lodge appears
as marrying again, to Margaret Parker of Wrottisley, and
having two daughters, whose marriages are recorded. But
Lady Anne Lodge died in 1579, when Sir Thomas was
about seventy years of age. And no mention is made in his
will of Margaret or her daughters. The probability is, as
we shall see, that this marriage was Lodge's second marriage, but preceded his third and last marriage, to Anne.
We may reasonably doubt the authority of the *Visitation*
in this detail, and indeed in all matters relating to Sir
Thomas. The pedigree seems to have been furnished by
John Kenrick, an alliance by marriage of the Lodges, and
no coat of arms is tricked in the manuscript, contrary to
its normal practice.

What I learn of the Littletons of Frankley, who held the
Manor of Cresset or Cressage, is equally disconcerting.
The *Inquisition Post Mortem* upon Sir William Littleton,[2]
who died in 1508, informs us that he had bequeathed the
Manor of Cressage and other lands in trust to Richard,
Thomas and Edward Littleton and others for his son John

1 *Gentleman's Magazine*, 1834, II, 157.
2 C 142/78/140.

until he came of age. John was then fifteen years of age. It is impossible to fit a Thomas Littleton or Lodge, born between 1508 and 1511, when Sir William's only son was between fifteen and seventeen, into these facts. The Thomas Littleton mentioned here is obviously of age in 1508.

A *Visitation of Worcestershire* of 1569 [1] confirms the evidence of the Inquisition. A certain Thomas Westcott married Elizabeth, daughter of Thomas Littleton. Their son Thomas, it was agreed, was to have the honour of the Littleton name, and was known as Thomas Westcott alias Littleton. He is known in legal history as the author of *Littleton's Tenures*, and he married Joan, daughter of Sir John Burley.[2] Their son, Sir William Littleton of Frankley, was hardly likely to add a further alias of Lodge, without any such honorific significance as that which led his father to accept the name of Littleton for himself and his heirs. Once more, no William Littleton of the second generation appears. If Sir Thomas was a scion of the Littleton family, it could surely only have been with a bar sinister.

Strype, in his account of the Lord Mayors of London, describes Lodge simply as 'son to William Lodge of Cresset in Shropshire,' with a cut of his arms.[3] Arms were granted to Lodge on 15 August 1556.[4] They may be found tricked in colours in MS. Harl. 1349,[5] a collection of citizen arms, showing azure, a lion rampant argent, crusilly gules, within a bordure flory de lis of the second. It is evident that

1 MSS. Harl., 5841, f. 17^b, 5814, f. 71^b.
2 The *Visitation of Shropshire* records Joan Burleton as wife of William Littleton alias Lodge and mother of Sir Thomas, a further indication of confusion. The history of the Littletons of Frankley and Cressage may be further studied in the following *P.R.O.* documents: C 142/22/36, 48, 78; C 1/1022/55–56; C 1/1025/45–46, among others. Sir William held nearly 4,000 acres.
3 Strype's *Stow, Survey of London*, from Munday's 1633 edition of the *Survey*.
4 Add. MS. 16940, f. 208.
5 F. 30^b. Cf. MS. Harl. 1396.

Lodge himself did not assert any claim to use the Littleton arms, which bear three scallops, with a crest of a Moor's head in profile, and mermen as supporters. There is no reason to doubt Strype's account, as far as it goes. Lodge was probably a Shropshire man, though of humbler origin, from Cressage, a few miles north of Much Wenlock on the Shrewsbury road. Late in life we find him purchasing land there to leave to his younger sons. And he had several transactions in property in Staffordshire, the neighbouring county, as we shall see. He married his son William to a Blagrave, of a Shropshire family. But I can put no faith whatever in the suggestion that he was a legitimate member of the great Littleton family. A thinner story can rarely have been told, even in the annals of heraldry.

City records, the records of the Grocers' Company, State Papers, the proceedings of the Courts of Equity, and parish registers, all conspire to furnish embarrassingly full details of the life of Sir Thomas Lodge, to compensate for the obscurity of his origin.

On 4 March 1528 he was apprenticed to William Pratt,[1] a year after that great Grocer Richard Grafton was apprenticed to John Blag, and a year after William Lane took his freedom,[2] whose widow was to be Lodge's second wife and the mother of the poet. By 1534 a Richard Lodge had taken his freedom, along with Grafton and Lane, and Nicholas Loddington, one day to be Lodge's brother-in-law, was apprenticed.[3] In 1535, four months after the martyrdom of his father-in-law Sir Thomas More, Giles Heron, son of Sir John Heron, was received a freeman of the Company, on 15 November.[4] And at some time between 1537 and 1539, years for which the records are miss-

---

1 *Quires of Wardens' Accounts*, Grocers' Hall, Vol. 403, f. 281[b].
2 *Ibid.*, ff. 238[b], 236[a].   3 *Ibid.*, Vol. 404, f. 14[a].
4 *Ibid.*, f. 39[b].

ing, Lodge had taken his freedom, paying 'Brotherhood Money' in 1539.[1] On 6 March 1541 his first apprentice, Richard Harris, was bound and sworn.[2] Of Lodge's many apprentices, of whom he bound as many as five at a time, one may well have been his kinsman Richard's son, and possibly cousin to the poet, Anthony Lodge.[3]

It is evident that Lodge was prospering in his business, and that he was resident part of the time in the Low Countries, where he had important interests. From 1544 onwards his name occurs frequently in State Papers, beginning with the record of loans of £200 to Henry VIII and of £80 to Otwell Johnson.[4]

He was then married, to his first wife, the sister of Stephen Vaughan, and was living in Cornhill, opposite St. Michael's Church.[5] Lodge was evidently closely associated with this well-known merchant, reformer, and government agent, who had served Cromwell and had been employed by Wolsey and by Henry VIII. As a member of the Company of Merchant Adventurers Vaughan's business took him frequently to Antwerp, where in 1530 he negotiated a loan for the King from the Fuggers. In 1531 he was instructed to obtain a retractation from Tyndale, and in 1536 sought to save him from his fate. In 1532 he was busy there seeking to capture the famous Franciscan, William Peto, a defender of Queen Katharine, then in flight after an over-bold sermon to King Henry at Greenwich. Both as Merchant Adventurer and as diplomatic agent Vaughan had a busy and successful career, with no small rewards, and died in 1549 in London, Under Treasurer of the Mint, and Member of Parliament for Lancaster.

1 *Ibid.*, f. 94[a].
2 *Ibid.*, f. 124[b].
3 *Ibid.*, f. 274[a], 27 July, 1547.
4 *Letters and Papers, Henry VIII*, xix, i, 891; ii, 140.
5 *Ibid.*, xix, ii, 765.

Lodge's activities during Vaughan's life are somewhat similar to those of his brother-in-law. Along with Vaughan and all resident English merchants, Lodge was arrested on the Emperor's orders in retaliation for the seizure of his ships by the English, and cast into prison on 6 January 1545.[1] After this imprisonment, the first of several in a chequered career, we find him engaged upon espionage, tracking down a certain suspected person, John Yong, an envoy of the French King, from Antwerp to London by way of Calais, and carrying letters to the Council about Yong. Lodge ended his task at Calais, where he presented his letters to Lord Cobham and where Yong was captured and examined.[2] In 1553 Lodge was one of a group of prominent London merchants who had raised a huge loan of £15,000 for Queen Mary and who had to submit to losing heavily on exchange, being repaid at Antwerp in Flemish money.[3] In 1558 he was thanked by Queen Mary for becoming surety for the ransom of Sir Henry Palmer, taken prisoner in France.[4] These transactions are evidence of his civic and financial standing and of his value to the government of the moment.

The records of the parish of St. Michael's in Cornhill give the information that one would have expected to find there. Lodge was a predestined Churchwarden, and attained this dignity in November 1547 at latest.[5] He also audited the Church accounts in later years. Changes of State religion did not affect his services to his Church, and his transactions illustrate the common attitude of the average Laodicean Tudor Englishman, who took the winds as

1 *Ibid.*, xx, i, *passim.*
2 *Ibid.*, xx, i, 250, 267.
3 *S. P. Dom. Mary*, p. 30.
4 *Ibid.*, xii (54).
5 *Accounts of the Churchwardens of St. Michael's Cornhill*, ed. W. H. Overall, *passim.*

they blew, where possible to his private advantage. Under Henry, Edward and Mary alike, Lodge paid his rent of £4.6.8 for a Church house in the Churchyard. Under Edward he bought, at a bargain price, first candlesticks and brass, over four hundredweight in quantity, for which he paid £4.6.0 in 1548, then copes and vestments for £15.14.0 in 1550, and finally the Church plate, 660 ounces for £222.17.10, on 28 February 1551, all of which, no doubt, he resold at a profit. Under Mary he was equally zealous in negotiating on behalf of the Church the repairing of its organ for the service of the Mass. A Mr. Pliable in religion if in nothing else, he was likely to advance his estate in such troublous times.

City records bear witness also to his growing fortunes. In 1548 he was elected a Warden of the Grocers' Company, under the Mastership of Sir William Laxton.[1] In the same year his first wife died, for we then find him paying five shillings for a gravestone and six shillings and eightpence for a grave in the Church. And the burial of 'Mrs Mawdleyn Lodge' is recorded on 25 July 1548 in the register of St. Michael's, Cornhill. A further payment of six and eightpence in 1552 'for breaking ground for his wife's grave' seems to indicate a second marriage and a second bereavement, both somewhat precipitate.[2] This probability is increased by the records in the same parish register of the christening of Sara and of Susan Lodge on 20 December 1549 and 11 October 1551 respectively, and of the burial of Mrs Margaret Lodge on 26 April 1552. The *Visitation of Shropshire*, it will be remembered, records Lodge's marriage with Margaret Parker and the birth of two daughters, one unnamed, the other Sara, who married Edward White the printer. White entered for publication

---

1 *Quires of Wardens' Accounts*, Vol. 404, f. 318^a.
2 *Accounts of the Churchwardens*, pp. 65, 103.

the poet's first work in 1579, and the connection with the family is further indicated by a legacy of £10 left to Sara, 'now the wife of Edward White,' by Sir Thomas in 1583. On 24 October 1553 he was elected to represent Cheap Ward on the Bench of Aldermen,[1] having recently married again, as we shall see, this time the wealthy young widow of a brother Grocer, William Lane, and daughter of Lady Joan Laxton, and was able to make a settlement of two Shropshire Manors, Edgemonde and Newport, upon the family to come.[2] And in September of that year his first son was born, named William after Sir William Laxton. A year later Lodge was Master of his Company,[3] and his election was celebrated at a two days' feast worthy of the Grocers. It involved the attendance of 'Currans the mynstrell . . . for both daies.' Thirty gallons of hippocras, nine gallons of beer and ale, two and a half hogsheads of wine, a barrel of sturgeon, a total of over four hundred capons, geese and quails, ' 120 Long Marybones,' three sirloins and a rib of beef, a sheep, half a calf, and sixteen bucks, of which one was sent by Queen Mary to grace the occasion, furnished the board. No wonder that three women were engaged for three days each to wash dishes. Never could three shillings, the total cost of their labours, have been more fully earned.

Alderman Lodge was well on the way to the height of his ambition. A merchant of wealth and consideration, Master of his Company, richly and happily married, with a son and heir in his house beside St. Michael's in Cornhill, he had cause for pride. I find something of an omen and a warning in a wager that he laid about this time with a shrewd fellow-Grocer, George Stoddard, who was his fac-

1 *Repertory* 13, f. 87^b.
2 *Cal. Pat. Rolls, Ed. VI*, p. 271.
3 *Quires of Wardens' Accounts*, Vol. 404, f. 454^a.

tor for seven years in his foreign trade in Flanders, Russia and Ireland, and whose *Diary* records a steadily mounting bill of expenses against Lodge. Thus Stoddard enters the bet: 'Item. . . . my Master owes me for a wayger layde upon a boye or a girle, the which I have wone, so that he owyth me £1 10ˢ 3ᵈ.'¹ I cannot doubt that this shows us Lodge exulting in his good fortune, declaring his confidence in the future, and in particular in a second son and heir to follow William. But his next-born child was a daughter, Joan, and he lost his bet. The odds in all probability were three to one in angels, long odds indeed for what was at best an even chance. But he would have it so, and would back his luck. It seems to me to have significance. A certain reckless masterfulness may well be thought to emerge here and to be borne out in events to come. The odd threepence was possibly his factor's charge for interest at the rate of ten per cent (the normal rate) on thirty shillings for a month. And the shrewd, cautious men in the long run overbore Lodge, though he outlived Stoddard and many another. Stoddard's bill rose to £1198 in the end, and Lodge was reduced to promising to pay hereafter if God spared him life. For the present, however, the tide of fortune still flowed strongly.

We cannot doubt his enterprise as a speculative trader, ready to share in any new venture whence wealth might accrue, a pioneer in world-trade. In 1555 he is to be found on the list of adventurers in the trade to Russia, and an Assistant Governor of the Muscovy Company, though not, as it has been suggested, taking part himself in the voyaging.² His son Thomas did not, as I have seen it argued from this reference in Hakluyt, inherit any love of the sea from his father. Five years later he and his relative Peter

1 Hubert Hall, *Society in the Elizabethan Age*, p. 50.
2 Hakluyt, *Voyages*, II, 307.

Osborne were projecting a scheme for refining base money for the Mint,[1] a scheme possibly suggested by his association with its late Under Treasurer, his brother-in-law Vaughan.[2] In 1561 he and two other London merchants were financing the voyage of a certain Portuguese to the West Coast of Africa,[3] a voyage that was in all probability connected with the lucrative Slave Trade to America. And a year later he and others financed another voyage to Africa and America,[4] Hawkins' first slaving voyage, in which Hawkins sold very profitably three hundred negroes for the benefit of a Lord Mayor of London and his associates. And in the same year, 1562, Lodge was able to lend £560, no small sum, to the Earl of Westmorland,[5] whom he 'knew very well,' along with other Northern gentry.

There were darker moments to be supported, however. In 1556 the desired second son was born, and baptised by his father's name on 23 May. But less than a fortnight after, on 4 June, the infant Thomas Lodge was buried, the first of many blows to his father's hopes in his children.[6] On 9 August Lodge was the chief mourner at the burial of Sir William Laxton (who had died on 27 July) in great pomp, with all the aldermen in violet. And on the morrow three Masses were sung, and a sermon preached by Doctor Harpsfield, followed by a dinner, as Machyn tells us in his *Diary*:[7] 'for ther was a grett dener as I have sene at any berehyng, for ther dynyd mony worshepfull men and women.'

In August 1557 Lodge moved from St. Michael's into

---

1 *S. P. Dom. Eliz.*, xiv, 55.
2 In 1546 I find him buying lead in Yorkshire, probably in partnership with Vaughan on behalf of the Mint (C 24/27, 28).
3 *Ibid.*, xix, 31.   4 *Ibid.*, xxvi, 43–45.   5 C 24/72.
6 *Parish Registers of St. Michael's, Cornhill* (Harl. Soc. Publ.), pp. 78, 181.
7 *Machyn's Diary* (Camden Society), pp. 111–112.

the neighbouring parish of St. Peter's, into a great house there of which Laxton had been landlord. The lease was granted to Lodge by the Grocers' Company for sixty years, in recompense for money he had spent on repairing it.[1] He had also a country residence at Plaistow, in the parish of West Ham, which came to him from the Laxtons through his wife Anne, daughter of Lady Laxton, probably from the time of his marriage with her. There, I think, was born his poet-son, the second Thomas, between May 1557 and April 1558. And with the coming of Queen Elizabeth Lodge rose still higher in the civic world. On 25 July 1559, at the Mercers' supper, with the Lord Mayor and Lords of the Council present, 'ther was chossen the shreyff for the quen master Logee, altherman and groser, for the yere to cume and nowe.'[2] The Grocers, conscious of the honour, presented him with £30 on 16 August to trim the house of the new Sheriff, to make it fit for his dignity.[3] And Machyn describes his journey in a barge to be sworn at Westminster Palace, with a dinner with the Companies to follow.[4] A third son, Nicholas, named after Mistress Anne's brother Loddington, was born.

Finally, in 1562, Lodge reached the summit of his ambition, and became Lord Mayor of London. Once more his grateful brother-Grocers trimmed and beautified his house.[5] And on 29 October the new Mayor went to Westminster by water to take the oath to the Queen. Machyn describes at some length the festival.[6] There were barges and a foist decked with banners, with drums and trumpets. On the return to the City he was met with a goodly pageant and music near St. Paul's. Dinner in the Guild-

---

1 *Calendar of Minutes of Court of Assistants*, pp. 13, 15.
2 *Machyn's Diary*, p. 205.   3 *Calendar of Minutes*, p. 34.
4 *Diary*, p. 213.
5 *Calendar of Minutes*, p. 71. Grant of £50 on 1 October.
6 *Diary*, p. 294.

hall followed, and a procession in state thereafter to St.
Paul's. The cup of Lodge's reasonable pride was filled to
the brim. On 3 November he presided for the first time as
Lord Mayor over a full Court of Common Council at the
Guildhall, attended by twenty aldermen.[1] And when a
fourth son, Benedict, was born to him, to the christening of
the Lord Mayor's son, in the afternoon of 18 April 1563,
came a great Lord of the Council, the Earl of Pembroke,
to be his godfather.[2] We may perhaps take it as a symbol
of Lodge's sense of power that he defied tradition in civic
fashions, for

syr Thomas lodge, beynge Mayr of london ware a beard, & was yᵉ fyrst
that (beynge Mayr of london) evar ware eny. yᵉ whiche was thowght
to mayny people very straynge to leve yᵉ cumly aunsyent custom of
shavynge theyr beards, nevartheles he ware yᵉ comly auncient bonet wᵗ
iiij cornars as all othar his predysesowrs had done before hym.[3]

It is most regrettable that no portrait of Sir Thomas has
come down to us.

At the very moment of Lodge's triumph, however, the
imposing edifice of his wealth and dignity was crumbling
away under him. Twenty years and more of life still remained to him. But from various sources we can put together a lamentable story of the decay of a great citizen,
the burden of these twenty years. Before he had even
taken off his chain of office, worn during a year of heavy
visitation by the plague, his credit broke, and we shall see
that by the end of 1563 he was for the second time in
prison, this time in the Fleet, and for debt. Twice does
Stow refer to the shock of the Lord Mayor's downfall:

1 *Repertory* 15, f. 138ᵃ.   2 *Machyn's Diary*, p. 305.
3 Stow, *Historical Memoranda*, in Lambeth MS. 306, f. 46ᵇ, printed inexactly
in *Three Fifteenth Century Chronicles* (Camden Society, 1880). His successor,
Sir John White, went further, wore a long beard, and took to an unseemly
and insignificant round cap.

this s^r T. lodge brake and professe to be banqwerooute in his maioralitie to the grete slandar of ye citie.

That same ser Thomas lodge (to ye great slaundar of ye wholl city) in ye ende of his maioralitie professyd to be banqerowpte.[1]

It is clear that the City was scandalized, felt Lodge's failure as a slur upon London, and had even its suspicions of the Lord Mayor's rectitude in the matter. Here the proceedings of the great Courts of Equity, preserved in the Record Office, furnish abundant material relating to Lodge's financial transactions. The well-known story[2] of his quarrel with the Queen's purveyor, Edward Skeggs, who seized capons intended for the Lord Mayor's table and was arrested by Lodge, whereupon great officers of state bestirred themselves on both sides, illustrates Lodge's masterful ways, but has no bearing upon the disasters that overtook him.

LODGE v. BANKS (1)

A surprising piece of evidence is given in a suit in the Court of Requests[3] by a reliable witness, Lady Jane Mewtis, the widow of Sir Peter Mewtis, neighbours of Lodge at West Ham, where he had a country residence, to the effect that Sir Thomas was a prisoner in the Fleet not long after the death of Sir Peter. Sir Peter died on 8 September 1562,[4] and the indications suggest at first sight that the imprisonment actually belongs to the period of Lodge's Mayoralty. The information available comes from this suit in Requests, brought by Sir Thomas against Thomas Banks in 1576, and from a letter, preserved among the Burghley Papers, from the Marquis of Winchester to Burghley and dated by him on 3 December 1563.[5]

---

1 *Ibid.*, ff. 46^b, 70^a.   2 Strype's *Stow*, Bk. I, p. 289.
3 *Requests*, II, 297.   4 C 142, 133/140.
5 B.M. MS. Lansdowne 6, No. 42. I owe this reference to Miss Margaret Dowling. The document is reproduced in full in Appendix I.

In the Requests suit Lodge's case is that in June 1562 Sir Peter Mewtis, Lord of the Manor of Bretts in West Ham, leased some property there to Thomas Banks, a London Skinner, for twenty-one years. At some time early in 1563 or late in 1562, Lodge agreed with Banks for £200 to have the lease of part of the property, a house with eight acres of land, transferred to him, by surrender and re-grant. Possession was given and Lodge held the property and took rents for half a year before Banks made a claim. A certain John Wyatt, it seems, had been Lodge's agent, and Banks denied the validity of the transaction. He, therefore, resumed possession. Lodge, seeking relief in Requests, maintained that Banks had defrauded him. Lady Mewtis, aged sixty, giving evidence on 2 February 1576, stated that after the death of her husband she met Banks and said to him:

Mr Bankes you shold do well to goe now vnto Mr Lodge for that he lieth prysoner in the ffleet and take some order with hym for the money which is Betwene you.

Banks replied, 'Madame I will,' but in fact did not go to Lodge to settle the matter. I cannot offer any explanation of the long interval between the claim and the consequent litigation, unless it was due to the involved condition of Lodge's financial situation at the time. Wyatt, an essential witness for Lodge, had died in the meantime. But it seems clear that Lodge was in the Fleet, in a debtor's prison, in the autumn of 1563, towards the end of his term of office as Lord Mayor, or immediately after. The Privy Council and the Queen herself took the matter seriously, as we may see from the long letter from Winchester, Lord High Treasurer, to the Earl of Pembroke, Lord Robert Dudley and Burghley, the Principal Secretary. It appears from this that Sir Thomas himself was allowed to approach

the Lords of the Council at Windsor and to bring a letter
from them to Winchester at Westminster, concerning his
situation. Winchester replied, in what is evidently a holo-
graph letter, on 3 December. He describes Lodge as 'Sir
Thõms lodge, last yere maior of the Cite of london.' The
year of office, it will be remembered, ends on 14 November.
Lodge, he writes, has been before the Lords and has put his
case before them, and they, considering

his good service at all tymes . . . have moved the quenes matie therof.
And thervpon induced her grace to haue gret pitty of the case. And that
her hyhnes by yor mediacõn is verry well inclyned to stay hym in his
Credit Wch shalbe a worthy dede ffor that he is a wise man and a gret
Occupier as any is in the Citie & shall wth the quenes favor and helpe,
shortly recouer this lakke.

Winchester goes on to discuss three projects put forward
by the Council to give Sir Thomas breathing space. The
main point is that he is to have an advance of six thousand
pounds in ready money, which is apparently his urgent
need. We may well take the size of this sum, and the terms
of this letter, as indications of the high respect in which
Lodge was held by the Queen and her Council, of the vast
extent of Lodge's trade as exporter and importer and general venturer in commercial affairs, and of the important
position he held in the economic life of the country. But it
is sad to think that when the younger Thomas Lodge in
turn got into financial difficulties of a lower order and
fetched up in prison, as he did, he might well have been informed of his father's misadventure when he himself was a
child of five or six years of age, and have had his answer
ready if his father had been alive to reproach him with his
prodigality.

I do not think, however, that Sir Thomas Lodge's imprisonment can be referred to the period of his office as
Lord Mayor. It is true that Lady Mewtis dates the inci-

dent by her husband's death in September 1562, and that
the Lord Treasurer's letter bears a memorandum of one of
Burghley's clerks which, while repeating the date of the
letter, yet refers to Lodge as Mayor of London: '3 10bris.
1563. L.Tres^r. Sr Thomas Lodge maior of London, wanting a Supply of money to keep vp his credit, obtained
favour from sevral Lords, being a wise man & great
trader.' But it was easy for the clerk to continue Lodge's
title for a month after he had ceased to hold it. And Lady
Mewtis might well date events from such a landmark as
the death of Sir Peter for more than a year, especially at a
distance of fourteen years. The probability is that Lodge's
embarrassments came to a head during his mayoralty, and
that immediately he ceased to hold office as Mayor, his im-
munity came to an end and his creditors took legal action,
in the latter part of the month of November 1563. The
visit of Sir Thomas to the Fleet prison was doubtless a
temporary arrangement and intended to ensure a mora-
torium from claims that could not be met immediately. It
was conceivably even a collusive arrangement. Nor was
such imprisonment inconsistent with a considerable degree
of comfort and liberty of movement for a privileged in-
mate.

There can be little doubt that Sir Thomas was in a situation familiar in all ages to the bold and venturesome
financier. He was over-invested, and, like Antonio in *The
Merchant of Venice*, he needed ready money pending the
delayed arrival of some of his financial ships. It is evident
that he went on speculating up to the last moment, and up
to the hilt, in landed property in England as well as in
trading ventures to Muscovy, Africa and the Netherlands.
A Chancery suit of 1563 and a Star Chamber suit of 1570
throw some light upon this aspect of his dealings and may
help to explain in part his need of ready money in 1563,

when we bear in mind also the inevitable cost in mayoral expenditure of the honour of this highest of civic offices. In this respect, we may observe, Lodge had a family tradition to keep up, for he followed to the Mansion House, at a distance of twenty years, his father-in-law Sir William Laxton. And Sir William had been a fellow-Grocer of great wealth.

LODGE *v.* UNWIN

Both these suits concern land in Staffordshire leased from Henry Touchet, Lord Audley. In the Chancery suit [1] we find Lodge, then Lord Mayor, at odds with Mrs. Ursula Unwin, widow of Edward Unwin. And Lodge appears in the unexpected capacity of an ironmaster. In 1558, his Bill avers, George Touchet, Lord Audley, leased for twelve years the Manor of Tunstall with other lands to Robert Luce, a London leatherseller, including all the 'mynes, delphes, and quarries of stone,' and the right to mine the 'yron stone' in them. Luce died bankrupt, in Ireland,[2] and his widow Katherine conveyed the lease to Sir Thomas, for 'great sums of money,' and he has been exploiting the mines ever since. George, Lord Audley, died in 1559 and his son Henry confirmed the lease to Lodge, according to whom, in 1563, there are still seven years of the lease to run. It was evidently a considerable enterprise, for five 'Smythes or Iron Mylles' were kept working as part of the property. Sir Thomas now complains in Chancery that Mrs. Unwin has taken unlawful possession of one of his Tunstall mines, and 'doth by

1 C 3/116/35.
2 C 24/167/28 (*Gardiner* v. *Luce*, 1584), 'being pore and bankrupt he gatt him into Irelande out of the waye.' The parties to this suit are William Gardiner, the Surrey Justice, and the Luces, who are involved in Professor Hotson's recent discovery of Shakespearian interest (*Shakespeare* v. *Shallow*, 1931). See also below, *Lodge* v. *Yardley*, and C 24/224/1. Both Chancery suits add considerably to our knowledge of these persons.

nighte as by day, digg, delve, myne, Spoyle, waste, and
carry away the Iron, stone, and other ower,' [1] working under forced draught, he asserts, because she knows that her
time is short before the law steps in as a result of this complaint. He concludes with the special plea that in this
present year of his mayoralty he is kept in constant service
and attendance upon the Queen, and cannot defend his
property in Staffordshire.

Mrs. Unwin's Answer to his Bill is dated 29 September
1563 and alleges a former lease of a third part of the Manor
from George Lord Audley to her husband in 1549 or 1550,
comprising the mine in the fields called Wylflatt and Newe
Hey, and the 'stone mine' called Tunstall Field. The lease
has still seven years to run, having been confirmed by the
new Lord Audley. Her husband died in 1561, leaving the
lease to her. Luce's lease was made in 1555, by her account, comprising only the remaining two-thirds of the
Manor, and it had only one or two years to run. Issue was
finally joined, after a series of Pleadings, apparently on the
question of the validity of the respective leases. I have not
found any depositions, but there is a long series of Decrees
and Orders,[2] beginning in 1563 with an emergency injunction granted to Lodge against Mrs. Unwin and her mining
activities, 'ne tu . . . devastes vendas aut asportas . . .
lapides ferrum et le ower . . . in quadam miner̄ siue quarr̄
vocat̄ Tunstall myne,' until the case brought by our beloved and faithful Sir Thomas Lodge shall have been discussed and decided, dated from Smalbridge on 4 September. Neither party seems to have been anxious to get on
with the case, and orders to produce witnesses had to be
repeated. On 7 November Mrs. Unwin was licenced to re-

1 = Ore.
2 C 33/29, ff. 77, 119, 161, 173, 416, 445; C 33/31, ff. 2, 298, 322, 489; C 33/33,
ff. 53, 108.

turn home, but on 22 November she was ordered to appear
on 18 January following before the Master of the Rolls,
who was then to hear and settle the case. On 23 January
1564 the obviously proper course was taken, and the Court
dismissed the case to be heard at Common Law, by arrangement between the parties. The injunction, of course,
was dissolved. Sir Thomas was to make an 'open entry'
upon Mrs. Unwin's mine, and she was to bring a suit for
ejection before Queen's Bench, to be tried at the next
Staffordshire Assizes. It would seem, however, that
neither she nor Lodge was happy about this, for in July the
Court imposed penalties in case she delayed proceedings,
to correspond with those already imposed in January upon
Lodge in the event of delay on his part. But there is no indication that Lodge took the necessary first step. On 28
November 1564 this phase is over. No suit was brought or
tried, and the case returned to be settled in Chancery before the Judges. On 6 February 1566 it appears that Mrs.
Unwin had her case ready drawn to present, but Lodge had
failed to prepare his for the Court, and he is ordered to do
so within five days; in default the suit would be dismissed.
The final decree was made on 12 February by Sir Nicholas
Bacon, dismissing the suit absolutely from Chancery and
relegating it to the Courts of Common Law. The decree
was made with the agreement of both parties, and I presume that no costs or damages were allowed on either side.
But it seems clear that Lodge could not establish his case
in any Court and that Mrs. Unwin continued to enjoy her
rights in the mine and to diminish seriously the profits that
Lodge had anticipated from his speculation. Possibly
Lodge bought her out. Certainly these two and a half
years of litigation in Chancery must have cost him considerable sums of money, to add to the loss on the Tunstall
Mine.

LODGE *v.* YARDLEY

Nor was this even more than a minor part of Lodge's speculations in Staffordshire property, as we learn from the Star Chamber suit which he moved against John Yardley, his wife Agnes, and Roger Toft, in the Hilary term of 1570. We are informed in his Bill [1] that in July 1563, at a time when Lodge's difficulties were already increasing, he purchased Luce's lease from Henry, Lord Audley, of the Manor of Heley Castle in Staffordshire, of which Audley was seized in fee tail. This was a considerable property. To ensure the legality of the lease, it was agreed that Audley's wife Elizabeth should also acknowledge the fine paid upon the conveyance, for the property had been assured to her for life before the date of the lease to Lodge. Audley died before this was done, and Lady Elizabeth remained in possession. There was a further claim by Sir William Snede on account of an existing mortgage. On 18 May 1564, however, both Lady Elizabeth and Sir William completed the lease, for which Sir Thomas had paid, as for his mines, 'great sums of money.' He entered into possession, and received the rents and other profits peaceably for four years, until John Yardley, one of the tenants of the Manor, set up a claim to part of the land on the pretext of a former lease to him from George, Lord Audley. In pursuit of this, Yardley made a forcible entry upon Heyes Meadow, part of the land he claimed, driving out and impounding Lodge's cattle pasturing there. And now a legal battle was set on foot, in which we may distinguish a series of campaigns.

Lodge began by proceeding in the Court of Common Pleas, and recovered both his cattle and damages against

---

1 *Star Ch. Pro.* 5, H (*sic*) 28/31. Cf. C 24/167/28.

Yardley. Fearing for his life, moreover, and disturbed by 'this desperate and contemptious person' and his 'threates and manasses to kill' his landlord, Sir Thomas went to three Justices of the Peace for Staffordshire, Sir Walter Snede, Sir William Aston, and Ralph Adderley, and procured an order against Yardley to keep the peace and be of good behaviour. So ended the first round of the fight, in favour of Lodge.

On 10 August 1570 a second campaign began. Yardley, his wife Agnes, Roger Toft their servant, and eight others entered the field again and drove out Roger Stubbs, Lodge's servant, in great terror before their bows, arrows, pitchforks and other weapons. Stubbs reported the matter, and the forces of the law came on the scene. Ralph Jenson the constable, bearing the warrant for good behaviour, arrived with the bailiff of the Hundred, and arrested Yardley. Yardley went peaceably until approaching his house, which stood near Heyes Meadow, and then broke away, thus making 'a rescous,' and fled to his house, aided by Roger Toft. From thence he reviled the officer in safety, and refused to come forth to be re-arrested. The second round had ended with honours even. And now Yardley found an ally.

Venturing forth to seek out Walter Stafford, another Justice, he managed to elude arrest on his way, and found Stafford a sympathetic hearer. Stafford sent for Jenson, took away his warrant from him and bound him to appear from day to day until discharged. Yardley, on the other hand, he discharged absolutely, and Yardley returned in peace and triumph to his home. The third round was Yardley's.

Sir Thomas, however, now unmasked heavy guns, and early in the following year made a Star Chamber matter of it, involving the sympathetic Justice in it, complaining against Yardley for violent entry, conspiracy and breach of the peace, and against Stafford for improper exercise of his magisterial functions and for maintenance of illegal actions. His Bill, drawn up by William Daniel, set up a good case, which Stafford for his part was not inclined to combat. In his Answer Stafford hastens to submit himself to the Court with humble apologies. But he stands up for Yardley. His attitude is that which came naturally to the older feudal gentry of England, with their obligation to protect their tenants against any oppression but their own, and with their hatred of the new gentry who made lands and tenants the pawns of their speculations. Yardley, he urges, is a poor man, who cannot resist the power of riches, the overwhelming weapon of his enemy Sir Thomas Lodge. It was Lodge's aim to get Yardley into prison, in order that he, a new Ahab, might possess himself of Naboth's vineyard and ruin him utterly. He himself, Stafford, was ignorant of the law, wherein Sir Thomas was skilled. But he was deeply moved with pity for Yardley. For the rest, the facts were, he avers, that he did not bind the officers to appear; on the contrary, he bound Yardley and his family to keep the peace. Stafford would go far to defend a son of the soil, in which he himself was so deeply rooted, against the intruder. But he knew something of the power of London. And he could not face the penalty of recalcitrancy, the dishonour of being no longer enrolled upon the Commission of the Peace, the ancient distinction of a country gentleman, and the measure of his local reputation.

Yardley's Answer has a preamble in the same vein, urging his poverty, his inability to combat the wealthy Lodge, and the constant vexation of a series of processes, whereby he is 'utterly undone for ever.' He then asserts his claim to the land, by virtue of a lease of Nether Heyes, including Heyes Meadow, from Sir George Audley, dated

29 March 1556, and bought by Agnes, Anthony and John Stubbs. Agnes was to hold during life, with reversion to the others in turn. She is still alive, and is Yardley's wife. And the land is her freehold, which they have held quietly for five years after the date of the lease. Nevertheless Yardley has paid rent

as well for the said meadowe as for other lands by the said Henry demysed to thands of one Thomas Lodge gent sonne of the said Sr Thomas Lodge Synce the making of the said lease by the said Henry Lord Audley to the said Sr Thomas Lodge . . . to thuse of the said Sr Thomas wch Thomas the sonne did quietlie accept the same Rent clayming then to haue a lease of the said premisses made to hime the said Thomas by . . . Sr Thomas Lodge his father for terme of dyvers yeres then endewringe.

And now young Thomas has combined with his father by a covenous agreement, and has surrendered his lease back to his father, who molests Yardley to evict him from his holding.

Here we have the first discoverable function in life of young Thomas Lodge, taking his part in a legal fiction at some time between July 1563, the date of his father's lease of Heley Castle, and 1570, the date of this suit. It would seem most probable that it was actually late in 1563, in the period of financial stress in Sir Thomas' affairs, when the transfer of the lease in trust for his young son would protect it from his creditors. So we may judge that Thomas was involved in legal devices at the tender age of five or six, and certainly not more than twelve or thirteen. When he came to maturer years, as we shall see, he rivalled the litigiousness of his father, as became one thus early blooded to the law.

The action of Sir Thomas, Yardley continues, for replevin of his cattle was improperly taken from the Staffordshire County Court to the London Court of Common

Pleas, where Yardley lost his case by the negligence of his attorney Robert Ethell. The case was not tried, but went by default. Lodge therefore obtained a decree with execution for £6.10.0 'wch hath ben th utter vndoinge of this def^t his wyef and famylie.' There was no riot such as Lodge describes. The truth is that on the day in question Roger Toft, Yardley's man, was mowing his hay on his land. Yardley and his wife were also there. Roger Stubbs, Lodge's servant, accompanied by Richard Lodge, Thomas Noden and others, came and riotously sought to expel Toft and the Yardleys. Toft was forced to flee, leaving his scythe behind. Finally, Sir Thomas Lodge is 'a veraie Rigorus man And one that altogether desyreth and preferreth his owne pryvat lucre and gayne,' and used his power in the Lordship of Audley to get Yardley improperly arrested by the bailiff of the Lordship. Stafford was justified in giving Yardley a supersedeas to the warrant against him.

We may, of course, write off what we think proper from Yardley's description of Lodge's character, but we cannot deny authenticity to it as the reflection of Yardley's view of his character and of his attitude towards the Staffordshire yeoman whose rights conflicted with his. And I do not know that Yardley is unworthy of credence here. Certainly young Thomas was to find his father 'a veraie Rigorus man' before he was twenty years old.

A minor point of interest here is the mention of Richard Lodge. This was apparently a kinsman of Sir Thomas. He had doubtless gone to Staffordshire, if he were not indeed resident there, on behalf of Sir Thomas, who was unable to leave London, to act for him in his quarrel with Yardley. We may notice from Winchester's letter that the Staple was heavily engaged in the measures proposed for the relief of Sir Thomas. It is, therefore, tempting to identify Sir

Thomas' kinsman with Richard Lodge, a Draper and Sta-
pler who died before 1577, leaving only a son Walter and
a daughter Margaret.[1] But there is a certain Thomas
Lodge of Lincoln's Inn to be accounted for who fits in best
as a nephew or second cousin of Sir Thomas, older than his
own sons, and I imagine that we must seek for another
Richard for his father. I shall return to this Thomas
Lodge later, for he has darkened counsel concerning both
the poet and Sir Thomas.

Lodge's case against Yardley went on to the taking of
evidence, of which the record remains, and we find Yardley, but not Stafford, appearing before the Court of Star
Chamber in London on 21 November 1570.[2] He now gave,
in some respects, a different account of the riot. His man
Roger was ordered to cut the hay in the meadow. Lodge's
men drove him out. Then Yardley went back with him,
Yardley with bow and arrows, Toft with a pitchfork, and
in turn drove Lodge's men away. And this, I think, rings
true. There was, says Yardley, no arrest and escape. For
Yardley, seeing Jenson coming, ran away at once to his
house and refused to budge, until he could get away to see
Stafford. Finally, the greatest indignation is plainly to be
read between the lines when Yardley replies to questions
concerning the warrant. Yardley had always been a respectable man of good repute among his neighbours, and
he felt very bitterly the indignity of being bound to be of
good behaviour. Twice he insists that Stafford, at any
rate, knew him 'to be a man not worthie to be bounde to
the good abearing.' To each man his sense of honour, as
well as his sense of justice. Whatever the rights of the case
in law, there can be little doubt that the dealings of Sir

---

1 C 24/128, *Keyes* v. *Barnard*. Walter seems to have been a most interesting
and attractive young man of unusual principles.
2 *Star Ch. Pro.* 5, L 27/6.

Thomas Lodge in Audley disturbed ancient dwellers and an ancient order of things, and we may judge, in the absence of any decree, that in all probability he carried his case against the Staffordshire yeoman, and rounded off his estate there. I do not, of course, commit the error of considering the English provincial yeoman to be innocent of guile or attached to justice more than to law. And he certainly resented the intrusion of the London speculator in his land. But I have the impression that here certain words written at a later date by the son of his enemy, who was initiated in this suit into the legal hunts-up to which he subsequently became inured in the course of his long and litigious life, would have seemed to Yardley, not without cause, to sum up the situation.

> The Lord looks down, and cannot see one good,
> Not one that covets to obey his will;
> But wicked all from cradle to the crutch. . . .
> Where merciless men rob the poor,
> And the needy are thrust out of door . . .
> The ploughmen lose the crop for which they toiled.[1]

There can be no reasonable doubt, I think, that Sir Thomas never recovered fully from the difficulties in which he found himself in 1563, and which were not diminished by such expensive litigation.

A significant act of the Court of Common Council, at which Lodge was present, on 3 February 1564, forbids the entry of suits for debt against Sir Thomas or any alderman of the City without the consent of the Lord Mayor.[2] On 10 February it was held by the Court

very mete and expedyent for Mr Alderman Lodge to purchasse the quenes ma^{ties} wrytt for the stay of such accon as shalbe comensyd ageynste him by eny suche person as he otherwyse shall not be hable to intreate or stey.[3]

---

1 *A Looking Glass for London and England.*
2 *Repertory* 15, f. 309ᵇ.   3 *Ibid.*, f. 313ᵃ.

On 22 February, however, both these orders were revoked, probably as inequitable.[1] But on 30 January Lodge was respited from payment of a debt of £600 to the City until 1571. It is clear that the City was most anxious to succour 'the right worshipful Sir Thomas Lodge, Knight and Alderman,' in his difficulties.[2] But they were piled up beyond help. On 7 February 1566 Lodge was ordered to answer to a debt of which the Court was informed by the Mayor of Dover.[3] Doubtless it was one of many.[4] On 22 June 1565 Sir Thomas sat on the Court of Assistants of his Company for the last time, and at last, on 3 December in the following year, came a tragic submission to fate.

At this Court Sir Thomas Lodge an Alderman of this Cytie dyd frankly in his owne person Surrender and yeld vp his Rome & offyce of Aldermanshipe of the Cytie into ye hands order and disposicon of the same Court which his genteel Surrender of the seid rome and offyce the seid Court for good consideracons movyng the same dyd thankfully accepte receve and allowe.[5]

And on 12 December Thomas Ramsey, Grocer, sat in his stead as Alderman of Cheape.

In this year of renunciation of civic dignity Lodge's last child was born. Henry, his fifth son, was baptised at St. Peter's in Cornhill on 14 April.[6] Young Thomas was now eight years old. And the Lodge children must have formed some vague but lasting impression of the instability and insecurity of civic fortunes, when so great a man could so soon fall into decay, so great a structure topple so soon.

By July 1567 Sir Thomas was actually in a debtor's prison again. On 17 July the Court of Aldermen, led by the Lord Mayor, considered his case. The Mayor and ten aldermen undertook to lend Lodge £20 each to satisfy his

1 *Ibid.*, f. 314ᵃ.   2 *Ibid.*, f. 416ᵇ.
3 *Repertory* 16, f. 8ᵃ.   4 Cf. *ibid.*, f. 131ᵃ.
5 *Repertory* 16, f. 142ᵇ.   6 *Parish Registers*, p. 12.

creditors 'and set hymself at lybertie.' Three aldermen
hesitated, desiring time for consideration. One refused,
having already respited Lodge for a debt of £25. Two,
White and Harding, would even give Lodge freely £10
each.[1] On 17 September the matter came also before his
Company, whom the Lord Treasurer approached with a
request for a loan of £200 for Lodge 'for the helpe of his
present necessytie.'[2] And the Company agreed to raise a
subscription. Effective relief was not given, however, for
two years. The subscribers demanded security, which
Lodge could not find. On 29 March 1569 the Aldermen
decided to deposit their loans with the City Chamberlain,
pending the provision of sureties for Lodge.[3] On 12 July
security was found for £60, which was paid to Stoddard.[4]
On 7 May 1570 the Grocers were further pressed to complete their collection for Lodge, and they agreed to do so,
and also to lend £100 to help towards his release.[5] Not
until 7 July 1570 was it reported to the Grocers that Lodge
had been 'clerely delyverid and owt of pryson' before 24
June.[6] He had thus been under arrest for debt for three
years. He was now able to pursue more actively his Star
Chamber suit against Yardley. And for the remainder of
his life our information comes mainly from other law-suits
in which he was engaged with some frequency.

For the rest, there were many events to chronicle in the
life of his family circle, recorded in the Registers of St.
Mary Aldermary, in which parish he was now living, in one
of the Laxtons' houses. On 30 March 1574 his elder daughter Joan married a brother Grocer, Gamaliel Woodford,[7]
and went to live with him in Lodge's old house in St.
Peter's. A few months before, on 19 December, his second

1 *Repertory* 16, f. 254ᵇ.   2 *Calendar of Minutes.*
3 *Repertory* 16, f. 461ᵇ.   4 *Ibid.*, f. 485ᵇ.
5 *Calendar of Minutes*, p. 194.   6 *Ibid.*, p. 204.
7 *Parish Registers*, p. 5.

daughter, Anne, was buried in St. Mary's.[1] On 10 September 1576 his mother-in-law, Lady Joan Laxton, followed her grand-daughter there.[2] Next year his eldest son, William, married Mary Blagrave, daughter of the temporary Master of the Revels, on 14 October.[3] And on 15 January 1578 his first grandson was born to Gamaliel and Joan Woodford, and was called Thomas after the old knight, a Thomas of the third generation.[4] The poet was now at Oxford. In 1579 two grand-daughters were born, and both bore Lady Anne's name and were her godchildren, Anne Woodford in May and Anne Lodge in June.[5] The knight and his lady might well seek consolation and new pride in contemplation of the young generation coming to life around them. But in the very first years of this happy sequence of marriages and births death also invaded Lodge's house. In the year in which her first grand-daughters were born, in December 1579, Lady Anne Lodge died and followed her mother Lady Laxton to the grave in St. Mary Aldermary.[6] His remaining daughter, Joan Woodford, died also some six months before Sir Thomas, in July 1583.[7] Truly Sir Thomas had many joys, and suffered many and great sorrows. Never, I think, can there have been a man in whose life joy and grief were more closely related, more exactly proportioned, or more suddenly sequent. We shall see, for example, how his pride in his five sons was sadly turned to disillusionment. Add to this a debtor's prison succeeding his year of glory, and the irreparable loss of such a wife cancelling the gain of three grandchildren, and we may well see in Sir Thomas Lodge a figure of tragedy.

1 *Ibid.*, p. 139. 2 *Ibid.*, p. 140. 3 *Ibid.*, p. 6.
4 *Parish Registers*, St. Peter's, Cornhill, p. 19.
5 *Ibid.*, p. 20; *Parish Registers*, St. Mary Aldermary, p. 59.
6 *Ibid.*, p. 142.
7 *Parish Registers*, St. Peter's, Cornhill, p. 131.

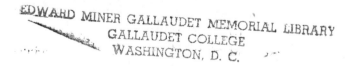

For there was something of heroic quality in him too. Not all the blows of fate could tame his spirit in his old age. From the City records comes the story of an explosion of thwarted will which landed Lodge into prison once more on 8 November 1576, no debtors' prison this time, but Newgate, and a visitation of the disciplinary censure of the Court of Aldermen.

Item Sir Thomas Lodge knighte for that he this presente daye did vnadvysedlye give vnto Mʳ John Braunche Alderman of this Cytie a blowe on the face, nere vnto the vtter Corte of the Guyldhall of this Cytie, was by the Corte here this daye comytted to Newgate, for the sayd offence, there to remayne vntyll this Corte, shall take furder order not only for his delyvery, but for his further fyne and poonyshment, as this Corte shall thincke meete for his sayd offence.[1]

The Court was jealous for the dignity of its Aldermen; Branch was to be Mayor in the following year; and to Newgate Lodge went. One may well wonder what turned Lodge into a brawler at his reverend age, assaulting thus violently a no less reverend dignitary. For Branch was over sixty, and Lodge nearer seventy, on this day. The Repertories of the City explain Lodge's anger. He was a suitor to the City for a lease of the house in which Lady Laxton had lived, and in which she had recently died, on 15 August.[2] The Court had decided on 28 August to grant him the reversion, but only on payment of a fine or premium of five hundred marks for a lease of twenty-one years, failing which 'Mʳ Braunche Alderman, shall have A leasse to him made of the same howse, for xxj yeres, before any other person.'[3] If Mr. Branch also refuses, then Alderman Langley shall have it. There was no lack of suitors for the house, and Lodge probably considered that Branch and

1 *Repertory* 19, f. 137ᵇ.
2 The Parish Register of St. Mary Aldermary records her burial on 10 September. The date here given for her death is from the *Inquisition Post Mortem*, and is consistent with the grant of the Court on 28 August.
3 *Ibid.*, f. 109ᵇ. Cf. *Ibid.*, f. 135ᵇ, 137ᵇ.

Langley were raising the market against him. As the first item of business on 8 November the Court reaffirmed the conditions, and demanded a decision from Lodge. I think I see the Court resting awhile from its labours, issuing into the outer Court Room of the Guildhall, the Mayor's Court, Lodge awaiting the news there, a little knot of elderly citizens in heated discussion, voices and hands raised, and at last the hasty blow, and the fall of a velvet hat; thereafter the old warriors separated, Lodge seized and arrested; the reassembled Court, on which sat Branch as Alderman, presided over by Langley, now Lord Mayor, and the swift decree, 'Sir Thomas Lodge knighte Comytted to Newgate' by his rivals for the fair house that launched one of the few blows recorded in these pacific annals. There was, we may see, in the heredity of the poet no small measure of the self-will that cannot brook opposition, of the ungovernable temper that meets obstructing circumstance with violent egotism, which we will find in the son of the old Grocer who was capable of this Homeric wrath.

Sir Thomas did not remain long in Newgate. On 22 November he appeared before the Court and agreed to pay the premium stipulated, and £20 over and above, apparently the cost of his obstinacy.[1] And so he entered after all into Lady Laxton's house, and in due course died in it. The City was very forbearing with Lodge, for in 1577 a similar debate arose with the Grocers, over another house in Cornhill, in which he had lived in his days of greatness before he moved to Lady Laxton's house, and which his daughter Joan and his son-in-law Gamaliel Woodford now occupied. Once more Lodge had his way, indomitable to the end.[2] And now he disappears, as far as I know, from the records of the City and of the Grocers.

1 *Repertory* 19, ff. 144$^{a, b}$.
2 *Calendar of Minutes*, pp. 281–285, 6 March–12 July 1577.

When Lodge died, early in 1584, he had a very restricted estate to dispose of, as will appear, and even the modest legacies therein devised could only be met from the proceeds of the sale of the leases of two estates, of the Manors of Sulton in Shropshire and Perryfelde in Essex. He had long since ceased to play any part in civic affairs, except as a petitioner. And it would seem certain that he had retired from active business, except in meeting his debts and dealing with his investments in landed property. We may fairly assume that he spent most of his time on his West Ham estate, enjoying the dignity that yet remained to him, that of a suburban knight in retirement. There remained to him also no small reputation for probity, to judge from the frequency with which, from time to time, he appears as executor of the wills of his friends, or as godfather to their children. In 1574, for example, Sir Thomas appears in Chancery as defendant against William and Margaret Wicksteade,[1] in his capacity as co-executor with Roger Evans of the will of Anne Hunt, widow of Thomas Hunt, a London upholsterer. In this instance Lodge had resigned to Evans the active management of the will, taking from him a bond to discharge Lodge from his duties and responsibilities. Thomas and Anne Hunt were evidently Shropshire people, as the legacies suggest, and we have here further indication of Lodge's connection with this county, in which, and in Staffordshire, the lands he purchased himself were mostly situated.

The Essex properties came to him through Lady Anne from the Laxtons, and he had only a life-interest in them after her death. The history of these lands concerns the poet and his brothers, and will be discussed later. But it may be observed here that there is no difficulty in identifying the actual house which Lady Anne brought in marriage

1 C 24/112, *Lodge* v. *Wicksteade.*

to Sir Thomas, in which the poet seems to have been born and brought up, and to which the old knight retired in his latter years. The house is frequently described, in a series of law-suits to be dealt with, as being situated on Le Hide in Plaistow. Lysons, writing in 1796, in his *Environs of London* [1] refers clearly to the house and gives its history: 'At Plaistow there is an ancient mansion called Hyde-house (now in the occupation of Mr John James).' It was said to have been the refuge of the monks of Stratford Abbey after the Dissolution. It was held by Richard Tailor, Doctor of Physic, in 1605. (We shall see that Lodge's house was, in fact, conveyed by his son William to Tailor.) It subsequently passed in the eighteenth century to Sir Thomas Foot and from him to the Onslows. The house bore the date 1559 on a wall and over a gateway the date 1579. The gateway bore the inscription 'This is the gate of everlasting life.' We may take it that these dates indicate additions to the house made by Sir Thomas. The gateway was surely built to commemorate the death of Lady Anne in 1579, and stood there for over two hundred years, a monument of enduring love and faith, long after its purport had been forgotten, as it soon was forgotten. The evidence of the coats of arms blazoned in various stained-glass windows is conclusive. With the Royal Arms we have also the Grocers' Arms, and another which from Lysons' description can be readily identified as that of Sir Thomas Lodge. [2]

This, then, was the country seat of the Lodges, a house with ample gardens and orchards, in which young Thomas and his brothers and sisters were brought up and which, after the death of Sir Thomas, his heir made haste to alienate, despite its associations and despite the gateway raised as a symbol of grief to the memory of a beloved

1 IV, 256.   2 *Ibid.*, Note 51, No. 4.

mother. A doctor of physic and a Flemish brewer in turn passed through the gate and sat in contemplation of the dissipated glories of a great house of Grocers. Here was a theme fit for the elegiac musings upon human vanity, upon the bubble that is man, of a Jeremy Taylor:

those into whose possessions their heirs or kindred are entered, are for-gotten, and lie unregarded as their ashes, and without concernment or relation, as the turf upon the face of their grave.[1]

The house has vanished. No trace remains today of either Hyde House or The Hide in Plaistow, which has long since been swallowed up in the spread of industrial London. West Ham is no longer a pleasant country resort for City magnates, but a crowded mass of streets jostled by fac-tories and docks.[2]

Little remains to be told of Sir Thomas. The last few years of his life were chequered with further law-suits and with the waywardness of his famous son. The first of these suits illustrates once more that combative obstinacy in the father which is so marked in the character and actions of the son.

LODGE v. BANKS (II)

In 1576, as we have seen, he was engaged in his suit against Thomas Banks in the Court of Requests, and it is evident that the case went against him. For in 1578 he

---

1 *Holy Dying*, I, ii.
2 Katharine Fry's *History of East and West Ham* (1888, pp. 245–248) locates Hyde House in Cordwainer Street (now High Street), opposite the Black Lion Inn, at the beginning of the nineteenth century, when it was pulled down. The gateway and inscription were still there, and part of the old brick wall, surrounding the property, which Lodge had built. An inscription over the mantelpiece of the 'best parlour' ran thus: 'Prosperity and adversity. Life and death. Poverty and riches come all of the Lord.' Aaron Hill lived and wrote in Hyde House about 1738. The book gives sketches of the house and the gateway, of which the date and the source are not given, and which are here reproduced.

LODGE'S BIRTHPLACE

GATEWAY, 1579

brought a second suit, this time in Chancery,[1] upon the same question. His son Thomas had just entered Lincoln's Inn. One might think that young Thomas, with this domestic interest to stimulate him, would have entered with the greater zest upon his legal studies. But he was deep in other matters, and probably busy already with such pursuits as made him apt and ardent to reply, a year later, to Stephen Gosson's attack upon the stage. He was only a boy of twenty, just down from Oxford, a fresh Bachelor of Arts, a scholar with the peculiar and all-absorbing ambitions of young scholars, especially in the days of Elizabeth. And we may reasonably surmise that he failed to show a proper interest in his father's affairs. His law-suits were probably burning questions with the old man, who was now approaching seventy years of age, and it may well be that his sense of grievance and his absorption in his cases wearied his hearers. Lady Anne Lodge, now fifty years of age, and soon to make a will commenting upon the conduct of Thomas, and to die, doubtless had to listen. But I imagine that the knight was disappointed of his most competent audience, of his expected escort to and from Chancery Lane, so conveniently close to Lincoln's Inn, and of the young apprentice lawyer's constant presence in Court with him, which would surely have been a source of pride to the old man. Who shall say what bitterness lay behind his mother's will and codicil, and his father's damning advice, soon after her death, that Thomas was not fit to be trusted with lands? In a Chancery deposition of 1573 [2] I find the fine flourished signature of the other Thomas Lodge of Lincoln's Inn, aged thirty-one, a lawyer in good practice, telling how he pleaded a cause before the Lord Chief Justice in the Guildhall on behalf of

1 C 24/131, *Banks* v. *Lodge.*
2 C 24/111/26.

Richard Thornehill, a member of Sir Thomas' own Company of Grocers. Such was the career that Sir Thomas had planned for a younger Thomas Lodge, and in the last years of his life he watched his cherished hopes vanish, shaken indeed in the very beginning of his son's entry upon London life. How much more galling if this other Thomas Lodge were indeed the son of his own kinsman Richard! It is this Thomas Lodge who has made historians attribute to the Lord Mayor in his later years high office in the Society of Lincoln's Inn, and also, it seems, an early marriage and progeny to the poet.

The pleadings in Lodge's Chancery suit against Banks explain a good deal of the action of Banks, to which I have already referred. Lodge's Bill states that Banks agreed to assign to him the lands in West Ham for £200, £40 to be paid at once and £160 when Lodge took possession. Banks took the £40 and refused to carry out his agreement, keeping both the £40 and the lands. Banks' Answer, dated 23 November 1575, gives a different account. He agreed with John Wyatt for the assignment of the lease to Wyatt. £40 was to be paid at once, and this was done. But the agreement was to be void if the remaining £160 was not paid, as it was not in fact. Banks had no agreement with Lodge, but only with Wyatt, whose money the £40 was. Lodge replied that the lease was in fact assigned to him, not to Wyatt. For proof, Lodge had received the rents for half a year. The agreement was made before the death of Sir Peter Mewtis, since when Lodge had been unable to get either the confirmation of his assignment or the return of the £40, which was his money, not Wyatt's. I do not see that we can escape the conclusion that either Banks or Lodge was seeking to turn to profit the death of Wyatt. In such cases, it is well to seek for devious paths trodden by both parties. Lodge may well, for example, have lent £40

to Wyatt to enable his servant to set up a holding for himself in West Ham near Lodge. Thus, when Wyatt died,
Lodge sought to recover his debt by claiming the lands,
and Banks saw his chance of pocketing £40. The evidence
on the whole supports this interpretation. But there are
complications.

There are depositions on both sides in the Court of Requests, and for Banks only in Chancery. In Requests,
Lady Jane Mewtis deposes on 7 July 1576, on behalf of
Lodge, and makes a confusing and possibly confused statement. But the point is clearly made that Banks borrowed
money from Lodge in order to pay Sir Peter for the lease
of the lands, for she,

Comynge into the Chamber vnto hir said late husband did ffynd there
wᵗ hym the said Wyatt and there did see certayne money in the some of
forty markℓ there left by the said Wyatt, and then this deponent asked
hir said husband is Wyatt now become so Riche to leve so moche money
heare, and hir said husband saide nay this is Sʳ Thomas Lodg is money
that is borowed for the vse of Bankℓ for his Lease.

Apparently, therefore, Lodge assisted Banks to buy the
first lease of the lands from Mewtis. On the death of Sir
Peter, Lady Jane confirmed the lease to Banks without
further payment, except that Banks undertook to have one
of her foreign servants made a free denizen. The rest of the
evidence in Requests on the whole supports Lodge's account of the intention of the second transaction, this time
between Banks and Wyatt. Anthony Bowes, a butcher,
and Margaret Wyatt, Wyatt's widow, both report dying
speeches of Wyatt. So Margaret says that

hir said husband beinge at Barwicke and there lyinge vpon his deth bedd
the said Thomas Bankes Comynge vnto hym the said Wyatt saied vnto
hym good sonne Bankℓ. Remembr̃e Mʳ Lodge for the fortie poundℓ wch
I had of hym for you and I paide you and he then saied ffather lett no
worldlie matter trouble you ffor I will pay hym and se hym answered it.

Bowes adds Wyatt's reply:

> good sonne lett it not be in worde but in deade.

Three scriveners concerned in the instruments, William
Dawtrey of St. Saviour's, Southwark, Thomas Wrightson
and Henry Etheridge, all former servants of Thomas Martin, a kinsman of Banks, who drew them up, give the date
of the indenture, April 1563. It set up a transfer of the
lease of 'the farme called Crissmas' only to Wyatt, not for
the use of Lodge. But two tenants make it clear that they
looked upon Lodge as their landlord.

In the Chancery depositions [1] Banks is evidently trying
to establish that the evidence of Margaret Wyatt favoured
Lodge's case in defiance of truth, and that she had been
suborned by Lodge to give false evidence in the Court
of Requests, through Anthony Bowes, a Westminster
butcher, as intermediary. Did not Bowes, Banks asks,
urge you to agree that he also had been there and heard
Wyatt's words and to depose to that effect?

Margaret, now a widow living in Hackney, thirty-eight
years of age, and servant to the Countess of Lenox, having
formerly served Mrs. Agnes Gibbes of West Ham, is a remarkably decided and fluent witness, with a fine sense of
dialogue. Sir Thomas, she replies, certainly asked her to
give evidence in Requests; she also knows Bowes; but as for
the alleged conversation and its effect upon her, she is clear
to the contrary and gives the conversation verbatim. It
may well be reproduced in the dramatic form which it deserves:

Bowes.   Sir Thomas will have vs both examyned in the Court of
    Requests to declare what your husband said when he laye upon
    his death bedd of the xl li he borowed of him for Mr Banks
Margaret.   why you were not there then

---

1 C 24/131, *Banks v. Lodge.*

Bowes.　　yes that I was
Margaret.　Nay that you were not
Bowes.　　Yes that I was indede
Margaret.　y faith you were not
Bowes.　　no? why say you so; you do forget your self. Remember
　　　your self better
Margaret.　Na; I do remember well ynoughe you were not there then;
　　　nor I will not for an C li saye that you were there and was not.

And she goes on to make it yet more clear, 'indede the said Bowes was not there at that tyme for she doth well remember the tyme and who were present with her said husband while he laye sick,' nor could she be moved even though Bowes 'did threape vpon her that he was there.'

There is a fine gradation of emphasis of denial, rising from 'why' through 'Nay' to the asseverative 'y faith' and the final 'Na,' in Margaret's side of the dialogue. She is surely a Scotswoman, or perhaps North Country. Her final 'Na' is, of course, not conclusive, for I find it not infrequently without indication of Northern origin; but Bowes 'threaped' upon her; she is in the service of the Countess of Lenox; and I think I see her in the Court before the Examiners, sturdy, with a little rasp in her voice, not to be intimidated by Southern lawyers, and utterly unchanged by the seven years she 'reckons' she has been in London, a forerunner of the great Northern invasion that descended upon London with James I twenty-five years later. She recalls, by the way, the arrival of her husband John Wyatt at Berwick 'the yere the king of Scotts was borne,' in 1566, and I think she married him there.

It is a great pity if young Lodge did not in fact attend the Court with his father and his counsel, had he had an eye to character-study for the good of his dramatic ambitions. A Margaret like this would have made a play live, as Lodge's extant plays do not live. But Chaucer was long since dead; Shakespeare and Ben Jonson had not yet come to the London stage; and Lodge was not the man to build upon the Wife of Bath or to anticipate Mrs. Quickly.

Mrs. Gibbes, I may add, corroborates Margaret's evidence. Two years ago, during the Requests suit, Margaret told her all about Bowes' attempted subornation, and she tells us herself that Lodge had discussed her present evidence with her that very day in London. And we may wonder whether the Court of Requests had disbelieved Bowes, and so found against Lodge as a result of his misguided desire to strengthen his case. I cannot say what was the end of Lodge's second attempt to vindicate his position, for I can find no Decrees or Orders in the records of Chancery in connection with this suit. I trust that the matter was amicably settled in the end. It had, after all, dragged on for some fifteen years in all. And there had been litigation long enough and costly enough to satisfy even a neighbourly quarrel. For Banks and Lodge were neighbours in West Ham.

LODGE v. KYNASTON

A property that Lodge owned in Shropshire brought him into Chancery in the same year on a second suit, in which he was defendant against Roger Kynaston, John Astley, Andrew Lewes and Anthony Lewes of Sulton. The Bill [1] recalls the history of Sulton Manor, of which Edward Twynhoe owned the freehold. Twynhoe leased it to Sir George Cotton and, in 1539, in reversion to George Rows and John Parrott from 1556. Sir Thomas, Lady Lodge and Lady Laxton purchased Rows' and Parrott's interest in the property and, in 1565, leased it for twenty-one years from 1567, for £99, to George Lewes. In December 1573, it is claimed, the whole interest of the Lodges was sold to Lewes for £200. Lady Laxton died, and Lewes died, leav-

1 C 3, 212/84.

ing the Manor to his two sons, who are now suing Sir Thomas through Kynaston and Astley, executors of the will of their father. The sale of the whole lease cannot be proved, and Sir Thomas has defrauded the Leweses. Sir Thomas and Lady Lodge have, in fact, made a secret grant of the Manor to their son William, who has entered upon the Manor.

In reply, Sir Thomas admits the lease of 1567, at a rent of £40 for twenty-one years, but under a condition forbidding sub-leases for more than three years. On 8 November 1568, however, Lewes broke this condition by several sub-leases, and his lease was therefore forfeit. Lewes then sought to buy the whole interest of the Lodges for £200, in January 1573, but would not agree to any terms proposed. There was no assignment of the Manor to Lewes on 22 December 1573. The £200 was paid by Lewes, but was left by him in Lodge's hands as an investment, and Lodge is ready to pay interest as the Court directs. Lodge was justified on all counts in authorizing his son William to take possession.

The depositions [1] on behalf of Lodge add some interesting details. The opposing case is not presented in the extant files of depositions of these years. William Tipper, a London Grocer, aged thirty-five on 18 November 1578, tells us that he had been Lady Laxton's servant, and that he had several times seen her in consultation upon this grant with Lewes and Sir Thomas Lodge in the parlour of her house in Budge Row in London. But Lewes, it seems, raised difficulties. The mill, leased with a farm to him, needed expensive repairs, and he thought they were making the bargain out to be a better pennyworth than he esteemed it. In the end he asked to have his £200 back, with interest.

1 C 24/138, *Lodge* v. *Kynaston*.

Gamaliel Woodford, Lodge's son-in-law, aged forty-four, also deposes. He was at Wem, near Sulton, in Shropshire, about November 1577, on business, and there learned that Lewes had in fact sub-let part of the lands to various people, whereby his lease was forfeited. Lewes had died since. Woodford leaves no doubt of Lewes' qualms about the proposed conveyance, and his desire to have his money back, in an account of a meeting at Lewes' lodgings near Charing Cross about 1572 or 1573:

Sʳ Tho: qd he there is no haist in the matter, I wold you wold paye me my money againe it [1] standeth in, and lett the lease allone, Marye, qd the said Sʳ Tho., I wold I had the money, and yf I had, it shold be the first bargayn I wold make.

Sir Thomas even proposed to his son-in-law that he should buy the lease, as it was such an excellent bargain, and point the moral to Lewes. Woodford, however, told Lodge and Lewes that as he 'was otherwise gyuen to ymploye his money, he wold not deale wᵗ it, or ells it shuld haue bene the first bargaine that he wold haue made.' With such protestations from two eminent authorities, one is surprised at the hesitancy of Lewes, who is said to have put his whole trust in Sir Thomas.

The records of the Court throw no further light on the case. It might seem that Lewes considered that he had paid for the property and could therefore dispose of it, though he had not completed the transaction. Sir Thomas, on the other hand, had his £200 and considered that he might keep both money and lands. It is impossible to believe that Lewes had willingly left the money in Lodge's custody. It is only too easy to believe that, having once paid it over, he could not extract it from Lodge, and to accept Lodge's statement that he no longer had the money

---

1 = yt (that).

to pay back. Both Tipper and Woodford were disconcertingly truthful on this point, and it seems to have been a grave lack of tact to introduce the question into the Interrogatories put to them in support of Lodge's case.

I cannot be certain, therefore, what was the upshot of it all. But when Lodge died in 1584, his will deals with a sum of £200 in the hands of his son William arising out of a sale of Sulton Manor. It would seem that the Court had upheld the protested assignment after all. But how, or when, or why the £200 had been entrusted to William are questions that could only be answered by one versed in the more devious ways of the law. And I am disposed to doubt whether William ever paid over to his younger brethren their shares in this £200 which had led such a precarious existence for ten years.

LODGE v. WILFORD

Less than a year later, Sir Thomas is again in Chancery,[1] this time defending himself against Francis Wilford, who is reviving claims on him dating back to the days of Queen Mary. On 27 July 1579 Richard Leedes, Grocer, aged fifty, gives us the facts as Lodge would have them appear. Leedes had been Lodge's 'factor and serũnt also . . . in his trade and affaires in the Countrye of fflaunders a xxiij yeres past, and remayned there in that forme and seruice about 6. yeres and vpwards.' Now Leedes in this capacity received letters from Lodge, then in London, to the effect that Lodge had Wilford's bills for a total of £463.17.1 Flemish, and instructing Leedes to pay the money to Wilford at Antwerp on the due dates, from 18 July to 7 September 1555. The letters were brought to Leedes at Lodge's house in Antwerp by Wilford, who had 'fled the

1 C 24/137, *Lodge* v. *Wilford*.

Realm for Religion into fflaunders.' Wilford asked Leedes
to arrange to invest £450 at interest for him with a Ger-
man merchant, Sebastian Libmore. This was done with the
help of Thomas Donne, an English broker there, and
Leedes paid over to Wilford the remainder. From that
day to this Leedes has heard no more of the transaction,
though Wilford has long since returned to England, until
now, twenty years after, Wilford is suing Lodge for part of
the money. Nor do the records of the Court of Chancery
carry the matter any further, and one may merely wonder
that such an action should have got as far as the taking of
depositions. But it is satisfactory to find Lodge aiding and
comforting a fugitive for conscience' sake in days when
there was danger in so doing. I daresay, however, his
profit on the transaction had been commensurate with
the risk.

I may perhaps conclude these memorials of Sir Thomas
Lodge with an account of the joint dealings of Lodge and
his neighbour Banks with a third neighbour of a humorous
turn of mind in the extremity of death, John Shipman of
West Ham. With this we come to the last year of Lodge's
life, for Shipman died in 1583,[1] and Lodge early in 1584.
Shipman was the copyholder of lands adjacent to those
held by Lodge in various Manors situated in the parish of
West Ham. He had no direct heirs, and his nearest relations were his cousins John Pragle and his wife, who were
friends and neighbours of the Lodge family. But he per-
sistently refused to make a will leaving any of his lands to
the Pragles or to their sons. Both Lodge and Banks used
all their influence to persuade Shipman, but in vain. The
land consequently reverted to the Crown, the Lord of these
Manors. Banks was asked by Pragle to intercede with the
Lord Treasurer on his behalf; indeed, as Banks tells us

1 Lysons, *Environs of London*, IV, 262.

himself when the case came up in Exchequer in Easter
1592,[1] when he was sixty years of age, Pragle had offered
him a third of the land for himself if he succeeded in getting it all for Pragle. From his evidence, and that of
Thomas Smith, a West Ham tailor, we learn that Banks
and Lodge together approached Shipman on behalf of the
Pragles, and Lodge met with a reply which makes me desire Shipman's better acquaintance. Smith tells the story
thus:

Sir Thomas Lodge Knight did move John Shipman lyenge vpon his
death bedd to dispose his landes by his will and to give some parte of it
to the yonger John Pragles eldest sonne who was godson to the said Sr
Thomas Lodge. John Shipman aunswering said he is yo[r] godson give
him somthinge of yo[rs] if you will, for myne happie man be his dole, let
him catch it that can.

The various versions of the incident all unite in remembering the capricious phrase 'happie man be his dole.' And
one version suggests an expiring flicker of humorous loyalty
in Shipman's reply to Lodge's insistence that if he dies intestate the land will only fall to the Queen: 'happie man be
his dole she is best worthie of it.' I fancy that the former
Lord Mayor found old Shipman too much for him, even in
Lodge's own parish, in which he was clearly a notability.
But Shipman, if he left nothing to his kinsmen, left £6 a
year for ever to the poor of West Ham.[2]

The tests of memory applied in this suit, and recorded
here, to certain very aged West Ham witnesses, are particularly interesting. They are asked whether they remember 'a feelde called flowden feelde' and the execution
of the Duke of Buckingham under Henry VIII. Isabell
Spaight, aged ninety-eight, tells us that she was in the
North when Flodden Field was fought. She was then

1 E 134, 34 Eliz. Essex, Easter 27. *John Pragle* v. *Regina*.
2 Lysons, *Environs of London*, IV, 270.

fifteen years old, she says. And she remembers well the
death of the Duke, for she married her husband, who had
been his servant in his Wardrobe, a year after, and came to
West Ham on Corpus Christi Day following his execution.
She has, I fear, overestimated her age in 1592 by some four
years, anxious to reach the hundred. Thomas Allison,
aged eighty, was at the house of his father Henry Allison in
the Bishopric of Durham when Flodden was fought, which
he 'well remembereth for that he had some of the points
that were on his vnckles Jacke [1] at his retourne from the
said feild.' I suspect Allison of being a distant ancestor of
my own, on the distaff side. If his estimate of his age in
1592 is right, he was obviously born only a year before the
date of the battle. But he doubtless heard the story of it
often, later on, and cherished the relics of his uncle's
soldiering. It is clear that Sir Thomas had some interesting neighbours at West Ham, and that there would be no
lack of matter for conversation and the exchanging of tales
of the past among them, in those remote days when conversation was still a lively pleasure, when men still found
adequate interests in their own affairs and doings, and before men dreamt of mortgaging their leisure hours beyond
recovery to the march of progress in commercialized dis-
tractions. I wonder if Sir Thomas told his neighbours
whether he ever received from his ancient friend Anthony
Hussey, his daughter Joan's godfather, whose executor he
was in 1560, the 'greate game of Swannes' which he was to
have after his death from Hussey unless it was sold in his
lifetime, as well as £20 in money and a ring of £6 value.[2]
I do not even know where he would have put the swans if
they had come to him. There was no pond in the West
Ham property, and in London they could not even have
served to grace a Grocer's feast, being a royal cate.

1 = tunic.
2 P.C.C., 52 Mellershe. I owe this reference to Miss Julia McCorkle.

We may be sure that there was in Lodge's later life in West Ham, with his troops of friends, with the general respect of his neighbours, with his past greatness and present modest sufficiency, much to set against the vexations of his law-suits and the loss of his wealth.   But it is equally certain that his later years were heavily darkened by the loss of his wife Lady Anne Lodge, in 1579, and by the grievous disappointment of his hopes in the son named after him, for whose sake I have sought to trace as much as possible of his life.   Sir Thomas Lodge made his will [1] on 14 December 1583, died on 28 February 1584,[2] at the ripe age of seventy-four, and was buried by his wife's side in a vault in the church of St. Mary Aldermary, in which Lady Anne had been laid on 30 December 1579, and her mother, Lady Joan Laxton, three years before on 10 September 1576. The inscription on the tomb read thus:

Here lyeth buried Sir Thomas Lodge knight, and Dame Anne his wife. Hee was L. Maior in the yeere of our Lord God 1563, when God did visit this Citie with a great plague for our sinnes. For we are sure that our Redeemer liveth, and that we shall rise out of the earth in the latter day, &c. Job 19.[3]

But the tomb and its inscription have long since vanished, and no man can say where it stood.

1 P.C.C., 29 Brudenell.
2 C 142/203/76.
3 Strype's *Stow*, Bk. III, p. 19.

II. A GROUP OF GROCERS

SIR THOMAS LODGE, as I have already remarked, was not
the only Lord Mayor or the only knight in Lodge's immediate family circle. Sir Thomas had married a second wife,
Lady Anne Lodge, the mother of the poet, from the family
of another great Grocer, Sir William Laxton, in his day
Master of the Grocers' Company, and Lord Mayor in
1544. Sir William died in 1556, having made provision by
a codicil to his will for the foundation of a free school at
Oundle in Northamptonshire, endowing it with lands and
houses in the City of London.

GROCERS' COMPANY v. WANTON

Something may be added to the well-known facts of Laxton's foundation of this famous school from a Chancery
suit brought in 1572 by the Grocers' Company against
John Wanton.[1] The depositions recall the circumstances in
which Laxton's proposed benefaction came before the
Company for discussion. The only witness produced on
behalf of Wanton is one of the most famous of Grocers,
Richard Grafton, whose age is given as sixty-six years on
27 February 1572, and who is brought on that day to depose on behalf of Wanton's side of the case. Grafton tells
us that he knew Laxton very well, and remembers how,
two or three years before his death in 1556, Laxton proposed his gift to the Company in trust for the School.
Grafton was present in his capacity as Warden of the Company and Assistant, and subsequently was deputed with
others to inspect the properties and to report. The report
must have been unfavourable, for the Company 'did

1 C 24/101/26; C 24/103, *Grocers* v. *Wanton*.

utterly refuse' the trust, despite Laxton's repeated insistence. The Master, Sir John Lowin, was especially obstructive. The reason for the refusal was the awkward conditions of tenure of the lands, because of which they and the trust might become a burden upon the Company. The project was revived by the Company, however, during Sir William's last illness, and a deputation was sent, comprising Sir William Ayloff, Edward Foulie and Grafton. Laxton was not in a fit state to deal with business and 'his aunswere was that he was very euill at ease and desired them therefore not to trouble hym with any such matter at that tyme.' So they came away, and about two days later Sir William died.

Grafton was asked further about a codicil to Laxton's will, leaving the lands and houses in question to the Grocers, the rents of which were to provide permanently £18 for a schoolmaster, £6.13.4 for an usher, and funds for the relief of the poor and for necessary reparations. And he states that he has no knowledge of any such codicil.

I find from other documents that John Wanton was the grandson of Sir William's brother John, whose daughter Joan married Thomas Wanton, also a London Grocer, and that Wanton was Sir William's sole heir by inheritance from his mother. It seems clear that Wanton, in the alleged absence of definite provision in the will, is disputing the codicil and claiming the property in question, whereas the Grocers are seeking to establish the intention of Laxton to form the trust and so to take possession for that purpose. But the evidence brought by the Grocers in support of the will and codicil which they brought into Court was conclusive. John Southcot, Justice of the Common Pleas, aged fifty-eight on 26 April 1572, deposed that he drew up both will and codicil, in his own handwriting, which he identifies, and that both were approved and

signed by Sir William. The will was written by Southcot
in Sir William's bedchamber, ten days before his death.
Five days later Laxton conceived the project of the school
for Oundle, 'where he was born,' and in a few days the
codicil was brought, read to him, and signed, not long before his death. Southcot had won a suit for Laxton against
one Knell, concerning lands purchased by Laxton in the
Cinque Ports, and Laxton had thereafter paid Southcot an
annual retainer of £1.6.8 or £2 as counsel in his law-
affairs. Sir Thomas Lodge also appeared to give evidence,
confirming that of Justice Southcot. The codicil was
brought by Southcot and read to Laxton and approved
by him in the presence of Lady Joan, Nicholas Loddington,
Sir Thomas and others. Sir Thomas then recalls the effect
of the codicil in detail. The lands devoted to the purpose
were those purchased by Sir William and Lady Joan
jointly of M^r. Weldon, and the bequest was to take effect
after the death of Lady Joan. Sir William charged Lodge
'by the name of his Sonne Lodge' to further the scheme
with all speed. And within a year after Sir William's
death Lady Joan purchased the 'house callyd the brother-
hed at oundell,' the upper floor for a school, the lower for
rooms for seven poor men, and placed a schoolmaster there
with twenty marks a year, as she still does. Edward Dawson, Grocer, aged forty on 4 April, formerly a servant of Sir
William, was also present in Laxton's chamber, gives further confirmation, and adds that he heard Wanton's
father, Thomas Wanton, 'A potycarye decessed beseeche
and praye in verie earnest manner' his uncle to go forward
with the foundation. And Dawson tells us that Laxton
adjured those present to see to it that no 'lack-latin' master should be given the post by undue influence; none below the rank of Master of Arts should ever be Master of
Oundle.

Such evidence could not be withstood. For the rest, Laxton's extant will [1] contains the codicil in which the school is provided for, and a list of the properties is given. It is dated 11 November 1556, and the *Inquisition Post Mortem* [2] upon Laxton's estate, on 14 May 1557, which recites his will, dating it 17 July 1556, also quotes the codicil. The history of this great school would never have been written had Wanton succeeded in his suit. And it owes something to Sir Thomas Lodge, who encouraged the project and defended the provision made for it by his father-in-law.

Grafton was dead a little more than a year after he gave evidence, in May 1573, and this was probably his last appearance in a Court of Law. At the time of his deposition he was in great distress and poverty, and on exceedingly ill terms with the governors of the City in which he had once been so great a figure. [3] Were it not Richard Grafton, one might almost believe that he was wilfully thwarting the great City Company, his own Company, whose ungracious treatment of him, as it seemed to him, he resented most bitterly, and which, at the end of this year, was to provide him with a compassionate pension of twenty pence a week for the last few weeks of his life. It may be that his memory had failed him on this one point, though it was so fresh on most things, even in detail, and that Wanton was making use of him to make his own case good. But it is more likely that he was in fact not acquainted with Laxton's actual will and the final disposition of his property.

Thus our first glimpse of Lodge's remoter parentage shows us a wealthy London citizen devoting no small share of the property he had accumulated to the philanthropic

1 *Cal. of Wills, Court of Husting*, II, 665.
2 C 142/112/93.
3 'Grafton and the London Grey Friars,' *The Library*, September, 1930.

intention, so ancient and honourable a tradition of the City, of maintaining religion, education and charity, in the form which it so often took, the benefaction applied to the foundation of a school in the citizen's native town. Sir William's will makes it clear that there are two lines of inheritance of his property. His residuary legatee is his 'cousin Johane Wanton, my ryght heyre.' But special provision is made for the heirs of his wife, Lady Joan Laxton. After her death the manor of 'Rosshalle in Sarett,' Hertfordshire, is to be entailed upon Nicholas Loddington and his heirs, and his lands in Stoke Nayland in Suffolk and Essex upon Anne Lodge, wife of Alderman Thomas Lodge. We shall find Stoke Nayland in due course bequeathed to the poet.

It is certain that Sir William was a native of Oundle in Northamptonshire. His will suggests that the parent branch of his family belonged to Gretton in the same county. The name, however, indicates the first origin of the family in Laxton in Nottinghamshire. And there is no doubt that Lady Joan was of Nottinghamshire birth. *The Visitation of London* of 1588 [1] describes her as daughter and heir of William Kirkeby in Yorkshire and of his wife Alice, daughter and heir of one Whettell. But we shall see that the manor of Rolleston, between Nottingham and Newark, near Southwell, was part of Lady Laxton's property. And the parish registers of Rolleston record the existence in the sixteenth century of a numerous swarm of Kirkebys, evidently a family of considerable standing in the parish. William, Joan and Anne are frequent Kirkeby names. A Nicholas Kirkeby gave £10 for the poor of the parish. And when Joan Kirkeby came to have children, Nicholas, Joan and Anne were their Christian names. The

1 MS Harl. 1463.

Herald's reference to Kirkeby in Yorkshire was merely a mistaken guess.

We are apt to forget that London has been built up by immigration from the provinces. And the provincial in London has always had a tendency towards clannishness and loyalty to his native county. Especially in the Elizabethan age was he inclined to look upon London as his market and temporary abode, while his roots remained firmly fixed in his provincial home. A 'countryman' was always welcome, to be patronized and helped, or to be allied in marriage. The Tudor confidence man knew this, and practised upon it. Shakespeare remained a Warwickshireman all his life, and Stratford from first to last was his home and the seat of his ambitions. Strongly as the tide of life has ever set towards the opportunities of London, no less significant is the reflux towards a settled estate in the country among Tudor Englishmen. In this respect, as in his portraits of country folk compared with those of a Ben Jonson, Shakespeare represents the sanest and most stable elements of Elizabethan England.

The Laxtons, like Shakespeare, were Midlanders. Joan Kirkeby's two marriages illustrate this provincial clannishness. Incidentally, they have given rise to some confusion, only her second marriage having been recorded hitherto. Lady Joan Laxton survived Sir William until 15 August 1576, when she died at the age of seventy-eight. Her will, together with other wills and Inquisitions, clears up some intricate family relationships arising out of several remarriages. It has always been stated, for example, that Lodge's mother, Lady Anne Lodge, was Sir William Laxton's daughter. This is not true, however. She was the daughter of Lady Joan (who married Sir William as her second husband) by her first husband, Henry Loddington. There is a village of Loddington in North Leicestershire.

And I find a Thomas Loderington or Loddington as vicar
of Rolleston from 1557 until his death there in 1571.[1] By
Loddington she had three children, a son Nicholas and two
daughters, Joan and Anne. The group of Grocers connected with Lodge thus widens, for both Henry and
Nicholas were Grocers. The *Visitation of London* confirms
this history.

Anne Loddington, the second daughter, in time married
Thomas Lodge, and became the mother of the poet. But
she also was married twice. Her first husband was another
Grocer, William Lane, by whom she had four children,
Luke, Gabriel, Anne and Elizabeth. This marriage is not
mentioned in the *Visitation*. Her sister Joan Loddington
married John Machell, afterwards Alderman, also a Grocer,
and after him Sir Thomas Chamberlain. Her brother
Nicholas continued the family tradition in his calling.
When Lane died in 1552, Anne married yet another Grocer
in Lodge, and brought him no small fortune, towards the
end of the year. She was born, as we shall see, in 1528, and
consequently was still only twenty-four years of age. Sir
Thomas was about forty-two years old at the time of his
third marriage to Anne Loddington. I know nothing of
any family he may have had by his first wife, the sister of
Stephen Vaughan. We have seen that his second marriage
brought him two daughters. By Lady Anne he had two
daughters and five sons, Joan, Anne, William, Thomas,
Nicholas, Benedict and Henry.

Their eldest child, William, was probably named after
Sir William Laxton. He was thirty years old on 8 July
1584, the date of the Inquisition upon Sir Thomas' estate.[2]
His parents were living at the time of his birth in the parish

1 E. H. S. Longhurst and E. B. Freckingham, *A Short History of the Village and
Church of Rolleston*, p. 13.
2 C 142/203/76.

of St. Michael's, Cornhill, and a William Lodge is entered
in the parish register as having been christened on 29
September 1553. The two records confirm each other.
Joan was the second child. Anthony Hussey, in his will [1]
dated 12 January 1558, refers to her as his god-daughter,
leaving her 'one portegue of gold.' I presume that Lady
Joan Laxton was her godmother. She is not entered in the
parish register, but there is evidence, as we shall see, that
she was born in 1555. Thomas, the second son, was born
between May 1557 and April 1558, if we may depend upon
his statements of his age in certain depositions already referred to. The parish register records the christening of a
Thomas Lodge on 23 May 1556, and his burial on 4 June
of the same year. It is clear that the sad fate of this first
infant Thomas did not deter the Lodges from giving their
next-born child also the same name, and that Lodge's depositions fix the date of his birth accurately. We may believe, in the light of future events, that Sir Thomas may
often have regretted the death of this baby, wondering the
while whether he would not have been a more worthy
perpetuator of his father's name. Nicholas, named after his
uncle Nicholas Loddington, was of age, and Benedict
under age, on 14 December 1583, the date of the will of Sir
Thomas, and so Nicholas was born before 1562, and it was
Benedict who was christened on 18 April 1563, as we can
conclude from what Machyn tells us.[2] We should therefore in all probability place the births of both Nicholas and
Anne in the interval between 1558 and 1562. Finally,
'Harry Lodge son of Sy^r Thomas Lodge' was christened in
the church of St. Peter in Cornhill, as recorded in the registers of this parish, on 14 April 1566. Evidently the Lodges

1 P.C.C., 52 Mellershe.
2 *Diary*, p. 305. It is pleasant to find the Lord Mayor expressing his sense of his
blessings in such graceful fashion.

had moved out of the parish of St. Michael into St. Peter's hard by, nearer to the Woodfords, whose family history is told in its registers. Before 1573 they had again moved into the parish of St. Mary Aldermary, the registers of which give further information.

Joan, the elder of the Lodge girls, married Gamaliel Woodford there on 30 March 1573. Gamaliel Woodford, yet another of the notable Grocers of this extensive London clan, figures very largely in numerous Chancery suits as a trader and financier on an immense scale, and finally as a bankrupt distinguished by the size of his debts. Their son Thomas, born on 13 January and christened at St. Peter's on 15 January 1578, like his uncle Thomas Lodge, played his part in the history of the London stage, a course which Sir Thomas could by no means approve for either of his namesakes, but which, in the process of revolution of that whirligig Time, has become the sole source of men's interest in the life and affairs of Thomas Woodford.

His first theatrical venture was tentative. Soon after Christmas 1600, he bought a play from Chapman, *The Old Joiner of Aldgate*, written upon the topical scandal of the profits made by a Londoner from the disposal of his daughter in marriage to several suitors. Woodford paid twenty marks for it and re-sold it to the Children of Pauls'. In due course, along with their Master Edward Pearce and the dramatist, Woodford was called upon to answer for his actions in Star Chamber in 1603.[1] Later on, we find him speculating more heavily in theatre-property. In 1608 he shared with Michael Drayton a lease of the Whitefriars, whereby they became the landlords of the King's Revels company, and Woodford became involved in litigation in 1609 and again in 1622. Finally, in 1612 he invested £50 in the Red Bull Theatre, with consequent law-suits in Chan-

---

1 *Star Ch. Pro.* 8, 8/2. I hope to publish an account of this lost play shortly.

cery and in Requests in 1613. It may well be that his uncle Thomas led Woodford into the treacherous path of dealings in theatrical concerns. He was only twenty-three when he lightheartedly dealt with Chapman for his play, a bargain that brought him into question as a publisher of libels. And he showed notable lack of foresight when he bought shares in theatres in the intervals of a regular business which kept him abroad and so invited fraud on the part of such a partner as Aaron Holland of the Red Bull. His sister Anne, godchild of Lady Lodge, was born on 17 May 1579. A son William followed, on 8 January 1580, and another, John, in 1582.[1] On 24 July 1583 their mother, Joan Woodford, was buried in St. Peter's, and the register gives her age as twenty-eight, which would fix the year of her birth as 1554-5. Gamaliel married again, and had a son Fulke, born in 1589. He predeceased his second wife, who was buried in St. Peter's on 17 May 1613.

In the meantime, the registers of the neighbouring parish of St. Mary Aldermary record in turn the burial of Anne Lodge, Joan's sister, on 19 December 1573; the burial of Lady Joan Laxton, inexactly, it would seem, on 10 September 1576; the marriage of William Lodge, the eldest son, with Mary Blagrave, daughter of Thomas Blagrave, on 14 October 1577; the birth of their first child Anne, another godchild of Lady Lodge, on 18 June 1579; the burial of Lady Lodge six months after, on 30 December; and the burial of Sir Thomas on 17 February 1584.[2]

From these landmarks of family history we may turn back once more to such further information and commentary concerning the lives of the earlier generation of Lodge's circle as can be furnished by legal records.

1 John is aged 17 on 20 November, 1599 (C 24/273/65; C 24/283/10).
2 The *Inquisition Post Mortem* upon Sir Thomas gives 28 February as the date of his death, and I have preferred this authority, as for Lady Laxton (15 August).

LODGE v. WYTBROKE

A Chancery suit in which Thomas' grandmother and mother give evidence on behalf of his father in 1563 [1] fixes the date of their birth. Sir Thomas was here involved in his capacity as Lord Mayor, together with other Aldermen, against John and Margaret Wytbroke, nephew and niece of Lady Anne's sister Joan by her marriage with Alderman John Machell. The story that emerges from the depositions throws an interesting sidelight on the risks and perils of a time when the changing religion of the State, as Mary succeeded to Edward, and Elizabeth to Mary, interfered so violently with men's desire to worship according to their faith.

Katharine Machell, sister of Alderman John Machell, daughter of a Grocer, sister-in-law to Sir Thomas and Lady Anne, and the widow of another Grocer, Thomas Londe, was a resolute Protestant, and feared the consequences of the advent of Mary upon the throne. Her nephew, John Machell the younger, the cousin of young Thomas Lodge, tell us that in the days of Mary

she was of a moche contrary Religion than was then set furth and vsed and seemed not to passe whether she lyved or dyed being of an other mynde and conscience in matter of Religeon then was at that tyme embraced or allowed in the Realm.

According to Robert Offley, son of a former Lord Mayor, Katharine was

a woman merveleouse addict vnto the Religion now embraced and allowed, for in all Quene maries daies she never came to the Churche but ij seuerall tymes and then taried there but a short tyme and thereby was in moche fere of her lief and this deponent hard the parson of the parish wherof she was to threaten hir for hir Religeon . . . if she had been then put to it she wold haue died in yt.

---

1 C 24/63, *Wytbroke v. Lodge.*

Now Katharine had a fortune, and was exercised more about what would happen to it than to herself if she were 'apprehended and executed for hir Religeon.' She was naturally anxious that it should not be confiscated, but should be saved for her child Margaret. Her brother John Machell, Joan Loddington's husband, was a Catholic, or at any rate conformed. Therefore Katharine lent him some £700 or £710. But she could not, for obvious reasons, appear on any bond for repayment. Machell, therefore, entered into bonds with the Lord Mayor and the City and Commons of London to repay the loan to them, it being understood that they were to act in trust for Katharine. The Lord Mayor named is Sir Thomas Offley, which gives the year 1556 as the date of the transaction. Now, in 1563, in the year of Lodge's mayoralty, Katharine's daughter Margaret, with her husband John Wytbroke, are claiming £710 from the Mayor and City, alleging that the money had not been repaid. Young Machell, twenty years of age on 30 June 1563, was 'servant in house' to his aunt Katharine, and relates in precise detail how the money was in fact paid to Katharine at her own house in 1560, when both he and Margaret were present. Lady Joan Laxton, aged sixty-five, and Lady Anne Lodge, aged thirty-five, appear on the same day, and we learn at once from their evidence exactly how the Laxtons, Lodges, and Machells were inter-related, and how Margaret and John were suing their uncle.

The preambles to the wills of Lady Laxton, Sir Thomas and Lady Anne Lodge are all Protestant in tone. But none of these was of the stuff of which religious zealots are made. The conversion to Catholicism of the younger Thomas Lodge, and his consequent exile, was of a piece with his general refusal to conform to family traditions and influences. Whatever John Machell's religious views, he cer-

tainly stood by his sister, it seems, though not altogether
to his disadvantage, in this transaction. It is true that,
had his share in it been known to Queen Mary's officers, he
might have paid dearly for it. Lady Lodge tells us that her
sister Joan, his wife, knew nothing of it, and that it was
kept very secret. It is significant that the Mayor and
Aldermen were willing to be parties to such a transaction,
if indeed they had accepted the trust and it had not been
laid upon them without their knowledge.

The two ladies both state that old John Machell on his
death-bed, at which they were present with Nicholas
Loddington, Lady Joan's son and brother to Lady Anne,
avowed a debt of £700 to his sister and charged Nicholas
to go at once 'to the Chapel,' the Chapel of the Rolls, near
by, and set the debt on record in writing. But this was
probably merely to make the transaction valid and to
prevent any demand for return of the money. For Lady
Laxton is very clear that Sir Thomas Lodge and the others
are such men as would discharge justly any trust laid upon
them as they understood it. And young Machell's evidence seems conclusive.

Both Lady Joan and Lady Anne sign their names to
their depositions with evident ease and even a certain
grace, indicating a high level of literacy. And we are
helped to see still further into what manner of family circle
and society Thomas Lodge was born, a family with wide
ramifications in the educated and comfortable class of London citizens of distinction. It is also clear that Lady Joan
Laxton has the highest respect for her son-in-law, Sir
Thomas, and a firm conviction of his probity. Sir Thomas
himself was at this very time, as we have seen, befriending
in similar fashion a Protestant refugee from Mary's England, Francis Wilford, who repaid Lodge for his help by a
claim in Chancery more than twenty years later.

The suit against Wytbroke evidently arose in the course of the settling up of John Machell's estate, for which Sir Thomas was responsible as executor to his brother-in-law. He was involved in another suit in the same connection, this time as plaintiff.[1] Machell owned land in Sandbach in Cheshire, which he left to Lodge in trust for the purposes of his will. A certain Dowce Hodgkinson and John Kent had usurped the land, and Lodge appealed to Chancery, being a stranger to Cheshire and unable to cope in Common Law there with the powerful protectors of his opponents. Kent, a local man, was in fact acting for Sir William Ratcliffe of Ordeshall in Lancashire, and I have little doubt that he found the influence of such men of worship as efficacious in its way as the more magic powers experienced by his famous namesake in Munday's romantic comedy of witchcraft,[2] the scene of which was laid in this very region of Cheshire. Kent replied with evidence of a prior title dating from 10 January 1537, and I can find no decrees or any further trace of the suit.

Chambers v. Warfield

Another suit of the same year[3] confirms the evidence that Lady Anne had been married before she became the wife of Sir Thomas, and introduces us to the Lane group of Grocers in Lodge's family. The suit is brought by Thomas Chambers and John Mere against Roger Warfield in their capacity as trustees for the estate of William Lane, as appears from Lane's will, during the infancy of his children. Lane had bought for £80 the leasehold of a house in Bucklersbury in London, called the Red Lion, from Edward Jackman, and had leased it to Warfield. Warfield is seek-

---

1 C 3/109/68. 2 *John a Kent and John a Cumber.*
3 C 24/63/*Chambers* v. *Warfield.*

ing to prove ownership, however, and Chambers and Mere
are demanding either possession or the £80 paid. Their
principal witness is Lady Anne Lodge, who gives evidence
on 20 June, being then aged thirty-five, the age stated
again ten days later, in the Wytbrokes' suit against Sir
Thomas. Her connection with the matter in dispute is at
once explained. William Lane was her late husband. In
1552 he bought the house from Jackman and gave the key
to Warfield's wife, Warfield being then in Flanders. Lady
Anne herself heard Lane say that he had bought it for the
use of the Warfields, and had seen it noted in his Journal,
in his own hand, that Warfield was to pay him £80 for
the house by Christmas 1552. Two of Lane's former apprentices and servants, George Badcock, aged forty, and
Thomas Fisher, aged thirty-seven, give confirmatory evidence. It appears that Warfield had also been Lane's
servant in business, and Fisher had heard Badcock say
how he wished that Lane would be as good to him as he
had been to Warfield. Evidently Warfield was serving
Lane as his factor abroad, and Lane was helping him to
provide a residence for his family in London. Thus we see
yet another group of Grocers closely allied to Lodge, by his
mother's first marriage with the wealthy William Lane.
His will shows us that Lodge had two elder half-brothers,
Luke and Gabriel, and two half-sisters, Anne and Elizabeth,
all adequately provided for, and in charge of the City as
orphans of a freeman. The names of the first three occur
frequently in the City records, chiefly with reference to the
portions due to them under Lane's will. On 12 May 1562
Anne was licensed to marry at her pleasure, and was therefore eighteen years of age.[1] On 23 June Peter Osborne was
licensed to bind Gabriel apprentice and on 17 November
to send him to school in the country.[2] By 18 September

1 *Repertory* 15, f. 70ᵇ.   2 *Ibid.*, ff. 90ᵇ, 144ᵃ.

1567 Luke was of age, and by 8 December 1569 Gabriel also.[1] From these indications it appears that Anne was born early in 1544, Luke in the summer of 1546, and Gabriel in the autum or winter of 1548. Lady Anne must have been married to Lane in 1543 at latest, at the early age of fifteen, and had her first child at sixteen. The evidence is clear that these were in fact her children. The youngest of these half-brothers and sisters of Thomas Lodge must have been at least six years older than he. Luke certainly survived until 1584 at least, when I find him giving evidence, as Luke Lane of London, Grocer, in a Chancery suit.[2]

Thus the pursuit of Lodge's immediate family connections takes his biographer back to the days of the first Tudor king. His grandmother Lady Joan Laxton was less than a generation later than Sir Thomas More, being born eighteen years after him, in 1498, in the reign of Henry VII. Eleven or twelve years later, between 1509 and 1510, in the days when More became Under-Sheriff of London, Lodge's father was born, at the beginning of Henry VIII's reign. His mother was a year old when More became Chancellor in 1529. Lodge himself was born in the last year of Queen Mary's reign. In the interval the great clan of Grocers, of which the Lodge family formed one branch, had built up a vast structure of wealth, respect, and position second to none in the City of London. With such an imposing heritage Thomas Lodge was born, having at his command, had he chosen to use it, the influence of the powerful and affluent group of Laxtons, Lanes, Lodges, Loddingtons, Machells and Woodfords, united not only by their common membership of the great Company of Grocers, but also by the common connections

1 *Repertory* 16, ff. 279ᵃ, 520ᵃ.
2 C 24/170/80.

with the Midlands of the Laxtons, Lodges and Loddingtons. Sir Thomas, we have seen, was probably of Shropshire origin, and was attracted to his investments in that
region by local knowledge and family associations. And it
is worth noting that his last deal in landed property was
the purchase of certain manors from Alban Lodge, alias
Broomley, of Asheley, Staffordshire, and that they were
entailed by his will, in equal division, upon his two youngest sons, Benedict and Henry, and to his heirs in remainder.
The elder sons, William, Thomas and Nicholas, had been
adequately provided for by Lady Anne.

It would seem clear that the rise to fortune of Sir
Thomas was in no small degree assisted by his marriage
with Lady Anne. For she brought with her a handsome
dowry of which we may judge the value from the will of
her first husband, William Lane, which was proved on 14
December 1552.[1] He is described as William Lane the
elder, Grocer, of London, and son of Thomas Lane of Fishburne near Chichester. Other family connections which I
have been able to trace, however, lead once more to Northamptonshire and the Midlands. His brother and nephew,
John and William Lane, were also Grocers. And it is clear
that he had a former wife, a sister of Peter Osborne, the
head of yet another influential family of London merchants
thus brought into the Lodge circle. Bequests of gold rings
to Sir William Laxton his father-in-law, and to Lady Joan
his mother-in-law, make it evident that his wife Anne
Lane is the future wife of Sir Thomas Lodge, as also when
he refers to John Machell, the husband of Anne's sister
Joan, as his brother-in-law. His first bequest is to Anne,
and consisted of a legacy of £2400, to be paid in six months
after his death, of which £2000 was in money and £400 the
value of the lease of his house and of household stuff in it.

[1] P.C.C., 33 Powell.

He left a further £2236 to be divided among his four children, Luke, Gabriel, Anne and Elizabeth, his children by
Anne, and who were then minors. In addition he entailed
upon Luke and Gabriel and his heirs certain houses in
Bucklersbury, of which the chief was 'Servis Toware'
then occupied by Edward Jackman, Grocer. The 'newe
erectyd ospitalls in London' were given rents of houses to
the value of £26 for nineteen years, and St. Bartholomew's
received £40. To the Universities of Oxford and Cambridge he left £60 each. A good deal of feasting must have
followed Lane's death. He left £5 for a memorial dinner
for the Grocers' Company. And for five years two sheep,
two calves and two lambs, with such bread and drink as
was meet, were to be provided for the parishioners of Fishburne at Whitsuntide, 'to be eaten by the people on the
High Street called Fishburne Street.' All Fishburne children under fifteen were to have twelvepence each. And
ten Fishburne maids were to have £1 each upon their marriages. Surely the memory of William Lane was to be a
sweet savour in the nostrils of Fishburne. I can find no
trace of William or of Anne or their children in the frag-
mentary parish registers [1] of Old Fishburne, but a considerable colony of later Lanes is recorded there, and a
Lane from Fishburne died for his country in the Great
War, three and a half centuries after the death of William.
In addition to these public charities, he had private charities to distribute. There is a bequest of £50 Flemish to
Elynor 'my bastard doughter in flaunders,' living at Antwerp. So we see that Lane preceded Vaughan and Lodge
in residence in the Low Countries, and like them did not
while there confine himself strictly to business activities.
His estate of 'Fre Croft' in Fishburne, no longer traceable
there, was entailed upon his father Thomas and his heirs.

1 Kindly placed at my disposal by the Rector, the Rev. N. F. Shaw.

Lady Anne's knowledge of England may well have been extended to Sussex by visits to her father-in-law and to her husband's property near Chichester.

Certainly her husband's bequest of £2400 made her much too eligible a young widow to be left long undisturbed. She was only twenty-four years of age. And a dowry that could have provided for nearly five hundred City dinners might well have tempted even an Alderman. Lady Anne's fortune was still further augmented upon the deaths of Sir William and Lady Joan Laxton.

From her step-father Sir William Laxton, in 1556, she inherited in remainder after the death of Lady Joan Laxton Sir William's lands in Stoke Nayland, in Suffolk and Essex.[1] From Lady Joan, her mother, who died in 1576, she inherited her lands in Plaistow and West Ham, including the house and estate upon which she and Sir Thomas lived, and which Lady Joan had bought of John Quarles, Draper, and a manor in Barking called Malmons, the former being valued at £4 per annun amd the latter at £20 per annum.[2] These were entailed upon Anne and her heirs. In addition Anne came in for all Lady Joan's apparel and household linen, plate to be chosen to the value of £400, her mother's 'great bed in the Chapel Chamber,' and certain intimate possessions with which Thomas must have been familiar in his youth, Lady Joan's great crucifix, and a 'Book of gold' which arouses one's curiosity, and which Lady Anne left at her death to Mary Blagrave, wife of her eldest son William. Something of the splendid scale of living at the house of Lodge's grandmother may be gathered from the description of six damask table-cloths which came to Lady Anne, patterned with the King's Arms, with the story of Cain or with the Holy Ghost, and

1 C 142/112/93, and C 142/177/69.
2 P.C.C., 23 Carew.

each seven yards in length. And we may note that Lady
Joan's quilt was of silk, her bed-curtains of taffeta, and her
pillows of cloth of gold and silver. Nothing was forgotten
in her will. She gave generously to the poor as also to the
London Hospitals, which owe so much to many a great
Grocer, and left £20 each to Oxford and Cambridge Universities for poor scholars. She provided for her old maid
Elizabeth Bedill, who was to stay with Lady Anne and to
have £40 and a bed to take with her so that she might not
be beholden for mere charity even to the child whom she
may well have nursed. Lady Joan was surely a kindly and
understanding soul. Thomas Lodge drew a fictitious picture of an old family servant, Adam Spencer, in his *Rosalynde*. But where is the old Elizabeth who moved helpfully
about the West Ham house when he was a young man of
twenty or so? I think I see Elizabeth and Isabella Spaight,
two old cronies at West Ham, exchanging stories, London
memories of the gallant early years of Henry's reign in return for Northern memories of Flodden Field, and both
sharing later London days when Sir Thomas More went to
the scaffold with a smile, and terror followed terror. How
many such tales did young Thomas hear from the old
lady? Elizabeth outlived Lady Anne and was bequeathed
by her to her eldest son William, with her £40 intact after
two years.

Lady Joan had a considerable manor, Barrow Hall, and
other lands in Essex which she entailed upon Lady Anne's
brother, her son Nicholas Loddington, in addition to
legacies in money amounting to £2351. Nor did she forget
the numerous younger generation of Lodges, Loddingtons
and Machells, several of them her god-children. To Joan
Lodge, now Joan Woodford, she left £40 in plate. To
William she left £100 at the age of twenty-one 'Vppon
condicōn that he be ruled by his frendes for his educacōn

vntil his said yeres of xxi.' Possibly William, like Thomas
later on, was showing signs of youthful unruliness. To
Thomas, as to her three other Lodge grandsons and to
three Loddington grandsons, Lady Joan left £100 each to
be paid when they reached the age of twenty-one, with no
minatory condition. Thomas, still at Oxford, had not yet
betrayed his tendencies. She also left £20 to 'Mary Lodge,
wife of Thomas Lodge' and £10 to their daughter Joan, her
god-daughter, upon her marriage. It is this bequest that
has led biographers of Lodge, I gather, to endow him with
a wife and a daughter in 1576 at latest, when he was at
most nineteen years of age, and when he was still an under-
graduate. It is clearly impossible. Nor could the 'Thomas'
be a slip for 'William.' William certainly married a
'Mary' Blagrave, but not until a year after the death of
Lady Joan. It would seem most likely that the Thomas
Lodge in question was the other Thomas Lodge of Lincoln's Inn, born in 1542, and apparently related to Lady
Joan, by her daughter Anne's marriage with Sir Thomas.
The suggestion is, therefore, plausible that he was the son
of Sir Thomas' kinsman Richard. Sir Thomas, we may recall, married Lady Anne late in life, when he was over
forty years of age, so that a brother's children might well
be considerably older than his children by Lady Anne.

By the time Lady Anne died, the considerable accumu-
lation of ready money which came to her from her first
husband had vanished. There is, at any rate, no trace of it
in her will or in the will of Sir Thomas. Much of it, no
doubt, had been lost in the disastrous year of Sir Thomas'
mayoralty. But some of it certainly appears to have been
invested in land, of which Lady Anne had a great deal in
joint possession with Sir Thomas. The total value of her
estate appears to have been about £3000, the amount of
the bond into which William as executor had to enter to

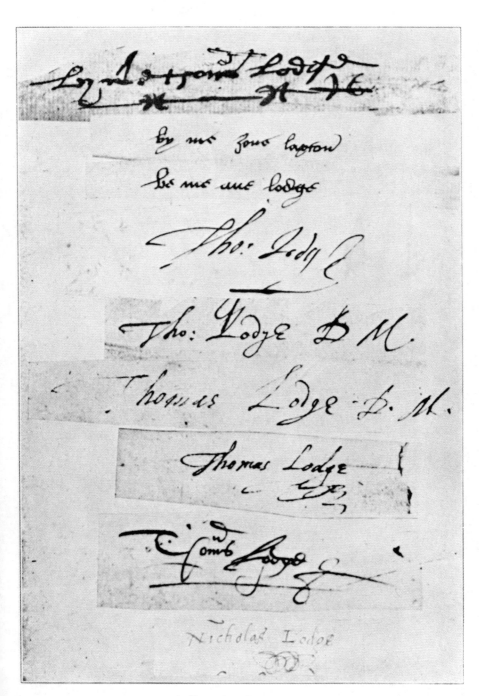

A Page of Signatures

secure due fulfilment of her will. The preamble to her will [1] indicates, I think, that Sir Thomas and Lady Anne were happily united. For she states that Sir Thomas has authorized her to dispose of her property. And when dealing with her lands she writes that she cannot convey them except by fine, yet she is content to leave them to come to her heirs after the death of Sir Thomas, confident that Sir Thomas will carry out her wishes. One may well read into this a pleasant reciprocity of wifely dutifulness and of marital respect and love, which helps us to understand something of what the loss of Lady Anne must have meant to the old knight, something of the significance of the memorial gateway at Hyde House, and perhaps also how the atmosphere of the great house at West Ham may have altered in the few last years he still lived after her death. The younger children were sent away, Nicholas and Benedict to live with their sister Joan Woodford and her husband, and Henry to Rolleston, in Nottinghamshire, to his brother William and his wife, it appears.[2]

Lady Anne's will was dated 15 September 1579, with a codicil dated 17 September, and it was proved by William Lodge on 26 January 1580. Little as she had to leave in money, and much even of this was held by her in trust as executor to carry out the money bequests of her mother, Lady Joan Laxton, not yet fulfilled, she did not forget the Universities, to which she left £20 each. The cost of her funeral was not to exceed £100. And she desired to be buried in the Church of St. Mary Aldermary, in the tomb made for her mother, in which Sir Thomas joined her five years later. Her apparel and linen she divided between her daughter Joan Woodford and her daughter-in-law Mary Lodge. To her grandchildren, her god-daughters Anne

1 P.C.C., 2 Arundell.
2 C 24/236/24.

Lodge and Anne Woodford, she left a gold chain and a gold cross respectively. Her household stuff at West Ham was to remain for the use of Sir Thomas until his death and thereafter to pass to William and his heirs, with remainder to Thomas. And the residue of her effects was to be sold and divided equally among her five sons, of whom Nicholas, Benedict and Henry were still under age. Their shares were to be paid in trust to certain London merchants and the interest used for their maintenance. So it would appear that Nicholas was then in wardship to Gamaliel Woodford, Benedict to Richard Culverwell, and Henry to Thomas Waterhouse. The share of Thomas was not to be paid until he reached the age of twenty-five. This restriction is as significant as the change in the disposition of lands revealed in the codicil to her will, which was witnessed by John Lane and signed by both Lady Anne and Sir Thomas. Her executors were Sir William Cordell, Master of the Rolls, who, with Lady Cordell, was evidently an intimate family friend, and her son William. Sir Thomas and Peter Osborne were overseers of her will, which was signed by both Sir Thomas and Lady Anne. And William was charged to act as executor throughout under the advice of Sir William Cordell. We shall see that Sir William had to shoulder this responsibility and to make serious decisions when the affairs of young Thomas came into question.

In Lady Anne's original disposal of her lands she entailed upon Thomas and his heirs the manor of Malemaynes or Malmons in Essex, and all her lands and houses in Barking and Dagenham, to be conveyed to him within a half-year if Cordell approved. The remainder falls to William, Nicholas, Benedict and Henry and their heirs in turn. The rest of her lands are entailed upon William and his heirs. In the codicil to her will, however, she revokes this bequest, but makes an alternative legacy, 'myndinge yet thadvauncement of my seconde sonne to some convenient porcon of lyvinge,' and leaves to him instead her property called 'the late ffree Chappell in Nayland in the Countie of Suffolk and the Advowson of the same.' With this went other lands in the same district, 'Preists feilds' in Nayland, thirty acres or so, sixteen acres in Great Horsley called 'Woodfenne,' a capital messuage in Stoke Nayland called Bakers, with other lands there held by claim from the Laxtons and others. All this property was to be assured to Thomas or to remain in trust for him according as Cordell decided.

The remaining lands, entailed as before upon William, are enumerated in the Inquisition [1] held upon the death of Sir Thomas. They include a house with six acres of land in West Ham, which I take to be the family dwelling-house, four other houses and sixty-four acres of land also in West Ham parish, and the manor of Malemaynes or Malmons in Dagenham and Barking. Of these, the West Ham lands had been entailed upon Lady Anne by her mother, together with Malmons, and the Nayland property by Sir William Laxton. One important property had apparently been settled upon the Lodges by Lady Laxton, or bought from her, the manor of Rolleston in Nottinghamshire, of which no mention is made in any will. This property, as we shall see, furnished an estate for William Lodge, and it seems to have been conveyed to him, doubtless upon his marriage with Mary Blagrave, before the death of Sir Thomas, as part of the marriage-settlement.

There remains, finally, the will [2] of Sir Thomas Lodge, dated 14 December 1583, but not proved until 7 June 1585, by Gamaliel Woodford, his son-in-law, and Thomas Pigott,

1 C 142/203/76.
2 P.C.C., 29 Brudenell.

his cousin, also a Grocer. The household stuff at West Ham has been inventoried and is to be divided between the three younger sons, as is also a sum of £200 in the hands of William realised by the sale of a lease of the Manor of Sulton. His lease of 'Perryfelde' and a recent purchase of land at West Ham are to be sold to carry out the provisions of the will. Sir Thomas has little to leave, and most of his legacies are in the nature of memorials to friends, cousins, servants, grandchildren and godchildren. He leaves pieces of plate to the youngest Thomas Lodge, his godson, and to Anne Lodge (the children of William), to his three younger sons, to his godson Thomas Woodford and to William and Anne Woodford, children of Gamaliel and Joan Woodford. The total sum of all his legacies in money is less than £70, which seems to me a pathetically small amount to be at the disposal of the man who was once a financial power in the land, who had been Lord Mayor of London, and whose affairs had been a matter of serious concern to the Queen and her Privy Council. What money he had, had apparently been expended recently upon an estate in Staffordshire bought of Alban Lodge, which was now entailed in equal halves upon his two youngest children, Benedict and Henry, who were left unprovided with land by their mother. Nicholas still remained landless, except in the hope of remainders from his elder or younger brothers. Little as Sir Thomas had to leave, however, he can still afford £5 for the poor of West Ham. He provides further £3 for six anniversary sermons. And seventy-eight poor men are to have two shillings each and a pair of gloves each to accompany him to his grave. The gloves have been bought ready for this — Sir Thomas saw to it himself — and there are enough to supply also a pair for any neighbours who care to come to see him buried. And so 'Sir Thomas Lodge, Knight, late Lord Maior of Lon-

don' died on 28 February 1584 and went to his rest beside
Lady Anne in the Laxton vault.[1] The number of poor men
who are to form part of his funeral gathering is, as usual,
intended to represent the number of years of his life. But
Sir Thomas, when in the prime of life, gives us 1509 or
1510 himself as the year of his birth. I have observed
not infrequently that old Elizabethans tend to exaggerate
their age when they once pass seventy, or indeed earlier,
and we need not examine this discrepancy more closely.
It is an odd, whimsical, and entirely pardonable vanity of
extreme old age, which has so few occasions for vanity. I
wish I could accept Sir Thomas' seventy-eight. There was
not much in his last years to comfort him. His glory had
departed, and there was no hope, as far as he could see, of
any revival of that glory in his sons. Even his last will and
testament was not to go unchallenged. His third son,
Nicholas, contested it with pretended letters of administration, which the Court rejected on 22 May 1584.[2] And
it was not until 7 June 1585 that probate was granted.
When we turn to Thomas Lodge, his second son, we shall
find that the earliest records of his life show him in conflict with his father and reveal one of the sorrows of his old
age. It has often been observed that Thomas is not mentioned in his father's will. This in itself will not perhaps
bear the implications drawn. For Thomas was fully provided for by his mother. But there is corroborative evidence that Sir Thomas had cut him off as an unfruitful
branch.

1 Parish Register, St. Mary Aldermary.
2 P.C.C., Sentence, 26 Brudenell.

III. THOMAS LODGE AND HIS BROTHERS

IN THE younger generation of this solid clan of London grocers we may see the dissolution of the traditions upon which it had founded its wealth and position, in the careers of the two elder sons of Sir Thomas and Lady Anne. It may be that Lady Anne's ambitions were turned towards gentility. The Laxtons bore arms, duly blazoned in the *Visitation of London*, and Lady Anne bequeathed to the most distinguished of her friends, Sir William Cordell, Master of the Rolls, her mother's skink-pot of gold with Lady Joàn's arms embossed upon it. Perhaps she looked forward to seeing William or Thomas following in the Master's footsteps rather than in those of the great business men of her own family. At any rate, her eldest son was given a legal training at Lincoln's Inn,[1] and was married outside of the clan, to Mary, the daughter of Thomas Blagrave, a Court official, and acting Master of the Revels, on 14 October 1577. Thomas was sent to Oxford and thereafter to Lincoln's Inn. It was evidently intended that the Lodge family of the second generation should, in its elder sons, be raised above trade. William was married into the gentry and provided with an estate in Nottinghamshire, the manor of Rolleston. Here the new head of the family was established in a country seat. Thomas was similarly provided with the estate of Stoke Nayland, in the hope that a second branch of the line might be founded there. Thus provided, and trained in the law, either might have risen to fame in the service of the Queen or in their great profession, with a secure position in Nottingham and Suffolk as country gentlemen and Justices of the Peace. So

---

1 He was admitted on 30 July 1573 (*Records of Lincoln's Inn: Admissions*, I, 80). Thomas entered on 26 April 1578 (*Ib.*, p. 87).

the Lodge family would have transcended its citizen foundations, with two lines of gentry to fall back upon, firmly rooted in the land. No parents, one would say, could have builded more surely and more substantially for the honour of their family name. But an essential part of the structure was the character of the sons destined to fulfil their hopes, and in this lay its weakness. Neither William nor Thomas had the necessary stability, as we shall see.

The circumstances of the education of Thomas Lodge must be included in the count of the disturbing factors in his life that were adverse to the influences of his family and his environment. Lodge passed from the Merchant Taylors' School in 1573 to Trinity College, Oxford, where he was withdrawn from the sober, settled and conventional circle at the great West Ham house and the Aldermanbury mansion, and came into contact with new and unconventional ideals of life, based largely upon self-assertion, and worship of scholarship which had in it a strong flavour of complacency and intellectual snobbery, and an implicit contempt for citizens, the City, and trade. The scholar and the gallant were cater-cousins, and gallantry hoped for maintenance by virtue of scholarship. Thomas was up at Oxford at the same time as a lively group of young men, of whom John Lyly was the senior, and George Peele a junior with Lodge. Lodge tells us himself in *Rosalynde* that he was intimate with the two Carey brothers, Edmond and Robert, sons of Lord Hunsdon, who were at Trinity with him. There can be little doubt of his association with the University Wits. Lyly and Peele, like himself, were Londoners. Peele's father, James Peele, was Clerk of Christ's Hospital under Sir Thomas Lodge as Mayor or Alderman. Lodge's career in London indicates a similarity of tastes, and he wrote a play in collaboration with Greene, a Cambridge Wit, who also saw through the press Lodge's *Eu-*

phues Shadow, when Lodge was on his voyage to Brazil. His friendship with the Careys may well have fired him with visions beyond the gentry of the robe. The citizen's son was dazzled by the twin ambitions of wit and gentility, and desired to consort henceforth with Town and Court instead of City. Altogether Oxford seems to have unsettled Lodge, and made him singularly disinclined to pursue the career marked out for him by his parents. Armed with his learning, and helped by patronage and literature, he hoped to shine in a new way of life, above the vulgar element of Lodges, Lanes, Loddingtons and Laxtons, buried in old-fashioned smugness. It is a story familiar in all ages, and the ambitions and contempts of lively youth are re-born daily. It is true that the career of Sir Thomas, at this stage, suggested that citizen life was beset with pitfalls, and sadly insecure.

When Lodge came back to London, after taking his degree on 8 July 1577, and was admitted to Lincoln's Inn on 26 April 1578, he seems to have given little attention to his law studies, and much attention to other matters, living the life of a scholar as these young men conceived one worthy of their quality and ideals. We shall see how Lodge's family thought of his way of life, and what effect their views had upon his fortunes. We shall also see that, if Lodge refused to take his studies at Lincoln's Inn seriously, and neglected to follow the safe and certain career open to him, the circumstances of his life and temperament kept him in and out of law-courts during a long period of at least thirty years, to the great benefit of his biographers to come. In this respect, at any rate, he was the worthy son of his father. For if he showed no signs of the commercial talent of Sir Thomas, the great Grocer, or indeed of the overwhelming heredity that was concentrated upon the children of the Lodges, he certainly inherited litigious

tastes and found in the law the opportunity of expressing
the marked stubbornness of his disposition and that passion for having his own way which his whole life betrays.
In this, it seems to me, he was not unlike his father. It
may be also that we should bear in mind the indications in
the career of Sir Thomas of speculation, ending in disaster,
and read into the career of his son something of the same
self-confidence that defies control and circumspection.

The main outlines of Lodge's life have long been known
and put on record by Sir Sidney Lee in the *Dictionary of
National Biography*, and by Sir Edmund Gosse in his edition of Lodge's *Works*.[1] But there is little in these accounts
that brings us in any way into intimate touch with the details of such a life. A great deal may now be added to fill
in the picture and to enable us to see the man himself as he
appeared in his doings and sayings, in his relations with
contemporaries, in their opinion of him, and in the practical concerns of a complex society. From this additional
knowledge, derived from the records of a series of law-
suits in which he was involved, we have material enough
to enable us to judge of his character and to throw considerable light upon his books. It is significant that the
more we learn about Lodge the more his writings seem
to be a direct reflection of the actual course of his life.
Successful research into the life of a man like Lodge grat-
ifies in itself the inquisitiveness of pure curiosity or the
detective instincts of the normal human busybody. But
in the end it is mainly the bearing of such knowledge upon
literature that compensates for and justifies the time and
labour spent in research or in reading of its results. It is
true also that even the records of law-suits, in so far as
they set before us the intimacies of human life three hun-

1 They have now been set forth again, with additions, in Professor Paradise's
Thomas Lodge (1931).

dred years ago, have their own interest apart from their relation to the thoughts and the character of a man of letters. Much of this information is derived from records that bear upon Lodge's unhappy relations with his own family.

LODGE v. COOPER

A Chancery suit of 1594 may serve as a preface to the long debate, which we are to chronicle, between Lodge and his brother William, inasmuch as it not only gives an example of the young poet's frequent indebtedness, but also suggests the course of life that led him into this condition. In this suit Lodge is plaintiff against Samuel Cooper and his wife Anne. His Bill of Complaint [1] is dated 20 November 1594, and he is praying a Court of Equity to intervene in a suit at Common Law for the recovery of debt brought against him by the Coopers. On 13 December 1588, it appears, Lodge made a bond to Peter Suckling, a London vintner, for £100. He owed Suckling £16, and Suckling had agreed that if Lodge could get his brother William Lodge, of Rolleston, to enter into a bond of £32 for payment of the debt of £16, Lodge's bond would be cancelled. Lodge, however, paid the debt on the date fixed on his own bond, but no receipt was given, and his bond remained with Suckling. Suckling died, his widow Anne married Cooper, and the Coopers, having the bond, are now suing Lodge at Common Law for the full amount of his bond.

It is clear, I think, that William did not give the alternative bond, and this part of Lodge's statement is introduced to argue that his debt was only of £16, whereas the normal amount of a bond is for double that of the debt. It is true, of course, that heavier security might be demanded of an unsafe debtor. In the absence of evidence upon this point

1 C 3/244/75.

it is difficult to judge of the probabilities. But a bond of
£100 for a debt of £16 seems to me excessive, and it would
hardly have stood in law if claimed on forfeit.

Evidence, mainly on the question of payment, was
brought by Lodge on 11 December 1594.[1] Suckling, it appears, kept a tavern frequented by Lodge. George Moreland, yeoman, of Barking near Tower Hill, aged fifty-two,
deposes that he has known Lodge for ten years. He also
knew Suckling 'as he might knowe any other vintener by
comyng now and then to drinke at the Taverne,' in this
instance the famous King's Head in Fleet Street, at the
corner of Chancery Lane, where a plaque may be found
today to mark the place it occupied since the thirteenth
century, close to the Chapel of the Rolls, next door to
Serjeants' Inn, and most convenient for the gentlemen of
Lincoln's Inn.

Lodge owed Moreland money too; and Moreland relates
a conversation with him:

he remembreth well that on a tyme which was about v or vj yeres agon
this deponent seeing the said Complainant (Lodge) and Peter Suckling
going together into the Taverne called the kings head at Chancerye lane
end in ffleet street went presently after them into the Taverne to gett
some money iff he cold of the said Thomas Lodge who was then indebted
to this deponent. And comyng vnto them he called the said Complainant a syde and told him he was come vnto him being a pore man that
wold fayne have his owne and therfore prayd to have some money And
Tho Lodge made answer in theis or the lyke words in effect saying I cannot lett yow haue any money now ffor here I have dispatcht a matter
with Mr. Suckley and have paid him all the money I have And I hope
he ys satysfyed now the said Tho Lodge speaking theis words in the
hearing of the said Suckley who therto answered and sayd vnto Tho
Lodge [I am answered] I have nothing to do with yow And as yt then
seemed to this deponent the said Tho Lodge had then satysfyed some
debt which he owed to the said Peter Suckly ffor Suckly the same tyme
had a great deale of money in his hand which to see vnto he had newly
receyved.

1 C 24/243/56.

I have been unable to find the final decrees in this suit. There are interim decrees.[1] On 28 November 1594 the Coopers failed to answer to Lodge's Bill, and a writ of attachment was awarded against them. On 12 July 1595 they were admitted to plead *in forma pauperis*, on account of their 'extreme poverty.' There is nothing further, apparently. I cannot therefore narrate the outcome, or presume an opinion on the facts. Moreland is unable to swear, 'dare not absolutely depose' that the transaction he witnessed bore upon the bond in question, though he thinks it did.

What this suit shows is that certain views concerning Lodge's way of life held by a wide variety of persons who knew him well were amply justified. He seems to have been one more to add to the number of young men about town of whom Nashe said 'who among us but is subject to debt and deadly sin?' Even before he left Lincoln's Inn in 1580 he had betaken himself to literature and the drama instead of to the law. After five years of this we find him at sea with Captain Clarke, on his way a-pirating to the Canaries.[2] It may well be that debt drove him upon this adventure. It will be remembered that he published *Rosalynde, Euphues Golden Legacy*, soon after Moreland saw him, late in 1588 or early in 1589, settling up his debt to Suckling, and hoped in vain to have his own debt settled. It was then also that Lodge declared his intention to seek higher literary ambitions than the stage could inspire, and to

> Write no more of that whence shame doth grow,
> Or tie my pen to penny-knaves delight;
> But live with fame and so for fame to write.[3]

---

1 C 33/87, f. 683; C 33/89, f. 405.
2 Professor Paradise gives convincing evidence that Lodge sailed with Grenvile on 9 April 1585, along with his cousin Thomas Loddington and with Cavendish, as far as the Canaries at any rate (*op. cit.*, pp. 36–37).
3 *Scillaes Metamorphosis*, 1589.

Once more he set forth on a sea-venture with Cavendish, on an ill-starred expedition, to which we shall refer again, whence he returned to London by 1593, to find the Coopers with his old bond, pressing him for £100, a claim which his sonnets to Phillis could not enable him to meet. In desperate need for money, he turned to his brother William, now a country gentleman in Nottinghamshire, and their conversations led them to debate certain matters at issue between them in the Courts of Chancery and Star Chamber. In the course of these suits, in which the evidence takes us back to earlier years, it appears clear that Lodge's family shared in part the derogatory views of Stephen Gosson, who in a well-known passage stigmatised him as 'a playmaker, an Epicure and an Atheist.' They certainly considered him to be a very unsteady young man, unfit to carry on the family traditions or to inherit the property conditionally left to him.

THOMAS LODGE v. WILLIAM LODGE

If we were to accept the statements of Thomas Lodge, made in a Star Chamber Bill[1] of 16 May 1593, in which he lays an information against his brother William, we should find in his story a prototype of Shakespeare's Orlando in his relations with his elder brother, though Lodge would have been hard put to it, even in a Star Chamber Bill, to have asked with any grace, 'What prodigal portion have I spent, that I should come to such penury?' For this was, in fact, precisely what he had done. He relates, however, that there had arisen

diuerse controuersies questions and debates betwene your sayd Subiect and one Wm lodge of Rolleston . . . Nottingham Esquier being the eldest brother of your sayd Subiect of for and Concerning diuerse

---

1 *Star Ch. Pro.* 5, L 26/18.

legacyes gyfts and bequests as well of goods and Chattalls as allso of
lands bequethed vnto your sayd subiect by one dame Anne lodge late of
london deceased to be performed and satisfied by the sayd Wm lodge
vnto your sayd subiect as by the will of the sayd Dame Anne Lodge may
appeare for the appeasinge whereof your sayd Subiect being a student
at Lyncolnes ynne . . . did by Reason of Brotherly love and affection
. . . and for auoydinge of suits and trobles trauell from Lyncolnes ynne
. . . into Nottingham shire to Rolleston . . . being above the space of a
hundred miles to have taken some good and loveinge End with Wm
lodge.

It may seem strange for Thomas Lodge, the Atlantic voy-
ager, to lay such stress upon the arduousness of a journey
to Nottingham from London. It is true, however, that to
travel a hundred miles by road in Elizabethan England
was a considerable undertaking, and very expensive. And
in any case Lodge was making the most of it to show his
spirit of good will. The Courts liked to be told, even if
they did not believe it, that litigants had exhausted all
peaceful means before going to law.

Lodge, it will be remembered, had recently returned
from his voyage with Captain Cavendish. It is probable
that he had sunk some money in this disastrous venture.
There is a possibility, as we shall see, that those who sailed
with Adrian Gilbert in the *Dainty*, probably including
Lodge, did not lose on the voyage. But there is no doubt
about Lodge's situation early in 1593. He was certainly
in low water. It is evident that he therefore set to work to
revive old claims on his brother William arising out of the
will of his mother, Lady Anne Lodge, of which William
was an executor. Lady Anne had died fourteen years before, on 31 December 1579, and Sir Thomas on 28 February 1584. And with this in mind he journeyed northwards to see William. I have often wondered whether
Lodge had William in mind when he drew the picture of
that 'covetous caterpillar,' the Usurer in *A Looking Glass
for London and England*, in a scene which we may reason-

ably take to be the work of the young lawyer rather than
of Greene.

At any rate, as Lodge saw the matter, the words of
Alcon to Thrasybulus might have been applied to the subsequent conversations: 'Friend, thou speakest Hebrew to
him when thou talkest to him of conscience.' So he related the outcome of his painful journey. For William,
'careless of love and affection which he ought to have
borne and vsed towards . . . [Thomas] in respect of his
longe trauell,' refused to agree to his proposals, and 'gave
. . . dyvers and sundrye evill and malicious words and
threatnings to the great terror of [Thomas].' Nay more,
he conspired with strangers unknown to Thomas to have
him set upon as he was travelling homewards to London
on leaving William, 'and by force of Armes to mayme or
otherwise to bereve [Thomas] of his liff,' so that William
might be finally freed from the risks of law-suits to come,
upon which Thomas was bent. Indeed, he was on his way
to institute them. Once more we find the parallel in *As
You Like It*, in the words of Orlando's elder brother
Oliver:

I'll tell thee, Charles, it is the stubbornest young fellow of France; . . .
a secret and villainous contriver against me his natural brother; therefore use thy discretion. I had as lief thou didst break his neck as his
finger. . . . I speak but brotherly of him.

It would have been a pity if Lodge had missed seeing that
play; he would surely have had a warm fellow-feeling with
Orlando, along with many another younger brother.

So, he goes on, these hired ruffians of William's, 'about
the number of three,' assaulted him as he journeyed on the
highway 'in February last' with his man William, whom
they beat and very sorely wounded, and very evilly entreated both of them and did them divers hurts. He

therefore charges William with riot, and prays that he be brought to book for it.

His Bill is dated 16 May 1593. William put in his Answer on 23 May, a week later, which is remarkably prompt. I think we may take it that when Thomas set out from William's inhospitable house at Rolleston he declared his intentions very clearly, and that William immediately girded up his loins also for the journey to London, with counter-suits simmering already in his mind. I see in my mind's eye, indeed, two small groups of pilgrims, Thomas and his man William on their horses, and William and his three men, or maybe two, also on horseback. It may even be that there was a race to London to get the first Bill in and the first shot fired. There would be untoward meetings at inns at the nightly stopping-places, with fresh explosions of high words. They might, of course, have travelled together for mutual protection against the perils of the road, and the riot charged against William might have been simply a wayside quarrel more acrimonious than the average level of ill-temper, the general burden of the journey. But I think each party would have preferred its own company, and would spend the time formulating schemes, seductive ways of manipulating the facts, and damning interrogatories; the time would thus have passed very pleasantly till London was reached and till a pair of lawyers and some sheets of parchment could be brought together.

William's Answer dismisses Thomas' Bill as the figment of mere malice, planned only to trouble him and to force him to come to London from his far-off dwelling-place. His complaints are 'moste faulse and maliciouslye and unnaturally supposed and contryved.' There is no evidence of riot or of anything proper to the Court of Star Chamber. He therefore demurs in law and asks for costs.

It is only rarely that we find traces of the outcome of suits in Star Chamber. In this instance, however, the rest of the story is told by William when he in turn, a year later, made his complaint against Thomas in the same Court. His Bill [1] is dated 12 May 1594, and he takes the opportunity of surveying the various legal assaults made upon him by Thomas, his natural brother, being moved by his envy of William's good estate. Imprimis, Thomas has proceeded against him in Chancery. William has done his duty, without any obstructive delays, the matter has gone forward to publication of evidence, and now awaits trial and judgement. But Thomas has also procured in that Court a writ 'de securitate inveniend quod se non divertat ad partes exteras sine licencia,' unreasonably, as William has no intention of evading his responsibilities or of flying abroad to escape the jurisdiction of the Court, nor does he need to do so. However, he has put in the requisite heavy bonds to the Sheriff of Nottingham.

Secondly, Thomas has put in a Bill in Star Chamber in Easter Term of last year. William's demurrer was referred to Mr. Justice Fenner of the Queen's Bench, who upheld it. The Court awarded £8 costs against Thomas. William's subpoena to Thomas for recovery of these costs was, however, contemned by Thomas, whereupon William proceeded, in the Hilary Term of the present year, to procure a writ of attachment against him returnable in this present Easter Term. Thomas still refused, and William now went to extremes, with a writ of attachment with proclamation of rebellion returnable in the coming Trinity Term. Thomas at last was moved with fear and a guilty conscience, but being still 'ledde by the instigacion of the devill' and determined to pay no costs, came to Court on 23 April, about three weeks ago, and made an

1 *Star Ch. Pro.* 5, L 44/4

affidavit which justifies William's charge of perjury now brought against him. The affidavit is now cited at length. 'Thomas Lodge of Lyncolns Inne in the Countie of Middlesex gentleman aged xxxvj yeares' admitted the fact that £8 costs were awarded against him in the Star Chamber on behalf of William Lodge. But there were reasons. Thomas did not pursue the suit as he might have done. William was his own brother, for one thing. Moreover, Mr. Tonge, a clerk in Mr. Shuckburgh's office in Chancery, who was also William's man of law, asked Thomas to drop the suit and to 'spare' his brother, on a promise that if he did so William would answer to the suit in Chancery which Thomas had initiated. It was understood that William also would withdraw from the Star Chamber suit. But he broke faith, pursued the matter, and got his costs of £8 awarded. Therefore Thomas refused to pay them, and felt that the Court would agree with him.

William, having cited this affidavit, is indignant at its lying statements, intended solely to defraud him of the costs lawfully due to him. He therefore prays for a subpoena, 'for that the saide Thomas Lodge hath not yett receaued any punishment for the same.' The quarrels begun at Rolleston in Nottinghamshire, growing to heat and violence on the highway to London, have reached their height. For what William now prays for is, in effect, a sentence of imprisonment upon his brother in the Gatehouse or even the Tower, for defiance of the Court.

Thomas answered William's Bill on 16 May, asserting the truth of his affidavit and relating its consequences. It was referred by the Court to Mr. Mill, its Clerk, 'whoe consideringe the great pouertie of the defendant (Thomas) and the long delaies and exceedinge troubles which this plaintiff (William) iniuriouslie sought to inforce against his said brother the defendant,' fixed an audience for hearing objections. On the day appointed, Tonge failed to appear, nor was any objection made. Mr. Mill came to the conclusion that the Court was being used to satisfy malice and therefore discharged Thomas of the contempt of Court and of the costs which William was seeking to recover. Thomas was not trying to plague William with suits, only to enforce his rights. As for the writ 'ne exeat regnũ,' this was obtained 'onlie for that he this defendant well vnderstoode that he was determined to pass beyonde seas . . . and so meant to do, for he would not come to hearing or ordering of the suit now depending in Chancery.' The matter proceeded to the taking of evidence from Thomas,[1] in reply to interrogatories from William which probe further the matter of the affidavit, and to which Thomas replies as in his Answer. William puts further questions. Some suggest that Thomas is being maintained and paid by some other person, and has been instigated to obtain the writ 'ne exeat regnũ' against him. Another insinuates contempt of the Court and its order for costs against him: 'what were the scornefull words you used touching the same and whether did you not clayme a priviledge in Powles, alleadginge that it woulde serve well enoghe to stay a Starr Chamber Subpena?' This clearly hints at some wild talk by Lodge in the common meeting-place in St. Paul's Cathedral. William also asks him whether he had not, before he began these suits, 'made a Release of all demaunds' upon William, and whether William had not maintained him and given him apparel until the suits began. Whatever the facts, Lodge was wise enough to refuse to answer these irrelevant questions, and was content to reply that they might be discussed in the Court of Chancery, where they were relevant.

The final outcome of these Star Chamber proceedings is

1 *Star Ch. Pro.* 5, L 6/3.

bound up with the conclusion of the Chancery suit then in
progress between the two brothers and with the agreement
reached in the end with the help of that Court.

I have been unable to find the pleadings in this Chancery
suit, which first emerges among the depositions taken before the Examiner at the Office of the Rolls in Chancery
Lane. They comprise two files of evidence, given respectively on behalf of Thomas[1] and on behalf of William,[2]
from October 1593 to January 1594. The main issue is
the claim that Thomas has upon William in respect of the
settlement of the estate of their mother Lady Anne Lodge,
who had lent certain lands and money to Thomas, the bequests to take effect after the death of her husband Sir
Thomas, which occurred early in 1584. William Lodge was
an executor of the wills of both Sir Thomas and Lady Anne.

The dominant note of the evidence is struck by William's first witness, Nicholas Markham of London, Ironmonger, aged 45. Thomas Lodge, he says,

was indebted to divers persons and for that he tooke no stayed course of
life for the mayntennance of his estate with credyt therefore he the said
defendant (William) for the good of the plaintiff made stay of the conveying of the lands mencioned in the Interrogatory.

The second main point is made by William Payne of London, Haberdasher, aged 34, who states that on 23 February
1583 Thomas made a formal release to William, which
Payne signed as witness, of all his responsibilities to
Thomas under the wills of Lady Joan Laxton or Lady
Anne Lodge, or under any suits that might be brought
against him by Thomas concerning them, in return for
money furnished by William to pay Thomas' debts.

On 21 January William's coadjutor in the execution of
the will of Lady Anne appeared to give evidence at length

1 C 24/236/24.   2 C 24/235/20.

concerning the provisions of the will and its administration. Gamaliel Woodford, then aged sixty, brother-in-law of the two litigants, was also an old friend of the family, having known both Sir Thomas and Lady Anne for forty years, and William and Thomas from their infancy. Lady Anne had left £400 at her death to each of her children as their share of her residuary estate, and her mother, Lady Joan Laxton, had also left legacies to her grandchildren. Gamaliel now goes on to mention the various children concerned. Nicholas and Benedict have had their portions paid since Lady Anne's death. They have been for some time living in his house with him and have made no complaint. If they had not been paid, he goes on, he 'thinketh he should have hard thereof' in these circumstances! Henry also seems to be contented. As for Thomas, his portion has been gradually exhausted in the payment of his debts from time to time, and he has signed a release to the executors, which Gamaliel has seen, from all claims under both wills. William has been a good brother to Thomas, for Gamaliel 'hath knowen the defendant alwayes well affected and to have an honest and brotherly care towards the plaintiff and so towards the rest of his brethren.' There remains the question of the lands left to Thomas under the wills of his mother and grandmother, the Free Chapel of Nayland in Suffolk. This property was entailed upon Thomas, and was left to the disposition of Sir William Cordell, Master of the Rolls, now deceased. But the lands were never conveyed to Thomas. The Master constantly refused to do so, the cause being 'the disorderly kynd of lyffe that he sawe or deemed to be in the said Complaynant.' William was indeed anxious to clear up the estate. He had actually asked Gamaliel to speak to Sir Thomas Lodge, in the hope that he would use his influence with the Master

to be a means to Cordell for his consent to convey the lands Naylands
as limited in the will, and was very earnest with him (Gamaliel), because
he (William) had none other lands holden in capite that were entayled
but only Naylands and yf the same were not passed over to his brother
Tho Lodge the same after his decease might drawe his the defendant's
heire into wardshippe.

Certainly the last thing William would wish would be for
his own estate to fall into wardship under the Crown, on
the ground that it included an unsettled property held
of the Crown, as Nayland was. Gamaliel did as he was
asked, and so did Sir Thomas in turn. But Cordell stood
firm that the lands should 'remayne as they were to Wm
Lodge.' The views of Sir Thomas, moreover, coincided
with those of the Master of the Rolls:

because his sonne Tho Lodge he sayd did take such a disordred Corse of
lyffe as he did, & that he sawe no lykelyhood that yt wold be otherwyse
with him he wold neuer graunt that the said lands should be conueyed
vnto Tho Lodge & therfore prayed this deponent not to move him anye
more in that matter also declaring vnto this deponent as he best remembreth that the cause why the said Sir Wm Cordell sayd he wold not consent to th assuring of the lands to Tho Lodge was because the said Com-
plainants then Conuersaĉon of lyffe was not agreeable to the lyking of
the said Mr of Rolls as he then sayd yt was not to the lyking of him the
said Sr Thomas Lodge.

Woodford leaves no loophole for misunderstanding the
dislike of the two authorities for Lodge's way of life.

An interrogatory in William's case, to which, however,
no witness replied, suggested how some of the legacies upon
which Thomas was basing his claims had been dissipated.
His grandmother having left him £100, which still remained unpaid at the death of Lady Anne, William gave
Thomas a bond for £100 and a bill for £10, presumably for
interest, which Thomas sold to one Richard Tompson of
London, in order to raise ready money. William bought
the bond and bill back from Tompson, cancelled them,
and debited Thomas, I presume, with the full amount, to

be charged against his expectations. William, doubtless, paid Tompson somewhat less than the full amount, and Tompson much less to Thomas. Ready money was a most expensive commodity in those days, especially on expectations; and things have not changed much since, in that respect.

We have full information concerning what appears to be a further Deed of Disclaimer or Release, by which Thomas freed William from his claims on Nayland in particular, from one Edward Johnson, goldsmith, of London, aged thirty-four on 27 October 1593, giving evidence on behalf of Thomas. Apparently Johnson's real trade was that of a scrivener. The Deed was drawn up by Serjeant Owen, and it was brought to Johnson to be engrossed, by John Drawater, 'then servant and famylier to one Tho Blagrave Esquier father in lawe to the defendant (William).' It was then sealed by Thomas and delivered to William 'in the lodginge of the said Mr Blagrave within the precinct of St Johnes and where the defendant and his wief then soiourned.' It was signed by Johnson, Drawater and one Luke, William's man, as witnesses, and none others were present, except the parties concerned. Blagrave, it will be recalled, was acting as Master of the Revels from 1573 to 1579, when he was superseded by Edmond Tilney and reverted to the Clerkship of the Revels, which since 1560 had its Office and lodgings for its officials in the former Hospital of St. John of Jerusalem in Clerkenwell. John Drawater appears in the records of the Revels as acting Clerk during Blagrave's Mastership.

Johnson helps Thomas by saying that he saw no sign of money paid as consideration for the deed. But he also reports that William then said that it was all for the good of Thomas, 'and that so longe as he the defendant had A grote to spende, the Complainant his brother sholde never want.'

Evidence was given at the same time by John Rutt, carpenter, of West Ham, aged forty on 21 January 1594, concerning Lodge's heritage of land there, which should have come to him by the Custom of the Manor. He was present, he says, at a Court 'at which Court the said Tho Lodge did surrender all the title & right he had in any lands within that mannor vnto the said William Lodge his brother.' He also has no knowledge of any consideration for the surrender, but 'the said W lodge did promyse in the hearing of this deponent that he would be as good to the said Tho lodge as the land surrendered.' Thomas also produced a young clothier of Stoke Nayland, aged twenty-four on 22 January, Thomas Crysall, whose father Thomas has a lease of the lands in question there. He does not know whose the lands are, but his father pays his rent to Thomas Coe. He describes the property as consisting of three tenements, eighteen acres of meadowland, thirty of arable, a chapel and a little yard. His father pays a rent of £36, but if the lease were out, the rent would surely be raised by ten pounds, and the lands would be well worth it.

Lodge seems to be making what case he can by bringing evidence to show the value of the properties he had lost, the little consideration he has had for giving them up, and the high hopes William has raised in his breast. There is a certain note of urgency in the terms of that interrogatory in which he adjures his witnesses to declare the truth, 'particularly and faythfully as you iuge with A good Conscience to God warde.' One may not unreasonably think that he himself had a hand in drawing this up, in his double capacity as lawyer and dramatist. But all he really proves is his own great folly.

It is evident that none of the literary triumphs of Thomas Lodge drew to him the respect of either of the two solid merchants, his father and his brother-in-law, or of the grave lawyer their friend, in the absence of a stable profession. The Master of the Rolls judged, I suppose, that if Thomas were put in full control of the property, he would straightway sell or mortgage it, and thus defeat the purpose of the legacy, intended to settle him and to found a family on the estate of Nayland which should be a credit to the Lodges. It may well be that William drove a hard bargain with Thomas when he obtained from him the release discharging him from his obligations under the will. It appears clear at any rate that William had some time before obtained possession and control of the Nayland estate, which crops up in a further Chancery suit, and had sold it, to meet a debt of his own, in 1587.

The final decree[1] of the Court in the suit between Thomas and William, in which the disposal of this property was an important factor, suggests that the Court was not clear upon the legal aspects of the question, but had come to the conclusion that Thomas had not had his full due from the executor of their mother's will. The decree is not couched in these terms, but I read this suggestion into it. The hope is expressed in an earlier decree that the brothers would come to an agreement, in consideration of the poverty of Thomas.[2] They have in fact compromised upon a payment by William of £200, of which £40 is in respect of his legacy and the rest was yielded by William in deference to the wishes of the Court. This has actually been carried out by William, and the Court now closes the case absolutely, declaring William finally released of all responsibility, and ordering George Carey and Jane Allington, executors of Sir William Cordell, late Master of the Rolls, to bring into Court for disposal the bond for £3000

1 C 33/88, f. 401. Professor Paradise, who has not found the Chancery depositions, appears to quote this decree as a decree of Star Chamber (*op. cit.*, p. 45).
2 C 33/85, ff. 515, 542; C 33/86, f. 394.

which William had executed to guarantee the fulfilment of the will of Lady Lodge. The decree is dated 14 October 1594, and may be quoted in full:

Whereas vpon the hearinge of the matter the first daye of this terme before the right worshipfull the Mr of the Rolls calling vnto him Mr Justice Owen one of the Judges of her Maiesties Court of Common plees The said Mr of the Rolles and Mr Justice Owen (not myndinge to determyne of the Right to the landes in question betwene the saide parties moved the said parties beinge brothers that they woulde fall to some fryndlye end betwene themselves And that the defendant would in compassion Relive the said plaintiff with some money or other pencion for maynetenance beinge wholly decayed as it was then alledged wherevppon the saide parties haue since fallen to suche agreement as aforesaide And the said defendant tendringe his said brothers estate was content in Comisseraĉon to geve to the plaintiff the some of CC li where of xl li was for suche parte of his legacy which (as it was then alledged) the said plaintiff was then vnsatisfyd of And the resedewe there of was to satisfye the mocion of the said Mr of the Rolles and Mr Justice Owen And for that yt ys informed that the said defendant hathe fully satisfyed the said CC li to the said plaintiff in full satisfacĉon and Recompence of all debtes dewties Legacies Demaundes and assurances of lande whatsoeuer demaund by his bill in this Courte or any way els to be demaunded by the plaintiff herafter Yt ys therefore ordered That the said defendant be from henceforthe cleerly and absolutely dismissed out of this Courte of and from all tytles and demaundes which the said plaintiff shall or maye make or clayme against the defendant for or by reason of the last will and testament and the Codycill therevnto annexed of Dame Anne Lodge their mother And where also the said defendant here to fore became bownden in a bonde of 3000 li vnto Sir William Cordell knight deceassed for the trewe performance of the said will and Codycill (which as it ys alledged the said defendant hathe well and trewly performed) It ys also ordered that a Subpoena with a ducens tecum be awarded against George Carye esquire and Jane Allington widowe Executors of the last will of the said Sir William Cordell to bringe the said bonde of 3000 li into this Courte To th end yt may here safelye Remayne to be disposed hereafter as this Courte shall thinke meete.

The original order, of which this is a copy entered in the Decree Book, was signed by the Master of the Rolls and apparently by both William and Thomas:

signatur manibus tam Magistri Rotulorum Quam partium predictorum.

LUXTON v. COE

The property which Lady Anne had originally intended for Thomas, in order that he might settle upon it and found a family there, never came to him. For he had long since anticipated his interest in Nayland under his mother's will, with the help of William, who evidently had advanced money to him upon this security, thus defeating the purpose of the conditions imposed upon the legacy. And William, armed with his brother's deed of release, soon disposed of Nayland to an outsider. A Chancery suit of 1589 [1] refers to William as having been seized of this property for some years when, in July 1587, he sold it. It was the only piece of landed property which was not entailed, and William took an early opportunity of selling the freehold, with the advowson of the rectory and the lands attached, to Thomas Coe, a clothier of Boxford, Suffolk. William, it seems, was in debt to one John Luxton of London, for £400. As purchase money, he received £200 cash, and £400 to be paid in four yearly instalments of £100, a total of £600. He assigned the deed and the instalments to Luxton to meet his debt. The first instalment was paid on 25 July 1588, after which Coe evaded further payments. So Luxton alleges in the suit he brought against Coe. Coe, answering, ignores Luxton's claims, and thinks it a matter for Common Law between himself and William. The Court, however, thought otherwise, as appears from a conclusive decree dated 5 February 1590, which makes the matter clear. Luxton, it seems, was acting as agent for John Heale, a lawyer friend of William Lodge. Lodge sold the lands to Coe under the agreement stated. 'And the said Lodge standinge in present neede of money the said Mr Heale vpon specyall friendshippe without any interest

[1] C 2 Eliz., L 4/14; C 2 Eliz., L 3/12; C 33/79, f. 447.

did lend and deliver CCCC li to the said Lodge to be Re-
payed in fower yeres,' taking as security an assignment of
the debt of Coe. Coe came to Heale and asked for respite
in paying, which Heale granted, whereupon Coe took advantage of Heale's kindness by tendering the money at the
time and place stated, knowing that Heale would not be
represented, as a device to escape payment. The Court
therefore ordered Coe to pay the money to Luxton for
Heale, Heale to give Coe Lodge's acquittance when the
payment is completed.

It is clear not only that William sold Nayland, but that
he must have been in no small financial straits, despite the
extent of the property he had inherited from his family in
1585, in addition to his Rolleston estate. So that, as far as
the intentions of Lady Anne Lodge were concerned, there
was little to choose between the spendthrift, dissipated
Thomas and the trustworthy William.

It is well to observe how considerable was the fortune
that Thomas Lodge had exhausted in a few years after the
death of his mother in 1579, when he was only twenty-one
years of age, and how complete was his destitution in 1594.
Payne, giving evidence in his suit against William, tells us
that already in the twenty-fifth year of Elizabeth, in 1583,
he had signed a release to William, having received the
value of his legacies from his mother. Now William sold
Nayland in 1587 for a total of £600, and Thomas was left
£400 in money from Lady Anne and £100 from Lady
Joan Laxton. We may not assume that William had un-
derpaid him to any considerable extent. The Court judged
that the deficit might be assessed at £40. At any rate it
seems clear that Thomas ran through approximately a
thousand pounds between 1579, when he had recently
entered Lincoln's Inn as a law student, and 1583, a period
of four years, between the ages of twenty-one and twenty-

five. Half the amount of his fortune, be it remembered, would have saved Antonio, the wealthy Merchant of Venice. A quarter of it was the legacy of Orlando from Sir Rowland de Boys. And Lodge himself speaks of forty pounds a year as an ample allowance for a young gentleman, in his *Alarum against Usurers*. When we bear in mind the magnificence of waste of money on this scale, we may the more readily understand the significance of Lodge's debt to Peter Suckling, the keeper of the King's Head Tavern in Fleet Street in 1588 or 1589, a few years later. We may also read once more, and with renewed interest, the pamphlets of Robert Greene, in which he describes in vivid and dramatic detail the course of life led by dissipated young men from the Universities who had plunged into the dangerous and expensive pleasures of London, seeking a precarious livelihood by literature or the stage. The life of Francesco or of Roberto, as Greene narrates it, is in essentials the life at this period of Lodge, the companion of Greene and Nashe, 'young Juuenall, that byting satyrist, that lastly with mee together writ a comedie,' as Greene speaks in 1592, probably of Lodge, in his *Groatsworth of Wit*. And we may perhaps understand how it came that Lodge was attracted by the theme of the *Tale of Gamelyn* which he developed into his *Rosalynde*, *Euphues Golden Legacy*, and so furnished Shakespeare with material for his story of Orlando in *As You Like It*. He can hardly have failed to read into it something of his own relations with his elder brother William.

It was precisely at this period of dissipation that Lodge had entered the lists in defence of the stage against the attacks of Stephen Gosson, with his *Honest Excuses* in 1579, which was suppressed, as Lodge tells us himself in 1584 in his *Alarum for Usurers*, by 'the godly and reverent that had to deale in the cause, misliking it.' Gosson heard of it while it was in the making, and dealt with it fully in his *Playes Confuted in Five Actions* in 1582. Addressing his *Epistle* to Sir Francis Walsingham he writes of his opponent as one who 'is (as I heare by hys owne frendes, to hys repentance if he can perceiue it) hunted by the heauy hand of God, and become little better than a vagarant, looser than liberty, lighter than vanitie it selfe.' In the interval Lodge had been called before the Privy Council,[1] to answer to charges which are not stated, on 27 June 1581, and was ordered to attend daily until discharged, just as Marlowe was ordered to attend on 20 May 1593. Later in the same year we find Lodge in the King's Bench prison, on an unknown charge, possibly a sequel to that of June, and becoming involved there, in September 1581, with a slanderous informer, Mirfin, and his associate Clement Draper, to whom Lodge introduced Mirfin when all three were prisoners together.[2] It may well be that Lodge was taking altogether too active a part in the growing controversy between City and Court concerning the stage. And there can be no reasonable further doubt what Lodge meant in referring to the 'long distress' he had suffered, when he contributed his *Poem Dedicatory* to Barnabe Rich's *Don Simonides*, which was entered in the Stationers' Register on 23 October 1581. On all counts, the activities of Thomas Lodge could not commend themselves to his father or to the other 'godly and reverent fathers' of the City. It was in these very years that the attitude of the City towards the stage was hardening into violent opposition, when the arms of the City were emblazoned on *A second and third blast of retrait from plaies and Theaters* in 1580, and when the City began to use all its power and influence with the Court to put a stop to plays. No wonder

1 *Acts of the Privy Council* (1581–82), p. 110.
2 Strype, *Annals of the Reformation*, Vol. III, Bk. I, Chap. 12, pp. 141–142.

Sir Thomas Lodge and Sir William Cordell disapproved of his course of life after 1579. One may, however, reasonably speculate upon the views of William Lodge in this respect, for he had, as we know, married the daughter of Thomas Blagrave, who acted as Master of the Revels for six years from 1573 to 1579, whose duties brought him closely into touch with the players, who indeed derived revenue from them, and who may in fact have helped to bring Lodge into contact with the stage, perhaps even into the stage-controversy. It was in December 1581, we may recall, that the Master of the Revels was empowered to exercise general supervision of the public stage, as a far-reaching extension of his functions. Lodge's polemics certainly tended to serve the interests of the Revels office.

It is of some importance to observe the earliest definite date given in the course of these suits in the years 1593 and 1594. Lodge's Star Chamber Bill is dated 16 May 1593. He was on his way back from Rolleston in February 1593, when his brother's servants assaulted him, according to his own account. He must have been in England for some time before that date, to allow for his journey into Nottinghamshire, and I think he actually came back to England much earlier. Lodge's biographers have hitherto assumed that he left Plymouth with Cavendish on 26 August 1591, and returned on 11 June 1593, when the first survivors of the expedition landed in the *Desire* at Bearhaven in Ireland.[1] This is, however, open to considerable doubt. Lodge's name is not to be found in the list of survivors. He was, moreover, back in London already in February of that year at latest. The story of the voyage as told by John Jane, who sailed with Captain John Davis on the *Desire*, informs us that on 24 January 1592 the fleet, having left Santos in Brazil, set a course for the

1 Hakluyt, *Voyages*, XI, 389 ff.

Magellan Straits, the rendezvous being Port Desire. But one of the ships at this stage deserted: 'master Gilberts barke came not, but returned home to England, having their Captaine aboard the Roe-bucke.' The Captain of Adrian Gilbert's *Dainty*, Randolph Cotton, was a close friend of Davis, Captain of the *Roebuck*, refused to be a party to this desertion, and left her when she set sail homewards. It is quite possible that Lodge was aboard the *Dainty* and with her returned to England, arriving home about May 1592. It would seem to be the likeliest ship to carry him on this expedition, for one may guess that he had been brought into it by his connection with the Careys and through them with Adrian Gilbert and Cavendish. If this is true, then Lodge was present at the taking of Santos on 15 December 1591. He was lodged, with Knivet and the captains and gentlemen of whom Knivet writes, in Friars' cells in the College of Jesus at Santos.[1] Lodge relates this himself in his novel *Margarite of America*, published in 1598, which purports to be translated from a Spanish story found by him in the College there. But he probably did not share the bitter hardships, the numbing cold, and the terrific storms that were the lot of those who went on with Cavendish into the famous Straits. An easy voyage westwards, an easy triumph at Santos, and a safe and easy return home, may well have been Lodge's experience, and no more, whatever his command of rhetoric may have induced his readers to believe. Sir Edmund Gosse bids us turn to Lodge's preface to his novel, written when he was 'storm bound among the icy cliffs of Patagonia,' or, as Lodge puts it with less decorative unveracity, 'being at sea four years before with Master Cavendish in passing through the Straits of Magellan.' But Lodge may never have got beyond Brazil. Had he,

[1] Purchas' *Pilgrims*, XVI, 181.

in fact, continued with Cavendish he might well, as Sir Edmund imagines him, have returned cured of his vivacity and sobered. But he could hardly have written *Margarite of America* as we have it. He would have had more notable matter for literature, to justify his friend Greene's promises on behalf of Lodge to readers of Lodge's *Euphues Shadow*. The copy for this book had been left by Lodge, on his departure with Cavendish, in charge of Greene, as Greene tells us in his editorial dedication when he saw the book through the press in 1592 during Lodge's absence. Lodge could hardly have been back in London by the time it was entered in the Stationers' Register on 17 February 1592, but he was already on his way. Greene promises that on Lodge's return 'what laboures his sea studies afforde, shall be I dare promise, offered to your sight.' What Lodge actually had to offer was a collection of sonnets to Phillis, dedicated to the Countess of Shrewsbury by 'her poore and affectionate Sheepheard,' and a *Life and Death of William Longbeard*, both printed in 1593. His *Margarite of America* was probably not born, in fact, until 1596, the year of the printing of the novel, and it would be difficult to find a less exciting reflection of an Atlantic voyage in the heroic age of such ventures.

Nor may we accept Gosse's account of Lodge's hereditary love of adventure, based upon an imaginary voyage of his father Sir Thomas to Guinea in 1562. The interest of Sir Thomas in this slaving expedition was purely financial. And it would seem most probable that expediency had no small share in dictating Lodge's departure on his two voyages, with Clarke and with Cavendish, enabling him to escape for a time from a country in which he was cumbered with debts and pursued by creditors. The *Dainty*, John Jane tells us, had freighted herself with a satisfactory cargo of sugar and so departed homewards, the only ship probably to make a profit on the voyage for the venturers aboard her. If Lodge shared in this profit and returned with his share safely, his pockets were nevertheless empty again before many months had passed, and he was driven to set the match to this remarkable and informative explosion of law proceedings against his brother.

Soon after 14 October 1594, the date of the Chancery decree, we may assume that William paid Thomas the £200 agreed upon. And we may take it as reasonably certain that the poet returned to his former manner of life in London, seeking a precarious livelihood in literary work and trying his luck once more as a dramatist. His renunciation of the stage so often quoted from *Scillaes Metamorphosis*, written in 1589, is of very little weight when compared with the fact that Henslowe paid a debt for him in 1597. As once before we found a tavern-keeper's bill oppressing him, so now a tailor, we may fairly conclude, drove him once more into exile. Beyond question he continued to be in touch with the world of the theatre long after 1589, and as late as 1619, when we find him again in debt. Collier's *Memoirs of Alleyn*[1] tell us that his unsatisfied creditor is Edward Alleyn, possibly as the inheritor of a debt due to Henslowe.

It is known that during Lodge's first exile in Europe he became a qualified physician at Avignon. It is not known how he maintained himself during these years of study in France. Oxford, his own University, granted him the degree of M.D. in 1602, on his return. And a suit in the Court of Requests,[2] in which he appeared as a witness, describes him on 8 May 1604 as Thomas Lodge, of the parish of Christ Church, London, Doctor of Phisicke, aged forty-six. There are two signatures, to both of which

1 Pp. 46–47.
2 *Req.* II, 436. I owe this reference to Mr. Mark Eccles.

he appends his title in the form D.M., and which prove beyond question that the signature and indeed the whole of the letter to Edmondes,[1] dated 17 January 1611, and reproduced in Dr. Greg's *Literary Autographs*, are in Lodge's own hand. The suit is brought by William Jenison, a friend of Lodge, against Gervase Sunderland and Thomas Reynolds. It concerns bills of exchange sent from Ireland and received by Lodge on behalf of Jenison, who was, like Lodge, a Catholic recusant.[2] The bills are dated 17 July and 3 August 1602, so that it is evident that Lodge was in residence in London by July of this year. Lodge's second exile, due to his conversion to Catholicism and his need to evade the penalties of recusancy, must therefore have begun between 8 May 1604 and 1606. In the interval he wrote his *Treatise of the Plague*, printed in 1603, from which we learn of Lodge's resentment at the unprofessional conduct of a neighbour doctor who set up printed bills on posts near Lodge's house, promising miracles 'ill beseeming a Phisitian and Philosopher' such as Lodge, who nevertheless suffers from an influx of patients attracted by these advertisements and is therefore driven to print this book to mitigate the nuisance. It is a queer story, and one would be glad to know to whom the printer sent his account for the printing of these bills which brought to Lodge such an unexpected windfall of patients. One is apt to recall here Lodge's career as a romancer. The whole tone of the treatise, indeed, suggests rather indignation at the success of less learned practitioners. I am tempted to believe that the *Treatise*, which Lodge seems to be so anxious to sell, was an attempt to make up from Lodge's real profession of literature what he was failing to achieve

1 B.M., *MS*. Stowe, 171, f. 352.
2 For a letter from Jenison to Lodge, dated 9 March 1606, concerning his investments and recusancy, see *S.P. Dom.*, James I, 1603–10, XIX, 298.

in his new profession. Many are the Elizabethan and Stuart physicians whom I have met in Chancery suits giving evidence concerning the deaths of their patients, but I have never chanced upon Lodge in this capacity. I would not, of course, lay much stress on this negative indication. Heywood, after all, refers to him in 1609, in *Troia Britannica,* as one of the best-known of London physicians. But Lodge certainly seemed to have ample leisure for miscellaneous literary work, as well as for this medical treatise, and was also kept busy with further lawsuits concerning the estates he inherited from his parents, upon his return to England from his second exile abroad, at the age of fifty-two.

LODGE *v.* GRACE

Lodge was allowed to return early in 1611, as appears from an Act of the Privy Council of 28 January 1611, protecting him from indictment for recusancy,[1] and from the letter dated 17 January 1611 in which he expressed his thanks to Sir Thomas Edmondes for help in bringing about his repatriation. It appears from a Chancery suit of 1614 [2] that he returned in poverty, and that one of his early activities in England was to see his brother Nicholas, apparently in London, from whom he had borrowed a hundred pounds in November 1610. William was no longer available, having fled to Ireland and died in the meantime, and the lot fell naturally upon Nicholas, who reigned in his stead at Rolleston. The circumstances of this loan are instructive, and both parties agree concerning the main facts.

Nicholas was very chary of lending the money to Thomas, whose reputation among his brethren was evi-

1 F. P. Wilson, in *M.L.R.*, ix, 99.
2 C 24/410/99; C 24/432/49.

dently none too good. The Interrogatories suggest that
Nicholas 'doubted the Complainant [Thomas] would not
be carefull for the repaiement,' and that he made certain
elaborate arrangements in consequence. One of the witnesses on behalf of Thomas, Gervase Molineux of Lincoln's Inn, aged forty-seven on 3 December 1614, reports
Nicholas as saying, 'he would be loath if his brother doctor
Lodge should dye to pay the same money out of his owne
purse.' Brother though Thomas was, Nicholas would not
lose his money if he could avoid it. He therefore pretended
that he had not sufficient ready money to make the loan,
and told Thomas that he would borrow it himself for the
use of Thomas from the Rev. Robert Grace, then parson
of Aram or Averham, in Nottinghamshire, the next parish
to Rolleston, it appears.[1] He therefore entered into bonds
for £200 to John Grace, the parson's son, then a student
at Cambridge,[2] for the repayment of the loan of £100, and
Thomas got his money. On 26 December 1611 Nicholas,
who had come up to London for the purpose, made Thomas
become bound jointly with him in a new bond. And finally,
the money being still unpaid, this bond was replaced by a
third with both brothers bound, for £100 and £10 interest
on 28 January 1612. The bonds were drawn up by Robert
Blackburne, of Newark-on-Trent, a servant of Molineux,
aged forty-eight on 3 December 1614.

   The bond is long since expired. Nicholas Lodge is dead,
and John Grace is suing Thomas at Common Law.
Thomas is moving Chancery to stay the proceedings and
to decree that he owes Grace nothing. For the point on
which the parties differ is whether the £100 was actually

1 Since 1576. He was inducted on 22 July, as recorded in the parish register of
  Averham, kindly communicated by Mr. E. H. S. Longhurst, by permission of
  the Rev. J. C. Wheeler.
2 Yet John was thirty-one years of age, having been baptised on 17 November,
  1579, as appears from the same register.

lent by Grace or by Nicholas himself, and Thomas maintains that the whole transaction of the bonds to Grace was
fictitious, no money having passed between Nicholas and
Grace. The bonds were only intended by Nicholas, so an
Interrogatory puts it, 'to keepe his brother in awe for that
the money was his owne.' Thomas argues that the bonds
in question remained in the possession of Nicholas in his
study at Rolleston. During the last illness of Nicholas,
and before Thomas arrived there to take possession, the
study was ransacked and some bonds were taken. So, at
any rate, says Sutton Lodge, who further remarks that
Nicholas 'never borrowed the hundred pounds in question
or any other summe of money . . . [of Robert Grace] who
was a more likely man to borrowe' £100 from Nicholas
than Nicholas from him, and that Nicholas on his death-
bed, at which Sutton was present, said he, 'he thanked
God, was not indebted to any body whatsoever.' Molineux bears witness that Nicholas was a man of wealth, but
that he was 'not any Comon Lender out of money'. . . 'Bycause he had vse for his moneys himself, he being one that
dealt vpon Bargaines for Catall and Corne.' A series of
orders of the Chancery Court [1] illustrate the gradual emergence of the true facts of the case.

The first of them, dated 21 February 1614, relates
Lodge's case as presented to the Court by his counsel,
Mr. Towneley, and makes it clear that John Grace is suing
Lodge in his capacity as executor to his brother Nicholas
in Common Law, though admitting in his Answer that he
knew nothing at the time of the loan from his father.
Lodge is given his injunction. At various times until
5 April 1616 the orders show the parties jockeying for
position over depositions, Lodge arguing that Grace is wil-

---

1 C 33/126, ff. 533, 751; C 33/130, f. 66; C 33/132, ff. 27, 63, 142, 330, 412, 680,
698.

fully delaying bringing evidence, and Grace that Lodge has brought evidence without giving him notice and has obtained publication unfairly before evidence on the opposite side could be produced. At last Grace resorts to a petition, finding himself in a bad tactical position, on 5 April 1616. His father, as he tells the Lord Keeper, lent Nicholas £100 at short notice 'in ready money which was intended for the defendants onely good beinge a Scholler at Cambridge for his keepeinge and maintayneing him there at his study.' Nicholas gave Grace's father his bond, and shortly after both Nicholas and his father died. Nicholas made Thomas his executor, 'leaveinge vnto him a great personall estate,' but Thomas failed to pay this debt. Being sued for it, he promised several times to pay, but never kept his promise, and finally

gave out in speeches that he would shewe the defendant a Tricke which he pursued, for that shortly after beinge about 3 yeares since the defendant being then busy at his study the plaintiff obtayned an Iniunction to stay the defendants suit.

Lodge's only object has been to delay proceedings and to keep Grace out of his money, which is his only means of maintenance.

Upon this petition, the Court seems to have made up its mind that Lodge was in the wrong. It orders that he shall at once show cause why he should not pay his debt, and damages in addition at the rate of twenty marks 'because the defendant is a Scholler' and Lodge has 'slept' three years on the injunction. On 30 April 1616 a further order states that the Lord Keeper is 'well satisfied' with Grace's petition, as a full answer to Lodge's allegations, and bids Lodge proceed at once to a judicial hearing or in default to obey the order to pay.

It seems fairly clear that the Court had come to the right conclusion. The evidence which John Grace at last produced, in November of this year, was circumstantial and convincing, and bore out the view of the Court. On 11 November 1616 two Nottinghamshire men, who had witnessed the signing of the bond by Nicholas, testified to the reality of his transaction with Robert Grace: Richard Bradford, of Kellam, yeoman, aged twenty-six, and John Smithe of Bilsthorpe, Clerk, aged thirty. According to them, Grace's father made a regular business of money-lending. They produced an account-book which recorded his transactions from 1565 onwards in his own handwriting, one leaf of which bore the note of two loans to Nicholas of £60 and £40 respectively and of the bond relating to them. It had been his practice of latter years to have all bonds made out in favour of his son, so that his debts were to furnish John's 'portion.' Smithe was given charge of the book, and of this bond among others, shortly before Robert Grace's death in November 1612,[1] on behalf of John. When Robert was in shaky health, and Nicholas also lay very sick, Robert sent Bradford to him to remind him of the matter he knew of, and Nicholas replied that if he were to die on the morrow he would leave behind him those who would meet the debt. They both died, in fact, and the immediate result was this law-suit between John Grace and Thomas Lodge, concerning which Bradford relates an anecdote which bears the stamp of truth. Either John sent him to Lodge to arrange a meeting to discuss the matter, or Lodge asked for an interview. At any rate Bradford met Lodge at Newark in pursuance of this attempt at an agreement, whereupon, he proceeds,

---

1 He was buried at Averham on 21 November, aged 68, as parson of Averham and of 'Braimson' in Leicestershire, and a prebendary of Southwell since 1592 (parish register of Averham). He was, therefore, born in 1544, and evidently set up his account-book as a lender of money as soon as he reached years of discretion.

he the said Complainant being a doctor in Phisike and the defendant
but a bachiler of dyvinity the plaintiff as yt semed toke himself to be the
better man and loked that the defendant should haue Come to him
rather then he to the defendant for this deponent telling the plaintiff
that if yt pleased him to Come to the white hart Inne in Newarke which
was hard by the place where the plaintiff was they might speake together the plaintiff aunswered that he was a little the better man and
therefore thought yt more fytting for the defendant to come to him and
withall vsed to this deponent these words viz If your master had not
taken this strict Course but come to me in friendly maner I would haue
payd him every grote and he should not haue lost a peny by me but
sythence he taketh this course he shall see that I have some braynes.

Lodge stood on his dignity. Apparently so did Grace. And
this knotty problem of precedence as between a Doctor
and a mere Bachelor was solved in the end by a compromise, for Smithe tells us that he saw the two high con-
tracting parties in conclave at the Talbot Inn in Newark.
But this elaborate diplomacy clearly left Lodge determined after all to show the provincial young parson the
quality of his brains, and in particular, one is obliged to
conclude, to show him and the Court of Chancery a taste
of his ancient skill as a writer and planner of fiction and as
a lawyer trained, however unwillingly and imperfectly, in
Lincoln's Inn and, more assiduously, in the active pursuit
of the law as a party throughout a long and busy career of
litigation. Bradford's anecdote depicts to us a man of stiff
vanity, led by a marked streak of obstinacy and egotism
into difficulties and devious ways, and typically Elizabethan in his subordination of moral scruples to the at-
tainment of his will at all costs, and in his conception of a
Court of Equity as a mere means to that end and the field
of a battle of wits.

Incidentally, it will be observed that Grace was by no
means above special pleading, which was not unsuccessful.
For the Court was much moved by the lamentable picture
of the hopeful young scholar being deprived by an un-

scrupulous adversary, who had cozened his poor old father, the parson of Aram, of the means of his education. Yet John Grace was thirty-seven years of age, and a Bachelor of Divinity, in 1616. And the poor old parson his father was a veteran and businesslike money-lender, in the intervals of his holy calling.

It is only fair to add, however, that in another case [1] in which Lodge was involved as executor to his brother, he succeeded in proving that a certain William Birkett had died owing Nicholas £655 and that his executors, despite an order in Chancery in a former suit brought by Nicholas, had failed to pay some £138 of this. Lodge obtained judgement on 19 May 1614, though he had not got his money by 5 October, when the Sheriff of Nottingham was empowered to attach Brian Birkett, son of William, for disobedience of the decree. Nicholas, it seems, had been an overseer of Birkett's will, and in charge of his estate, apparently for some eight years, during which he had supervised the upbringing and education of Brian and other sons of Birkett. So Thomas added to his claim charges, which the Court accepted, for these expenses too.

Sutton Lodge is something of a puzzle, and I cannot place him in the family. He states, when giving evidence, that he was nineteen years of age on 16 November 1614, being then described as apprentice to Gamaliel Woodford, who had married Joan Lodge and was therefore brother-in-law to Nicholas and Thomas. In January 1611, he tells us, he was servant to Nicholas, and set his hand as a witness to the bond. He has known Thomas for three years, evidently since his return from exile, and knew both Nicholas and Robert Grace before that, but did not know John Grace. This points to a Nottinghamshire upbringing.

1 C 24/396/84; Chancery Reports and Certificates 19; C 33/126, ff. 231, 253, 357, 648, 788, 1042.

Was he conceivably an illegitimate son of Nicholas, who left no heir? The name Sutton has no parallel or link with any in the wide sweep of the Lodge family connections. And there is a village of Sutton not ten miles from Rolleston. It was not an uncommon practice to call bastard children after the name of the place where they were born or put out to nurse.

I find Sutton Lodge once more in 1617 in the *Acts of the Privy Council*.[1] He was now servant to Thomas Woodford, son of Gamaliel, resident in Southwark. On 4 April a warrant was issued to have them both brought before the Council for some offence not stated. There is no later reference to the matter.

The Fates had at last been kind to Thomas Lodge beyond his deserts. He arrived back in England early in 1611, in need of money, as ever, and alternating from poverty to indebtedness or both. And within a short space we find him not only executor, but heir, of the estate of his brother Nicholas, and a man of great possessions, for Nicholas had died at Rolleston in 1612. It is clear what this implies. By the wills of Lady Anne and Sir Thomas, all the landed property which they owned, with the exception of the Free Chapel of Nayland which was left conditionally to Thomas, was entailed upon the eldest son William and his heirs, with remainders to the younger sons excluding Thomas, and their heirs, and finally to the right heirs of Sir Thomas and Lady Anne. Here we find Nicholas, the third son, seated at Rolleston, having inherited from William in default of heirs to William. And Thomas succeeds Nicholas. Inasmuch as both Benedict and Henry were superior to him in the line of entail, it is clear that they also had died without heirs, as well as William and Nicholas. Can any black sheep of a family ever have enjoyed more astounding luck?

1 *Acts of the Privy Council*, 1616–17, p. 218.

IV. FOUR BROTHERS AT ROLLESTON MANOR

THUS three of the five Lodge brothers came, in succession, to Rolleston as Lords of the Manor, heirs to that Joan Kirkeby who had left the village many years before, in days when the great family of the Nevills had owned the manor, until Henry VIII and the Reformation between them drove them and many another from ancestral holdings. The ancient Manor House was demolished in 1813, but its site is still to be traced, with its moat and fishpond. Two stones survive in the structure of a barn-door, bearing the arms of the Nevills. And an old sketch has been preserved which shows the very house in which the Lodges reigned in turn over Rolleston, the successors in their manor of such great men as Earl Godwin and Odo of Bayeux, supplanter of his house in the days of William the Conqueror. The parish church near by is of no less antiquity, in a region of ancient churches, with Southwell Minster two miles away. In it stand the considerable remains of an eleventh century stone cross which bore the now defaced inscription 'Radvlfvs me fecit.' To such great traditions William Lodge, the lawyer-son of the great London Grocer, succeeded when he brought his bride Mary Blagrave to Rolleston. His father, Sir Thomas, had been there. For his generosity is commemorated on a board set up in the ringing-chamber of the tower, recording the gift by him of £50 for ever to the poor of the parish, along with a similar gift of £10 by Nicholas Kirkeby, a benefaction which to this day, at Christmas-time, recalls his name at Rolleston when it has long been forgotten in London. On the north wall of the chancel stands a marble monument to Nicholas, who died there in 1612, set up by his brother Thomas and recording his benevolence. The inscription

MEMORIAL TABLET IN ROLLESTON CHURCH

runs thus, under the Lodge coat of arms cut upon the beautiful pink marble, which Thomas must have had executed by no mean craftsman:

Inveni portv̄ spes et fortuna valete
Nil mihi vobiscv est, Ludite nunc alios

Heare vnder lyeth bvried the body of Nicholas Lodge Gent: the third sonne of Sr Thomas Lodge knight, in tymes past Lord Maior of the honorable cittie of London, and some tymes Lord of this Mannor of Rovlston) whose pietie towardes many orphans his Allie' & frendes are extant in his will to ye poore of this parish notified by his bequest, his vpright dealing testified by all yt knew him: He died ye 25th of Septēb: 1612 Thomas Lodge Doctor medicus testamenti svi solvs execvtor Charissimo fratri hoc amoris testimonium Mærens Posvit [1]

A great deal of information concerning William Lodge, and some concerning Nicholas, is to be found in the parish registers of the Church, which are of almost unique interest on other grounds. There are many indications here of the loving care for their Church of a succession of vicars, and not least the careful preservation of a considerable part of the original paper registers from 1584 to 1615 as well as the 1597 transcript in exceptional completeness. The paper registers bear on every page contemporary notes by the vicar, Robert Leband, including character-sketches of parishioners and comments upon them and upon his task

---

1 The Latin couplet is a translation of a Greek epigram, *Anth. Pal.* ix, 49, which is quoted by Goldsmith in the preface to *The Citizen of the World*. The most authoritative text runs thus:

Ἐλπὶς καὶ σύ, Τύχη, μέγα χαίρετε· τὸν λιμέν' εὗρον.
οὐδὲν ἐμοὶ χὐμῖν· παίζετε τοὺς μετ' ἐμέ.

I owe this identification to Mr. H. E. Foster and Professor M. T. Smiley. Mr. Eccles adds that Gil Blas (at the end of Book IX) resolves to place a Latin version over the door of his country retreat, in letters of gold; that Burton in *The Anatomy of Melancholy* (Part II, sec. iii, mem. 6) quotes the Latin as engraven on the tomb of Fr. Puccius the Florentine, in Rome (S. Onofrio), citing the *Deliciae* of Chytraeus (1594); and that the form Lodge used is also found, with a variation of one word, under the name of Sir Thomas More, and, with a variation of another, under the name of William Lyly, among the renderings from the Anthology prefixed to the 1520 Basel edition of More's *Epigrammata* (cf. *N. and Q.*, series 9, ii, 41, 229).

as vicar. There is also a series of records of prices, weather, and notable events, such as helps the reader to understand better the contents of an Anglo-Saxon Chronicle. And in particular there are illuminating comments upon the vicar's relations with William Lodge, as well as the official record of his family affairs.

The first Lodge entry records, on 12 October 1585, the baptism of a daughter Joan, followed by that of a second daughter Mary on 2 January 1587. A son, Blagrave Lodge, was baptised on 13 July 1589. Joan and Blagrave both died in childhood; Joan was buried on 28 May 1592, and two days before her 'Blagraue Lodge a childe allmost three years ould, the sonne of Willm Lodge armigeri departed this life on ffriday morninge May 26 and was buried the next day.' And the worthy vicar, who frequently exercised himself in verse, broke here into eight lines of elegiac comment upon the sad event. The dreaded plague seems to have made its appearance at Rolleston in 1590, and the two Lodge children fell victims to it. Two more daughters were born at Rolleston to the Lodges, Damaris being baptised on 7 December 1591, having been born on 27 November 'nata ante solis occasu,' and Debora on 12 August 1594. In 1594 there was also a marriage in the family. Henry Lodge, William's youngest brother, who had been sent to Rolleston in William's charge after the death of their father, was married there on 15 April to Dorothy Mering, a widow, and a member of a notable local family of knightly rank. I know nothing further about Henry except that he was dead before 25 September 1612. Had he survived Nicholas he would have succeeded to Rolleston.

But the vicar had other matters to record concerning William Lodge, pouring out his grievances against him and stigmatizing him not only as one of his principal enemies in the parish, but as a Papist. In January 1588 we find, in confidential Latin, the following entry: 'Homo homini fera pessima, vt Mr Lodge & Eduard Barham ... et Mr Lod papista et Eduardus Barham neut̄ et ambo dexter mihi iniurissimi.' Two years later, between entries dated March and April 1590, the vicar repeats his accusations, in English this time. Mr Barham has fawned as a friend upon him but has bewrayed himself as an enemy, 'but gods rod I will take patientlie,' he adds in philosophic mood. He then apostrophises Lodge: 'farewell I wish thy prosper-itie, for seavẽ yeares intertainment I hartilie thank thee,' whereby we learn that William had been Lord of the Manor and patron at the time of Leband's coming to the parish in 1583, the earliest reference to William at Rolles-ton. Leband is evidently in great straits, and is thinking of resigning his benefice: 'God send thee a (parson *deleted*) more woorthie thẽ I yet haue I not hurt thee as god knowes on hie.' And hereupon he explodes into seven rhymed couplets, accusing Barham of hypocritical shows of friend-ship, and Lodge of fraud upon himself whereby his cunning has sought to subvert the vicar's temporal estate, and end-ing thus:

> If I had then knowne his nature as now
> his fraude had been feeble my estate for to bow.
> But god my defence protecte me frõ hence
> that life may be freed from greater offence.

It is evident that William had involved his vicar in some speculation in which Leband had been overreached. A further entry a few pages later serves to illustrate the sad limitations of Leband's poetic talent and the desperate distress to which William and Barham between them had reduced him:

> Sweet Jesus Christ, who on the crosse ⎫
> for mans salvation nayled wosse ⎬ Amen
> Pray for Robt Leband vicar of Rolston ⎭

There must have been something of a truly Christian
spirit in the man who, two years after writing this, could
cudgel his brain to strike out, for his own private satisfaction, a consolatory elegy upon the death of little Blagrave Lodge, the son of his tormentor. It is therefore not
unpleasing to record that Leband not only emerged from
these trials, but long outlived William and Nicholas and,
still vicar of Rolleston, survived by a year even Thomas,
who rivalled the tough indestructibility of his father. The
Rev. Robert Leband, immune to old age and disease,
finally fell off a bridge over the little River Greet and was
drowned, in 1626, at the age of seventy-two. The fact is
recorded in this remarkable parish register by his successor.

The son of John Leband, a husbandman of Morton in
Lincolnshire, as he himself writes, he had lived through
stirring days, both in public and domestic affairs. The
Spanish Armada in 1588 is recorded in Latin in general
terms as a putting to flight of the enemies of the English
Church, whether Spaniards, Italians or French, as a sal-
vation from papal tyranny and enslavement to idolatry,
and as a matter for thanksgiving. The floods and scarcity
of that year are also described at length. In 1589 he quotes
the contemptuous lines of a popular catch which he dates
1326:

> the Scotchmē to ye Englishe
> Longe beardes hartles
> painted hoods witles
> daintie fare needles
> gay coats gracles
> maketh England thriftles.

Leband was a Greek and Latin scholar of a kind, and had
some scholarly impulses, for he gives variants of this tag
in the margin. In 1603 he was to come into closer contact
with the Scots, and records the passage of King James and

his lodging at Newark on 21 April. Grieving at the death of Elizabeth, of which the news reached him on 26 March, two days after the event, doubtless as a result of Carey's precipitate ride northwards to bear the tidings to James, he now trusts, in Latin, and with some uneasiness, that the new King may 'study the prosperity of the English.' He records the triumphant Cadiz voyage of Essex in 1596, 'victoriam navali terrestriq̃ bello (si non mentiatur fama).' We hear of this again in October, for a Rolleston man, Robert Oliver, a gentleman attending upon Essex, was slain there and left by his will £15 to the poor of Rolleston, Stoke, and Farringdon. In February or March 1598 he mentions a war in Ireland, remarking 'Bellũ ex virtute spolia multa ducit Stilpo.'[1] The virulence of the plague in August 1604 inspires in him a terror that is expressed with tragic brevity: 'Furit pestis Da opẽ imploremus,' and we may realise something of the dislocation of life caused by the plague from the christening of one Edward Parke, who, on 5 May 1612 'was baptysed tempore pestis in Rolston Church-yard.' He records the changing extremes of weather, a great flood on 2 January 1610, and ten months later

Then viz festo Michaelis beeing Sunday was a verie greate snow, which bended & brake manie branchs from trees with the waight therof & so followed three or foure nyghts & daies extreeme froste on earth & waters.

In September 1612 was 'an extreeme droughtie sumer,' at the end of which William Lodge's successor at Rolleston died: 'Nicholas Lodge gent was buried on ffriday Septemb 25 1612 Jacobi 10,' too soon for the 'new Bible,'

---

1 This, I fear, is beyond me. I offer the following variants: for *bellũ* read *bellorum* or *bellũ:*, for *Stilpo* read *Stilicho*, as a starting-point for exegesis. But the last word may indicate that the first six words were a saying of the Greek philosopher in question. And I can find nothing like it in Claudian.

which was 'bought and brought from Newark' on 14 October and 'first red on at Yarwards buriall' on 16 October.

The name of Nicholas Lodge first occurs in the Register on 14 October 1596, when he appears as a churchwarden signing a deed of receipt for Oliver's bequest, and we may believe that he had been resident there for some years before being made a churchwarden. Henry, we know, was with William at the Manor House, and was married at Rolleston Church in 1594. When Thomas went there in 1593 he probably found all three in Rolleston, with ample material either for a revival of brotherly love or of family dissensions among the four brethren. On his next visit in 1611 he found Nicholas Lord of the Manor in William's stead. It is not easy to decide the date of his succession. The main facts are clear, however. It appears from certain Chancery records of a suit in which Thomas became involved in 1621, to which I shall return, that when William was so pressed for money in 1587 that he sold Nayland, he also effected an illegal sale of part of the West Ham property. And one of the witnesses, Thomas Pollard, who claims to have known Thomas for thirty years, gives the surprising information that William had gone into Ireland many years ago. In the normal event, departure into Ireland was an escape from the consequences of misdemeanour or bankruptcy, and we may be sure that this was in fact the end of William's career. The last reference to William in the parish register occurs on 16 September 1594, when the burial was recorded of his servant Walter Chamberlain, possibly one of the assailants of Thomas on his way from Rolleston to London. In 1621 there had been no news of him for at least ten years. Between 1594 and 1611, therefore, William had fallen into decay and exile, hastened no doubt by his recusancy in which he set the example for Thomas, and had died in Ireland.

The margin of years may, however, be considerably reduced with the help of a series of law-suits in which William was engaged in connection with his Rolleston estates.
From the third of these it appears that he was still in possession in 1599, and all three throw light upon the affairs
of an Elizabethan landowner.

TINGLE *v.* PILGRIM

We have a glimpse in the year of the Armada of the
affairs of William Lodge in his capacity as Lord of the
Manor of Rolleston in a Chancery suit between John
Tingle with others and John Pilgrim.[1] Pilgrim, it appears,
has sold certain lands occupied by Tingle and the other
defendants to William. The suggestion is made that Lodge
used undue influence to induce Pilgrim to sell at a price
below the value of the lands. And it is clear that Lodge is
enforcing the payment of rents by his new tenants, who
are refusing the demand. The principal witness is John
Blagrave, of Grafton Court in Wiltshire, Esquire, aged
thirty-eight on 30 June 1588, Lodge's brother-in-law. He
has known Lodge for thirteen or fifteen years, for some
years before the time of his marriage with Mary Blagrave
in 1577. Blagrave was spending the Christmas of 1586
with William and Mary at Rolleston. While he was there
he saw Pilgrim come to Rolleston and heard him ask William if it was true that he was about to seize some of Pilgrim's land. William denied this, but said it was within
his power to do so, 'for qd he you hold yor land of me you
ought me Sute & seruice and you ought to pay me vj s
Rent by yere And for the nonpaymt of my Rent I maie
lawfullye entre vpon the same.' Pilgrim replied that no
rent had ever been paid by his father or his ancestors.

1 C 24/224/54.

And the said Willm lodge did bring vnto & shewe vnto the said defendt
A certen auncient dede made betwene one of the lords of Rollston and
one of the auncesters of the defendt, as he tooke it, named *lepylgryme*,
wherin̄ these tenem̄ts and lands were comprysed, and made menc̄on of
A certen Rent payable to the lorde of Rollston for the sd lands.

The deed provided for forfeiture of the lands on non-pay-
ment of rent. Pilgrim, much abashed, asked Lodge to deal
lightly with him, and either to remit the rent or to buy the
lands from him. Blagrave interposed here and advised
Pilgrim to take counsel, 'for both their credits.' So Pilgrim brought in one Piell, 'an honest substanciall yeoman
and a freeholder in that Manor of Rolston.' It was agreed,
finally, that Lodge should remit past rent, except a sum of
eleven shillings, on condition that Pilgrim paid rent in
future. 'And so they parted in frendlie Maner.' Next day,
Pilgrim and Piell came and again offered to sell the lands.
A bargain was struck by word of mouth for a sale at the
price of £35 or £45, and earnest money paid, in the presence of Blagrave, two of the tenants, and Edward Maplesdon, the Deputy Seneschal of the Queen's Manor of West
Ham, of which the West Ham property of the Lodges was
held,[1] who was also spending Christmas with William. And
the tenants were instructed to pay rent to William henceforth. Blagrave states that William had a good bargain,
for the lands were worth five pounds or perhaps six marks
more than he paid. It would seem that even during the
Christmas holidays, with a house party of friends to spend
the season of goodwill with him, William could still attend
strictly to business. It is very likely that he and Blagrave
and Maplesdon, three lawyers together, went over all the
muniments of the manor, discovered this ancient deed,
and made the most of it, reviving an old claim. One might
wonder why Thomas, William's next brother, was not one

1 *Court Rolls*, 172/41.

of the Christmas party. But it does not seem likely, from
all the indications we have, that Thomas and William
could have wished each other a Merry Christmas, at any
time since 1583, with any great heartiness. Blagrave, by
the way, refers in June 1588, to Rolleston as the place
'where the said Lodge then dwelled,' at Christmas 1586.
Apparently William had left Rolleston temporarily, probably on a visit to West Ham, and possibly to complete the
negotiations for the sale of the greater part of the family
property there. But he was mainly resident at Rolleston,
as the parish registers show, and he was certainly there in
May 1593, when Thomas went to visit him on his expedition in search of money. An inveterate borrower or
beggar is not, as a rule, a welcome guest either in spring-
time or at Christmas, even at a brother's house. A little
before Christmas in 1588, we may remember, Thomas was
trying to get William to back his bond to Peter Suckling.
He probably had some other bill to be backed in 1586. Not
that indebtedness was an unusual matter in the second
generation of the Lodge family. Even the solid structure
of Gamaliel Woodford's affairs was shaken in 1597, when
he was arrested for debts of £450 and was bailed by his
son-in-law William Moulton, in circumstances suggesting
fraudulent concealment of assets. And the suit that reveals these facts shows us Woodford proceeding against
his own daughter Anne, grand-daughter and god-daughter
to Lady Anne Lodge.[1]

LODGE v. PALMER

William seems to have been kept fairly busy with the
preoccupations arising out of his Nottinghamshire estates.
In Michaelmas 1595 he complains in Star Chamber [2] that

1 C 24/273/65; C 24/274/18; C 24/283/10.
2 *Star Ch. Pro.* 5, L 27/2.

his quiet enjoyment of his manor of Rolleston has been recently disturbed, on 24 March, by the forcible entry of a group of rioters armed with bills and glaives on Marsh Close, part of his property, and by the breaking down of several enclosures of his tenants, whose names are given. It was doubtless one more of the many instances of the usurpation of common lands by an Elizabethan landlord to the serious discomfiture of the villagers, ending in revolt and subsequent repression by the law. The sympathies of the vicar, we may believe, were with the rioters in this instance. The records of Star Chamber bear witness to a hundred such cases and to the despairing outcries of the village folk in their answers to charges of riot. They plead ancient rights of common, they lament the loss of immemorial free rights of grazing for their cattle, and they resent bitterly the rapacity of the new landlords, merchants and lawyers from London, men of business and speculators, strangers in the land, who have taken the place of the old feudal landlords. William Lodge was one of many such.

Lodge v. Bevercotes

We find him speculating in other property in Nottinghamshire, in Perlethorpe or Peverillthorpe and Thoresby, about five miles west of Tuxford and as far north of Laxton. At some date not long before 1599 Sir John Byron, Lord of the Manor of Perlethorpe, made a lease of some part of his arable and pasture land to William and Mary Lodge. They at once set about ejecting the tenant, the widow of Nicholas Russell, who owned a lease of the parsonage of Perlethorpe and Thoresby. Mrs. Russell denied his title, asserting that the land belonged to the Dean and Chapter of Lincoln, as part of the parsonage. She then married David Watson, who gave possession to

Lodge. Watson died, having in the meantime sold his lease of the parsonage to Samuel Bevercotes, who proceeded against Lodge at Common Law. Whereupon Lodge retorted in 1599 in Star Chamber,[1] charging Bevercotes with maintenance and conspiracy. The records of this Star Chamber suit yield these facts, and show John Markham of Halam near Rolleston in Nottinghamshire and Henry Tamworth of Holborn, London, but formerly the owner of property in Thoresby, as Lodge's friends and neighbours, coming to give evidence on his behalf. There is, as usual, no record of the decree of Star Chamber in either of these suits. There can be no reasonable doubt that all these legal proceedings reflect an active career of speculation in land. William's country estate was his vantage-ground from which he dealt in a busy market. His heredity broke out in another field, after all. In the end, like Sir Thomas, he overreached himself and fell into irremediable disaster.

The period of William's flight to Ireland may therefore be dated between 1599 and 1610. When Thomas, at some time before May 1594, obtained a writ to prevent William from leaving the kingdom, his fears may well have been based on some knowledge of William's plans and of an earlier crisis in his affairs. William seems to have survived this crisis, despite the heavy costs of the litigation between the two brothers and the final award of £200 to Thomas, all of which must have aggravated his difficulties. But his fall was only delayed. In the meantime it seems reasonable to assume that Nicholas and Henry had found a home and occupation with their eldest brother at Rolleston, and that William had in a measure provided for both of them. He certainly provided an eligible widow for Henry, and on the whole it would seem that he was a good brother to Nicholas

1 *Star Ch. Pro.* 5, L 37/5, L 24/13.

and Henry, and that Thomas may well have been unreasonable in his demands upon him.

Nicholas, a churchwarden in 1596, served again from
1606 to 1608, and we find his signature at the foot of two
pages of the parchment copy of the parish register. By
this time, we may fairly assume, he was reigning in William's stead, and was evidently a more satisfactory parish-
ioner than William. He is described in Thomas' suit
against Grace as a dealer in corn and cattle and as a man
of some wealth, and he was apparently more successful in
his speculations, or more conservative, than William. At
any rate he died a benefactor of the parish and of his
brother Doctor Thomas Lodge, who succeeded him as
Lord of the Manor in 1612, and raised a grateful monument to his memory.

No trace remains in the parish register of the advent of
Thomas at Rolleston. He was, of all the Lodges, least
qualified for the office of churchwarden, and was not at all
likely to follow in the satisfactory steps of Nicholas. Above
all, he was a Catholic recusant. And he was accustomed
to less rural ways of life, happier in the whirlpool of London than in this backwater of Nottinghamshire. It is clear
that Rolleston was never his place of abode, and he took
an early opportunity to dispose of his estate there. What
further may be learnt of Thomas Lodge at Rolleston arises
out of his dealings with the Manor lands and the inevitable
suits at law consequent upon them.

V. THOMAS LODGE (1612–1625)

By 1612, then, Thomas Lodge had at last come into his heritage, and was lord of this important property, and also of what was left of the principal seat of the Lodge family at West Ham, where his father and mother had lived and brought up their family. In addition to these properties, he had his profession as a physician. And we actually find him, two years later, setting out for the Archduke's country to collect debts due to him. The case, it would seem, was altered.[1] Yet despite these apparently comfortable and prosperous circumstances, three years later, in 1619, we find him owing money to Edward Alleyn, the great actor and founder of Dulwich College, and having to be rescued from a debtor's prison. There is a considerable volume of litigation which indicates the way in which Lodge exercised his rights in his inheritance. It throws no light upon the waste or loss of money which must have occurred, but it certainly suggests that Lodge, like his brother William, was anxious to turn his property into ready money as far as the entail permitted. The suit against John Grace arose out of Lodge's executorship to Nicholas, and other suits followed. It is worth noting that the conclusion of this suit was reached during the early months of 1617, when Lodge was abroad with Savill. Little more than a year after the final decree in this suit, we find Lodge once more at law, this time in the Court of Requests, defending himself against a complaint of George Raye, of Highgate, Middlesex, yeoman, whose Bill is dated 20 June 1618.[2]

1 *A.P.C.*, 1616–17, p. 116. On 10 January, 1617 the Privy Council sanctioned a pass for Lodge and for Henry Savill, for a period of five months, with two servants. It is clear that they were travelling together.

2 *Req.*, II, 424.

RAYE *v.* LODGE

Some time before his debt-collecting tour abroad, Lodge, it appears, was anxious to realise on his property at Rolleston, which he had inherited from Nicholas in 1612, and which included the mansion and its lands, and the Rectory of Rolleston. Some he had leased, and he had also set to work to sell the reversion of his interest in the whole property. He therefore approached Raye with proposals, assuring him that it was worth £300 a year and having got a valuer to support this estimate. Raye, 'a meere stranger in those parts,' put his full trust in Lodge and was drawn into an unprofitable lease, according to his version of the matter. On 20 July 1616 Raye agreed upon a fine of £100 and a rent of £120 for a lease of the house and lands for seven years, and a rent of £80 for a lease of the Rectory for twenty-one years, both leases to begin from the following Lady Day, in March 1617. Accordingly Raye took possession. He has now held the property for a year, paying the fine and £150 rent so far. And he repents him of his bargain, and seeks for relief. The meadows he has leased are near the Trent, and 'one other small River which hath his Course through parte of the said grounds.' The rivers have overflowed their banks and the lands, and have ruined Raye's grass and the tithe grass, corn and hay of the Rectory: 'he could not make nor reape anie profitts or Comodityes . . . for that whole yere to the value of Twentye Poundes.' The parish register of Leband refers frequently to such floods drowning the low-lying meadows of Rolleston, and the small river Greet went so far as to drown the vicar himself, as we have seen. On more than one occasion Leband had to take boat from the vicarage to the church, as in the summer of 1588, when the floods were continuous and devastating, and called forth the vicar's most pious ejaculations in a series of mournful notes.[1] And a year before Raye leased the lands, in the worst floods in local memory, they had lain under water for over nine weeks together. Raye's fortune was no better. Consequently, he complains, he has been obliged to surrender his estate in the lands to one Mr. Bales, to whom Lodge, he informs the Court, has recently assigned his whole interest and estate in the property. Yet Lodge now demands £50, the rest of the year's rent due, and threatens a suit at Common Law, though he has been a great gainer, both by the £250 from Raye (if he gets it all), and by the new assignment to Bales. It all seems unconscionable to Raye. Surely, he argues, in justice the rent he pays ought to be calculated retrospectively in proportion to the profit accruing to the lessee. He is a little doubtful, not without reason, of resting his argument there, and urges redress on account of the exaggerated valuation of the land, his misplaced trust in Lodge, and the equitable implications of an act of God.

Lodge filed his Answer on 25 June, and riddled Raye's Bill with contempt. What has Raye to put forward, after all? His Bill is based on his own negligence and ignorance. And he imputes the overflowing of rivers to the act of God. The Bill is bad in law. But it is also untrue. It was Raye who pressed for a lease, which he got on the same terms, with a small increment of £15, as had been paid by former tenants. He was moreover a bad tenant, very dilatory with his rent, and so led Lodge for the sake of peace to part with his interest to Bales. As for the rent, it was by Raye himself 'thought very reasonable being himselfe a man of iudgment in such thinges and a grasier by his trade of life.' Lodge pours scorn on Raye's attack on the valuation which

1 *Parish Register of Rolleston.*

he accepted. Raye, moreover, knows the place well, spend-
ing much of his time at or near Newark, which is only two
miles or so from the properties. And how should Raye, a
grazier by trade, trust Doctor Thomas Lodge in a matter
of this sort, for Lodge is no grazier? May he not, he asks,
go forward in justice to demand his rent according to the
Common Laws of this land? His Answer is signed by
Anthony Dyot, but its peculiar tone and rhetoric reveal
the hand and art of Thomas Lodge.

In the records of the Orders of the Court of Requests we
find an entry dated 23 June 1618.[1] At Raye's humble request the matter is referred to Sir Christopher Parkins as
arbitrator, and Lodge is commanded to appear on the following Saturday. Two days later, Lodge swore his formal
Answer. Nothing more is to be found concerning the suit
in the Court of Requests. But the sequel is on record elsewhere.

Lodge made the obvious reply to Raye's suit, exchanging
the defensive for the offensive, and launched a countersuit in the Court of Chancery at the earliest possible date,
in the Michaelmas Term following. Orders and Decrees in
Chancery relate his progress.[2] On 15 October 1618 Raye
is ordered to answer to the suit. A Report of Master Heywood finds for Lodge on 22 November. But interim orders
show that the Court, on 1 February 1619, was nevertheless inclined to find for Raye, and to mulct Lodge in heavy
costs. On 8 March the matter is again reviewed by Master
Heywood, in the light of these proceedings and of the documents from the Court of Requests, and he reports in
favour of Lodge, who has suffered 'this his double vexačon
and delaie.' And on 14 April 1619 a final decree orders
Raye to pay £50, with costs and damages. I dare say

1 *Req.*, 1, Misc. Books 29, f. 213.
2 C 33/135, ff. 47, 220, 489, 645, 702.

Lodge was glad of the money, if he ever got it, for it was about this time that he was pursued for debt by Edward Alleyn and driven into prison once more.

LODGE *v.* WILMORE

We have now reached the last stage of Lodge's restless life. When he obtained his verdict against Raye, only to find his own debt to Alleyn his next pressing concern, in 1619, he was an elderly man of sixty-one years of age, with but six more years of life to run. But he was not yet finished with Courts of Law. In the following year at latest he plunged once more into Chancery, in an attempt to vindicate his rights in certain lands in West Ham, part of the property which had long before been the principal seat of his father Sir Thomas.

It is instructive to observe how his father's property had been dissipated by his sons. The Nayland property in Suffolk, destined for Thomas, to whom it was denied by the trustees, passed to the hands of William. And William hastened to alienate it. It was the first to go, in 1587, only three years after the death of Sir Thomas. The Rolleston estate in Nottinghamshire, entailed as it was, passed to William, Nicholas and Thomas in turn. And Thomas sold it to Bales in 1618. We may now turn to the West Ham property, and trace its history in the records of proceedings in Chancery between Thomas Lodge and Andrew Wilmore, which seem to have begun in 1620, possibly before. I have not found the pleadings, but there are very full depositions which enter into great detail.[1] The wills of the elder generation of Lodges, and Inquisitions after their deaths, together with Surveys and Court Rolls, supplement this information.

1 C 24/480, *Lodge* v. *Wilmore*; C 24/481, *Wilmore* v. *Lodge*; C 24/482/54.

This very valuable estate came to the Lodges through Lady Joan Laxton, mother of Lady Anne Lodge, even as the Nayland estate came to them from her step-father, Sir William Laxton. It is described in the *Inquisition Post-Mortem* upon the death of Sir Thomas as consisting of two parts: one including a mansion house with six acres of land, the other of four messuages with a total of sixty-four acres of land, in Plaistow in the parish of West Ham, and held of the Queen's Manor of West Ham. In a survey of the manor, made on 8 April 1605, the annual value of the first part of the property together with about one fifth of the other lands is rated at twenty pounds, and again at about the same rate in a later survey of 1615.[1] I gather that the Royal Manor was put together out of two dissolved manors, of Playes and West Ham Burnells, of which the lands formerly held.

The mansion of Sir Thomas Lodge, referred to in Court Rolls as the 'great house,' must have been of considerable size, a dignified residence in the country, with extensive and pleasant grounds, with its garden and two orchards. It must have been expensive to maintain. And William, the heir to this estate, was settled at Rolleston in a far country, and was soon to be in need of ready money. Consequently, three years after the death of Sir Thomas, at about the time when we find him disposing of the Nayland property in Suffolk, he conveyed the property to Richard Taylor, a Doctor of Medicine who may well have set the thoughts of Thomas moving in the direction of the profession of his later years. The transaction is recorded in the surveys mentioned already, which quote a conveyance dated 8 October 1587, and also in the Court Rolls of the Manor of West Ham.[2] In the Court Rolls it is stated that

1 E 315/425 contains both, and mentions Thomas Bales as owning land in West Ham.   2 *Court Rolls*, 172/41.

William and Mary Lodge, of Rolleston, Nottinghamshire, on 8 January 1588 demised the property into the hands of the Queen's Seneschal of the Manor,[1] the Court being held by Edward Maplesdon, his Deputy, and disclaimed all title in it for themselves and their heirs, in favour of Richard Taylor. A summary of the property involved follows: a great house or mansion in Plaistow, with garden, two orchards and six acres and one rood adjoining as a small park in a close called the Hide; another piece of land, formerly part of the orchard, of one rood; one acre and three 'dayworks' of land in Post Mead; three acres of land in the Holme in Post Mead; one more acre of land; and a cottage in Balam Street. An earlier statement in the record of the Court Baron of 5 April 1584, held to admit William as heir upon the death of Sir Thomas, adds to this one rood called Burnthawes, two acres and three roods not specified, and a 'bent' and garden in Plaistow formerly part of the grounds of the 'great house.' The cottage is described as being in Newbarn Street. Further variations may be found in the descriptions contained in the Surveys of 1605 and of 1615, the latter copied from the deed of 1587. To all this, it appears, the other brothers, Benedict, Henry, Nicholas and Thomas, who were involved in the succession, had renounced their claims to William at an earlier Court. The renunciation of Nicholas is recorded at the Court of 5 April 1584, at which he appeared, was admitted to his share, and remitted it to the use of William, who paid the fine for admission for the whole property. I may remark that a list of the Homage of the Manor, which, unfortunately, is not dated, includes Nicholas, Benedict, and Henry, though not Thomas, as well as William. I presume that this list antedates the conveyance to William and to Dr. Taylor. The land, it will be further observed,

1 Jasper Cholmondeley.

is said to be copyhold. Here again, therefore, the most valuable part of the West Ham property of Sir Thomas has
been alienated by William at about the same time as his
disposal of Nayland. It appears, however, that part of the
West Ham land continued to be held by William and his
heirs. For the survey of 1615 states that William held
twelve acres of pasture called 'Bowyers,' after its former
owner, and a mansion with lands, including a close called
Milking Hawe or Porters Field, three acres in all, of all of
which no mention is made in Court Rolls. This was freehold land, and I presume it was in fact held by Thomas.
Possibly the survey gave the name William by error for
Thomas, as Stephen Gosson did in the first uncorrected
copies of his attack upon Lodge.

Now it is precisely upon the question of the legality of
William's transactions with these and other lands at West
Ham that Lodge bases this, his last suit in Chancery. He
attempts to establish the case that Sir Thomas and Lady
Anne owned the great mansion, its grounds and other lands
in West Ham, that they were copyhold lands, that according to the custom of the Manors all sons shared alike after
their death, that the sons were in fact admitted to their
holdings in the Manor Court, and that Thomas himself
was the only surviving son and therefore the sole heir. He
maintains that he was himself admitted to hold certain
parts of the land called Barnhawes or Burnthawes and
Barnard's Hope in New Marsh in the Manor of Playes, as
his share of the lands. He then argues that, when William
disposed of this property, it was an illegal transaction. He
therefore seeks to recover it, as his inalienable inheritance,
from Andrew Wilmore, who has succeeded the original
purchaser. This appears to be his case, to judge from the
trend of the interrogatories and depositions in his favour.

The land in question is described, and its history given,

by Paul Waldegrave, who had formerly been Steward of both Manors and still kept the Court Rolls in his possession. It is impossible not to be moved to curiosity concerning the vicissitudes of these documents between the year of this suit, when Waldegrave was quoting them in Court, and the year 1915 when fragments of them were presented to the Public Record Office by Mr. Frank Marcham and so came under the eyes of the present writer, three hundred years after Lodge based his claims on their authority.

The property was a 'Toft,' comprising an orchard at the back of the great house, three acres of land at Barnhawes in New Marsh, formerly belonging to Sir Christopher Hatton, one acre in Barnard's Hope, formerly belonging to Isabel Gresham, widow, one acre in Barnard's Hope in Middle Marsh, formerly belonging to Sir Nicholas Barker, Garter Knight, and one acre formerly belonging to John Pragle. In 1567 these were all surrendered in Court by John Quarles, Draper, to the Lord of the Manor, to be transferred to Lady Joan Laxton and her heirs. In 1576 Lady Laxton surrendered them to have them regranted back to her for life only, with remainder to Sir Thomas and Lady Anne Lodge and to the heirs of Lady Anne for ever. In the following year the Jury of the Court presented the death of Lady Laxton, and the Lodges came to Court and were admitted as copyhold tenants. After the death of Sir Thomas in 1584, William Lodge came to the Manor Court to claim his inheritance, and was admitted, paying a fine of £5.6.8. Nicholas also came, and was admitted, but returned his share to be regranted to William. No mention is made in the Court Roll of the other sons, though evidence is given that Thomas was then 'admitted Tennant of a (fiveth *deleted*) Childes part of the Coppiehold . . . landes.' John Palgrave, for many years Bailiff of the Manor of Playes, reports a statement of the then Steward,

Mr. Higham, to that effect. There were then four other sons living, as we learn from most of the witnesses, who are called upon to say what they know of the Lodge family. John Pragle, an ancient of the district, and a neighbour and friend of the Lodges, Laxtons and Wilmores, gives the names of the children in the following order of seniority: Joan, William, Thomas, Nicholas, and Benedict. He does not seem to know of Henry, and he believes that Lady Anne was the daughter of Sir William Laxton and Lady Joan, whereas she was a Loddington. Thomas Stubbs, an old man of sixty, knew better. He adds Henry to the tale of sons, and also mentions a second daughter Anne. He had been Sir Thomas' gardener at West Ham for a dozen years. We might believe that his memory of the young people who walked in his garden forty years ago or more had in his mind confused Lady Anne's god-daughter Anne Woodford with her own offspring, were it not for an entry in the parish register of St. Mary Aldermary. There we find that on 19 December 1573 'Mrs Anne Lodge, daughtr to Sr Thomas Lodge' was buried in that church, a few months before her sister Joan was married there to Gamaliel Woodford, on 30 March following. All the children, it is stated, are dead in 1621, except Thomas. The only question is of William, of whom nothing certain is known, except that he went to Ireland many years before, and may therefore be presumed to be dead by now. Stubbs has been unable to hear news of him for ten years, at any rate. Stubbs also gives the fullest version of the history of the whole property, including Sir Thomas' 'very fair House,' after his death. He heard talk in the house, among the servants presumably, that already before his father's death William had disposed of his reversion to Richard Taylor, Doctor of Physic. After the death of Sir Thomas a lease was made by Dr. Taylor to Mr. Catesby of the

King's Bench. Catesby 'put off his estate therein to the late Earl of Oxford,' and the Earl assigned his interest to Peter Haughton, Alderman and Sheriff of London.[1] Haughton disposed of his lease to Sir Henry Brunker and at the end of the lease the property reverted to Dr. Taylor, who lived there himself until his death, leaving it to his wife, who two years ago, in 1619, sold it to Jacob Wittrongle, a Dutch brewer. Court Rolls of 1622 confirm 'James Wittewronghe' as the owner of the estate at the time of this suit,[2] when Prince Charles was Lord of the Manor.

It will be observed that the process of dissolution and dispersal of the imposing landed estate of Sir Thomas Lodge, in the hands of his sons, had begun even before his death, and that the principal family seat at West Ham was the first to go, though the actual surrender in the Manor Court did not take place until 1587, three years later. It is evident that William had no mind to take his father's place as a local magnate near London, but had already determined to set up his rest at Rolleston. We may assume that he had been established in possession of the Nottinghamshire estate for some years, possibly since his marriage in 1577, and in residence there, before the death of his parents. In 1584, it appears, he was thirty years of age, and he may well have been at Rolleston for seven years by then. His later career, moreover, suggests that he stood in need of ready money.

The various accounts of the transactions which led to this suit are very involved, but the story may, I think, be disentangled and reconstructed upon the proper basis, that is to say, a basis of some measure of fraud and greed on two sides. To begin with, we are dealing here only with a certain part of the property of Sir Thomas, in Barnard's

---

1 For a quarrel between Haughton and Taylor concerning the house in 1591, see C 24/225/91.   2 *Court Rolls*, 172/19.

Hope and Barnehawes or Burnthawes. All witnesses concur in the view that the lands in question have become difficult to trace exactly, their boundaries have become blurred, and they have now become mixed with other pieces of land. The various names under which one of the properties is known may serve to illustrate this. James Dawbeny, a young West Ham lawyer, calls it 'Barnards hope alias Easthope alias Waylands croft alias Middleshott' and says it is now known as Butcher's Hedge! So within a few years work had been made for local antiquaries, and opportunities for litigation.

In 1587 these lands had been sold by William and Mary Lodge to William Townsend, a lawyer, who left them at his death to his son William. The younger Townsend in turn sold them to George Wilmore, who left them to his son Andrew, who now occupied them.

Somewhere about 1600 the Lord of the Manor seems to have discovered that such a sale was contrary to the custom of the Manor, whereby all copyhold lands of the Manor are divided equally among surviving sons or, failing sons, surviving brothers. On both counts, obviously, Thomas inherited. A Court was therefore held, and proclamation made that the lands were forfeited to the Lord and that any heirs should present themselves. Thomas came and made his claim. He was admitted to his share, four other brothers then being alive, and paid a fine to the Manor. Andrew Wilmore, who held the land claimed by Thomas, also came forward and challenged it as his, but nothing was done, says George Allen, 'monyer,' of West Ham, 'unles ther were something done in private betwene the Steward and him.' At any rate, Wilmore continued in fact to occupy the land. A further step was taken on 12 June 1620, when the land was granted by the Lord to James Dawbeny, who surrendered it to be granted to

Thomas Lodge, and these transactions were entered in the Court Roll. And thereupon Lodge proceeded to claim in Chancery the enforcement of his rights, against Wilmore.

The clue to the whole story lies in the evidence given that Wilmore had long since refused to pay rent to the Manor, denying that this land was held of the Manor. I am led to conclude that the Manor wanted its rent, Lodge wanted the land, and they were proceeding in harmony to prepare a case suitable to be taken to Chancery. It is highly probable that, when William originally sold the land to Townsend, Thomas connived at the sale and had some share of the proceeds, or that, like Nicholas, he had already in 1584 given up his claim to William, in return for immediate payment. Thomas and the Manor were seeking to profit by the obsolescent customary laws of manorial tenure, and Wilmore was taking advantage of the decay of these laws and the disappearance of ancient boundaries and landmarks, processes of the time which are here admirably illustrated. All this makes a story sufficiently shot with sharp practice and guile to be entirely credible and consistent, and it is probably the true story. As for the long delay between 1600 and 1620, it is probable that Wilmore in 1600 mollified the Steward for a while, until he felt that he had been long enough in possession to defy the Manor, and to deface the boundaries.

If this was indeed his view of the matter, he was justified in the end by the Court of Chancery. For the rest he founded his case on the validity of the sale from William Lodge to Townsend and from the younger Townsend to his father, together with his denial, supported by the confusion of boundaries, that the lands belonged to the Manor of Playes.

The successive decrees of the Court [1] are particularly

1 C 33/139, f. 1044; C 33/141, ff. 72, 472.

interesting, for they seem to me to illustrate admirably
that marked vein of obstinacy and wilfulness which once
more led Lodge to throw away the substance for the
shadow of self-satisfaction. The orders of the Court begin
on 11 June 1620, bearing upon the usual procedure of
pleadings and depositions before hearing. On 30 October
1621 the issue is defined. Lodge lays claim by inheritance
to lands actually in the possession of Wilmore. His title,
the Court holds, is clear. But the bounds of the lands are
in question. The Court orders certain Surveys to be
brought in to try to settle this point. On 7 February 1622
a final decree is given, after the cause has been heard, with
arguments from Mr. Stanwell for Lodge and Mr. Paul
Crook for Wilmore. The decree not only gives a decision
of the case, but also recites the failure of the Court to arrange a friendly compromise, its favourite procedure.
Lodge, says the Court, claimed four acres of land as copyhold, though they have been 'passed away as free Lands'
and by long occupation of the defendant cannot be distinguished now. Lodge paid only thirty shillings as consideration for his title. He has, in fact, purchased the land
from owners who were never in possession, basing his title
upon a supposed forfeiture. Against his title, we have to
set two descents, from William Lodge to Townsend, and
from Townsend to Wilmore; a fine paid for the transfer-
ence; forty years' quiet possession; and valuable consideration paid by the rival claimant. The Court sees no just
cause for relief to Lodge. Nevertheless, when the cause was
formerly heard in Michaelmas 1621 the Master of the Rolls
suggested to Wilmore that he should come to a compromise with Lodge, and Wilmore agreed. But Lodge refused,
not once, but twice, preferring the due course of law, on
which the Court has twice found against him. Considering
all this, the Court now thinks meet, and so decrees, that

the matter shall be clearly and absolutely dismissed. His counsel must have advised him to cut his losses. I marvel that the records of Star Chamber do not show some sequel to this suit. But Lodge was an old man of sixty-five, and a poor man. And two years in Chancery must have exhausted his resources, even if his combativeness remained undiminished.

In the meantime Lodge had married, probably during this last period of his life. It is evident that his choice of a wife was determined in some measure by his position as a Catholic recusant. And we may well wonder to what extent he was in touch with the powerful Catholic family of the Howards. For his wife was a Catholic and was at least an acquaintance, if not more, of Anne, Countess of Arundel. Our information concerning the marriage comes from a seventeenth-century manuscript life of Philip, Earl of Arundel,[1] at Arundel Castle, written probably in 1635. Lodge's name is familiar to the unknown writer, apparently a Jesuit Father attached to the Arundel circle, who tells the story of the Earl's imprisonment in the Tower and of various plots laid against him to convict him of treason or to discredit him. In one of these Lodge's wife played a part, in 1585 or 1586:

For besides the forging the letter above mentioned, which was before his comeing into ye tower; after his comeing thither they slandered him first; with incontinency, as tho' he had there got a woman with child, & suborned a base dishonest baggage servant to one Mr Pigeon dwelling in the Tower, to lay her child to his charge: and sent a certain catholick gentlewoman (Mrs Albridge afterwards marryed to Dr Lodge) with whom I was acquainted and whose husband was a dependent of Sir Francis Walsingham then Secretary, & had been his spye at Rome &

---

1 *The Life and Death of the Renown'd Confessor Phillippe Howard Earl of Arundel, etc.* I have to thank Mr. R. Cecil Wilton for access to this manuscript, by permission of His Grace the Duke of Norfolk. Lodge's treatise, *The Poor Man's Talent*, was dedicated to Lady Anne during this period of his life.

other places diverse years, to give notice to his Lady thereof vpon pretence she might take some secret order for the maintenance of the woman & the childe, lest otherwise the matter might come to light, & her Lord be disgraced.[1]

But Lady Anne knew her husband better. She was, moreover, a woman of sense, and pointed out to Mrs Albridge or Aldridge how straitly the Earl was imprisoned, how infirm he was at the time, and how unfortunately she had lent herself to what was manifestly a plot. 'Besides,' writes the biographer, 'had he been so wickedly disposed he never would have made choice (as himself did say) of one so base, so old, & so ugly as she was.' Mrs Aldridge was greatly abashed. But the historian is careful to assert her innocence of any treachery towards the Arundels. Her 'simplicity was much abused therein,' he writes. It is an odd story.

Her first husband, Solomon Aldred or Aldridge, had set her a sad example of double-dealing, as is abundantly evidenced in the State Papers [2] which record his career from 1583 to 1589. In 1583 he was responsible for the imprisonment at Milan of Edward Unton, and Henry Unton writes to Walsingham concerning him as 'one Aldred, the player of my brother's tragedy' and as one worth winning over, being 'better acquainted with Romish practices against England than any.' Aldred was, in fact, in receipt of ten ducats a month from the Pope, but was evidently considering a better bargain with Walsingham. After an unsatisfactory journey to England with this in view he lost his subsidy from Rome, but succeeded in reinstating himself 'into more credit than ever, being one of the inquisitors,' by December 1584. By September 1585 he was under

1 *Op. cit.*, pp. 45–46.
2 *Calendar of State Papers (Elizabeth), Foreign,* Vols. XVII–XXI; *Domestic,* Vols. XXVII–XXXI, *passim.*

grave suspicion of flying false colours in his dealings in France as an agent of Rome, and in danger of his life, and in 1586 we find letters from him to Walsingham from Rouen and Paris. By September 1589 he was evidently engaged upon diplomatic affairs of the highest magnitude on behalf of Walsingham in France. And now he disappears from the records. It would be charitable to believe that the preparations for the Armada roused a sense of patriotism in Aldred and led him to 'become a right Englishman,' as Unton put it in 1583. But he seemed to Unton a man 'of little honesty,' and to Lewknor, who had known him for ten years, 'a malicious fellow.'

Mrs Aldred may well have been of different mettle, however. The very fact that she was chosen for the errand to Lady Anne Arundel, as a woman beyond suspicion of treachery to her, makes it more likely that she was more loyal than her husband to her co-religionists. Nothing more is known of her except that her maiden name was Fernley [1] and that she survived Lodge as well as Aldred. She must have been a woman of mature years when Lodge married her, and there is no indication that there were any children of the only marriage of Lodge that is recorded.

Lodge's literary activities continued unabated. During the course of his protracted last struggle in Chancery, he published a translation of a French *Summary of Du Bartas*, in 1621. He had a sufficient command of French to write even French verse in earlier years. And in 1622 the last product of his pen appeared, a preface to *The Countess of Lincoln's Nurserie*, a short treatise, addressed to her daughter-in-law, in which Elizabeth Clinton, Countess of Lincoln, anticipates Rousseau's advice to mothers to suckle their own children. The Countess had ample experience, having had eighteen children herself, of whom one or two died

---

1 Hunter, *Chorus Vatum Anglicanorum*, B.M. MS. Add. 24487, I, p. 307.

'by the default of their nurses,' for she had not been allowed to nurse them herself. Lodge supports her thesis with medical and moral argument, and concludes his preface with the last of his verses, poor, angular and trite, beginning thus:

> Blest is the land where Sons of Nobles raigne
> Blest is the land where Nobles teach their traine,

verses which evoke, unbidden, memories of Blackmore and transport us by their rhythm and cadence into a later century. Some of Lodge's earlier verse is no better than this, however. The fact is that he was, except for a lyric or two, a poor poet and, in general, one of the many Elizabethans who were neither called nor chosen, but doggedly determined, to write literature.

The end of Lodge's long and varied career inspires a feeling of compassion, though this would be the least acceptable of tributes to that indomitable man. To be invited by so great a lady to give in print his learned sanction to her treatise was the last spark of the almost extinguished glow of his dignity. Three years later we have the final record that marks the end of his life. On 23 October 1625 letters of administration were issued to Joan Lodge, widow of Thomas Lodge, Doctor of Medicine, late of the parish of St. Mary Magdalene in Old Fish Street in the City of London, who had died intestate.[1] He had little to leave, though he had been the sole residuary heir to the great possessions of the Lord Mayor and his wealthy wife, Lady Anne. The line of Lodges, of which such fair and reasonable hopes were cherished by these admirable citizens, ended with Thomas, and with him foundered in poverty and obscurity.

1 P.C.C. Admon., 23 October 1625.

VI. THOMAS LODGE THE MAN

LADY ANNE LODGE was buried on 30 December 1579, and
in the Stationers' Register we find entered for printing an
Epitaph of the Lady Anne Lodge, her son's first piece of
literature. This has been spoken of as a proof of filial
devotion. It may be so — I hope it is — but it is an odd
kind of grief that can be solaced by precipitate print. For
the *Epitaph* was entered on 23 December, before Lady
Anne's death authorised even poetic grief. The facts seem
to be consistent with an intention to be ready for the
event, with a view to the market, though it may be that
Lodge was not responsible for the entry. But it is a queer
incident. And it shows us Lodge as an 'occasional' poet
in his beginnings, as in much of his *Fig for Momus,* the
indication, on the whole, of an inferior literary talent. It
points to a limited, less imaginative, more imitative type
of mind at grips with art, as compared with his fellows of
Oxford and Cambridge.

There is not, by the way, any real reason for suggesting
that Thomas was the favourite son of Lady Anne or grandson of Lady Laxton, though Sir Edmund Gosse urges it
upon us that he alone was especially provided for by both,
maintaining that 'he must have shewn some particular
powers of intelligence to be thus selected among six children as his mother's sole legatee.' The facts are that both
ladies provided for all the children, and that Thomas, as
second son, second in the line of Lodges, had to be given a
reasonable landed estate, 'some convenient portion,' as
Lady Lodge put it. And even that was left to him on
strict conditions, and so never came to him in the end.

What Gosse is naturally apt to admire in Lodge was precisely what both his father and mother particularly de-

tested in him, knowing the normal accompaniments of the life of the young scholar or man-of-letters in London. Lodge's real interests at this time are amply indicated by his next work, written in defence of the stage in 1579 or early in 1580 against Stephen Gosson, and called *Honest Excuses*, which was suppressed after printing. It was doubtless some similar escapade that brought Lodge before the Privy Council in June 1581. In the same year Lodge wrote a prefatory poem, before October 23, when the book was entered in the Stationers' Register, to Barnabe Rich's *Don Simonides*, in which he speaks of himself as dulled by his 'long distress,' 'breaking my pleasant vein.' Gosse will have it that this must be illness, not misfortune. But the facts surely are that Lodge had got into serious trouble, ending in imprisonment, had put himself irrevocably out of court with his father and his family, and was finding literature and the stage a poor support for wit and gallantry. Gosson wrote of him in 1582 as a man under heavy clouds, of a loose and worthless way of life, almost a vagrant. Such, says Gosse, is the 'worthless testimony' of Gosson, whose acrid zeal certainly seems excessive, coming from a young man of twenty-seven, only two years older than Lodge. Gosson was only twenty-four [1] when he wrote his first diatribe against the stage, and must have been very young when he himself wrote plays in his unregenerate days. But there is no doubt he was right about Lodge.

In February 1583, Lodge signed a Deed of Release to his brother William, freeing him of all his claims on legacies, including the Nayland estate, in return for money advanced and debts paid in anticipation of his expectations. And by 4 November he had ready for the press a notable piece of work called *An Alarum against Usurers*.

1 C 24/346/5, containing a deposition by Gosson which gives his age.

Less than ten years later Lodge was extremely busy in Star Chamber and in Chancery seeking redress for the advantage that, he argued, William had taken upon him in obtaining this Deed from him in his time of need.

Of Lodge's many and varied literary efforts, none perhaps is more closely taken from experience than *An Alarum against Usurers*, in which he sets forth the normal process of the degradation and ruin of young gentlemen brought about by dissipation in London. And all points to the probability that Lodge is in a large measure drawing upon experience when he paints this picture, though he defends himself in the *Epistle to the Gentlemen of the Innes of Court* against the strictures of Stephen Gosson. In this pamphlet Lodge inveighs against that class of merchant which has taken to usurious practices, by whose means

(the more is the pittie) the prisons are replenished with young gentlemen. These be they that make the father carefull, the mother sorrowfull, the sonne desperate: . . . that can close with a young youth while they cousen him, and feede his humoures, till they free him of his farmes.

He proceeds to explain how a young man with expectations or with land, but short of money, is exploited by a broker acting for a merchant. 'If you want money, you have creditt,' the broker suggests, and after an investigation of the young man's circumstances a loan is given on his bond. Not money is lent, however, but commodities to the value of the loan, which the young man has to turn into money. The broker kindly acts as his factor, and the young man finally receives in cash at best a half of the amount for which he has given his bond for repayment in full in three months, the penalty for forfeiture of the bond being at least double the nominal loan.

It will be observed that this is precisely the procedure in the play, *A Looking Glass for London and England*, written by Lodge and Greene. It was a well-known trick, of course.[1] But there can be no reasonable doubt that the young lawyer of Lincoln's Inn wrote the scene in which the Usurer deals in this fashion with Thrasybulus, having given him ten pounds cash and thirty pounds in lute-strings, which he sold for but five pounds, fifteen pounds in all for his bond of forty pounds. Indeed, later on in the pamphlet this very transaction is given as an example of fraud, down to the details of the amounts involved, forty pounds the amount of the loan, ten pounds cash, and thirty pounds' worth of lute-strings. The matter seems to stick in Lodge's mind.

The young man nevertheless repeats his indiscretion, and falls into more and more expensive dissipations.

> Truly, gentlemen, this that I write is true: I myself know the pay-master; naie, more, I myself know certainly that by name I can reckon among you some that have ben bitten, who, left good portions by their parents, and faire lands by their auncestors, are desolate now, not having friends to releeve them, or money to affray their charges. . . .
> Thus, thus, alas! the father before his eies, and in his elder yeres, beholdeth as in a mirror the desolation of his owne house, and hearing of the profusenesse of his ungratious sonne calleth him home, rebuketh him of his error, and requesteth an account of his money misspended.

There is not a word of this which is not strictly true when applied to Lodge's own life. We may find further auto-biographical hints in Lodge's references to the young gentleman who is obliged to seek his fortune abroad, with unhappy results, bearing in mind his own adventures with Clarke and Cavendish, or to the man of money ousting the gentry, and ultimately feasting 'in the halls of our riotous

---

1 Sir Thomas dealt with the Earl of Westmorland in this fashion in 1546, lending £560 in wares, 'the which being sold by the broker and converted into moneye was by the broker and the servants of . . . Sir Thomas Lodge delyvered at the late Erls house in the Charterhouse churchyard' (C 24/72). We are not told what the Earl received in cash. We are, however, given a specimen of his conversation: 'Yea, marye, quod the Erle, by Goddes faire foote'!

young spendthrifts.' For Lodge came of a doubly knighted family, though merchants on both sides.

There follows the discourse of the father, lamenting the evil ways of his once hopeful son. Sir Thomas Lodge, it may be observed, was probably a sick man when the book was written. He made his will on 14 December 1583, little over a month after the book was entered in the Stationers' Register. He died on 28 February 1584, and I think these dates exclude the possibility of a sudden death from plague. The book bears all the signs of rapid writing, and we may wonder what lay behind the producing of it. Filial piety was no light sentiment and tradition among the Elizabethans, and there is something more than dramatic rhetoric in the speech here set down:

O, my sonne, if thou knewest thy father's care, and wouldest answer it with thy well dooing, I might have hope of the continuance of my progeny, and thou be a joy to my aged yeres . . . my name shall cease in thee, and other covetous underminers shall injoye the fruites of my long labours.

Sir Thomas had several sons, it is true, and this was a dramatic touch hardly justified in 1584. Yet, strangely enough, it was Thomas who outlived all his brethren and did, in the end, stand alone to represent the progeny of the old City knight, who goes on here to refer to the young man's mother:

How tenderly, good boye, in thy mother's lyfe wast thou cherished! How deerely beloved! How well instructed! . . . Report, nay, true report, hath made me privie to many of thy escapes, which as a father though I cover, yet as a good father tenderly will I rebuke.

Sir Thomas, as we have seen, was in fact less reticent about his son's faults, in private at any rate.

The father continues, reproaching his son with wasting an allowance of forty pounds a year, and in two years running a hundred pounds into debt, and with haunting expensive courtesans. I have no evidence upon this last charge. But there is the clearest evidence that within three or four years of his mother's death Lodge had exhausted the legacies left to him under her will, and had completed the process just a year before the printing of this book, in 1583. It is probable that the three enemies enumerated by the father here were all known to Lodge, as two of them certainly were: 'first prodigalitie, the enimie to continencie; next lasciviousness, the enimie of sobrietie; and thirdly, ill company, the decayers of thy honestie.' Finally, having met his debts this time, the father warns him that if he falls again from virtue, 'I promise thee this, that as now I deale with thee as a father, so then will I accompt of thee as a reprobate.' So the son returns to the Inns of Court, repentantly, but at once returns to his old ways, to his usurer and his mistress Minxe, and in the end is completely ruined, whereupon 'his father refuseth him, dispossessing the ryghte heyre of what hee maye, and poore hee is left desolate and afflicted in prison.' Lodge was in prison, in fact, in 1581, and his account runs close to the facts. His father, as we have seen, had no small share in preventing Lodge from coming into possession of the lands left him by his mother on condition of good behaviour.

This may perhaps suffice to show that there was much more than mere literary art in the outcry of the young man that now follows:

Alas! unhappie wretch that I am, that having a good father that did cherish me, a tried mother that tenderly nourished me, many friends to accompanie me, faire revenewes to inrich me, have heaped sorrowe on my owne head by my father's displeasure, refused of my friends for my misdemeanour, and dispossessed of my land by my prodigalitie.

We come closer than ever to the actual details of Lodge's affairs, as they appear in the series of law-suits in which he was involved with his brother William, in certain suggestions which he makes for the remedying of usury and the removal of temptation from young gentlemen to have recourse to usurers. For, considering the case of such heirs as are 'wardes unto her Majestie, or else by the tender provision of their parents they are left to the discretion of their kinsfolke,' he argues that if they are kept short of money they are likely to borrow. Either condition of wardship may stint the heir, 'for nowe a dayes kinsfolkes are as covetous as others, and as crafty as the best.' Let such guardians be bound to supply the young man with the largest possible income, and they will then be satisfied with his conduct!

Now it was precisely the condition of Thomas Lodge that the lands left to him by his mother were left under trustees, and that having been paid less than their value, as he maintains, he brought suit against William Lodge, his elder brother and one of the executors of his mother's will, some nine years after the publication of this pamphlet in which he sets forth the unhappy career of just such an heir as himself. One cannot help feeling that some of the outrageously righteous indignation with which Lodge ends the pamphlet, calling upon the wicked usurer to repent, must have been composed to the address of his brother, who had lent him money, taken his bond of release in respect of his legacies, and usurped the estate left to him by his mother. At any rate, we may observe the strongly fraternal note struck in the concluding paragraph, wherein he 'for brotherly amitie counsailed' the usurers, and does 'brotherly admonish' them! Lodge's reliance upon his own actual experiences throughout increases the possibility that the pamphlets of Greene, for example, may be taken as genuinely autobiographical.

It is characteristic, again, of Lodge, that he finds Gosson's strictures, to which he refers in this book, incomprehensible. Nothing but prejudice, ignorance and unfairness can account for Gosson, or anyone, opposing Thomas Lodge. Lodge went his own way, secure in his own rectitude and the excellence of his motives, and convinced that he knew best. Sir Thomas died shortly after this book was published, and there is no mention of Thomas in his will, despite the excellent morality of the *Alarum against Usurers*, which may have been partly meant to soften the old man's heart towards his ill-used second son. But Thomas was deliberately excluded from the entail of the Lodge properties, as his succession to the Nayland estate had been deliberately withheld. It is probable that Thomas did now in fact go to sea to the Canaries. By 1588 or at latest by September 1589, he was back in London with a book ready for printing and no mean debt for wine to Peter Suckling, and probably another of £7 to a Strand tailor, Richard Topping. In 1596 Topping was still trying to get it out of Henslowe, who bailed Lodge in 1597.[1]

In 1590 his novel *Rosalynde* was printed, written before October 6, the source of Shakespeare's *As You Like It*. Has any one considered the choice of this theme by Lodge, and the working out of it? Yet it is most significant and apt to his career. It was written, he says, during his voyage with Clarke to the Canaries, and 'it is the woorke of a Souldier and a Scholler.' It has a double moral, pithily put in the postscript: 'Here Gentlemen may you see . . . that such as neglect their father's precepts, incur much prejudice . . . that yonger brethren though inferior in yeares, yet may be superior in honors.' The relations between Saladyne, the elder brother, and Rosader, the younger, are almost ludicrously parallel to those of William and Thomas. Saladyne is another picture of the 'covetous caterpillar,' the Usurer in *A Looking Glass*. He is in *Rosalynde* the 'weeping hyaena' who defrauds Rosader

1 *Henslowe Papers*, Arts. 21, 22, 23.

of his dues, makes havoc of his legacies and lands, and spoils his manor houses.

I need not labour the point. It is certain that the writing of *Rosalynde* must have been a great comfort to Lodge, and we may be sure that the underlying autobiographical facts in his life were not ignored by some of its readers. Rosader is therefore, in a measure, an artistic and idealised portrait of Lodge, and so Lodge served indirectly as a model for Shakespeare's Orlando. I cannot believe that Shakespeare and his circle of theatre-folk were not aware of the affairs of Lodge. And I am certain that Lodge went to see it, took parties with him and led the applause and groans at the right moments, which I think may readily be found.[1] I feel sure that Professor Dover Wilson, who suggests 1593 as the date of Shakespeare's first writing of the play, would rejoice to think that this fits in admirably with the year in which Thomas and William Lodge were fighting it out, Oliver and Orlando in Star Chamber and Chancery!

At the end of the postscript Lodge anticipated Ben Jonson's defiant retort upon criticism,[2] in the words 'If you like it, so:' — words which surely gave Shakespeare his title, and which also are characteristic of Lodge. He is incurably self-sufficient, assertive of his own point of view, and impervious to any opposing point of view. This characteristic runs through all his writings, and through all his law-suits.

Does he write a *Treatise of the Plague* in 1603? Then he warns readers against all the doings and sayings of all other doctors and their quackery, 'foolish Idiotes and ignorant Emperiques' who are not, like himself, Physicians and Philosophers. Yet he can write, 'Truly my resolution is to provoke no man, and those that know me inwardly of late time can witnesse . . . I thanke God I haue indured wrongs,

---

1 *E. g.*, I, i, 158 ff.; I, i, 138 ff., respectively.
2 *Cynthia's Revels*, Epilogue.

tho I haue had power to revenge them.' His object in writing this book is mainly to help the poor who suffer from
plague and cannot afford doctors. And he calmly requests
the Lord Mayor and City to buy his book up and distribute it broadcast. For the first time, apparently, when
there is something to be gained, he expresses here a belated
sense of 'the duetie and loue which I owe to this Citie
wherein I was bred and brought vp.'

Turn to his law-suits, to the ineffable self-righteousness
of his complaints against William, which have a more personal and dramatic note than even the average Star Chamber Bill. Here he is the friendly young innocent, hardly
used, but anxious to do the right thing between brothers.
See him again in a later character, the mature philosopher
in a noble mood, being troubled by a vulgar-minded
grazier, a peasant — George Raye, to whom he leased the
Rolleston lands at a most satisfactory rent, on which Raye
lost heavily when the Trent and the Greet overflowed his
fields. Lodge's Answer found Raye an easy mark. What
has Raye to say? It is a source of grief to him that Lodge
has made the best of his lands. He alleges that he paid too
much, that is, he alleges his own negligence and really
praises Lodge: 'that kinde of exception tendith rather to
commende a mans providence then to impeach him of
evill dealing.' Besides, Raye is in the trade, he is a grazier,
unlike Doctor Thomas Lodge, who has

never practised anie such course of life but the Cleane contrarie and
dwelte for the most parte of his life in the cittie of London, his practise
of life hath been but studie and contemplation for the most parte.

And Lodge ends with a peroration in good set terms:

and this defendant doth admire that the plaintiff should saie that this
defendant hath beene a great gainer by him and not acknowledge the
goodnes of his owne bargaine and shewe his turbulent spirit to stirr up
sute concerning that whereby he hath benefited himself and is behold-
ing to this defendant.

I must say that, at this stage of Lodge's litigious career, this picture of himself as the studious and contemplative man, withdrawn from meaner concerns in his pursuit of higher matters, excites a tickling of the midriff. It is his nearest approach to truly imaginative fiction. No doubt Lodge, at the age of sixty, looked the part admirably, and probably with a certain nobility and dignity. But it is strange how often our contemplative scholar, who had so recently, in 1614, translated Seneca's Stoic *Morals*, was thus beset with turbulent spirits.

It is also clear here that, when Lodge had an advantage, he drove it home, without any compunction. The turbulent spirit of George Raye resided in the withered body of an aged man over eighty years of age,[1] who could not even write his name. But Lodge, having overreached him, showed him no pity. The same bent of character led him into the obstinate rejection of compromise, and a refusal to admit defeat, which are strikingly shown in his last suit against Wilmore concerning the West Ham lands, that astute, unscrupulous, forlorn hope. When the case had been thoroughly heard, the Court, in Michaelmas, 1621, saw no cause to admit Lodge's plea. Nevertheless the Master of the Rolls suggested to Wilmore that he should pay £30 to Lodge as a solatium. Wilmore agreed. Lodge refused, and demanded a second hearing. Again the Court, in February 1622, found as before, yet again moved Wilmore to compromise, this time suggesting £20, to put an end to the matter. Wilmore, much protesting, once more agreed, but Lodge, 'being present in Court departed without giveing any consent to accept the same,' evidently in high dudgeon. And so the Court, upon this, clearly and absolutely dismissed the case, and Lodge got nothing.

Was ever man so blind to the direction of the finger of

1 C 24/221/37. George Raye, of Highgate, yeoman, aged 55 on 10 June, 1591.

fate? It was not in Lodge, one would imagine, to conceive that he might be in the wrong, or that he might be unable to have his own way. And when things went inconceivably awry, he satisfied himself with a gesture of contempt and rebellion.

When Lodge was a young man of twenty-one, and mounted his paper steed to tilt against Stephen Gosson, he could see nothing but error and animus in an incomprehensibly irreconcilable opponent. He had not changed forty years later, when he thought to carry away the Court of Chancery with an *alla stoccata*. I have no doubt he backed his own judgement against that of his counsel Mr. Stanwell in this matter. Indeed, this seems to be the dominant note of his whole life, the life of an incurably assertive individualist vindicating self-will and private opinion against all the forces of environment.

Born into a citizen family of wealth and standing, but with firm convictions upon its right and power to guide and dispose of its children, Lodge resisted the imposing influences leading him towards a steady, assured life of dignity and ease in the legal profession. Three generations of Laxtons, Lanes, Loddingtons, Lodges, Machells and Woodfords surrounded him in his youth, with two Lord Mayors and several Aldermen of London among them, all Grocers of name and fame, desirous of perpetuating the honour of the clan, and hoping great things from the sons of Sir Thomas and Lady Anne. From all this, Lodge turned away to join a group of young wits and scholars about town, regardless of warnings and threats, and unmoved by entreaties, to exploit his genius and to follow the impulses of the moment. So doing, he forfeited his patrimony in the end. He paid a heavy price for the privilege of writing a few charming lyrics, a poor play or two, some second-rate satires, a few novels, and a pamphlet in defence of the stage. Spendthrift or improvident to the end, there is never any sign even in his riper years of that settled course of life that was the only demand his clan made of him. At twenty-one he was in the lists against Gosson; at twenty-three he fell foul of the Privy Council; and in middle age, still pursuing his bent, he turned Catholic, in the teeth of a time of most violent persecution of a faith that seemed to involve disloyalty to the State. He went his own way throughout, whether it were to the tavern in Fleet Street, to the Terceras or to Brazil, to France in pursuit of a degree in medicine, or when he turned upon his heel, spurning the Court of Chancery. It is significant that when he died in 1625, leaving behind him a wife of whom we know little, he died intestate, having provided for the moment and no further. We may well be moved by a sense of irony when we consider how this man, having refused to follow the profession of the law, a truant from Lincoln's Inn, thereafter spent a notable proportion of his energies in an endless series of suits at law, involved in its processes in his very childhood, turning to it at intervals throughout a long life, till we finally see him resolute as ever in Chancery at the age of sixty-four. But we need not feel any incongruity in this pursuit of the law in practice. For the law to Lodge was but one more field in that wide and varied country which he explored with endless zest and persistence, seeking lists wherein to challenge circumstance and to vindicate and assert his own wit, his own powers, and his own desires. There was never a truer Elizabethan. Let Lodge state the moral himself, in his comments upon the misfortunes of his young rake, in *An Alarum against Usurers*:

Nature's gifts are to be used by direction: he had learning, but hee applied it ill: he hadde knowledge, but he blinded it with selfe-opinion.

APPENDIX I

AFTER my verry harty commendatoñ to yor good lordships. I haue receyved yor letts by thandę of Sir thoms lodge, last yere maior of the Cite of london, pceyving, by the same that yor ll., vpon the hering of his cause, haue so considered of his good seruic at all tymes, that you haue moved the quenes matie therof. And thervpon induced her grace to haue gret pitty of the case. And that her highnes by yor mediacon is verry well inclyned to stay hym in his Credit. Wch shalbe a wurthy dede ffor that he is a wise man and a gret Occupier as any is in the Cite & shall wt the quenes favor and helpe, shortly recoū this lakke. Wherof I pceyve the quenes highnes and yor ll be moch desirous and so am I for my pt to th vttermost I may do/And of yor iij devices for his helpe I think the staplers verry good for that wilbe redy mony wherof he hath most nede/ And I think the Sparing of his Customes vpon eūy of his shippingę in six yeres shall cause hym ship the more to his increase And of that Custom the quenes matie to be paid in the ij yere wch will not helpe hym at this prsent nede And therefor there must be as moch more aboue the staplers mony as must make the full of vj m li and so he shalbe well holpen And if it please the quenes grace to graunt to this then the quenes prie Seale to me to pay to Mr lodge the Staplers mony to be paid to her grace vpon the last shipping & as moch therto as shall make the full of vj m li I shall shortly despatch the matī aggrehable to the quenes pleasure when I shall know the same by yor lre: most hartely desiring yor good ll, to contynue yor favor to the said sir Thomas lodge that the quenes highnes may contynue her most gracious favor and ayde

---

[1] The letter and the second endorsement appear to be in Winchester's own hand. The first endorsement is written by a clerk.

to the end of this matť Wch shalbe as honorable and as charitable
as my hart can think of/ & thus fare you hartely well
Westm this ffriday the iijd day of december 1563
yor ll assured loving ffrend

            Winchester

(Endorsed)   3 10 bris. 1563
              L. Tresr
Sr Thoms Lodge maior of London, wanting a Supply of
mony to keep vp his credit, obtained favour from sevral
Lords, being a wise man & great trader. xviii

To my verry good ll and ffrendę therle of pembroke the
l. Robt Dudley and Willm̄ Secill the quenes principall
secretary
at Windsor

BARNABE BARNES

By MARK ECCLES

CONTENTS

BARNABE BARNES

I. PARTHENOPHIL [1]

A moving spirit pricked with Beauty's grace.
Parthenophil

WHETHER or not Barnabe Barnes was that mysterious being, the Rival Poet, it is clear that he was one of the rivals for Southampton's favor, and that he was occasionally a poet. All we really know is that the entry of *Venus and Adonis* in the Stationers' Register is followed a month later by *Parthenophil and Parthenophe*, and that Barnes addresses one of the dedicatory sonnets to Southampton. He has also 'A friendes gratulation, to his beloued friend Master Iohn Florio,' before *A Worlde of Wordes*, 1598, which Florio, the Earl's Italian tutor, dedicates to Southampton and two other patrons. Our knowledge of Southampton's circle is too slight to build upon; but whatever makes the character of any member of it stand out more vividly at least does a little, where so much is shadow, to fill in the picture.

Barnes' date of birth has commonly been given as 1569; but he was baptized on March 6, 1570–71, at St. Michael le Belfrey in the city of York.[2] One of the earlier christenings in the same year was that of Guy Fawkes, whose father was Register and Advocate of the Consistory Court. Barnabe's father had been living at York as Suffragan Bishop of Nottingham and Chancellor of York Minster. The entry of the christening describes him as Richard,

1 The preliminary work upon the Star Chamber Case was done by Mr. Eccles, Mr. R. W. Schmelzer, and Mr. T. M. Moore jointly. (*Ed.*)
2 *Yorkshire Parish Register Soc.*, 1, 9. In *N. and Q.*, CXLVI, 268, the year was quoted merely as 1570, which was turned into 1569–1570 in *The Year's Work in English Studies, 1924.*

Bishop of Nottingham, although he had been translated from that see to Carlisle the preceding June, and had entered upon his new charge by October. He owed his position to Burghley, who advanced him seven years later to the rich see of Durham. There, when Barnabe was a boy of ten, the Bishop lost his first wife: 'O Fridesmonda vale.'[1] He married as his second, in his castle at Durham during Lent 1582, 'Jane Dyllycote a french woman.'[2] By birth she was Jane Jerrard, a native of the Duchy of Anjou.[3] I suspect that her presence in Durham is explained by the fact that Whittingham, chief translator of the Geneva Bible and Dean of Durham, had married a wife from Orleans, Katherine Jaqueman; for by his will in 1579 he leaves a bequest to 'Mrs. Jane, the Frenchewoman.'[4]

'Barnabye Barness' was matriculated from his father's college, Brasenose, on July 8, 1586, the Oxford register with its customary inaccuracy giving his age as seventeen, instead of fifteen.[5] Among his friends who came up in the same year were Bastard the epigrammatist, known even as a student for his satiric verse, and John Thorie the translator, who later joined in praise of Harvey. Barnes took no degree, and it is possible, as Grosart suggests, that his residence may have been interrupted at the end of his first year by the death of his father in August 1587. On the other hand, it was not until 1589 that William Percy matriculated at the University, and since Percy was the chief friend of his early years, it seems more likely that Barnes was then still a student at Oxford. Grosart, and

1 Brass at St. Andrew's, Auckland, reproduced in *Archæologia Aeliana*, N.S. xv (1892), 81.
2 Sir Cuthbert Sharpe, *Chronicon Mirabile*, pt. i, 4.
3 On this, noted in Hunter's *Chorus Vatum*, Grosart remarks, 'no authority.' The authority is *Harl. MS.* 1995, f. 91; see also Foster, *Visitations of Yorkshire*, p. 50.
4 *Surtees Soc.*, xxxviii, 17.
5 Andrew Clark, *Register of the University of Oxford*, ii, i, 152.

Bullen in the *D.N.B.*, have followed the error of Malone in making Florio servitor to Barnabe, on the strength of his matriculation in 1581 as servant to Mr. Barnes.[1] This was the Bishop's eldest son, Emanuel, who in the same month had permission to cross the sea to become a Doctor of Sacred Theology at Basel.

Barnabe was of an age now to choose his career, but he had no desire to follow his eldest brother into the Church or his second brother, John, into the law. Then in 1591 came Essex's expedition to Normandy, promising action and adventure, and Barnes with a crowd of other ambitious youths volunteered. War did not strike him as a particularly intelligent occupation, if we may believe Nashe's chaff, but his pleasant company made him a special favorite with divers knights and captains. Among these may have been Sir Robert Carey, with whom we later find him, Northumberland's brother Sir Charles Percy and his brother-in-law Sir John Wotton — all knighted in this campaign. Nashe affirms that Barnes got leave of Essex to return to London, where he bragged of having killed ten men.[2] The score was too high by ten according to Campion, who seems also to have been a volunteer, perhaps under Carey.[3]

Barnabe's opinion of war was shared by Campion (*De Se*), and evidently by most of the gentlemen volunteers, from the speed with which they came back to England. Harvey's reference to Baskerville does not prove that Barnes served under him, as Vivian assumes; nor can Barnes have joined the army in February 1591–92, since Essex had by that time returned home. Many years later

1 Clark, I, 392; Wood, *Fasti Oxonienses*, 1, 218. By an opposite error Miss Dodds gives the verses on Florio's *World of Words* in 1598 to Emanuel, although they are signed 'B. B.'
2 *Works*, ed. McKerrow, III, 104.
3 *Works*, ed. Vivian, pp. xxxiii, 239.

Barnes praises Essex enthusiastically, and writes, 'I my selfe a Boy, haue seene him in the French warres to communicate in sports and sometimes in serious matters with men of mean condition and place,' to labor with the mattock, set watches, and often go walking the rounds.[1] From this passage Grosart superfluously infers an earlier visit to France, perhaps to his stepmother's relatives, forgetting that he could not have seen the Earl in any French wars before 1591, since Essex fought in none. Barnabe was still but a boy when he published his poetry, and Nashe never tires of referring to him as a 'chrisome,' a 'smattring pert Boy, whose buttocks were not yet coole since he came from the grammar,' and together with Chute as 'infants' and 'princockesses.'[2]

Barnes refers to his age in the curious zodiac sonnets of *Parthenophil*.[3] The first two take him from the age of fourteen, when he first fell in love, till 'now mine age had thrise seuen winters ronne.' In this year (which we can now place correctly as 1591–92) he forsook youthful fancies for studies and labors, and fixed his eyes 'On Pallas, and on Mars, home, and in field.' He had probably written much of his verse even before he came of age. Nashe speaks of his returning from France to finish *Parthenophil*.[4] When it came out about May 1593, it proved to be a more extensive collection of love poetry than an English author had ever before published. Not only were there sonnets, but madrigals, sestines, canzons, elegies, an eidillion, and odes in many meters, including asclepiads and anacreontics.

In his essay on Lodge[5] Sir Edmund Gosse remarks,

1 *Offices*, p. 180. Was not Shakespeare in *Henry V* thinking of this trait in Essex?   2 Ed. McKerrow, III, 108, 89, 109.
3 Sonnets 32–43.
4 Ed. McKerrow, III, 105.
5 Hunterian Club edition, and in *Seventeenth Century Studies*, p. 35.

'It does not seem to have been observed that the elaborate piece . . . [in *A Margarite of America*] is an example, the earliest in English literature, of a sestina formed on the exact plan of that form of verse, as invented by Arnaut Daniel and employed by Dante.' Whenever Lodge wrote this poem, he did not publish it until 1596, and Barnes had therefore preceded him by three years with five sestines. Spenser in the *Shepherds' Calendar* (August) had used a simpler variety of his own, but Barnes followed the intricate Petrarchan form in all his sestines except the second. In the fifth he even succeeded in constructing a vigorous triple sestine. The first English sapphics are said to be those of Webbe in his *Discourse of Poetry* (1586), where he 'turned the new Poets sweete song of *Eliza* [April of the *Shepherds' Calendar*] into such homely Sapphick as I coulde,' which was very homely indeed. Barnes had taste enough not to aim at observing quantity in English, but, with shorter lines, at producing the effect of Sappho's stanza, and he made a fair beginning in Ode 18, which indicates the difference between the work of a poet and that of a metrician murdering poetry. Sidney in the *Arcadia* had already given examples both of sapphics and of the sestine.

The first mistress who withdrew Barnes from his 'solitary studies' was light Laya (perhaps a Ley or Lee), who left him for a richer prize, a youthful courtier.[1] Then he laid siege to Parthenophe, and the best answer he got of her was 'That she was all vow'd to virginitie,' yet above all men she would most affect him.[2] It is equally unlikely, on the one hand, that these poems 'enshrine a real love-story' or 'love-tragedy,'[3] and on the other, that Barnes was thinking of no woman whatever. Some of the sonnets clearly refer to his lady as a Percy, with 'noble grand-

1 Sonnet 5.   2 Sonnet 37.
3 Grosart, pp. vii, xiii, and Dowden, *Academy*, x (1876), 231, who gathers together the actual incidents mentioned in the verses.

fathers of might.'¹ It has recently been suggested² that she was Northumberland's sister Eleanor, who later married Sir William Herbert. But Eleanor was only eleven years old at the time, having been baptized in January 1582,³ and the fierceness of the poet's passion is hardly appropriate to a fair Geraldine. In any case, we are not to take Barnes too seriously when he writes, 'This passion is no fiction.'⁴ The troubadour must have a mistress, and he naturally looks for one to the family of his chief patrons. That it was not all feigning, however, would appear from a madrigal in *Coelia* the following year in which William Percy demurs to Parthenophil's triumphant final poem on his conquest of Parthenophe through the magic spells of his verses.⁵

Whether or not Barnes was at Oxford with Percy, in London they were so intimate that he could dedicate *Parthenophil* 'To M. William Percy Esquier, his deerest friend.' In this privileged position he had every reason to pay his principal homage to the house of Percy, especially since, between 1587 and 1602, except for two brief intervals, William Percy was heir presumptive to the earldom. Barnes was also seeking the favor of Northumberland himself, who just at this time was blossoming forth as a patron of science and poetry, and (beside rewarding Peele for *The Honour of the Garter*) was gathering round him such asso-

---

1 Sonnets 44, 46, 78.
2 Madeleine Hope Dodds, *Ten Poems from 'Parthenophil and Parthenophe'* (Priory Press, Tynemouth, 1929).
3 Collins' *Peerage*, ed., 1779, II, 408.
4 Madrigal 17; cf. Elegy 16.
5   'I litle rue thy well deserued teares. . . .
          What tell'st thou me by spells th' hast wonne thy deare?
          Beleeue her, friend, no more then *Laya* past,
          Charm'd loue endures but whilst the charme doth last.'
   Coelia is not dedicated to Barnes, as is sometimes stated (Greg, *English Literary Autographs*, pt. i, no. xxv; M. H. Dodds, *N. and Q.*, CLXI [1931], 57). There is a note on Barnes' poem at 11 *N. and Q.*, II, 245.

ciates of Ralegh and Marlowe as Hariot, Roydon, and Chapman.

In *Have with You to Saffron Walden* Nashe advises a friend to apply to Barnes 'if you haue euer a chaine for him to runne away with, as he did with a Noble-mans Stewards chayne at his Lords enstalling at *Windsore*.'[1] Here 'his Lords' is ambiguous, but from the context it would seem to refer to Barnabe's lord. The only Knights of the Garter with whom Barnes had connections at this time were Essex and Northumberland, but Essex had been chosen as long ago as 1588, while the most recent installation when Nashe wrote was that of Northumberland and others on June 25, 1593.[2] At that date, therefore, he appears to have been a follower of Northumberland, whom he placed first among the patrons of *Parthenophil* in May of the same year; but from all we know of his actions it was probably not long before he had to seek another lord.

Nashe's inimitable pencil draws 'my yong Master *Barnabe* the bright' braving it through London and the Court in 'a strange payre of *Babilonian* britches,' and writing letters and sonnets to Gabriel Harvey 'from a farre, as namely, out of the hall into the kitchin at *Wolfes*, where altogether at one time they lodged and boorded.'[3] It is, however, 'From my lodging in Holborne,' June 1593, that Barnes dates the letter in *Pierce's Supererogation*, with his three sonnets on Nashe, 'the Confuting Gentleman,' and Harvey, 'the Sweet Doctor,' mentioning 'Diuinest morall Spencer.' Harvey bids him, 'be thou, Barnabe, the gallant poet, like Spencer, or the valiant souldiour, like Baskeruile; and euer remember *thy French seruice* under the braue Earl of Essex.'[4] If he saw any further service, it was

1 Ed. McKerrow, III, 103.
2 W. A. Shaw, *The Knights of England*, I, 28.
3 Ed. McKerrow, III, 116, 109, 102.   4 Grosart's *Harvey*, III, 22, 15.

probably at Brill, the only place abroad he later admitted having visited except Paris. In 1594 he was traveling in France, and 'by prescribed taske' devoting some time each day to writing spiritual sonnets. So he says in his dedication of the *Divine Centurie* to Dr. Toby Matthew, Bishop of Durham, 'From London this 30 of August 1595.'

In his *Praise of Poetry* the same year Churchyard mentions, of living English poets, only Spenser, Daniel, and these two:

> One Barnes that Petrarks scholler is
> May march with them in ranke
> A learned Templers name I mis
> Whose pen deserues great thanke.

Corser, who printed 'I mis' as 'I wis,' explained the whole stanza as referring to Barnes; [1] but Barnes was not, as he supposed, of the Temple. Churchyard throughout the work is hammering out his verse by couplets, so that Barnes and the Templar are clearly distinct persons. The allusion is interesting as evidence that Barnes had a certain reputation at the time when Shakespeare was probably writing his sonnets.

1 *Zepheria*, Spenser Soc., 1869.

II. STAR CHAMBER

Youth full of error, whither dost thou hale me?
Parthenophil, Elegy 7

THE most dangerous adventure of Barnes' life happens, by great good luck, to be the one episode of which a full and intimate account is extant. Till now we have had only tantalizing hints of this turning-point in his career. The register of the Privy Council tells us that in the spring of 1598 Barnes fled into the North to escape arrest for an attempt to poison the Recorder of Berwick, John Browne. At length he was caught and brought before the Council; but in July he broke prison, and the Privy Council ordered search-warrants to hunt him down throughout the North. With this all news of him ceased. In calling attention to these notices, Joseph Knight observed, 'Future biographers may care to follow up the clue thus supplied.'[1] Dr. Harrison in *The Second Elizabethan Journal* has lately rephrased the same entries, but in the many years between no one has taken the trouble to follow up the clue. It has not been asked why Barnes should be mixed up at all with the Recorder of Berwick, nor whether any documents in the prosecution for poisoning remain. Dr. Sisson answered the second question when he discovered the complete file of the case among the records of Star Chamber,[2] and he found the key to the first in sources long since available in print, the *Border Papers*.

Two men tell the story of the poisoning, from diametrically opposite points of view. The first is the greatest of English lawyers, Edward Coke, Attorney General for the Queen. The other is Barnes himself. Prosecutor and

1 *Athenaeum*, 1904, II, 240.
2 Star Chamber 5, A 20/25, bill, June 16, 1598; A 20/26, answer, June 26; A 36/32, interrogatories and examination, July 3.

prisoner, one eager, the other reluctant, between them they give us the history of the John Browne poisoning case. After we have heard them both, we shall still have a problem to solve: not the customary one, Who committed the crime? but the more important question which must always follow, Why?

First, then, for the case against Barnes as Coke presents it in the bill. He begins with a preamble on the Queen's great care and study to keep out of the realm the lewd practice of poisonings and the like hateful devices to endanger men's lives in secret and cunning manner. It is interesting to compare this with his speech as Chief Justice in opening the trial of the Overbury murderers, when he declared that of all crimes murder was the most detestable, of all murders, poisoning. Poisoning was still very rare in England, and struck with peculiar horror the imagination of a people which preferred death to be open and bloody. The prosecution of Barnes therefore furnished a useful background of experience to Coke when in 1615 he discoursed learnedly of the four ways by which the Devil taught poisoners to kill as they list: *gustu, haustu, odore, contactu.*[1]

Coke proceeds to inform the Queen:

That one Barnabye Barnes havinge ben a traveller in forren *partes* and countryes beyonde the seas, hathe in his sayd travayles throughe the corrupc*i*on and wicked disposic*i*on of his owne mynde chieflie framed him self to learne and intertayne the vyces and abuses of other nations, emongest wch he is growen moste expert and coninge in the mynistringe of poysons, whereby he can either presentlie rydde and depryve men of theire naturall lyves, or els wth grievous tortures kepe theym languishinge for a longe tyme, and yeat w^thout all hope of recoverye of theire lyves. wch sayd Barnabye Barnes beinge latelie retorned agayne into this Realme of Englande, and havinge conceaved causeles displeasure against one John Browne . . . (one that in his

---

1 Howell, *State Trials* (1816), II, 911.

place hathe don good services to yor highnes), partlie for that the sd
Browne metinge sometyme in companye wth the said Barnes (and
Barnes beinge emongest other vyces given to excessive drynkinge)
wold not pledge the said Barnes in carrowses, and unreasonable maner
of drynkinge, for wch the said Barnes hathe threatned to doe some
revenge vpon the saide Browne, As allso vpon his owne mere malyce
corrupt and wicked disposicion, Or throughe the procurement and
instigacion of some of the sayde Brownes enymies, dyd determyne to
practise his saide detestable skyll and feate of poysoninge vpon the
said Browne, and thereby to haue taken awaye his life.

To effect his purpose, continues the bill, Barnes came to
London and with many protestations of affection insinu-
ated himself into the company of Browne. Then, on
March 21, 1597–8, he gave Browne

as a token of his great kyndnes and love . . . a limonde [1] wch he had
taynted and venomed wth some subtyll poyson, wch should kyll either
by the eatinge thereof or smellinge therevnto, wch the said Browne
(litle suspectinge anye sutche villanye daunger or abuse) dyd p^rsentlie
in the viewe of the said Barnes deliuer over as a kyndnes to A frend
of his and thereby saved his owne life.

Browne's friend, through smelling it but once or twice, had
ever since been tormented with exceeding great and strange
pains in his head, and would doubtless have died had he
not used remedies in time.

Seeing that his first plot against Browne had failed,
Barnes resolved to use other means to make a speedy end
of him. The same day, accordingly, he bought 'A certayne
quantatye of marcurye sublimate wch he knewe to be verye
like to suger and yeat a stronge and forcyble poyson.' [2]
He then pressed again into Browne's company and im-
portunately desired that they might sup together, or at
least drink together, pretending that he needed Browne's
advice in matters of great importance. Having drawn him

---

1 Lemons were used to sweeten the air against plague infection.
2 Mercury sublimate was the poison which, after Overbury had survived
rosalgar and arsenic, was served in his tarts and jellies and finally put an end
to him.

into a Westminster tavern, Barnes called for claret and
sugar, filled a cup for Browne, and cunningly mixed with
the sugar he put in it a great quantity of the mercury.
Browne, having for a long time forborne to drink any wine,
said that 'if the said Barnes wold begyn to him he had
rather pledge him in a cuppe of beare,' and called for one;
but Barnes called for another cup and filled it with wine,
'sayenge that he was a frenchman & loved to drynck
w^thout suger.' At last by many importunate words and
friendly enticements, drinking to Browne and to 'one of
his especyall and honorable frend*es*,' he allured Browne to
drink a great draught of the poisoned wine. No sooner had
he taken it than Browne 'fownde a great inflamac*i*on tor-
ture and distemp*e*rature in his bodye' and affirmed that
he greatly disliked the taste and doubted that some offensive thing was put into it. Barnes, to win time for the
operation of the poison, still persuaded him that there
could be no evil in the wine, but on being entreated to
judge for himself, utterly refused. Browne, now beginning
to suspect him, called for the people of the house to taste
it, which two servants did, George Allen and Richard
Maffen, whereupon they grew exceedingly distempered,
and George became 'p^rsentlie inraged and allmoste madd.'
He would have died, and Browne also, 'beinge longe tyme
after mortallye sick,' had they not sought remedies in time
to expel the poison and so saved their lives with much difficulty and danger.

   Browne informed the company in the tavern how Barnes
had enticed him thither and put something hurtful in his
drink yet refused to taste it himself, all which, the bill
avers, 'Barnes att that tyme was not able to deny but
acknowledged and confessed to be true.' Finding his torments grievously to increase, Browne called for a constable
to attach Barnes, and requested to have the dregs in his

cup examined and safely kept, '(wch is yeat reserved and readye to be sene).' He directly charged Barnes with being the actor of whatever evil might befall from what he had drunk, and threatened that Barnes too should taste of the cup. Barnabe was now in a quandary, but seeing no other way, 'In thend throughe extreme feare . . . aft^r soundrye refusalls to drynck, he desyered the sd Browne to geve him his hand perswadinge the said Browne to thinck no ill of him, for he should see that he . . . had geven him nothinge butt what he wolde take him self.' He therefore tasted the wine and seemed to drink it up, but 'reserved the most parte . . . in his cheekes, and torninge his back to the said Browne dyd p^rvelye spytt owte the same wyne againe.' Then, while Browne was gone to fetch a constable and the others were busy viewing the mercury in the cup and wondering what it could be, Barnes seized the opportunity and escaped from the house to secret places, where he first saved himself by taking antidotes and then 'hydd and obscured him self for manye dayes togeather.'

In his answer Barnes has nothing to say for himself except to affirm that of all the misdemeanors charged in the bill he is 'Clerely not guilty in such Manner and fforme as in the saide Informacion ys verye vntrewly surmised and alleaged.' This sort of conventional blanket denial, especially the saving phrase 'in such manner and form,' was commonly used when no better defence was possible. The answer is signed by Wrightington: George Wrightington, one of the four Attorneys of Star Chamber, and brother-in-law of Lucrece Bryskett.

What Barnes did have to say is found in his examination, as 'Barnabye Barnes gent nowe prisoner in the Marshallsey in Sowthwarke aged xxvij. . . .' The clerk had written the first two letters of 'gent' when Barnabe insisted that he was properly an esquire. The designation was so written, but was crossed out in favor of the original word when the examiner decided that he was only a gentleman.

The first point Coke tries to establish is that the accused has traveled in Italy and France and other foreign countries. Barnabe will admit only, 'That he hath byn at Parrys in ffrance & at Brill in the lowe Contryes And further travelled not into any of the *par*tes beyonde the Seas.' He has known mercury sublimate for four years, and after an attempt to profess ignorance, cautiously admits that he now hears that it is a poison.

The prosecution next aims to discover whether the motive can have been personal revenge. Barnes testifies that his first acquaintance with Browne was last December, when together with Dr. Marbecke and Capt. Jackson they supped in Friday Street — at what sign he says he does not remember, but Coke specifies the White Horse. There he drank a 'carrowse, to wete a whole cupp of wyne' to Browne, whom he desired to pledge him in return. According to the questions of Coke (who has his information from Browne throughout) Browne refused, whereupon Barnes uttered speeches of anger, saying it was a base part in Browne not to pledge him, and that he would be even with him for it, or would not take it at his hands; and rising to his feet threatened him and behaved as though he would have thrown something at him or struck at him. Barnes denies this and says that Browne pledged him without refusal; but he well remembers that

Capteyne Jackson the morning following dyd reprove this def for pressing the sd browne at supper the night before to dryncke Sacke wch the sd Browne loved not, & to presse doct^r marbecke to dryncke Toebacco against his liking. And this def answered that he was sorry if such his demeano^r had byn offensive vnto them & prayed the sd Capteyne to make an attonem^t betwixt them & this def.

SMOKERS CAROUSING

The names of the persons next introduced give us our
first hint of the violent Border feud which actually under-
lies this apparently isolated crime. In March Barnes
traveled up from the North in the company of Sir Robert
Carey and Henry Woodrington, Esq. He does not remember asking Woodrington on the journey to pledge him a
carouse, but acknowledges that he took sugar in his sack
'much against his will to pledg one Geo: Wood being
therunto pressed' by Carey. When Wood drank a carouse
to him, he said that he 'would haue his Cupp washed after
the sd Georg had druncke thereof for that the sd Geo had
byn a traveller in Italy & might peradventure putt poyson
into his Cupp.'

As soon as he had alighted at the Swan Inn in the
Strand, he repaired to Woodrington's lodging near the
Savoy, and there met Browne, 'vnthought of & vnlooked
for.' He denies that he delivered Browne kind commendations from the Bishop of Durham or told him that he had
special business wherein to take his advice. Browne and
his friends offered to procure him a lodging at the same
house, which he accepted with thanks, but on the sudden
departed without saying whither, and went to the Swan
to accompany Mr. Saunderson, his countryman, who provided him a lodging there.

On the day of the poisoning, about five of the clock in
the afternoon, the two men met betwixt Charing Cross and
Whitehall near the lodging of William Waad, Clerk of the
Privy Council. To Browne's question whither he was going so speedily, Barnes replied that he was going to the
Court at Whitehall to be a suitor to the Lord Treasurer for
letters to travel beyond the seas, and showed his petition
directed to Burghley. He promised to sup at Browne's
lodging that night if his business would permit, and at his
departure toward Westminster he gave Browne a lemon

'at the request of the same Browne & not otherwise.' By the oath he has taken, it was not 'taynted infected or impoysoned,' nor did he, as the interrogatory supposes, see Browne deliver it over to the said Mr. Waad.

After despatching his business with the Lord Treasurer in Whitehall, he went to a grocer's shop in Westminster, where he bought two pennyworth of figs and one groatsworth of mercury sublimate, bruised small. He denies that he asked to have it white, small, and clean, and asserts that he bought it to apply to a sore leg that had been bruised with riding post. As he went out of the shop he remarked that it was good for a galled horseback, 'bycause he would not haue the Grocer to thincke that yt was for this def^{tes} sore legg.' The grocer would know well enough what it was commonly used for.

After going 'to a howse in Tuttlestreete in westm^r to dryncke & repose himself,' he then returned toward the Strand. On his way, 'betwixt the Co^{rt} gate then at whitehall & the post*es* or rayles next to Charinge Crosse,' he sent his man, Bonaventure Darbishire,[1] to tell Browne that he was waiting to have his company to supper. Browne, who was walking with Sir William Bowes towards the gate of St. James Park, sent word that he 'was then a lyttle busyed but would come presently.' For a whole hour (two, according to Coke) Barnes and his man waited, 'looking on Bowlers w^thin the sd p*ar*ke,' till 'thevening was closed vp & supper tyme past.' Seeing Browne leave the park and go with Bowes into Whitehall, he sent Darbishire to fetch him over to the Court gate, where he told Browne that he had some things wherewith to acquaint him. Browne said it was too late to sup at his lodging and

---

1 Evidently an old family servant, the Adam to Barnabe's Orlando. His son Henry was christened in 1579 at St. Mary-le-Bow, Durham, Barnes' parish (*Dur. and Northumb. Par. Reg. Soc.*, xxvii, 2).

that he was to sup with Woodrington at the Bull's Head in the Strand, but that Barnes should be welcome to him some other time. The pertinacious Barnes then suggested that they might sup at Whitehall with his friend Mr. Browne, Clerk Comptroller, and being answered that it was too late, proposed some tavern or cook-house in Westminster. Browne was unwilling, saying he did not wish to be so late abroad, but at length was persuaded to stay but a little while and drink a quart of wine so that Barnes could talk with him. Barnes meant, he says, to inform Browne what he had done in his business with the Lord Treasurer.

He brought Browne first to the Rose Tavern in Westminster,[1] but his companion 'dyd dislike wth that howse for that yt was an obscure corner.' At the Queen's Arms in Westminster they went upstairs to a private room, where the drawer brought a quart of claret, two silver cups, and a groatsworth of sugar in a brown paper, some of it bruised small like powder and some in little round pieces. Barnes testifies that he has already confessed before Coke that he could not charge the vintner or his house with any fault in the sugar or with bringing mercury instead. The mercury he had bought was then in his pocket, but he denies putting any of it amongst the sugar or into the cup, holding the paper of sugar under the table about his lap, or tearing the mercury wrapping and casting it under the table; nor did he request Browne to drink to him or to the Bishop of Durham in the sugared cup, or say that he was a Frenchman and would drink without sugar. He did temper the wine with sugar in the cup he did not intend to drink of, and began the drinking out of the unsugared cup.

As soon as Browne drank, he affirmed he was poisoned. Barnes answered, 'god forbydd, how can yt be so for the

---

1 In St. Peter's Street, according to *Taylors Travels*, 1636.

wyne wch I drancke in the other Cupp was good.' Browne
then charged him before Henry Berry [1] the vintner,
Mr. Fynche, and others, with poisoning the cup, but he
denies confessing it. At last, being urged by Mr. Fynche,
Barnes tasted of fresh wine put into the cup, 'wherewith
he dyd nott mislike save only yt tasted somewhat of Sugar
wch is a tast that this def for his owne parte canott well
away with.' But he did not drink the grounds in the cup,
and on Browne's insisting that he should, Fynche stirred
them up with a knife and Barnes drank again, turning his
back to spit some of it out 'for that in deed he cannott
away wth any sugar in his dry,nckes for that he dyd heretofore surfett of wyne & Sugar.' The cup with the sugar
seemed to be 'more paler' than the other, and he thought
he saw something among the sugar whiter than sugar and
like mercury, but the vintner was of a contrary opinion,
and Barnes says he now thinks it was only sugar that was
in the cup, because it did not make him sick at all. He
confesses that he took 'sallet Oyle' in the tavern presently
after drinking and that on the way to his lodging he
stopped at a tavern near Durham House and called for
more salad oil and a feather, purely as a precaution, he
says, for he thought then that there had been poison in the
cup, the rather for that there was something hot in his
mouth, and because Browne had made such a great ado
about it. He denies telling Coke and Waad, 'That if he
this def drancke Sallet oyle in any place except in the sd
Taverne at westm^r that then this def was guilty of all to
weet of the poysoning. . . ' In a writing given them con-

<hr>

1 It is curious that in this very year the Guildhall presentments for defective
wine record Henry Berry as vintner of the Three Tonnes in Fleet Street
(Kenneth Rogers, *The Mermaid and Mitre Taverns in Old London*, p. 22), to
which he may have removed from the Queen's Arms. The Three Tuns,
though few writers on Herrick give it its true name, was the 'Triple Tun'
whose clusters made poets nobly wild, and where Jonson's verse 'out-did the
frolick wine' (*Hesperides*, no. 912).

taining the truth of all he knew of these matters, he has
confessed that he 'vsed mercurye viij dayes eare he came
out of the Contrye,' and that he 'had at dyvers tymes for
his owne necessary vse carryed mercury about him till the
nowe L. Bishop of durham' reproved him or advised him
to the contrary, which was at his last being in the country,
since the Queen's Arms affair. But he denies that he gave
Browne mercury, or did any such vile fact.

His one idea now was to vanish, no doubt the end he had
in view in applying to Burghley for license to travel.
Woodrington came after him very speedily to the Swan
and desired the chamberlain of the house to take him in
charge, but Barnes prayed that no such course might be
taken with him and promised on his credit to be forthcom-
ing the next morning in his chamber, or else to be held
guilty. His reason for leaving is worthy of a stage clown:
'the next morning being Wensday for that the sd m^r wyth-
erington came nott this def about eight of the clocke dyd
dep*art* from the sd howse thincking if he should haue
stayed he should haue byn p^{r}iudyced one waye or other'
by means of Browne or Woodrington. He feared, too, that
if he were once in custody, one Felton, Principal of Furnival's Inn, would lay an execution on him for a debt of
three hundred pounds.[1]

Late that night Barnes supped in the house of Thomas
Horden, ironmonger,[2] willing the servants to conceal his

1 Anthony Felton of Great Felton, Northumberland, who had been M.P. for
Morpeth in 1586 and steward to Lord William Howard and to the Earl
of Northumberland (Elijah Williams, *Early Holborn*, 1, no. 496; De Fon-
blanque, *Annals of the House of Percy*, 11, 593; *S.P.D. Eliz. Add.* 30/26, 43,
107; *Border Papers, passim*).
2 In 1596 a servant of Lord Henry Seymour, Thomas Shaw, sued Thomas Horden of St. Clement Danes (as occupant of a house there) and two others,
'beinge men well acquainted wth the dealinges' of Admiral Seymour and the
only living witnesses to a lease by him to his nephew Lord Henry. Horden
demurred that the Admiral was 'beheaded to dead many yeares before this
Defend^t was borne'; that he was only one of thousands of undertenants to the

being there. According to Coke, he bade some of them hold back their candles lest he were seen going out, willed them to say that he was gone to Dover, and the servants at the Swan to say that he was gone to Gravesend. Barnes says that he does not remember doing so, nor being charged by Woodrington with an intent to poison him as well as Browne. That night and the next he lodged at the Star, an alehouse in Holborn, directing Darbishire and the people of the house to tell nobody of his being there.

The Attorney General, in conclusion, tries to find out whether Barnes was hired to do the job for someone else. He therefore asks, as an afterthought to the last question, from whom Barnes has received money since being committed to prison. Barnes gives a list: forty shillings of Thomas Jackson, an officer in the Marshalsea, for a mare sold to him, and twenty more as a loan; forty lent by Mr. Tailboys, his brother-in-law's uncle; forty which he had of Mr. Cowper, a counsellor in the Temple dwelling in the Bishopric of Durham; and forty pence of Mr. Gaylor, a clothworker dwelling at the Golden Key in Cannon St., part of forty pounds rent payable to him yearly within the city of London.[1] Barnes is then asked: Have you been dealt with by anyone to do some mischief to Browne, either by violence, policy, slander, accusation, poisoning,

forfeited estates; and that plaintiff ought to sue the Queen, Marquis of Winchester, Earl of Pembroke, Countess of Arundel, and other persons of account (C 2 Eliz. S 16/46).

1 Christopher Gayler of St. Mary Abchurch, clothworker, was married in 1585 and buried at St. Michael, Crooked Lane, in 1627–28 (*Harl. Soc.*, xxv, 140, and parish registers). Robert Tailbois was a London goldsmith, who had two sons at Merchant Taylors' School (*Register*, ed. C. J. Robinson, I, 4). Mr. Robert Cooper of the Inner Temple, Attorney General for Durham and later Seneschal for life and Master in Chancery, lived in Barnes' parish of St. Mary-le-Bow, Durham (Surtees, *Durham*, iv, ii, 150; Hutchinson, *Durham*, I, 478, 482, 490). His daughter Muriel married Cuthbert Sisson, gent., of the same parish, who appears to have been the founder of the Durham family from which Dr. Sisson is descended.

or any other means, and were you promised any reward or favor for so doing? Had you any conference with persons you have said to be or who are noted to be unfriends to Browne, in the country or in London? Were you at any of their houses late before or since the poisoning? Did you receive either gold or promises from them? and what speeches of dislike, grief, revenge, or discontentment did you hear any such persons utter against Browne? To all these questions he returns a plain negative, as he does to the final question whether Browne had not offered, or it was suspected would offer, wrong or injury to him or to some of his friends.

This completes the Star Chamber record, but we have also the entries in the register of the Council. Three weeks after the poisoning, on April 12, the lords wrote to the Bishop of Durham, 'Whereas there hath bin a very lewde facte lately comitted by one Barnaby Barnes, sonn to your Lordship's predicessor . . . in attemptinge to poyson John Browne, the Recordor of Barwick,' that Barnes had fled, it was thought to the North. He was to be arrested and sent up for examination, escorted at his own expense by some trusty person.[1] Bishop Toby, who was famous for his unquenchable sense of humor, cannot have missed the irony of having to arrest for 'fowle and odious' crime a Bishop's son who had lately dedicated to him *A Divine Century of Spiritual Sonnets*. He must have felt that the Bishops of Durham were unfortunate in their families, for in the very city of York where his immediate predecessor, Bishop Hutton, was now Archbishop, this same year of 1598 saw the hanging of Luke Hutton, the most famous highwayman of the age. This former Cambridge student, to whom were attributed such works as *The Black Dog of*

1 *A.P.C.*, xxviii, 393.

Newgate and *Luke Hutton's Repentance*,[1] was a nephew of the Archbishop and of Dr. Robert Hutton of Durham, whose wife Grace was daughter to the Dr. Leonard Pilkington who married Bishop Barnes' French widow. Bishop Matthew just at this time was violently disowning his own son, the friend of Donne; his pungent summing up of his three sons was that one had grace without wit, another (Sir Toby) wit without grace, while the third had neither wit nor grace.

The fugitive poet was caught and sent down from the North, and made his appearance before the Lords on Sunday, May 14. Next Sunday the Council wrote to Coke, Bacon, and Waad to examine Browne's complaint against him 'as well by the testimony of witnesses as by all other good meanes,' and if they found by proof or by pregnant presumptions that he was in any way culpable, to take the advice of the Chief Justice what course would be fit to punish so foul an offence.[2] They accordingly examined him and had him sign a written statement. This document was inconveniently quoted to him during his later examination on oath, and he had to retract one statement with the excuse that he had changed his opinion, and deny that he ever made another, which he had just contradicted. As to the punishment for poisoning, Coke at the Overbury trial reminded the jurors that by 22 Henry VIII poisoning was declared treason and it was enacted 'that wilful poisoners should be boiled to death.' He did not add, apparently, that this statute was repealed by 1 Edward VI.[3] At Middlesex Sessions or in Queen's Bench Barnes would presumably have pled his clergy and got off with at most a branding. He was therefore prosecuted in Star Chamber, the only

---

1 Cf. A. V. Judges, *The Elizabethan Underworld* (London, 1930), 506.
2 *A.P.C.*, xxviii, 441, 456.
3 Sir J. F. Stephen, *History of the Criminal Law of England*, 1, 476; W. F. Finlason, *Reeves' History of the English Law*, iii, 325–326.

court which could make certain that any crime, not capital, was punished as the offender deserved.

Star Chamber met on July 6 for the last time before the Long Vacation, and the Lord Keeper delivered the customary exhortation from the Queen to her justices now about to travel through the realm.[1] Barnes decided to follow their excellent example, and by his flight made quite clear what judgement he expected. On July 11 the Council wrote to the Archbishop of York, Bishop of Durham, and the rest of the Council in the North, that Barnes 'by all meanes seekeinge to fly from due tryall and escape the censure of the said Courte ys broken out of prison and fledd into the Northerne Parts (as yt is thought),' where he is to be pursued by search warrants.[2]

He probably knew that escape was the only thing that would save him, for the outlook before him in Star Chamber was not a hopeful one. Burghley, his father's patron, was ill and would never sit at a Star Chamber trial again; and Essex, who attended Council meetings regularly until the last day of June, just at this time had his ears boxed by Elizabeth and withdrew from Court. Nor can one envy the prisoner who was pitted against the combined wits of Coke, Bacon, and Waad. Waad was the most zealous of officials in tracking down fugitives and forcing unwilling confessions, and he would not be likely to let his talents sleep with Barnes, from whom came the lemon which had made him suffer exceeding great and strange torments in his head. Bacon was exerting himself to pass Coke in the race for office and for Lady Hatton. The ferocity Coke could show at a trial is well known, but we must not suppose that every prisoner called forth his thunder and lightning. Father Garnet after his examina-

1 John Hawarde, *Les Reportes del Cases in Camera Stellata*, p. 101.
2 *A.P.C.*, xxviii, 568, 576.

tion wrote to a friend that he had been treated with great courtesy by Coke.[1] Whatever Barnabe's experience, he was diplomatic enough in his next book to go out of his way twice to compliment 'that right worthy Lawyer of our time, Sir *Edw. Coke*, the Kings Atturney generall,' and the very learned Epistle to his *Reports*.[2]

That Barnes did his best to poison John Browne there can hardly be any reasonable doubt. If we had the bill only, we should reserve judgement, remembering that it takes two sides to tell a story; but we have the answer, in which Barnes makes no attempt at defence, and the examination, in which he acknowledges most of the facts without suggesting an alternative explanation. His story is consistent neither with itself nor with the confession formerly extracted. The truth is that a satisfactory defence was impossible after a crime so carelessly planned and carried out. In Elizabethan drama the villain had commonly a diabolical ingenuity which kept him from being suspected, or at least from being run to earth, until the fifth act. In real life this would-be Machiavellian succeeded in administering the poison only by a pertinacity that would mark him out at once for suspicion, which he did everything to attract and apparently nothing to deflect, and so left himself nothing to trust to but a fair pair of heels.

His admission of the principal facts and his unconvincing denials of the rest warrant the conclusion that Coke's narrative in the bill and interrogatories gives a very fair account of what actually happened. It could scarcely be more circumstantial in relating the events on the day of the poisoning. What it does not succeed in establishing is the motive. Coke suggests in the bill that it was partly

1 David Jardine, *A Narrative of the Gunpowder Plot*, p. 327.
2 *Offices*, pp. 137, 160.

revenge for Browne's refusal to pledge a carouse four
months earlier, or else that Barnes acted by the instigation
of some of Browne's enemies. Barnes is careful to deny
having any reason to wish ill to Browne. From the testimony alone, therefore, one could not tell whether he himself owed Browne a grudge or whether he was acting as
agent for someone who did. Fortunately, though no one
since the affair came again to light has inquired why
Barnes should choose the Recorder of Berwick out of all
the men in London whom he might have poisoned, this is
just the question that can be answered from other sources.
There is abundant material to construct a chain of evidence indicating that Barnes was only the tool of Browne's
most powerful and inveterate enemy, who had threatened
to take his life and had already attempted it. Posterity
will now enter its case against a criminal too great to be
brought to justice in his own time, and against whom, in
the written record, even Coke did not breathe a word:
Rafe, Lord Eure,[1] late Warden of the Middle Marches
against Scotland.

1 The richly varied spellings for this name show clearly that it had two pro-
nunciations, 'Ewrie' and 'Ever(s),' as in 'Lord Evers Players.' 'Eure' is the
baron's signature, but it should be remembered that, whether 'Ewrie' or
'Ever,' this was pronounced in two syllables. The ballad of *Lord Ewrie* in
Minstrelsy of the Scottish Border, though accepted as a genuine popular ballad
by Scott (and by the reviser of G. E. C.'s *Complete Peerage* in 1926), was written by Robert Surtees.

III. BORDER FEUDS

Out upon thee, Withrington!
And fie upon thee, Fenwick!
Thou hast put down the doughty one
That stole the sheep from Alnwick.[1]

THE Withrington of this ballad, head of the family which
we all remember from *Chevy Chase*, was no other than the
Henry Woodrington whom Barnes hoped to poison while
riding down from the North in the company of Sir Robert
Carey. Carey, who held Widdrington Castle as the jointure of his Cornish wife, the former Lady Widdrington, had
just appointed as Deputy Wardens of the Middle March
young Harry and his 'dear friend and near ally,' William
Fenwick of Wallington. The events of the ballad can
therefore be securely dated as during their term of office,
from 1598 to 1603. His appearance may be imagined from
Clarendon's description of his son, Lord 'Withrington,'
as 'one of the most goodly persons of that age, being near
the head higher than most tall men.'[2] It is easy to understand that Barnes would not look forward to his interview
at the Swan the morning after the poisoning. Woodrington, a 'squyre of notable desert,' was 'the only man of
action in all the shire, and therefore most followed . . . for
he carries the country absolutely as he will.'[3] This was
in 1617, but even as a young man in 1592 he had waged
open warfare [4] against Rafe Gray of Chillingham, whose
strength was the greatest of the shire and who had lately
led seven hundred men to defend a title against the Earl of

1 Child, *English and Scottish Popular Ballads*, IV, 140; C. H. Firth, *Trans.
Royal Hist. Soc.*, 3d ser., III (1909), 51. The ballad has the phonetic spelling
'Anix,' rhyming with the surname which it gives as 'Phœnix'!
2 *History of the Rebellion*, Book XIII, 69.
3 *Surtees Soc.*, LXVIII, 435.
4 Star Ch. 5, G 4/27, 9/5, 22/21, 30/1; *S.P.D. Eliz. Add.* 32/53.

Northumberland.[1] When Bothwell invaded Scotland in 1594 his chief ally was to have been Woodrington, who rode to the rendezvous at the head of a hundred well-horsed gentlemen, and but for Forster's forbidding him at the last moment would have joined Bothwell in chasing the King's troops 'even to Edenbroughe gates.' [2] In 1596, when Elizabeth raised a storm of protest at the famous rescue of Kinmont Willie, James pointed out that Buccleuch was not the only raider, and demanded redress for the 'Rode of Cavers in Tyvidale,' a town belonging to the Douglas, by Mr. Henry Woodrington.[3]

Lord Eure, whom the English Ambassador instructed to obtain this redress from Woodrington, had just been appointed Warden. As he reminded Burghley,[4] his father, grandfather, and great-grandfather had been Lord Wardens of the Middle March before him, and he himself was born in Berwick Castle. All this did not prevent him from making a fiasco of the wardenship. Under him the Middle Marches had their last fling, for his successor Carey's firm rule gave them five years of comparative quiet, until in 1603 the stormy history of the Borders suddenly ceased.

Unquestionably the Middle March was the most difficult of the three wardenries to govern, taking in as it did the wild and mountainous part of the Border from the Cheviot to Liddesdale, and indeed all Northumberland south and west of Flodden and Alnwick.[5] The warden had no strong garrison town like Berwick or Carlisle to command his frontier, but lay at places further inland,

1 Collins, *Peerage*, II, 420.
2 *Border Papers*, ed. Joseph Bain (Edinburgh, 1896), I, no. 940.
3 Rymer, *Foedera*, XVI, 309.
4 *Border Papers*, II, no. 131. References to *B.P.* will hereafter be understood to be to the second volume, and not to the pages but to the numbers, by which one may also refer to the originals, which I have used, at the Record Office.
5 Cf. D. L. W. Tough, *The Last Years of a Frontier* (Oxford, 1928); Howard Pease, *The Lord Wardens of the Marches* (London, 1913).

such as Hexham. His March bore the brunt of innumer-
able raids from Liddesdale and Teviotdale, often set on or
led by the bold Buccleuch or his brother-in-law Ker of
Cesford, the two 'fyrebrands' of the March.[1]

From his quiet Yorkshire estate Eure precipitated himself into the whirlpool by a letter to Burghley. He had
been at Durham Assizes on the bench with Bishop Matthew and Beaumont's father, and he describes how the
Scots or 'Scottishe imitating' outlaws penetrated even to
Durham, where the Queen's subjects were 'lefte as a pray
to the wylde boore' and the country people 'amaysed, and
moste doe forbeare to be actors in so honarable a trage-
dye.'[2] Burghley promptly cast him for the chief part,
sending him on September 1, 1595, the Queen's orders to
be on the March as Warden by Michaelmas.[3] The Border
had never lain so open as in the last years under Sir John
Forster, who had been Warden since 1560 and was now
within seven years of the one hundred and two he lived to
reach.[4] Woodrington and others in an hour's time reckoned up one hundred and fifty-five masters of families
slain in their own houses in defence of their goods since
1568; in all, there had been about a thousand murders, and
spoils in ten years amounting to a hundred thousand
pounds.[5] The chief spoilers of the English were not the
Scots, but the Englishmen who made alliances with them
against their own neighbors for the sake of plunder or revenge.[6]

Eure reported that to break up the alliances with Scots
clans he would need a hundred horsemen, levied in Yorkshire and Durham, and that he must remove the keepers

1 B.P., 786.   2 B.P., 103.   3 B.P., 119.
4 B.P., 129; Raine, North Durham, p. 306.
5 Hatfield MSS., v, 477; Raine, p. xlvii.
6 B.P., 672, 830.

of Redesdale and Tynedale, the bailiff and constable of
Hexham, and all other officers infected with toleration of
thieves, and put in Yorkshire or inland gentlemen who
need not fear the outlaws.[1] The theory was excellent,
but it did not commend itself to the officers he superseded.
He found that no one in Northumberland dared sell him
grain. Forster had to be commanded by the Queen to give
up his house at Hexham, and even then refused to let Eure
have hay or straw for any money.[2] Eure wrote that the
weather at Hexham was 'extreame tempestious,' and this
is the best description of his two years in office. Every
gentleman of worth in Northumberland, he found, was
near of kin or allied to Forster.[3] Fenwick, for example,
had married his daughter, and Woodrington was a grandson of his sister.[4] Eure declared that Fenwick, who soon
resigned the keepership of Tynedale, had been in league
with the Scots, and that he and Woodrington had made a
compact with the Bournes and with the Armstrongs,
'Bangtailes freindes.'[5] At first the Warden made some
effort to conciliate Woodrington, but the fiery young
squire refused to abandon his private quarrel with Cesford,
and Eure's letters soon began to denounce the disobedience of the race of Woodringtons, and their open bra-
vadoes.[6] He recommended for sheriff his kinsmen Rafe
or Edward Gray rather than the 'yonge fry' such as the
Woodringtons.[7] The upshot was that after a year Woodrington with some of his friends openly refused to live on
the March and resorted to Carey, and that a jury of the
chief gentlemen of the Middle March presented charges
of maladministration against Eure and his officers, demanding their removal.[8] Fenwick's signature is the first

1 *B.P.*, 131.
2 *Hatfield MSS.*, v, 494; *B.P.*, 138, 187.
3 *B.P.*, 209.   4 Raine, p. 306.   5 *B.P.*, 267, 164.
6 *B.P.*, 227, 292, 452.   7 *B.P.*, 422.   8 *B.P.*, 670, 756, 764.

of the twenty-four, and among the others is that of John Browne.

Here, then, we have the John Browne whose body, if Barnes had had his way, would so soon have lain mouldering in the grave. His name is not one which delights the investigator, but fortunately his identity is made clear by his friendship with Woodrington and his office as Recorder of Berwick. We have his own declaration of the causes that 'inforced John Browne gent to wthdrawe himself out of the Myddle Marches vnder the gouernment of the Lo: Eurye.' First, on taking office Eure without any cause replaced Browne as Clerk of the Peace for Northumberland by an incompetent servant of his own; and he vehemently labored until he had also displaced him from 'thoffice of learned Steward' of Hexham, putting in a man who never studied the law.[1] As bailiff or steward, a place of power not disdained by Woodrington's grandfather, Sir Reynold Carnaby, Browne had controlled the large regality of Hexhamshire (only in 1572 made a part of Northumberland)[2] until, as we have seen, Eure asked the Queen to remove him. The only John Brownes recorded at the right time at an Inn of Court were students admitted to Gray's Inn in 1571 and 1587, and our Browne is probably the later one, since Woodrington entered the Inn in 1590.

To repair the great spoils done on his father, Browne continues, by Cesford's followers, the Bournes, he surprised and took a principal man among them, old Jock of the Cote, whom he freed before Forster on bond to reënter when called. To force Browne to disclaim the bond, the Goodman of Elisheugh, chief of the Bournes, ran a day foray within half a mile of Alnwick and took twenty-two horses from men under the charge of Thomas Percy as

1 *B.P.*, 860.   2 J. C. Hodgson, *Hist. of Northumberland*, III, 56, 65.

Constable and of Browne as Steward of Alnwick. In the pursuit Browne encountered and slew the Goodman.[1] For this he incurred the deadly feud of Cesford, the Bournes, and Younges. When he entreated protection and justice, Eure refused, though 'confessinge that he had gotten Cesfords surance for his Cozen Tho: Percy; but as for the said Browne he could doe him noe good . . . as for the matter of bloud betwene them, yt would not end wythout bloude. . . .' Petitions to Eure through Percy and through Roger Conyers were equally in vain. Ker's servants and thirty-six followers came to Alnwick to have murdered Browne at his house, brought thither by a follower of Percy's, as was declared to Percy and himself. 'This Armed Company myraculouslie myssinge their purpose to murder the said Browne, spoiled his brother of goods to the value of C. markes, and in the pursuyte, wounded m^r Claveringe for dead.' Eure gave him no redress, and refused justice to his servant in a suit with Eure's kinsman Arthur Gray. Significantly he hints at the danger some of his friends and especially he himself have to fear from Eure: when Cesford, '(that border bloud sucker and State Enymie) . . . and his traine of theves faile in their purposes & pursutes for o^r bloud; that English moyners mynte at the same marke, and meane not to mysse yt.'

Woodrington in a like statement[2] tells how Ker surprised Meikle Swinburne Castle, rescued James Younge of the Cove, and forced his brother Roger Woodrington to enter bond as prisoner, while Rafe, the youngest brother, 'to saue his lyef lykewise, lept out of his chamber windowe beinge 3. stories highe, vpon a pavement where he was almost bruzed to death & hardlie escaped.' Ker rode home by daylight through Redesdale, being in league with its

[1] He had done above forty murders and two hundred robberies on the English (*B.P.*, 887).   [2] *B.P.*, 861.

keeper, Ralph Mansfield, whom Eure supports because he is his kinsman and officer, although (as Browne puts it [1]) Mansfield daily haunts the 'arche bloodye enymie' Cesford, whose 'alluring, wakeryfe, highe and malycious spirit' the whole Border feels. Eure has offered to draw his dagger on Roger Woodrington, sent servants to murder him in his Hexham lodgings and again at Hexham Fair, and has had him proclaimed in every parish church and market town as a March traitor. Fenwick was quarreled with at Eure's house and pursued into the town, where one of his men was murdered and himself struck to the ground. The chief assailant openly boasts of Eure's protection.

Eure in his turn declares that Woodrington from his infancy has been a rebel to all authority, even to his uncle and to Forster, and that except the Queen vouchsafe his ambitious humor 'an highe place of honor and an imperiall gouerm^t he cannot liue Contented.' [2] For himself, his conscience is clear; he has done as good service as he could, being a stranger and succeeding a man grieved to be displaced, of great possessions, and allied to the Woodringtons and others, who in revenge have opposed him. He has always been very careful for the safety of Browne, sending him soldiers from Harbottle. Whereas many of Forster's officers were notorious thieves, now 'Justice hath bene executed both vpon Scottes and englishe, even vpon men of speciall place nor hath the brother of Henrie Woodrington bene spared *hinc illae lachrimae.*' Beside himself, his conduct in office has one other vigorous champion, the freelance Richard Fenwick, who declares that Eure 'hath vsed all his godly wittes since he came' to reform the robbers and has brought to trial the gentlemen thieves Forster winked at, but that Woodrington and the rest of the jury would condemn none but the friendless. Such is the flat-

1 *B.P.*, 672. 2 *B.P.*, 652.

tery and dissimulation of the greatest gentlemen in the
March that 'if Jesus Christ were emongest them they
woulde deceaue him if he woulde heere trust & followe
theire wicked councells.' [1]

Browne, no less strenuous than Woodrington in his
efforts to discredit Eure, appealed the matter of Jock of
the Cote to the Privy Council. Their first letters brought
a promise which Ker did not perform, and the affair became one of international diplomacy. Ker had just been
called before James to answer for the surprise of Swinburne and for seeking to murder Carey. The Council now
instructed the Ambassador to deal very earnestly with the
King that 'Browne, his surname and freindes' be secured
against Jock and his partakers, Browne 'beinge a man of
good deserte and speciall service there.' [2] In the following
month, September 1597, since the Queen considered the
jurors' charges 'rather misunderstanding, then matter,'
she sent the Bishop and Sir William Bowes as commissioners to demand more direct proofs.[3] The jurors reaffirmed all their 'detects,' and Browne dealt with Eure's
answer both 'scholasticallye' and vigorously. As 'we y^e
naturall borderers' know, Black Will Ridley and such outlaws, 'whoe be as notoryous in this age . . . as eu*er* was
Robyn Hoode in his tyme,' are either spared by him or en-
listed in his garrison; 'indeed *hinc illae lachrimae* ye true
nourse of desolac*i*on, and ye twoe edged sworde of dis-
coragement on ye borders. . . .' As to Woodrington and
Selby, whom Eure accuses, 'They are vndoubted right
englishmen . . . twoe of ye chief pillers vpholdinge y^t
dwyninge people.' [4] Eure says that Browne provoked a
quarrel in the presence of the commissioners; Browne, that

1 *B.P.*, 762.
2 *A.P.C.*, xxvi, 560; xxvii, 340; *Hatfield MSS.*, vii, 239.
3 *B.P.*, 758. 4 *B.P.*, 672.

Eure openly denounced him 'to be his Enymie, and in termes of yrefull threat*es* bidd him speake no further, or els his Lo: himself would chamber Brownes tounge.'[1]   In October, when the great tryst at Norham Ford suddenly became a fray in the twilight, Browne and Fenwick were chosen by Bowes to guard Buccleuch (Sir Walter Scott of Branxsome).[2]   The plague, which had been sweeping the North for a year, now reached Hexham, and Eure retired across the Durham border to his house at Witton, leaving as deputy Edward Gray (ancestor of the Earls Grey and Viscount Grey of Fallodon).[3]

Browne now set out for London to tell his story to Burghley in full. He carried with him the Bishop's letter of October 29, warning Burghley that in taking Buccleuch and Cesford as hostages, 'You have . . . a brace of wolves by the eares.'[4]   Bishop Toby, himself an accomplished fox, goes on with indirect hints to inquire: Is it not strange that the Queen of England cannot come by Cesford, when Thomas Percy, Constable of Alnwick and Wark Castles, may entertain him when and where and how he list? Ask the bearer of this, yet forget not that Percy is 'my lord of Northumberland's both officer and kinsman, as also that Jo. Browne was sometime toward his lordship' (as Steward of Alnwick). Thomas Percy was of course none other than the leader of the Gunpowder conspirators.

When the news came to Eure at Witton Castle that at the Bishop's Palace, some four miles off, the most pertinacious of his enemies was consulting with the subtlest and most powerful, he determined that Browne should never reach Court if he could prevent it. Browne and his company spent the night of the 29th in an inn at Richmond. On Sunday morning,

1 *B.P.*, 820, 860.   2 *B.P.*, 784.
3 *B.P.*, 675, 694, 779; Raine, p. 326.   4 *Hatfield MSS.*, VII, 452.

after they had broken their fast, m^r Browne going to his horse at the doore, & having his foote in the Stirrop, one of his handes on the Saddle pum*m*ell, & his other putting towardes his pocquett for money to giue to a multitude of poore folkes that stode about him, sodainly Will*i*am Browneles housholde Seruaunt to the L. Eure wth his sworde ready drawen came behind him, & gaue him a great wounde on the hinder part of his heade, & another wound vpon his left arme, and a thirde vpon his shouldior, wth so exceading great force & furie,

that but for having to reach over the heads of the poor folk, he had slain him outright.[1] Brownles and Francis Wadley, another of Eure's servants, had been walking up and down near the door for an hour or more, watching for Browne; 'they pretended to seeke a fleckt graie hound wth a reade Collor, wch they saide they had lost, and wch they sought also in an Alehouse'! The inhabitants pursued them with clubs and captured them at the inn of one Mark Sober. At their examination they said that they had no quarrel of their own with Browne, but that 'they did it for theire lorde & M^{rs} causes and for causes knowne to the best in Englaunde, Browneles affirminge that he was sory for nothinge but that yt was no worse wth me.'[2]

Eure supported his retainers energetically. On Monday night Mr. Robert Tailbois of Thornton, Durham, arrived and offered to go bail for the two men. Here the scent we are following suddenly grows warmer, for if we inquire who Tailbois was, we find that he had married Bishop Barnes' daughter Elizabeth, and was therefore Barnabe's brother-in-law. The Alderman of Richmond, the town's chief official, said that he must wait to see what became of the life of Browne.[3] Refusing compromise, Tailbois 'in great Anger, & in a stormy night rode thence to ye Lo: Eurye,' and returned with Eure's gentleman usher and another of his chief followers.[4] He brought special letters from Eure

1 *B.P.*, 836, information of Browne's host, Cuthbert Cowling.
2 *B.P.*, 813, Browne to Sir William Knollys of the Privy Council.
3 *B.P.*, 838.   4 *B.P.*, 860.

requiring the Alderman and Burgesses not only to release his men on the bond of Tailbois, 'my frynd and kynsman,' but to take bond of Browne and his company (imprisoning them if they refuse) to appear to Eure's prosecution for 'trespasses and outragious attempt*es*.' That 'factious varlett John Browne,' he is informed, began the quarrel, and the 'hurt fallen to browne by the fortune of my man is as david saieth. fallen vpon hym that diggeth a pytt for an other.' [1] The poor Alderman was now bombarded with letters from the Bishop, bidding him take no bail for these 'manquillers'; from Eure, threatening to complain of him unless he took bond alike from both sides or neither; and from each of them, demanding to see the other's letters. The men, who had been among Eure's Durham horsemen at Hexham, were freed on entering a recognizance together with Tailbois and Sober, and, says Browne, were received into Eure's house with great acceptation, he having been their 'anymater and mover.' [2] He desires, 'if I ouer live these woundes,' to be protected against Eure, for he will continue to inform the Queen and Council how the Border is 'cast open to the theef and ill doer . . . though my blood paie for speakinge.' [3] The Council decided that the men might go without further imprisonment provided that they made Browne satisfaction. [4] Bishop Matthew demands that Eure be expressly commanded to forbear such bloody revenge toward the gentlemen jurors, 'a fowle spectacle whereof was lately seen vpon M[r] Browne, belyke for that he was the pen-man of those bookes' [5] — the indictments against Eure.

The whole affair leaves little doubt who was at the bottom of Barnes' attempt on Browne, and still less when one reads what Eure says of his enemy. Browne's conditions,

1 *B.P.*, 841.   2 *B.P.*, 860.   3 *B.P.*, 813.
4 *A.P.C.*, xxviii, 203.   5 *B.P.*, 862.

he writes Cecil, shall be made known 'to be moste vyle and in this Country apparauntlie knowne.' He has provoked quarrels both with myself and with my followers, and he 'hath avowed his threates of malice & murtherous intentions . . . by riding in the midle marche . . . armed on the body and carrying Peternell pistoll . . . to doe some notable mischeefe & so avoyde his Country wch in his conscience he knoweth he cannot long brouke' if he receive due measure of law. Even within a mile or two of my house at Witton, he riding with five men made most intemperate speeches, hoping to quarrel my followers, which he did not succeed in until he found two at Richmond on their necessary business and tried to shoot one with his petronel, but it pleased God that my servant wounded Browne with a Scots sword. Let me appear in person (his continual entreaty), to 'be tryed of the truthe of theese slaundrous informacons wch this *brauo* Browne thundreth against me.' [1]

Burghley had hitherto turned a deaf ear to Eure's earnest requests to be allowed to attend the new Parliament, but now that the feud had come to such a head, he sent for him. The immediate result of the attack on Browne, therefore, was that on November 19 Eure took his seat for the first time in the House of Lords.[2] On the same day he received news that Woodrington had been knighted, an unfounded rumor which has misled the modern historian,[3] for the knighting did not take place until 1603. Woodrington, who belonged to Essex's party, had embarked that summer for the Islands Voyage, and though the Queen ordered Essex to send back from the fleet the Withringtons and other principal gentlemen of the Border, 'upon hourly complaint of devastation by the Scots,' they kept their promise not to put themselves again under the rule of

1 *B.P.*, 820.   2 *Lords Journals*, II, 198.
3 *B.P.*, 831; J. C. Hodgson, *History of Northumberland*, IV, 280.

Eure. Only in December, when his enemy was in London, did Woodrington ask license to repair to the Border to succor his oppressed friends, many of whom had been slain or taken prisoner into Scotland.[1] Meanwhile he and Browne had been laying their complaints before Burghley, while Eure made his defence to the Council.

It was now that Barnes first met Browne, possibly by chance but more likely because Eure had already commissioned him to begin his tragedy of revenge. Certainly he tried hard to train Brown to empty the whole cup at one carouse, a habit desirable to induce in a man who is to drink poison. Woodrington said that Barnes urged him also to drink in that fashion and made an attempt to poison him, which may have been the object Barnes had in journeying to Durham and riding back with Carey. Eure was attending Parliament, and in January he wrote his last letter as Warden. He reported that Ephraim Woodrington and three of Henry's servants had besieged and threatened his deputy Gray. He therefore prayed that Burghley, after punishing the Woodringtons, would find someone more fit than he for the office.[2] Burghley did. Sir Robert Carey had sought the wardenship in Forster's time and in 1596 had volunteered to keep the Middle March quiet 'in spyte of Cesfordes teethe'; but now, in the light of Eure's experiences, he protested that he regarded the appointment as a disaster.[3] He came up to Court and accepted it, however, since he had already been superseded in the East March by Lord Willoughby. His success owed much to his making Woodrington and Fenwick his Deputy Wardens, and especially to his reliance upon Roger Woodrington, who combined a taste for painting (as shown in his will) with a knowledge of the

1 *S.P.D. Eliz.* 264/61; *B.P.*, 865.
2 *Hatfield MSS.*, viii, 73; copy in *B.P.*, 894.　　　3 *B.P.*, 281, 913.

Border 'Highlandmen' which made him the most expert
Borderer of his time.[1]

Carey in his *Memoirs* gives a very fair estimate of Eure
as 'a worthy nobleman,' 'who did his whole endeavour for
the good of the March' but trusted too much to men who
deceived and abused him.[2] He speaks of Eure's term of
office as five years, but it really lasted just half so long,
and that only through Elizabeth's favor and her obstinacy
in supporting constituted authority. A day or two before
Barnes came to London with the new Warden, Elizabeth
was unreasonably finding fault with Bowes, whose conduct
throughout had been admirably impartial, saying that it
was never her direction that a jury should inquire into
Eure's conduct.[3] On April 2 Bowes wrote from his lodgings in Greene's Lane, near Charing Cross, that he had
been sick these eight or ten days:[4] a time which goes back
so nearly to the date of the poisoning, March 21, as to suggest that he also had not escaped a whiff of the tainted
lemon.

Within a month after the poisoning Browne was well
enough to renew his petition against Jock of the Cote and
on April 17 to carry the Council's letters in his behalf to
Lord Willoughby.[5] Of Eure we hear no word after his
resignation until May 13, when Barnes had just been
brought back a captive and was to appear next day before
the Council. Walking the streets of London with his
brother Sir William and one page, Eure was set upon by
'fowre or fiue of the witheringtons about a country quarrell,' and hurt in the hand, while his brother was sorely
wounded in the shoulder, over the face, and quite through
the body.[6] The Council wrote the Lord Mayor to examine

1 B.P., 1078, 1265, 1281–1282; *Surtees Soc.*, cxii, 225; cxlii, 287; lxviii,
  passim.   2 Ed. 1905, p. 55.
3 B.P., 922.   4 B.P., 929.
5 A.P.C., xxviii, 405.   6 Chamberlain, in *S.P.D. Eliz.* 267/15.

diligently which side began the fray, and to hold the Woodringtons without bail, though they might be removed from
the Compter as 'noysome for their health.' An order a
week later allowing bail, since Sir William was likely to
recover, was stayed the next day on the surgeons' report
that his life was still in danger.[1]

Once more at least the feud blazed out, again in Eure's
territory. We hear of it only from the Star Chamber bill
of 'Henrye Wooderington . . . Esquire Deputye warden . . .
and keper of Rydesdale.'[2] In July 1598, he informs the
Council, William Brownles and other evil-disposed persons
to the number of thirty took an oath to surprise and murder him as he traveled home from London. They met at
Malton (one of Eure's residences) and by companies of
eight or nine together spent three days in riding through
Yorkshire to Bawtry, adding to their store of weapons in
every town and raising tumults by shooting off guns and
pistols. After some days 'in Awayte and Ambush' they
rode leisurely back through Doncaster and Pontefract.
While they were in an alehouse, they saw Woodrington
pass by, but better accompanied than they expected.
Following him in a manner described as 'Ragyous' to
North Allerton, where he lodged, they passed through the
town in the night season and spent the Sunday night riotously at a rendezvous 'called the lowsye Bush.' At Nesham
in Durham they sent abroad spies, who seeing him coming
down a long hill cried often with a great fury, 'he was
Cominge he was Cominge,' whereupon they rode to gather
all their confederates and lie in wait beyond Darlington.
However, they had aroused so much suspicion the past
week by asking at every town when he would come by,

1 *A.P.C.*, xxviii, 443, 458–459.
2 Star Ch. 5, W 77/19 (W 67/11, containing further documents in the case, is
missing).

and refusing to give their names or tell whose men they were, that travelers had warned Woodrington against them as far away as Newark-upon-Trent. At Nesham he was warned by Squire Lawson and persuaded to make stay there, being, as he very sensibly observes, 'loth to be Assaulted.' Brownles and the rest came in most furious manner to shoot at him, but finding him well accompanied and among good store of people, had to content themselves with swearing great oaths.

Eure's name no more appears in this affair than it does in the Barnes case, for to bring charges against a nobleman without full proof was to court a prosecution for libel. Nevertheless, he was clearly responsible for the ambush of Woodrington by his servants, and in the light of this and of the earlier assault on Browne it becomes impossible to acquit him of responsibility for the poisoning. No one who knew his threats and acts against Browne could have doubted it on hearing that this fresh attempt had been made by a Durham man. Barnes is not known to have been in Eure's service, but that made him the fitter man for the business: one who could pose as Browne's friend without suspicion, a gentleman, yet unscrupulous, Italianate, made desperate by debt. As he had once sought the patronage of the Bishop, so it was natural now that he should turn to Eure, the other great lord of the county of Durham.

Barnes could have had access to Eure through Thomas Percy, but the surest link between them is Robert Tailbois — on the one hand, Barnabe's brother-in-law, on the other, Eure's right-hand man in Durham. His promptness in offering bail for Eure's servants, without even waiting to consult Eure, suggests that he was following instructions given him in advance. He had once furnished Eure an important book of Border treaties which had belonged to

Bishop Barnes and which he secured from Emanuel. Eure
sent it to Burghley. Tailbois, who had been at the Middle
Temple with John Barnes, was Attorney General of
Durham under his father-in-law, and Attorney General
and Escheator under Bishop Hutton. When as Justice of
the Peace he got into very hot water by defying Bishop
Matthew, Eure wrote to Burghley interceding for his kinsman Tailbois.[1] He was being characteristically generous
with the word 'kinsman' — Tailbois was his fifth cousin
thrice removed! — but it was enough for him that his
grandmother, the wife of Sir Edward Dymock, had been
a Tailbois.[2] Besides, his kinsman was useful, being a lawyer as well as justice and custos rotulorum; and for another
sort of business, the kinsman had a brother-in-law.

Eure's private revenges are indefensible, but for his time
there was nothing unusual about them except their singular lack of success. Other Star Chamber suits show that
the Earl of Derby, for example, in the intervals of penning
comedies, would order his servants to ambush and murder
an enemy, promising to save them harmless, or would
muster men by the hundreds to defy the law on the Yorkshire moors. Eure, as the rest of his career shows, was a
very fair specimen of the cultivated Elizabethan nobleman, and highly regarded by both Elizabeth and James.
After studying, like Browne and Woodrington, at Gray's
Inn, he had traveled to Paris and the Emperor's court. It
is amusing to find that though Walsingham had warned
him by no means to visit Italy, by hurrying from Germany
he got in three weeks at Venice and saw Padua, Mantua,
and Cremona before letting Walsingham know where he
was.[3] After his wardenship he returned to York as Vice-

1 B.P., 382, 425; Hutchinson, Durham, I, 460, 471.
2 Surtees, III, 254, 382; Harl. MS. 2118, f. 43ᵛ.
3 S.P.D. Add., 1580–1625, passim.

President of the Council in the North. In 1601–2 he had to come before Star Chamber to explain his enmity to Sir Thomas Posthumus Hoby, which had culminated in his son and his brother inviting themselves to Hoby's York-shire house and there dicing, carousing, and during prayers making rude and strange noises in the nature, said Hoby, of a Black Sanctus.[1] At the Queen's death he was in Bremen at the head of an embassy.[2] Webster mentions him with the other courtiers who followed Prince Henry in becoming free of the Merchant Tailors in 1607.[3] He had a company of players traveling the country between 1601 and 1613, called sometimes Lord Evers' men and some-times the Lord President's,[4] for he spent his last ten years at Ludlow ruling over the more tranquil Marches of Wales. From a suit in the uncalendared Requests I find that he bought from Lord Morley a half share in the profits of *God and the King*, perhaps the only book which a sovereign has commanded to be purchased by every householder in Great Britain.[5] Lady Hunsdon, the kinswoman whom Spenser delighted most to honor (Charillis, 'the pride and prim-rose of the rest,' 'the fairest under skie'[6]), chose him for her second husband, which speaks well for his personal qualities. At the time of his death in 1617 they were en-gaged in a Chancery suit with the Admiral's son, Lord Effingham, for possession of Edmund Tyllney's former

1 Violet A. Wilson, *Society Women of Shakespeare's Time*, p. 238, and 'Shake-speare and a Yorkshire Quarrel,' *North American Review*, ccxix (1924), 653. I am surprised that Mr. Dover Wilson takes this seriously as having anything to do with *Twelfth Night* (ed. 1930, pp. 95, 150).
2 *Hatfield MSS.*, xiv; Nichols, *Progresses of James*, i, 43.
3 *Works*, ed. Lucas, iii, 323; Clode, *Early History of the Guild of Merchant Taylors*, i, 303.
4 J. T. Murray, *English Dramatic Companies*, ii, 44.
5 Cf. *D.N.B.* under Richard Mocket, and for the petition of Jaggard and others to be paid for the printing, *A. P. C. 1616–17*, pp. 145, 159.
6 *Colin Clout*, ll. 563, 559. Cf. *D.N.B.* under Elizabeth Carey; and P. W. Long, *Mod. Lang. Rev.*, iii (1908), 257, in favor of the identification with Charillis rather than with Phillis.

mansion at Leatherhead, where the Master of the Revels had once entertained his cousin and Queen.[1]

No sooner had Woodrington escaped Eure's ambush than he and Fenwick broke up that second hunting of the Cheviot described in Carey's *Memoirs* and in the *Border Papers*. The following year he gave Cesford the lie and was straightway invited to a meeting at the 'Hayr Craggs' on the Border with short sword and whinyard. The Queen next year in a gracious letter praising Woodrington's good service commanded their reconciliation. He was at Essex House on the fatal day of the rising, but urged that he had dissuaded Essex and Rutland from violence and extricated from the affair his kinsman the Earl of Bedford (a grandson of Forster). Coke produced him as first witness at the trial. Woodrington, the Scots' bitterest foe, was one of the first Englishmen to be knighted by James, who sent him with Selby and Fenwick at the head of a thousand horse to establish peace along the Border.[2] Cesford, that 'Pluto-like spirit,' 'that border bloud sucker and State Enymie,' [3] became Earl of Roxburghe, and it was for his wedding that Daniel wrote *Hymen's Triumph*.

John Browne completely disappears from the *Border*

1 Eure's grandfather Sir Rafe, the 'fell cruel man' who burnt Melrose and defended Scarborough, had been before Star Chamber for the outrageous kidnapping of Lady Salvayn from her private chapel in Egton (*Yorks. Arch. Soc.*, XLV [1911], 2). Eure's father in 1586 sued Bishop Barnes in Chancery over rights in the forest of 'Wardell' (C 2 Eliz. E 4/71). An oil painting of the time of Elizabeth, 'representing the Eure family dancing the Brawl' (not inappropriately), is mentioned in the *History of Witton-le-Wear* (p. 21) by Brig.-Gen. H. C. Surtees, who, however, cannot trace the present owner. After the Lord President's time the house of Eure never flourished. The last remnant of its possessions, Malton Castle, was actually divided stone by stone between two adamant coheiresses; and on the death of the seventh lord, who had been journeyman to a woolen draper, the barony became extinct (G.E.C., *Complete Peerage*; Foster, *Yorkshire Visitations*, p. 616).

2 *B.P.*, 1103; *A.P.C.*, xxx, 372; *S.P.D. Eliz.* 278/5; Spedding, *Life of Bacon*, II, 219; Nichols, *Progresses of James*, I, 68; Stowe's *Annals*, ed. 1615, p. 818.

3 Lord Willoughby, in *B.P.*, 1034; *B.P.*, 860.

Papers after Eure's resignation, but he is evidently the 'Mr. Browne of Gray's Inn' mentioned in a Berwick case in 1600–01, and he represented Morpeth in the 1601 Parliament.[1] On August 23, 1605, the Government paid ten pounds through Joseph Haidon to the use of John Browne, as his reward for apprehending certain priests and bringing two hampers of papistical books from Berwick to London.[2] He may have lost his eagerness for the bailiwick of Hexham after observing the fate of the bailiffs: Nicholas Whitfield, slain by the Scots in 1597–98, and John Whitfield, who, riding to surprise the Armstrongs at a great football match, was himself surprised, and had to be sewn together again. His office fell to Roger Woodrington, on the strong recommendation of Carey and of the West March officers, Richard Lowther and Lancelot Carleton.[3]

To pick up Browne's trail again after he had vanished from the Border long seemed hopeless, until in going through the records of Durham Chancery I recognized his signature (matching that in the *Border Papers*) to many of the pleadings. Of all the towns in England, therefore, he chose to practise law in the one where Barnes was living. A suit brought by Dr. Emanuel Barnes in 1607 against Lancelot Carleton of Wolsingham mentions that Browne had been Carleton's counselor at Durham Assizes in a land controversy against John Barnes and his brethren, doubtless including Barnabe.[4]

---

1 *A.P.C.*, xxxi, 201; *Members of Parliament*, p. 439. The town of Berwick chose Browne for a commissioner as early as 1592–3 (*B.P.*, i, 803, 810). He was no longer Recorder in 1603 (Nichols, i, 64).
2 *Declared Accounts*, E 351/543, f. 140.
3 *B.P.*, ii, 907, 1065–1067, 1078, 1281, 1282, 1285.
4 P.R.O., Durham 2/4, 7/5.

IV. BOON COMPANIONS

Frescobaldi.   And yet I love thee, rogue; ask, rogue, and have.
Baglioni.   Come and embrace: 'tis blithe when malt-men meet . . .
              Embrace fantastically.

The Devil's Charter, ll. 1553 f.

QUITE apart from the poisoning, the Star Chamber case
gives us occasional pictures from a poet's life in London:
watching the bowlers in St. James Park, avoiding the
candlelight at an alehouse door, pledging carouses at the
White Horse in Friday Street. Standing over the way
from the Friday Street entrance to the Mermaid in Bread
Street, the White Horse was the tavern where Peele helped
his hungry friend to a supper by throwing at him in a show
of anger two rabbits and a loaf.[1] The vintner of the White
Horse until 1582 was Arlington Kelley, who by his will of
that year bequeathed to his cousin William Hunys, Master
of the Children of the Chapel, 'my best Damaske coate
garded with velvett,' his best cloak and hose, twenty
pounds, and a pair of viols.[2] John Cordell, his successor,
was host in the time of Peele and Barnes. The White
Horse was one of the forty taverns allowed in London by
the city ordinance of 1554, and of all the forty it is the
only one which now survives. The Mermaid has vanished,
but one may still, after three hundred years, drink a health
at the White Horse.

The scene of the poisoning, the Queen's Arms, seems to
have been the one described on a token as 'in Whit Hall.'
The Swan in the Strand, where Barnes lodged, was probably the White Swan 'against Somerset House,' on the

---

1 *Works of George Peele*, ed. Bullen, II, 386.
2 Kenneth M. Rogers, *Trans. London and Midd. Archæol. Soc.*, N.S., v (1928)
  446. Arlington Kelley was not known to Mrs. Stopes, *William Hunnis and the
  Children of the Chapel Royal* (*Materialien*, XXIX, 1910).

north side of the Strand just west of Drury Lane. Great
kitchen ranges were set up at the Swan in 1606 for the
feasting of Christian of Denmark and his train; and the
next year we find in the Stationers' Register *Wofull newes
of the burninge of certen houses at the Swan in the Strand of
one Nicholas Blontz an Inkeper*. . . After a final burning
in 1812 the inn (not to be confused with Jonson's tavern,
the Swan near Charing Cross) gave way to the office of the
Morning Chronicle, and the place which Barnes had known
became familiar to Hazlitt and Dickens.[1]

As the son of a bishop, Barnes ranked socially above all
the professional playwrights of the time except Beaumont
and Fletcher; and accordingly the friends we find him associating with are all men of some dignity and position. The
three with whom he supped at the White Horse were a
physician, Dr. Marbecke; a lawyer, John Browne; and a
soldier, Captain Jackson. Dr. Roger Marbecke, once public
orator of Oxford and Provost of Oriel, was Censor of the
College of Physicians, physician to Elizabeth, and chief
physician to James. His life may be read in the *D.N.B.*,
together with that of his father John Merbeck, the Tudor
musician. I have shown elsewhere that he was the uncle
of Thomas Marbeck, the Admiral's player, and of Middleton's wife.[2] He wrote an excellent account of the Cadiz
voyage, on which he went as physician to the Lord Admiral. But he is, or rather should be, best known for his
mellow and good-humored *Defence of Tabacco* (1602), and
it is therefore amusing to find that Barnabe pressed him to
drink tobacco 'against his liking.' This confirms what he
says in the *Defence*, that he wrote it only at the request
of some friends that he would answer the attack called

1 Boyne, *Trade Tokens*, ed. Williamson, pp. 757-759, 797; *Harl. MS.* 6850, f.
    31; Arber, III, 345.
2 *Review of English Studies*, VII (1931), 440.

Worke for Chimney-Sweepers from the point of view of a quite impartial physician:

Touching mine owne particular fantacie and affection to *Tabacco*: I protest, it is no maner of way, tyed vnto it. For in all my life, either I did neuer take it at all: or else verie seldome.

Yet for the honor of his country, he declares, he will not see 'that poore simple' left without a fair trial,

for that this *Tabacco*, is a poore gentleman, and a stranger, and, as it should seeme, of some good account in his countrey, with the high Priests, and Rulers of the sinagogues there [in Virginia], and can speake no word of our language to defend himselfe.

And so, for pastime during the Christmas holidays, he wrote his little book (which is as merry as the season), and sent it to his friends, Sir Henry Cocke, the Queen's Cofferer, and 'Master Richard Browne Esquire, Clark of the Greene cloth.'

By the help of this dedication we can now identify another of Barnabe's friends, Master Browne, Clerk Comptroller, with whom he proposed to sup at the Court at Whitehall. From the *Journal to Stella* we remember the Green Cloth as 'much the best table in England . . . designed to entertain foreign Ministers, and people of quality, who come to see the Queen,' and as the place where the Clerk Comptroller who had invited Swift declared 'that I abused the Queen's meat and drink, and said nothing at the table was good, and all a d—d lie,' for Swift said only that the wine was small.[1] Richard Browne lived at Sayes Court, Deptford, in the rich meadows of which wandered Queen Elizabeth's cattle (of which his son Christopher was keeper), and where a century later Peter the Great in his wheelbarrow charged through Evelyn's hedges. When the Queen visited Harefield in 1602, 'Mr. Browne, Clerke

1 *Journal to Stella*, ed. Aitken, pp. 266, 308.

Comptrowler,' sent 'Peakcockes, ij,' 'Bustardes, ij,' and
'Freshe sturgion.' Knighted by James, Sir Richard burst
a vein in a vehement speech in Parliament, and he lies
with Marlowe at St. Nicholas, Deptford, where a long inscription was erected to his memory by Evelyn.[1]

Henry Saunderson, with whom Barnes chose to lodge
at the Swan, was Searcher for the port of Newcastle and
Constable of Brancepeth Castle. He was the terror of
smugglers and of seminary priests, and the most trusted
confidential agent of Bishop Matthew, who sent him to
inform Burghley privately on the charges against Tailbois
and against Eure, and at the time of the poisoning, on
customs business.[2] The energy with which he performed
his duties won him many enemies among the Catholics,
and one of the bitterest found relief by denouncing him
as 'Henry Saunderson, a bankrupt merchant, and base
companion; yet for his pretended zeal in Puritanism, and
Machiavelian subtlety, a special instrument to the President' — the Earl of Huntington, Lord President of the
Council in the North.[3] The King's surveyors reported in
1614 that in the twenty-two years since he had been
granted the keepership of Brancepeth the 'sweet walks
and pleasant Harbours' had grown ruinous, and that only
three hundred deer were left in the parks because of his
depredations of deer, roes, and conies, which he killed for
his own use and gave away to friends and followers.[4]

1 Lysons, *Environs of London*, ed. 1796, III, 366–367; Hasted's *Kent*, ed. Drake,
I, 7; *Egerton Papers* (Camden Soc., 1840), 356; *Diary of John Evelyn*,
ed. Wheatley, I, xcix. The attribution to Browne of *A True Report concerning the Worthy Accompt of Tobacco*, Ashmolean MS. 1148, in the catalogue
and in C. M. MacInnes, *The Early English Tobacco Trade*, p. 38, is unfounded.
A careful reading of the MS. shows that the author, R. B., was a clergyman
in the diocese of Durham who had used tobacco for forty years, and therefore
wrote long after Browne's death in 1605.
2 John Morris, *Troubles of Our Catholic Forefathers*, Third Series, p. 134; cf.
pp. 151, 154, 170.   3 *B.P.*, II, 442, 794; *S.P.D. Eliz.* 266/60.
4 W. Fordyce, *History of Durham*, I, 430.

Clearly it was worth Barnabe's while to be friendly with the lord of so much venison.

Captain Thomas Jackson, of the party at the White Horse, is to be distinguished from Thomas Jackson, officer of the Marshalsea, who lent Barnes money in prison and bought his mare.[1] The captain led a company under Essex in France, at Cadiz, and in Ireland. He was taken by the French and held for ransom, and on his return out of Brittany the Queen called him 'her honest captain.' His father had financed the 1560 invasion of Scotland, and he himself lent money to Hunsdon, Governor of Berwick, his native town, where he held a company but sought in vain to break the Careys' monopoly of the higher offices. After the death of Hunsdon (who described him in 1587 as 'a good talle fellowe') he seems to have been out of a place, and after the death of his other patron Burghley he got into a good deal of hot water: cashiered and lodged in Dublin Castle for his lieutenant's false accounts; engaged in a fray with a pensioner at Berwick in December 1600, and the 'mortal enemy' of several other captains and of Sir John Carey, whom he challenged for threatening at Theobalds to thrust him with a dagger; 'enforced to hew out new fortunes in foreign countries' and seeking permission of Cecil to offer his sword to Henry IV and to the 'Prince of Swethland,' who sent a special messenger to Jackson requesting his services.[2] His desperate straits led at length to 'phantasies and conceites' in his pathetic letters to Cecil, written 'imprysoned in my lodging in London, by want,' or again actually prisoner at Warwick Inn in Warwick Lane, hinting mysteriously at projects for the good of the State and the safety of the King, for

1 A third Thomas Jackson, born near Witton, owed his career as a scholar and President of Corpus, Oxford, to the encouragement of Eure (cf. D.N.B.).
2 S.P.D., 1591–1603; Hatfield MSS.; B.P.; S.P.Ir., 1599–1600; A.P.C., 1600–01.

which 'I am glad to be accovmpted a phantasticke foole,' lost 'in a wylldernes of conceit*es*, phantasyes, follies, illusyons and errores'; but if Cecil thinks him mad, 'yet imagine yt to be *sacer quidam furor*.' He resolves to accept a pension, that he may pass the remainder of his days in prayers and the contemplative life, 'and for a tyme to lyve a cloysterer'; generously pensioned in 1605, he appears twelve years later as Muster Master at Newcastle.[1] A soldier of fortune, sudden and quick to quarrel, he had also something of a taste for verse, and on Elizabeth's death he encouraged Cecil with a Latin sapphic. Very likely he was one of the captains with whom Barnes was a favorite in France under Essex.

The tracing out of Captain Jackson's career proves that the Thomas Jackson, officer of the Marshalsea, who aided Barnes in prison, was a different man. In January 1600–01, while the captain was still in Berwick, Thomas Jackson, servant to the Knight Marshal, found two bails for his appearance before Cecil to make answer concerning the escape of George Kendall from the Marshalsea.[2] He was plainly suspected of connivance with the prisoner, and this offers a very significant hint as to how Barnes also may have made his escape.

1 MSS. at Hatfield, 114/47–54; *S.P.D. Jas.*, 1603–10, pp. 208, 215; *A.P.C.*, 1616–17.
2 *S.P.D. Eliz.* 278/5; cf. 275/114, and *Hatfield MSS.*, XI, 402.

V. DURHAM

> O that I never had been born at all,
> Or being, had been born of shepherd's brood;
> Then should I not in such mischances fall,
> Quiet my water, and Content my food.
>
> *Parthenophil, Sonnet 65*

WHAT happened to Barnes after he broke out of the Marshalsea and fled to the North? His whole history between
1598 and 1606 has been a pure blank, and much of it must
remain so. I have, however, found two traces of him during this period. On February 9, 1598–99, 'Barnabe Barnes
of the Citty of Durham gent. of th'age of xxviij yeares'
deposed in Durham Chancery on behalf of his brother
John against his brother Timothy.[1] This is proof that he
was no longer a fugitive from justice, since he could safely
appear in the court of the Bishop who seven months earlier
had had orders to recapture him. It also indicates that he
can hardly have undergone sentence in Star Chamber, or
his address would not have been Durham, but the Fleet.
Had he been captured again, his appearance would have
been entered in the Privy Council register, but there is no
record of this nor of any further proceedings against him.
Influence alone could have brought him thus safe from the
danger he stood in. As to whose influence, we can only
conjecture that it was set in motion by Eure and that the
likeliest courtier to intercede was Essex, who when Thomas
Percy was in trouble two years earlier had written in his
favor to Justice Beaumont, at Northumberland's request.[2]
Essex had withdrawn from Court, but at this same time

1 P. R. O., Durham 7/2, pt. 2.
2 *Hist. MSS. Comm.*, III, App., p. 50. The Looking-Glass-Land editor tells us
  that though Essex asked a pardon for Thomas, he meant William, the poet,
  who was to wound Henry Denny the next week.

was doing what he could to obtain pardon for Southampton. Eure's chief favorite, Captain Ralph Mansfield, was an active follower of Essex; Anthony Bacon wrote the Earl in 1598 warmly recommending Eure's brother; and Eure might reasonably expect some favors, since he had shown that he knew well how to deserve them, by rewarding Anthony's advice with the gift of a Northumberland nag.[1] Certainly Barnes in his *Offices* praises Essex with an enthusiasm he shows for no one else. Whether through Essex or other friends at Court, Eure could be counted upon to see that his agent came to no harm.

The eventful year of 1598 saw several allusions to Barnes, beginning with an epigram in Bastard's *Chrestoleros*,[2] licensed a fortnight after the poisoning:

> *Barneus'* verse (vnlesse I doe him wrong,)
> Is like a cupp of sacke, heady and strong.

This little compliment (which incidentally suggests that sack came readily to mind when you thought of Barnes) shows Bastard as a friend, evidently from Oxford days; but it must have amused those who had heard of the poison-sugared wine. *A World of Words* belongs to the spring or summer of the year, since Southampton is addressed as being on his travels. Unless Barnes wrote his verses in prison, therefore, he must have sent them to Florio before the Browne affair. In September were licensed Marston's *Scourge of Villainy*, with its passing fling at Sonnet 63 of *Parthenophil*,[3] and Meres' *Wit's Treasury*, which makes no mention of Barnes. Harvey himself says nothing of his protégé in the 1598 copy of

---

1 *Hatfield MSS.*, VIII, 454, 470; *B.P.*, 805. Anthony had won Essex's approval for Eure's proposal to ally himself with the Earl by marrying his son to one of Stella's daughters (Penelope, Essex, Lettice, or Isabel): Birch, *Memoirs of Elizabeth*, II, 296, 331, 340.

2 Book VI, no. 40.   3 Satire VIII, 126-127.

Chaucer where he writes of 'owr florishing metricians.' [1]
It was natural that a suspected poisoner who was in hiding
from the Lords of Star Chamber should for a time be under
a cloud; but even this did not prevent the resolute Florio
from publishing his friend's verses.

After his Star Chamber adventure, Barnes probably
lived less in London and more in Durham, though his retirement was not so complete as that of Harvey at Saffron
Walden. The second reference I have found to him during
the long eclipse from 1598 to 1606 shows him once more at
Durham, as in the Chancery deposition of 1598–9. A
Court of Requests suit, one of the many brought by his
sister Elizabeth Tailbois, describes him as present when
the luckless Robert Tailbois died in Durham Gaol, 'after
a long and lanquishinge' [2] imprisonment for debt. The
date is established by the parish register as the first week
of 1604–5.[3] Together with another brother-in-law, Aristotle Knowsley, Barnabe witnessed the will of Tailbois,
who left to his brother John Barnes 'my manuscripts and
law Books,' and to his brother Barnabas Barnes 'my other
manuscripts.' [4]

At Durham Barnes resided, like most of the gentry, in
the parish of St. Mary-le-Bow, between the Cathedral and
the Castle. The register of St. Mary records his burial
there in December 1609. In all likelihood he lived, as we
know his sister Elizabeth Tailbois did during her hus-

1 *Gabriel Harvey's Marginalia*, ed. Moore Smith, p. 233.
2 *Sic*: Requests 2/476, uncalendared.
3 *Dur. and Northumb. Par. Reg. Soc.*, XXVII, 126.
4 Surtees, III, 382, supplemented by the Requests suit and by information from
    Durham. Barnabe was a party, with the other children and executors of
    Bishop Barnes, to many further suits, including: E 13/368 (for this reference
    I am grateful to Dr. Leslie Hotson); E 112/Eliz., Durham, 49, and Jas. I,
    Durham, 163; Star Ch. 5, B 19/19; Requests 2/104/57; Durham 3/87, mm.
    3, 4 (*Deputy Keeper's Report*, XXXVII, Appx. I, 316 f.); Durham 7/2, Pt. 2,
    containing a deposition by 'Jane Barnes wedowe', aged fifty on February 15,
    1593–4.

band's imprisonment, with his brother John, Clerk of the
Peace for the Bishopric, whose burial is recorded four
years later.[1] If Barnabe's last years must be left to our
imaginations, at least we can form some picture of the
house he lived in, for in *The Rites of Durham* we discover
that Mr. John Barnes' house in the North Bailey was the
same to which Dean Whittingham's widow had carried the
holy-water stone, 'very artificially maide,' which once
stood at the south door of Durham Cathedral. That
thrifty Frenchwoman found it useful in her kitchen, and
for building the walls of her house she appropriated with
equal coolness sundry 'blewe *marble*' gravestones that lay
over the ancient priors and monks, setting up two great
ones without her door, where they remained during the
time of Barnes. In the days of his successor (the Solicitor
General for Durham) 'an olde man wth comly gray hayres'
came by in the guise of a beggar and declared that, whilst
those stones stood there, nothing would prosper about the
house. Thereupon he vanished, and his words coming
true, the tombstones were restored.[2]

To John Barnes we owe the preservation of *Parthenophil and Parthenophe*. His signature appears on the title-
page of the sole remaining copy. Grosart did not identify
it, but it is the signature which one constantly meets as his
in Durham legal records. He has followed it with his
motto, 'Principium sapientiæ timor Jehouæ': a strange
companion to these pagan poems.[3]

1 *Dur. and Northumb. Par. Reg. Soc.*, XXVII, 127, 128; *Harl. Soc. Reg.*, XXIII, 82.
2 *Surtees Soc.*, CVII, 61.
3 Grosart gives a facsimile. Other signatures of seventeenth-century owners include the Northumberland name of Thomas Delavale and the Durham one of
  Cuthbert Creswell. The unique copy was bought by the Bishop of Rochester
  in the late eighteenth century 'for a mere trifle,' says Park, who himself about
  1792 secured for sixpence a copy of Barnes' *Divine Century*, offered in 1815 for
  £30 (Brydges, *Censura Literaria*, VI [1808], 120; *Bibliotheca Anglo-Poetica*
  [1815], p. 53).

VI. SATIRIC PORTRAITS

All wonders Barnzy speaks, all grossly feigned.
Speak some wonder once, Barnzy: speak the truth.
Campion, seventh elegiac epigram

WHETHER or not Shakespeare thought of Barnes in drawing the type of all liars and braggarts, Parolles, it must be
acknowledged that no contemporary whom the satirists
dared to name bore so close a resemblance as Barnes to
that equivocal companion. Nashe was the most brilliant
of those who amused themselves in sketching Barnes, but
not the only one nor even the first, for Campion had already published his epigram *In Barnum*, 'Mortales decem.'
In his *Observations in the Art of English Poesy* (1602)
Campion made merry with Barnes in three English epigrams, but they had evidently been written years before,
when lampooning Harvey was still in fashion. They picture Barnzy as a teller of feigned wonders, and 'Haruy'
and 'Dawson' as cuckolding him with his wife Matilda.
There is no record that Barnes ever had a wife, and none
is mentioned in the wills of his kindred; so that (unless a
marriage should unexpectedly come to light) one must be
skeptical of Matilda as anything but a fiction. Campion
explains that 'sometimes vnder a knowne name I haue
shadow'd a fain'd conceit,' which seems rather hard on the
known name. It is amusing to find Campion four years
later writing verses for the *Offices*, first in English and then
in Latin: 'liber hic viuet, habet Genium.' [1] In the 1619
edition of his *Poemata* Campion kept his uncomplimentary
In Barnum and included another early epigram on Sonnet 63 of *Parthenophil*.[2]

1 Ed. Vivian, p. 352. Cf. Jonson on the *Bosworth Field* of Sir John Beaumont,
   1629: 'This book will live; it hath a genius.'
2 Ed. Vivian, pp. 239, 284.

Since Barnes attracted the lightning first of Campion, then of Nashe and of Marston, it should be no surprise to find him the favorite butt of still another satirist, Sir John Haryngton. This discovery we owe to Professor Moore Smith, who in 1927 identified him with 'Lynus the writer' in Haryngton's epigrams.[1] The evidence is not so immediately decisive as in the equation of Paulus with Ralegh, but when one reads through the epigrams — more than Haryngton devoted to any other man — the parallels are certainly very numerous. We may accept the identification at least provisionally, remembering that we have no conclusive proof, but that it seems to fit the known facts. The likenesses will be readily recognized if we summarize what Haryngton tells us of Lynus, replacing the imaginary name by that of Barnes.

'Thow boasts and trewlie mayst of some nobillitye,' Haryngton writes. Barnes was the son of a spiritual peer, and so far as we know the only Elizabethan poet justified in making such a claim who at the same time led Lynus' shifting life. He does not seem to be allied to the temporal peers, for his personal opinion of them is that most are 'much decayd in valour and in wit' and very few fit for government. He wears on his back the greatest part of what he is worth, and borrows all he can of what he spends, offering to pawn even his raiment and his armor (compare Barnes' military service, and the pride he took in it, according to Campion). He is 'valiant as a Gander' — precisely the testimony of Campion and Nashe; and if poetry is lying (as Touchstone held), he is 'a passing poet.' This appears to be the trait that led Haryington to rechristen Barnabe Barnes 'lying Lynus.'[2] It was not any learning,

1 *Times Lit. Suppl.*, March 10, 1927.
2 He probably had also in mind the mythical poet Linus, of whom Churchyard writes that 'he was the sonne of Mercury and wrate the courses of the sun, moone, and spheres in excellent verse' (*Praise of Poetrie*).

says the satirist of 'impudent *Lynus*,' but his 'brute bold-
nes' which made people suspect that he was 'bred in
Brazen-nose.' [1]

The portrait gives us Barnes to the life, so far as we
know him, and it is only reasonable to suppose that the
further details are equally faithful. Compared with Haryngton's black but ruddy complexion, Barnes is 'somwhat
fayrer yet perhapps more bluddy.' He is often melancholy, 'alone in dumps and muses,' and so desperate in his
fortunes that he prays for civil warfare. Instead of robbing
authors, 'thou robst som thow dost meet in hope of pardon'
(which recalls Nashe's charge that he ran away with 'a
Noble-mans Stewards chayne at his Lords enstalling at
Windsore').[2] He once took pains to set down in a bond the
exact place at which he was to repay the loan; in order,
said the lender after waiting there on the day in vain, to be
sure to avoid the spot. Penniless again, he offered to give
any sort of bond in return for twenty pounds from the
same friend; that humorist bound him hand and foot to a
bench of four-inch plank, as the only bond he would not
break. For raising a slander on Lesbia, she threatened to
sue him, but was pacified by his saying that he spoke in
drink. Even when sober ('which is but seld'), he feigns
himself drunk and reels as he walks, in order that when he
is drunk his friends may say, ''tis but his fashion.' [3]

That Haryngton ran foul so often of Barnes shows that
they moved more or less in the same London orbit. Both
were followers of Essex; both were friends of Bastard, to
whom Haryngton addressed three epigrams; [4] and above
all, Haryngton was a close friend of Bishop Matthew, as he
proved by writing our best account of the Bishop and his

1 *Letters and Epigrams of Sir John Harington*, ed. N. E. McClure (Philadelphia,
   1930), nos. 138, 170, 184, 211, 243, 371.
2 Ed. McKerrow, III, 103.   3 Nos. 170, 253, 349, 371, 395.
4 Nos. 160, 180, 358.

wit.[1] The relations between Haryngton and Barnes seem to have known as many changes as an April day. Sometimes they are friends; then Barnes complains of being forgotten of late, and offers to be Haryngton's guest; but Sir John, who has had experience of this 'ill ghest,' finds it the chief consolation of living at Kew that he will see Barnes there but seldom. Barnes presses Haryngton to lend him twenty or thirty shillings, swearing 'God damn him, hee'd repai't to morrow,' and either goes off cursing Haryngton for refusing, or is happy to get fifteen (compare his many forty-shilling borrowings in 1598, as well as his debt of three hundred pounds). He seeks gain as an informer by reporting a remark of Haryngton's about Henry VIII, and by trying to draw him out on the succession to the crown. In friendly sort he comes to remonstrate that Haryngton has raised a slander of his keeping a great lady; it is notorious, Sir John retorts, that she keeps him.[2]

Of late, says Haryngton, presumably in 1593, Barnes is proud because the stationers sell his books, and thinks himself 'a great endyter' — an illusion of which the satirist tries to cure him. He begs rewards, perhaps for his verses. Finding him angered, 'Because I said, he wrote but like a scholler,' Haryngton hastens to assure him that the criticism did not mean to imply that he had any learning. As a woman selects for praise one who is in no danger of rivaling her, so Barnes praises Churchyard, not Sidney, Daniel, Constable, or Spenser.[3] He finds fault with *The Metamorphosis of Ajax*, but Haryngton on sinks is better

---

1 *Nugae Antiquae*, ed. 1804, II, 255.

2 Nos. 194, 217, 243, 270, 316, 351, 397.

3 As a matter of fact, Barnes praised Sidney and 'Diuinest morall Spencer' in Canzon 2 and in his sonnet on Harvey, and Sidney again in Sonnet 95 and later in the *Offices*. Haryngton, who declares of Lynus' verses, 'I read some three or foure, and passe the rest,' was probably thinking of some particular

than Barnes on scepters. The 'foolish Satyrist' out of his gall is planning a bitter satire against Haryngton, but no one will think it worth reading, for Ralegh 'sweares, That *Lynus* verse best suits with *Mydas* eares.' When Barnes 'thinkes that he and I are friends,' he sends Sir John all his poems to be criticized and corrected:

> His Disticks, Satyrs, Sonnets, and Exameters,
> His Epigrams, his Lyricks, his Pentameters.

Of all English poets in the 1590's, Barnes is metrically the most adventurous. Haryngton's judgement agrees with Ralegh's: his rime is harsh, his number uneven, 'His words too strange, his meanings are too mistick.'[1] All this fits Barnes to a T.

Haryngton also writes that 'Pure *Lynus*' accuses him and his writings as Papist.[2] We may say with Maria, 'The devil of a Puritan that he is, or anything constantly, but a time-pleaser.' After *Parthenophil*, however, in which he addresses the Virgin (or a virgin) in Ode 3, Barnes at least assumed a very Protestant attitude, and he utters fierce invectives against Papistry in the *Divine Century* and the *Devil's Charter*.

But the most vivid flashlight upon the life of Barnes, if indeed he is Lynus, comes in Epigram 212, 'Against an vnthrifty *Lynus*':

> Many men maruaile *Lynus* doth not thriue,
> That had more trades then any man aliue;
> As first, a Broker, then a Petty-fogger,
> A Traueller, a Gamster, and a Cogger,

---

occasion on which Barnes praised Churchyard; that he did so is a safe in-ference from the otherwise unaccountable fact that the old poet in turn praised him.

1 Nos. 10, 11, 14, 47, 68, 107, 196, 210, 378.
2 No. 365.

A Coyner, a Promoter, and a Bawde,
A Spy, a Practicer in euery fraude:
   And missing thrift by these lewd trades and sinister,
   He takes the best, yet proues the worst, a Minister.

These are trades in which men rarely leave records of their activities, but they accord well enough with Barnes' general character.[1] In becoming a minister, he would only be following the example of Fulwell and Gosson and setting still another for the Reverend John Marston and the Very Reverend John Donne and Robert Daborne, who 'died amphibious by the ministry.' It is certainly a career one would expect Barnes to have turned toward for a livelihood, remembering the rich preferments of his brother Emanuel, and above all the great power of their father's friend and executor, Bishop Matthew. Barnabe may have had a personal motive for writing divine sonnets and dedicating them to Matthew so soon after the latter became a bishop. It does not necessarily follow that he ever carried out his intention of taking orders. Haryngton probably wrote on hearing the first news of the matter, which is not always the last, and indeed the ground of his jest may have been the *Divine Century of Spiritual Sonnets* — 'such another deuice it is,' declared Nashe, 'as the godly Ballet of *Iohn Carelesse*, or the Song of *Greene sleeues* moralized.'[2]

We do not really know, however, what Barnes was doing after 1598, and in fact our information is not full enough to make the identification with Lynus absolutely certain. Yet the field is limited to a very few names by the fact

1 As to 'Petty-fogger,' he may have spent a year or so at an Inn of Chancery before going to the wars; cf. his love of legal metaphor. As to 'Spy,' his intimacy with Saunderson makes it likely enough that he may have occasionally been employed by Matthew or Burghley; but evidence is lacking. No relationship is traceable with the active spy Thomas Barnes; and 'Barnaby,' also employed in the Mary Stuart correspondence, appears too early, in 1576 (Conyers Read, *Mr. Secretary Walsingham*, III, 65 ff.).
2 Ed. McKerrow, III, 104.

that Lynus is one who has published books of verse, written in a notable variety of meters: moreover, he is a famous evader of the truth, and once a soldier yet 'valiant as a Gander.' Finally, Professor Moore Smith observes that the only poets of the time 'bred in Brazen-nose' were Barnes and Marston, to whom we may add Barnfield. Marston entered the Church, but not until 1609, five years after Haryngton wrote the last of his epigrams. Neither he nor Barnfield can be recognized in the very detailed description of Lynus, while this is a close enough likeness of Barnes, so far as we can judge, to make it at least a reasonable conjecture that it is his portrait.

A much more evident satiric sketch of Barnes, I believe, is found in Middleton's gay little pamphlet, *The Black Book*, published in 1604. The allusion here has never been guessed at, though the name is hardly at all disguised, but it becomes rather striking now that the Star Chamber case has thrown into stronger light Barnabe's passion for smoking. The Devil is making his will:

But turning my Legacie to you-ward, *Barnaby Burning-glasse*, Arch Tabacco-taker of *England*, in Ordynaries, vppon Stages both common and priuate, and lastly, in the Lodging of your Drabbe and Mistresse: I am not a little proud, I can tell you *Barnaby*, that you daunce after my Pipe so long: and for all Counterblasts and *Tabacco-Nashes* (which some call Raylers) you are not blowne away, nor your fierie thirst quencht with the small Penny-Ale of their contradictions, but still suck that dug of damnation, with a long nipple, still burning that rare *Phœnix* of *Phlegiton* Tabacco, that from her ashes burnt and knockt out, may arise another pipefull: Therefore I giue and bequeath vnto thee, a breath of all religions, saue the true one, and tasting of all countries, saue his owne: a brayne well sooted, where the Muses hang vp in the smoake like red Herrings: and looke how the narrow alley of thy pipe showes in the inside, so shall all the pipes through thy body.[1]

---

1 From the original; cf. *Works of Thomas Middleton*, ed. Bullen, VIII, 42–43.

The only editor who has offered an interpretation is
Mr. A. V. Judges,[1] who explains it thus:

> A dig at Barnabe Rich, author of *A Looking-glass for Ireland* (1599),
> and an enemy of tobacco-taking. His most vigorous denunciation of
> smoking appears in *The Irish Hubbub* (1617).

This seems a curious mode of reasoning, if it implies that
Middleton was satirizing an opinion first expressed, so far
as I can find, in a book published thirteen years later, and
then by '*an enemy of tobacco-taking*.' Unlike Captain
Rich, Barnabe Barnes was no enemy but a missionary too
ardent for even the author of the *Defence of Tobacco*, and
as the friend of Anthony Chute he, if anyone, belonged
to 'the smoakie Societie,' as Nashe christened it, of the
Knights of Tobacco.[2] Middleton, thoroughly familiar with
the works of Nashe, before he wrote of tobacco would
naturally remember these pages on Chute and Barnes, and
when he went out of his way to pun on Nashe's name that
Barnes, too, might remember, it would be with a deliber-
ate love of mischief.

1 *The Elizabethan Underworld* (London, 1930), p. 509.
2 Ed. McKerrow, III, 106-107, and see Robert J. Kane, 'Anthony Chute,
  Thomas Nashe, and the First English Work on Tobacco,' *R.E.S.*, VII (1931),
  155.

VII. BORGIA AND MACHIAVEL

Alexander VI. For in this Man there is a mind intelligent,
                 A quickening word and a celestial spirit,
                 That like a lightning every way diffused
                 All things which are made by the mighty power
                 Uniteth, moveth, and replenisheth.
The Devil.   These things should have been thought upon before.
                                                The Devil's Charter, ll. 3177–82

THE escaped criminal who in 1598 set at naught the authority of the Privy Council next reappears in London
dedicating to King James a book on the duties of a Privy
Councilor, as well as of a Lord Treasurer, judge, and general, and especially on the necessary moral virtues. *Foure
Bookes Of Offices: enabling privat persons for the speciall
service of all good princes and policies* was entered in the
Stationers' Register on February 3, 1605–6 and bears the
imprint 1606, so that presumably Barnes made a slip when
he wrote the date 10 May 1605 in a copy which he
inscribed to Northampton.[1] He mentions that he has already presented his work to the hands of the King, and no
doubt he also sent copies to the other Privy Councilors
and to all whose interest in government might be supposed
strong enough to pry open their purses. For it was a large
and expensive folio, published at the joint charges of
Bishop, Adams, and Burby, and to get it published at all
Barnes must have had either a subsidy from William
Percy or a strong subscription list.[2]

Of Offices was ushered in with verses by 'W. Percy
Mvsophilvs,' by 'Iohn Ford, in commendation of his very
good friend the Author,' and by what were to Grosart
'unknown names,' including 'Tho: Campion Doctor in

---

1 Facsimile in Grosart's edition of Barnes' poems; see p. 234.
2 The printer, Adam Islip, Wolfe's successor, had printed Percy's *Coelia*.

Physicke.' The other two were Thomas Michelborne (the friend of Campion and of Percy), 'To my singular good friend Master *Barnabe Barnes*,' and Robert Hasill.[1] Ford made his first appearance as an author in this volume, and his second in his *Fame's Memorial* on the death of Devonshire the same year, to which Barnes contributed a madrigal.[2] This friendship with a boy of twenty shows that Barnes still frequented London and had perhaps made one in Devonshire's literary following. His friend Bastard had found his chief patron in the Earl, to whom he dedicated *Chrestoleros*. Since even in complimentary verses there may reside some kernel of truth, let us see what can be winnowed. Campion praises the work, but says nothing at all of the author; Percy calls him the only writer on government to join divine with secular knowledge (praise appropriate if Barnes was then a clergyman); and Ford entreats him:

> Write on rare Myrrour of these abiect dayes;
> Thy good example others will aduise:

he will be a precedent to youth. Our ignorance of his manner of life since 1598 permits us to hope, if not to believe, that he had really become a changed spirit.

The book which Barnes calls his 'accedence to gouernment,' or 'true loue knot, and labyrinth of vertues with their opposites,' is little but a long display of edifying moral sentiment. The virtuous author marvels that the English should 'so much encline to that Dutch distemper-

---

1 The British Museum copy has no verses, but they appear in the Bodleian and Harvard copies. A Robert Hassall wrote in 1601 a *Lamentable Mone of a Soldier for the losse of his derely beloued Lorde*, apparently Essex (*Roxburghe Ballads*, VIII[2], clxx*).

2 This fact is overlooked when it is suggested that Barnes' friend was not the poet but his cousin of Gray's Inn. It has been pointed out that Ford remembered the name Parthenophil in *The Lover's Melancholy*, and the mechanical chair from *The Devil's Charter* in *The Broken Heart* (Grosart, p. 235; *Works of Ford*, ed. Gifford-Dyce, I, 302).

ature of drunkennesse'; and next to that vice the most
wasteful is the love of 'exterior new-fangled robes.' 'How
odious,' he cries, 'is the very name of homicide, by whose
violence man which is the goodliest artifice of nature is
dissolved!' He speaks of himself only fleetingly: of his
finding by good experience 'of my selfe and others most
neere vnto me' that nothing vanisheth sooner than remembrance of benefits; of his hatred of flattery, 'that
fault (for which I detest to conuerse in the houses of great
princes)'; how 'my practise in warres hath bene very
little,' and the time he did spend wasted 'through the
vaine weakenesse of my greene and vnstayed head.' There
is little in the book that escapes from commonplace except
the recurring praises of Essex and 'An Exhortation to
make famous and precious our English language amongst
all partes of Christendome.'

Yet one passage in the *Offices* has a curious connection
with the poisoning. Barnes is denouncing stratagems because they infringe faith and honesty:

as *Macrobius* captaine of the Carthagenians vsed the Assirians his
enemies, whom (being drunke with wine, and mandragoras) he most
insidiously slaughtered. [1]

This would tell us nothing did we not happen to have
Gabriel Harvey's copy of Frontinus, now at Harvard. The
same exploit, which Frontinus tells of Maharbal against
a tribe of Africans, sets Harvey to filling the margins with
authorities and examples:

Cunning Empoisonment*es*. Mercurialis de Venenis . . . Monsieur
Renes perfumid glooues, dublet*es*, apples, &c.
Ons deuise, to conquer Virginia, with Sugar, & Arsenick, cunningly
mixt. [2]

---

1 *Offices*, p. 208.
2 *Strategemes*, tr. Sir Richard Moryson, 1539, II, v, 12 (sig. F 4); quoted less
   accurately by F. Marcham, *Lopez the Jew* (1927), p. 17.

Barnes' absurd 'Macrobius' and 'Assirians' indicate clearly that he was drawing on his memory, and it would not be at all surprising if he had the story from Harvey years before, whether through borrowing Frontinus with Harvey's notes, or more likely through conversation which ranged from Carthage to Virginia. Whose ingenious notion it was (brilliantly anticipating modern chemical warfare) thus to abolish the American Indian, we cannot know; but I should be willing to wager that Barnes remembered it, as well as M. Réné's perfumed apples, when he chose as his weapons against Browne, first the perfumed lemon, then sugar and mercury cunningly mixed.

The Divils Charter, or *The Tragœdie of Alexander the 6*, was acted before James by the King's Men on Candlemas Night, 1606-7. Barnes corrected and augmented it 'for the more pleasure and profit of the Reader': the first dramatist, says Creizenach, to announce that he had taken pains to please the reading public.[1] He dedicated the play 'To the Honorable and his Very Deare Friends,' Sir William Herbert and Sir William Pope. The Library of Congress copy has a further address of ten lines to these patrons, not present in the copies known to modern editors.[2]

It is hard to imagine what induced Shakespeare's company to choose this crude melodrama for Court performance, to close a Christmas begun with *King Lear*. The explanation I should suggest is that James had liked *Macbeth* and wanted another play with even more demonology, which Shakespeare was in no mood to write. Shakespeare, going his own way, produced *Lear*, and Barnes, writing to order, *The Devil's Charter*. As with Spenser, the enthusi-

1 *English Drama in the Age of Shakespeare*, p. 86.
2 R. B. McKerrow, *Materialien*, VI, 1904; J. S. Farmer, *Tudor Facsimile Texts*, 1913.

asms which Barnes in his youth had shared with Harvey
seem to have endured, for in the *Offices* he treated Harvey's
central conception, the perfect statesman, and in his
tragedy he took the historical part from one of 'the sweet
Doctor's' two favorite books: '*Guicciardines* siluer Historie,
and *Ariostos* golden Cantoes.'¹ Guicciardine himself acts
as chorus, like Gower in *Pericles*.

Himself a practiser of the art of poisoning, Barnes had
no hesitation in choosing for his subject the most illustrious specialists in that art — the Borgias; and under the
guise of displaying God's revenge against murder and
against the papacy, he gloats over their virtuosity. Com-
pensating in literature for what was denied him in life, he
extinguishes characters by means of a poisoned cosmetic,
by aspics ('*Cleopatraes* birds,' 'proud wormes'), and by
'a noble Nipster' of wine mixed with poison, the efficacy
of which has already been scientifically tested at varying
strengths on three condemned criminals, with the most
gratifying results. His murderers like to explain what a
kindness they are doing their victims, 'To giue you waft-
age to the *Elisian* fields.'

For us, unless we share the taste of James for incanta-
tions, or of Barnes for poisoning, the chief interest lies in
the pair of rollicking bravos, with their conjurations by
mulled sack and Peter-see-me and by a remarkable list of
London courtesans. Barnes, like the bravos, had gone
'armed all in sacke' and inspired his courage by 'head
strong Maluesie' and the reward of 'a rich purse cram'd
with red crusadoes.' Throughout he draws with gusto
from his own experience, and does not even avoid the
mention of mercury sublimate: 'thou confectionary vil-
leine:' cries Baglioni to the slain apothecary, 'where is
your sublimatum now sir?' Barnes probably idealized

¹ *Harvey's Works*, ed. Grosart, I, 191.

himself as a master criminal much in the fashion of Fresco-baldi, who calls himself 'Secret as mid-night, sure as the sunne, quick as the waters' — into which Caesar Borgia promptly casts him after his victim. His soliloquy might almost have been spoken by Barnes:

> I was the first that from the *Swisse* quarter in the raigne of king *Ferdinand* brought vp in his army the fashions of bowsing and tows-ing *Greeke* and *Spanish* wines by the flagon . . . well I will second my Lord in any slaughter for his wages, and if any man will giue me better hiers (when I haue seru'd the Cardinalls turne) I will present my pistoll vpon his sacred person afterward for charities sake. . . .[1]

In the *Offices*, where he speaks of all the other courts, Barnes makes no mention of Star Chamber; but he was not sensitive about it, for in the very first lines of the play Guicciardine introduces himself as

> Sent from the Christall Palace of true *Fame*,
> And bright Starre-Chamber of eternall soules.

A MS. play, *The Battle of Hexham*, listed after *The Devil's Charter* under Barnaby Barnes, was sold with Isaac Reed's library in 1807,[2] and has not been heard of since. If this were extant, it would have an additional interest now that we know Hexham as Browne's bailiwick and Eure's residence while warden. From notes in British Museum and Harvard copies of the catalogue I find that while the *Devil's Charter* quarto brought a pound, the *Battle of Hexham* MS. went for one shilling. This suggests that it was either a fragment or in bad condition.[3] In 1624

---

1 Ed. McKerrow, ll. 1385–87, 1395–98.
2 Bullen remarks in the *D.N.B.* that he could not find it in the catalogue, *Bibliotheca Reediana*; but it is no. 7699, p. 348. Those writers are in error who call it *The Battle of Evesham*.
3 Thomas Park, who collected whatever he could find of Barnes, says nothing of *The Battle of Hexham*, even in 1815 (*Heliconia*, II). Colman the younger wrote a musical drama of this name, acted in 1789 and printed at Dublin in 1790 and at London not until 1808. It occurs to me that a MS. of his play

Herbert licensed '*The Madcap*: Written by Barnes,'[1] who may or may not have been Barnabe.

Since Barnes is not among the poets included in *English Literary Autographs*,[2] it may be useful to point out where examples of his hand may be seen. Beside the inscription to Northampton reproduced by Grosart, his signature occurs no less than twenty-eight times in his Star Chamber examination, and once each in his subscription to the Thirty-Nine Articles at Oxford and in his Durham Chancery deposition. I have found it also in a book now in the library of York Minster: *Il Prencipe*, in the edition which masquerades under a title-page dated at Palermo in 1584, but which was really printed by John Wolfe at London.[3]

It is appropriate that the volume to survive should have been Machiavelli, whom Barnes must often have discussed with Harvey and Wolfe. Indeed, *The Prince* is the very book which suggested his *Offices*, and in the dedication to King James he names it, with appropriate horror:

> Vile is that wretched analogie, which the corrupt Florentine Secretarie *Nicolo Machiauelli* seruant to Duke *Petro di Medici*, did in his puddle of princely policies produce betwixt a true Prince and a mixt monster; resembling him . . . vnto a lion & a fox.

His 'puddle of princely policies'! Indignation makes, if not verses, at least alliteration. The margin supplies the exact reference: '*Il Prencipe cap. 18 comme se debbe osseruar la fede.*' The lion, indeed, is very welcome: 'that aufull magistrate (if of his Maiestie men may so terme the Lyon . . .) is another portly representation of a perfect Prince:' but Barnes is firm as to the fox:

may have been catalogued by title instead of by author, in which case it would alphabetically follow the entry under Barnes, but this would have been a curious error.

1 Chalmers, *Supplemental Apology*, p. 218.
2 Cf. Moore Smith, *Mod. Lang. Rev.*, xxiv (1929), 215.
3 See authorities cited by H. Sellers, *4 The Library*, v (1925), 108.

BARNES' AUTOGRAPH IN HIS MACHIAVELLI

whereas it is well knowen, how no true prince can aptly be compared
to that vnsauory curre. . . .

Yet Michelborne declared Barnabe's book, which is all on
this level,

> NIL VLTRA, and the farthest continent
> That wisest statist euer yet did runne,
> Within this world of ciuill gouernment:
>   And as the woorke, so doth the style excell
>   That of *Boterus, Bodin, Machiauell.*

Il Prencipe came to York with the library of Archbishop
Matthew, and so did the dedication copy of the *Divine
Century* which Barnes presented to him, bound in vellum
with a gold border and each page ornamented.[1] This is
one of the earliest of a stream of similarly bound and dedicated books with autograph inscriptions to Matthew from
Coke, Casaubon, Saravia, and many ecclesiastics and
Oxonians. Florio sent *A World of Words* with an Italian
inscription; and Haryngton seems to have contributed his
1602 MS. *Tract on the Succession to the Crown.* Matthew
acquired many books which bear the signature and motto
of Bishop Barnes or of Emanuel or John; and we should
certainly find more of Barnabe's, had not lighter literature
been considered below the dignity of a cathedral library.

This turning up of one of the very books Barnes owned
leads to an interesting discovery as to his sources for *The
Devil's Charter.* Dr. McKerrow, in the excellent introduc-
tion to his edition, saw no reason to suppose that Barnes
had used any other source than Guicciardini for the historical part of the play. This leaves unexplained, however,
the striking situation in which 'warlike *Kate,* the pride of
Italie' (l. 2168), from the height of her citadel in Forli,
bids defiance to Caesar Borgia in spite of his threats to

---

1 James Raine, *Catalogue of the Printed Books in the Library of the Dean and
Chapter of York,* p. 282; Joseph Hunter in *Add. MS.* 24487.

kill her two sons. Barnes had doubtless read or seen on the stage the similar incident in *George-a-Green*, but he is not simply enlivening Guicciardini with a bit of effective theater. It was precisely at Forli that history or legend located this episode, in a siege eleven years earlier than Borgia's, and Katherine Sforza was, as Barnes represents her, the heroine. He has developed the situation in part from *George-a-Green* and in part from his imagination, but the book in which he found the historical basis for the story was probably his copy of Machiavelli's *Discorsi sopra la prima deca di Tito Livio* (iii, 6). For Wolfe did not issue *Il Prencipe* alone: he published the *Discorsi* at the same time under the same fictitious imprint, and the two books are generally bound in one volume. Machiavelli tells the story again in another of his works which Wolfe printed, the *Florentine History*,[1] and Lodovico Guicciardini has it in his *Hore di recreatione*,[2] but Barnes may or may not have known these books, whereas we can put beyond doubt his use of the *Discorsi*. On the name of Baglioni, one of Caesar Borgia's bravos in the play, Dr. McKerrow notes that it is frequent in Guicciardini; but if we look at the *Offices* (p. 175) we find that Barnes had already, a year earlier than *The Devil's Charter*, told an anecdote of the Baglioni when they were masters of Perugia. The marginal reference Barnes himself gives for the story is to Machiavelli's *Discorsi* (iii, 14).[3] This explicit citation completes the chain of evidence that Guicciardini was not the sole historical source for the play, but that Barnes found the kernel for one of his best scenes in the perilous but fascinating pages of Machiavelli.

1 Book viii; Bedingfield, in the *Tudor Translations*, p. 418.
2 Ed. Venice, 1610, pp. 207 f.
3 Not noticed by Edward Meyer, *Machiavelli and the Elizabethan Drama* (Weimar, 1897), pp. 109 ff.

VIII. THE POET

Behold, within that shady thick,
  Where my Parthenophe doth walk!
Her beauty makes trees moving quick,
  Which of her grace in murmur talk: . . .
  The blossomed hawthorn, white as chalk . . .
Sweet cypress, set in sundry places,
  And singing Atis tells
Unto the rest my Mistress' graces.
Parthenophil, Ode 9.

As a poet, Barnes has been something of a critic's tennis ball, tossed first too high, then volleyed back and forth, and now and then smashed to earth. Dowden called him 'one of the most exquisite' of Elizabethans;[1] Courthope denounced him as an 'idiot.'[2] Each critic has found in Barnes what he was looking for: Dowden, a 'passionate delight in beauty'; Bullen, that Barnes was 'a born singer'; Lee, that he had evidently read French; Courthope, that like other sonneteers he wrote nonsense. The true cleavage between the critics lies in their estimates of the Elizabethan sonnet, according as it leaves each delighted or entertained, bored or stirred to wrath: feelings which it is capable of arousing at different times even in the same reader. Barnes has been commonly singled out for criticism because, though the least typical, he is the most striking of the lesser sonneteers. There is no real question that among Elizabethan sonnet-sequences *Parthenophil* stands about midway. Some will care more for the craftsmanship and grace of Watson and Constable, others for Barnes' energy and sparks of poetic fire.

Anyone collecting examples of how not to write poetry would find Barnes a treasure-house: his triumphs of bathos

1 *Academy*, September 2, 1876.
2 *History of English Poetry*, II, 304.

and bad taste, his conceits from law and clocks and punctu-
ation marks, his seeking 'to take the heaven of poetry by
violence,' [1] his passion for apostrophe, echo, and feminine
endings, his parade of intimacy with the best families on
Olympus, and a hundred other absurdities that 'would
make merry Th'infernal souls.' [2] Many of his poems are
pure dross, and no one of them is free from it. He has been
so over-praised that it is necessary to make this perfectly
clear, granting at the same time that whoever goes to his
poems resolutely prepared for the worst will often be surprised by random beauty. Excellent critics have admired
his 'rare imaginative ardour,' his 'splendour of imagery,'
his 'fire and poetical virility and fullbloodedness,' his
thorough originality both in form and treatment.[3] For
while he naturally wrote on many conventional themes,
Barnes avoided translation or important borrowing of language and spoke with his own voice, in a far from conventional tone.[4] Breaking away from Petrarchan adoration,
he brought into English in several of his poems a frank
Hellenic passion. He further resembles Swinburne in ve-
hemence, and in variety, though not mastery, of meter.
Parthenophil, on the whole, is a somewhat remarkable
achievement for a boy hardly twenty-two.

The seeds of poetry that were in Barnes never ripened,
because there was no deepness of earth. For all his passionate striving after beauty, he attained only a confused

1 F. S. Boas, in *A History of English Literature*, ed. Buchan, p. 142.
2 *Parthenophil*, Ode 16.
3 Ward, *English Dramatic Literature*, II, 626; Gosse, in Garnett and Gosse, *English Literature*, II, 261; Saintsbury, *Elizabethan Literature*, p. 108 (cf. his *History of English Prosody*, II, 151); Boas, *loc. cit.*
4 Lee's assertions as to 'sources' have been superseded by the careful work of
Janet G. Scott, *Les sonnets élisabéthains* (Paris: Honoré Champion, 1929),
chap. v and pp. 217, 309. This is the best study that has been made of Barnes'
poems. For earlier writers on sources see the full bibliography in H. K. Has-
selkuss, *Der Petrarkismus* (Münster diss., 1927).

richness of sensuous imagery, no more to be compared with
the true poetry of Campion than Imagist verse with that
of Miss Millay. 'To none but to Prometheus me compare,' he wrote, but he was more like Phaethon, great only
in his desires; juvenile, impetuous, and mischievous as his
Cupid,

>   A fiery boy outmatching the moonlight. [1]

[1] *Parthenophil*, Elegy 10.

LODOWICK BRYSKETT
AND HIS FAMILY
By DEBORAH JONES

CONTENTS

I. BRYSKETT AND *LYCIDAS*

LODOWICK BRYSKETT, Sidney's congenial companion on the Grand Tour and Spenser's friend in Ireland, — the "lodwick" of the thirty-third sonnet in the *Amoretti* [1] — has, like other minor Elizabethans, been gradually coming into his own of late years. His *Discovrse of Civill Life* indeed has not yet received the new edition which it deserves, if only for its picture of his happy intercourse with Spenser and other friends during the Irish years. But in 1914 W. P. Mustard of Johns Hopkins University published an illuminating little article [2] called *Lodowick Brysket and Bernardo Tasso*, in which he showed that Bryskett's other two works, the elegies on Sidney, *The Mourning Muse of Thestylis* and the *Pastorall Aeglogue*, were paraphrased from Tasso's *Selva nella morte del Signor Aluigi da Gonzaga* and his first Eclogue, *Alcippo*, respectively. More lately, in 1927, Henry R. Plomer and Tom Peete Cross published their monograph, *The Life and Correspondence of Lodowick Bryskett*, based largely on re-

[1]   Great wrong I doe, I can it not deny,
            to that most sacred Empresse my dear dred,
            not finishing her Queene of faëry,
            that mote enlarge her liuing prayses dead:
        But lodwick, this of grace to me aread:
            doe ye not thinck th' accomplishment of it,
            sufficient worke for one mans simple head,
            all were it as the rest, but rudely writ.
        How then should I without another wit:
            thinck euer to endure so tædious toyle,
            sins that this one is tost with troublous fit,
            of a proud loue, that doth my spirite spoyle.
        Ceasse then, till she vouchsafe to grawnt me rest,
            or lend you me another liuing brest.

[2] *American Journal of Philology*, xxxv, 192–199.

search among the Elizabethan State Papers and certain other documents in the Public Record Office and on the Hatfield Manuscripts.

The present article also had its inception in the Public Record Office, where Dr. Charles Sisson found Bryskett himself deposing in a Chancery suit involving numerous members of his family, and where indeed there is an endless number of papers bearing on the ramifications of that family.

Bryskett's claim to our interest, beyond such little as he intrinsically deserves, does not rest solely on his relations with Sidney and Spenser. For in taking my dutiful way through the rather sparse woods of his elegiac fancy, I caught a sound that I knew well; and in pursuing it, came to think that of the haunting interwoven memories in *Lycidas* a few may have echoed from here.

I do not forget that in entering the realm of pastoral elegy, both Milton and Bryskett were walking on much-trodden ground; that often when Milton steps in the earlier poet's footprints it is only because there lies the common path. Consequently we must look rather for verbal reminiscence than for parallel of idea.

For elegies of this sort had an accepted ritual. Both mourner and mourned were shepherds. The mourner invoked the Muses for inspiration; reproached the local nymphs and deities for neglecting the dead shepherd; called for (and received) the sympathy of inanimate nature; and found consolation in believing that the dead had gone into a better world. Elegies, whether pastoral or not, set forth the gifts and accomplishments of the lamented, and if he had died young told what he might have done had he lived longer.[1]

Milton, as is well known, was bountifully acquainted

1 H. M. Percival's edition of *Lycidas*, 1914, p. 5.

with these, as with other kinds of literature; already sources and parallels for this single poem of that erudite young man have been found in Hesiod, Theocritus, Moschus, Bion, Virgil, Horace, Ovid, Dante, Petrarch, Mantuan, Sannazaro, Castiglione, Giambattista Amalteo, Vida, Boccaccio, Andrea Navagero, Giraldi Cinthio, Euricius Cordus, George Buchanan, Sir Edward Dyer, Campion, Drayton, Herrick, Peele, William Browne, Shakspere, Phineas Fletcher, and Spenser's *Astrophel*, *Tears of the Muses*, and *Shepherds' Calendar*.[1]

The numerous references to Spenser, and to his *Astrophel* in particular, make it seem curious that Bryskett's two elegies which were printed in that same volume with *Astrophel* should not have been considered in this connection.[2]

The Mourning Muse of Thestylis begins with a conventional invocation to the Nymphs,[3] significant to us only in

1 Except Drayton, all these are mentioned in Sir John Edwin Sandys's article (*Transactions of the Royal Society of Literature*, Second Series, xxxii, 233–263), which Professor Lowes tells me is the most thorough study so far. The Rev. W. Tuckwell in the notes to his edition of *Lycidas* notes many of these names, and adds Drayton (p. 59), and also (p. 61) the ancient hymn of Callistratus on Harmodius. H. M. Percival in his edition of *Lycidas* (p. 11) cites Jonson's *Sad Shepherd*, which was written before *Lycidas* but not published till after.

2 As a matter of fact, after reading many editions of *Lycidas* I have found in A. W. Verity's *Cambridge Milton for Schools*, 1891, the following notices:
On p. 128, note to l. 41 of *Lycidas*: "There is a similar passage in *The Mourning Muse of Thestylis*, 143–144."
On p. 155, note to l. 160 (he mentions Milton's changing "Corinneus" to "Bellerus"): "Cf. also *The Morning* (sic) *Muse of Thestylis*, 31, and *F. Q.* II. 10. 12."
On p. 158, "The *Shepheards Cal. November*, the *Morning Muse of Thestylis*, and the *Lay of Clorinda* all close on the same note of resignation and comfort." The first of these I had not already discovered for myself. I am glad of this editor's corroboration, and do not wish to seem churlish in saying that this appears to me the weakest of the parallels, because it is the purely conventional lament of nature (cf. p. 249 below). Verity does not mention the *Pastorall Aeglogue*. The parallels now strike me as so obvious that I live in the daily expectation of finding that someone else has noticed them long ago.

3 Imitated from Theocritus, 1, 66; and in Virgil, *Ecl.*, x, 9 (Tuckwell's edition of *Lycidas*, p. 33).

connection with other likenesses. Mars is then called upon:

> Ah dreadful *Mars* why didst thou not thy knight defend?

Sidney having died on the battle-field; just as Milton reproaches the sea-nymphs for their neglect. "Thou hast in Britons valour," continues Bryskett, "tane delight of old" — a line that would have caught Milton's attention, with his delight in ancient British history; and he answers himself, as Milton does, that the tutelary genius must have been far away:

> Thou hast estrang'd thy self, and deignest not our land:
> Farre off to others now, thy fauour honour breeds,
>   And high disdaine doth cause thee shun our clime (I feare).

Moreover, as "Lycidas is dead, dead ere his prime, Young Lycidas," so is Sidney too young:

> Whom spitefull death hath pluct vntimely from the tree,
> Whiles yet his yeares in flowre, did promise worthie frute.

There then arose an old and lamenting deity. Milton's was "Camus, reverend sire, . . . His mantle hairy and his bonnet sedge", and his lament was brief and bitter. Bryskett's, less appropriately, it would seem, was Corineus, that companion of Brutus's whom the legendary histories of Britain make the ruler of Cornwall, from whom her name derives:

> Vp from his tombe the mightie *Corineus* rose,
> Who cursing oft the fates that this mishap had bred,
> His hoary locks he tare, calling the heauens vnkinde.

One wonders whether possibly the common phrase "Hoary locks" here — the sound of "hoary" and the sense of "locks" — may have contributed to Camus's "mantle hairy." But Bryskett's Corineus, if my hypothesis is right, seems to have come into Milton's mind at another point as well; for in his original draft [1] he wrote,

> Or whether thou to our moist vows denied
> Sleep'st by the fable of Corinneus old,

later altering "Corinneus" in the margin to "Bellerus." [2]

In two other instances Milton has, whether intentionally or not, set himself further from his sources by the alteration of a word. His "rathe primrose that forsaken dies" originally died "unwedded," like Shakspere's.[3] Again, he seems to have checked himself in using the familiar rhetorical device of repetition, for his manuscript reads

> for [young, *struck out*] Lycidas is dead, dead ere his prime,
> young Lycidas, etc.,

as if he had been afraid of plagiarizing Spenser's

> Young *Astrophel* the pride of shepheards praise,
> Young *Astrophel* the rusticke lasses loue.[4]

Corineus's lament is followed by that of all nature, a pastoral commonplace.[5] Out of this universal grief, inter-

1 The Cambridge MS., edited by the Rev. W. Tuckwell, 1911.
2 Cf. p. 247, n. 2.
3 Tuckwell's edition, p. 53, notes.
4 Spenser, *Astrophel*, ll. 7–8. Verity (edition of *Lycidas*, p. 121) notes this as a recognized trick to gain the pathetic effect. Milton of course made this alteration primarily in order not to waste the force of his adjective on the first line, where, as Miss Erma Gebhart points out, it is less effective than in the second.
5 Tuckwell, *op. cit.*, p. 35. He compares Theocritus, I, 71, and Virgil, *Ecl.*, x, 13. The corresponding passages to *Lycidas*, ll. 39–44, are *Movrning Mvse*, ll. 34–44, and, as Verity says, ll. 143–145. Cf. also Tasso, *Selva nella morte del Signor Aluigi da Gonzaga* (Mustard, *op. cit.*):

> "Lui piansero le piante; e d'ogn' intorno
> Spogliar d'ombre il terren, lui dolcemente
> Pianser gli augelli; e'l gran padre Appennino
> Vscendo fuor del cauernoso monte
> Si uolse contra il cielo, e feramente
> Accusò i fati, e'l suo crudel destino;

rupted in Lycidas by the digression on fame, comes the
sea-deity with restraining speech: Milton's "Herald of the
Sea," Triton, "that came in Neptune's plea"; and Bryskett's "old father *Ocean* hoare,

> Who graue with eld, and full of maiestie in sight,"

merely tells the mourners that their tears are in vain.

For the next hundred and twenty lines no parallels appear, unless Bryskett's Medway "that wont so still to
slide" overflowed into Milton's "smooth-sliding Mincius";
and indeed one of the contrasts between *Lycidas* and the
other poems in memory of King is noteworthy here, that
whereas Milton insists upon the calm weather, Bryskett
indulges in the more obvious drama of a storm, his Aeolus
making war on Neptune instead of appearing as a sort of
ally. But through all this turmoil Sidney was on his way
to a Paradise of mingled Christianity and paganism,[1] to
endless bliss; and I wonder whether this contrast, lingering
and changing in Milton's mind, could possibly have been
the matrix of that incredible magic,

> Henceforth thou art the Genius of the shore
> In thy large recompense, and shalt be good
> To all who wander in that perilous flood.

Perhaps it is too far-fetched to think so. At all events,
after describing the eternal glory of the dead youth, each
poet closes the consolation with a brief apostrophe.

It is worth noticing that the sea washes the shores be-

> Et fece a i bianchi uelli oltraggi e onte:
> S'udi il Mincio lagnar pien di tormento,
> Et spogliato di gioia e di diletto
> Turbar il puro suo lucido fonte."

Sandys (*op. cit.*) cites a similar passage from Euricius Cordus, in whose poem
the mourner is named Lycidas.

[1] Sandys observes the parallel between this mixture in Milton and that in
Spenser's *Shepherds' Calendar.*

hind Bryskett's kingdom almost as perpetually as it does
Milton's, though for less apparent cause, since Sidney's
death was on all too dry land; it even appears from the
mention of Corineus and of "*Liffies* tumbling streames"
near Dublin to be that same perilous flood in which Lycidas
was drowned. It was a sea which Bryskett knew well from
many crossings; and its voice through his poem explains
further why Milton should be teased by these among
many echoes.[1]

The parallels with Bryskett's other elegy for Sidney are
more striking; in the first place because in this *Pastorall
Aeglogue* the author has given Sidney that name which he
had invented for himself, Phillisides,[2] and all through the
poem runs the refrain, "*Phillisides* is dead." "For Lycidas is dead!" Here not so much the idea as the sound is
arresting. It is exactly the sort of trick that one's mind
does play, holding and digesting the pure sound of a word
or phrase and later producing its own phrase curiously
like; rather as in writing fast one may substitute a word
like "permeated" for "terminated." [3]

For both poets it is a "constraint" to write — "this
hard constraint" in Bryskett becomes "Bitter constraint
and sad occasion dear." Both recall their earlier life with
the dead; but there is not much resemblance in subject
matter here, since Bryskett is remembering not college
years but the Grand Tour —

> Where is become thy wonted happy state,
> (Alas) wherein through many a hill and dale,

---

1 Compare the "hooked atoms" in Professor Lowes's *Road to Xanadu*.
2 Phili(p) Sid(ney), the lover of the star; from which "Astrophel" and "Stella"
   are derivatives (Cambridge edition of Spenser, note to *The Ruines of Time*,
   l. 609).
3 Tuckwell (*op. cit.*, p. 25) says that "For Lycidas is dead, dead ere his prime"
   is a reminder of *Shep. Cal.* XI, 37, "For dead is Dido, dead, alas, and drent."

> Through pleasant woods and many an vnknowne way,
> Along the bankes of many siluer streames,
> Thou with him yodest; and with him didst scale
> The craggie rocks of th' Alpes and *Appenine?*

The poem being a pastoral, Phillisides is of course a shepherd: and it is notable, by-the-by, that as the sea-element in the other poem was used more appropriately for King's death than for Sidney's, so also Milton has particularized this conventional pastoral imagery, more fitting to the intended minister than to the knight Sidney. But he may have found a suggestion for his hungry sheep who look up and are not fed in Bryskett's

> Vnhappie flock that wander scattred now,
> What maruell if through grief ye woxen leane,
> Forsake your food, and hang your heads adowne? [1]

Then there are numerous small parallels.

> Hear'st thou the *Orown?* how with hollow sownd
> He slides away

suggests the Mincius again; both poets mention the myrtle and laurel, which are, however, common elegiac property; Bryskett's "Honor my base words with his high name" has a vague suggestion perhaps of

> So may some gentle Muse
> With lucky words favour my destined urn,

though this is not worth insisting upon.

As in *Lycidas*, Neptune and the lesser deities of the sea appear:

> Loe father *Neptune*, with sad countenance,
> How he sits mourning on the strond now bare, . . .
> . . . His sacred skirt about

---

1 Possibly this may be cavilled at as *lucus a non lucendo*, since Milton's sheep looked *up*, and waxed bloated instead of lean! Tuckwell (*op. cit.*, p. 46) suggests that Milton may have been indebted to Dante, *Par.*, xxix, 112, and to Spenser, *Shep. Cal.*, ix. The latter is certainly a much closer parallel of idea, but may not preclude Bryskett from a small share.

> The sea-gods all are set; from their moist caues
> All for his comfort gathered there they be.

Moreover, they and various British river-gods [1] are assembled not only to comfort Neptune, but

> . . . eke to see
> The dolefull sight, and sad pomp funerall
> *Of the dead corps passing through his kingdome.* [2]

This means, of course, Sidney's body being brought home in state. But the line, especially with that imagination-stirring word "kingdome," was well calculated to set Milton's imagination, never hard to stir, a-roving with a body that actually the shores and sounding seas washed far away; and so he wrote,

> Whether beyond the stormy Hebrides,
> Where thou perhaps under the whelming tide
> Visit'st the bottom of the monstrous world;
> Or whether thou, to our moist vows denied,
> Sleep'st by the fable of Bellerus old,
> Where the great vision of the guarded mount
> Looks toward Namancos and Bayona's hold. . . .

For both, the thought of strewing the grave with flowers brought comfort — although for that no literary source was needed; and finally, both poems end with four lines in which the sun dips into the western waves and the shepherd goes home.[3]

Such reminiscence was the most natural thing in the world. Since the circumstances of *Astrophel* and the poems printed with it were almost identical with those surrounding *Lycidas*, a group of friends in each case contributing laments for a lost young comrade, it would have been more curious if Milton had *not* been haunted by these echoes.

1 Including the Severn. Cf. Milton's Camus, and Sabrina.
2 Italics mine.
3 That picture of the end of the day is quite common. Milton has it twice in
Lycidas.

II. LODOWICK HIMSELF

THE outline of Bryskett's life has been very adequately blocked in by Plomer and Cross. Their accurate and careful monograph, although not always convivial reading, has become the authoritative work on him, and presents perhaps as complete a picture as is necessary.[1]

He was the son of a Genoese merchant, Antonio Bruschetto, and his wife Elizabeth, also an Italian,[2] born about 1545,[3] perhaps in the village of Hackney, where his father had a house in addition to one in the parish of St. Gabriel Fenchurch.[4] He was the third son of five, the others being Sebastian, Henry, Michael, and Thomas, and of his three sisters Lucrece was the eldest. After schooling in Kent and a University career at Cambridge, not terminated by a degree (possibly because of his father's debts at the time), he was sent to Italy on business, first by his father, and again while yet a very young man by Sir Henry Sidney, Philip's father, whose household he had joined. Sir Henry was the Lord Deputy of the Kingdom of Ireland, and from now until the end of his days Bryskett lived as reluctantly as his friend Spenser in close connection with that troubled realm, from which he seems to have escaped when he could.

From 1572 to 1574 he was one of Sir Philip Sidney's two companions on the Grand Tour. In Ireland he held, not without complaint, the office of Clerk of the Privy Council;

1 Henry R. Plomer and Tom Peete Cross, *The Life and Correspondence of Lodowick Bryskett*, in The Modern Philology Monographs, Chicago, 1927. No slight to Cross is intended in my usually referring to the book for brevity's sake as Plomer.

2 Her name, not mentioned by Plomer, though he must have known it, appears in Anthony Bryskett's will, Prerogative Court of Canterbury, 31 Martyn; also in the London *Inquisitiones Post Mortem*, ii, 177.

3 See *infra*, p. 257.

4 See terms of Anthony Bryskett's will, *infra*, p. 270, Chapter III.

later that of Clerk in Chancery for the faculties under the
Statute 28 Henry VIII, afterward held by Spenser; that of
general controller of customs on wines in various Irish
ports; and finally that of Clerk of the Council of Munster,
which he had long desired for its better salary. He acted
also as sheriff for the County of Wexford — no easy task
in those rebellious days; apparently as steward to Sir
Henry Wallop for a time; and as Clerk of the Casualties.
In the horrid rebellion of 1598, in which Spenser lost his
castle, Bryskett and his family had to flee to England,
"ruined and broken"; subsequently (in 1600) the Queen
sent him on a mission to the Continent, where he was in
prison in Flanders for a time; but later years brought him
again to Ireland, where he died before the end of 1612;
for at that time we find his widow Ellen bringing suit
against the owner of some cattle which have destroyed
her oats.

As to his Irish offices, he was rather given to appointing
deputies in his place and going over to England, whence it
was sometimes difficult to recall him. Nevertheless those
for whom he worked praised him highly. His own letters
speak an intelligent and often an exasperated interest in
Irish affairs, which, as all now concede, were so stupidly
conducted by authority at home. Bryskett felt the stupid-
ity, and for all the flowery circumlocution necessary in addressing the Elizabethan great, his meaning was sometimes
uncomfortably blunt.

On its social side Ireland must have had its compensations, especially after Spenser came over. Our pleasantest
picture of this side of his life comes from his *Discovrse of
Civill Life*, written or translated, by the way, "to end to
frame a gentleman fit for ciuill conuersation, and to set
him in the direct way that leadeth him to his ciuill felic-
itie." Of course this sort of book was fashionable at the

time; still, it is not over-fanciful to connect his purpose with Spenser's in the *Faery Queene*. I do not know whether Bryskett noticed the similarity of the phrasing; that of the substance he did, and had Spenser mention it in the *Discourse*. In this book he reads his translation of Giraldus to a group of friends who gather for three days to hear him in his "little cottage" to which, after resigning one of his clerkships, he has retired.[1] These friends are Dr. Long, Primate of Armagh, Sir Robert Dillon, Mr. Dormer, the Queen's solicitor, Captain Christopher Carleil, Captain Thomas Norreis, Captain Warham St. Leger, Captain Nicholas Dawtrey, Mr. Edmond Spenser, and "Th. Smith Apothecary," Bryskett's attendant physician. The conversations which intersperse Bryskett's reading of his translation are filled with engaging chaff. On Bryskett's saying that he studies to find human felicity, the primate reminds him that it cannot be found in this world. "I crie you mercie, my Lord," answers Bryskett, "if I haue stepped into your marches before I was aware." Again, they threaten to "coynie vpon [him], and to eate [him] out of house and home." When he calls the meal a philosopher's dinner for its modesty, Dillon laughingly refuses to praise it as his host is angling to make them do. All in all it is a pretty picture, and one would be glad of more like it from the same pen; for it must be admitted that the ethical part of the *Discourse*, the very substance of the little book, is not exciting to read.

To Plomer's array of facts, newly discovered depositions of Lodowick Bryskett in a suit in Chancery add two or three.[2]

---

1 Plomer says that although Bryskett has telescoped several years, the account of these meetings may well be founded on fact.
2 C 24/277/7, 59, Thomas Wrightington vs. Michael Bryskett, discovered by Dr. Sisson. For a full account of this case, see Chapter V.

Plomer's plausible surmise that he was born about 1545 is corrected by the date given at his examination: in February, 42 Elizabeth, that is in 1599/1600, he was described as "Lodovik Briskett of London Esquier aged 53 yeres or therabowt℮." This means that he was born in 1547, new style — or, since we cannot tell on which side of the new year his birthday fell, in 1546.

It happens that information from his depositions also fits into two gaps acknowledged by Plomer. From June, 1593, to September, 1594, Plomer knows nothing about his movements; and in fact the gap quite probably goes back to April, 1592, since the 1593 entry is of very doubtful accuracy.[1] Now it was in 1592 or 1593, at any rate later than his brother Sebastian's death in August, 1592, that Lodowick was in England on a journey unrecorded by Plomer. "Seven yeres now past or therabowt℮," his deposition runs, "this dept being at the then howse or Chamber of one Mr Waferrer a Counselle^r at the lawe ... vppon some busynes of his owne There happened in the meane while of this dept℮ being there to be a certen deede pfected" by which Lodowick's brother-in-law Thomas Wrightington made over certain lands to his wife, Lodowick's sister Lucrece; which deed we shall consider at more length in a later chapter. Lodowick, being there by chance, "was requested & did at the tyme aforesd [to, *struck out*] subscribe his name as a wittnes to the sealing & delyvery of the same."

The happily named Mr. Waferer, by-the-by, seems to have been the family lawyer. Sebastian Bryskett in his will named him one of his overseers.

Again, after Bryskett's flight to England in 1598, followed within a few months by the deaths of Spenser and Sir Henry Wallop, Plomer loses sight of Bryskett until the

1 See Plomer, *op. cit.*, pp. 52–54.

end of March, 1600, when he surrendered his office of Clerk of the Council of Munster into the Queen's hands.[1] Here too his depositions help us, for his examination was held in early February, 1599/1600, and establishes his being in London not only at that immediate time but also, presumably, for some months earlier, since he is described as "of London." He speaks of his long absence: asked, according to form, whether his sister Lucrece or his brother Michael have tampered with his testimony, he replies that they have not,

but this dept having bene of long tyme a stranger in England & to theire Actions was hable to saye lyttle to any of the sd Articles yf she should haue offered to examyne this dept vppon them neither is he this dept to be wrought or practised w[th]all to straigne his Conscience for affection in any suche Cause.

This is as much as the Chancery suit in question can tell us of Bryskett himself, but further research in connection with it has brought a little more matter, the most interesting of which is the discovery of his two children.[2] On Thursday, the 5th of May, 1580, there was held at St. Peter's, Cornhill, the "Christning of Phillip Brisket sonne of Lodwicke Brisket gentleman the child born the 28th of Aprill being Friday." This event may account for the brevity of Bryskett's visit to Ireland in the spring of 1580, except for which he was absent from Ireland from June, 1579, till January or February, 1580/81; he had come to England in 1579 on account of his mother's death. The other child, Elizabeth, was baptized twenty years later almost to a day, on May 9, 1600, in the church of

1 Plomer, op. cit., pp. 61–62.
2 In this I have no share; they are the trove of Howard Paton Vincent, my collaborator in the earlier stages of this research. He found Philip in the Register of St. Peter's, Cornhill, Harl. Soc., 1877, and Elizabeth in the Register of St. Antholin, Budge Row, London, Harl. Soc., 1883. Plomer says there was an Edward Bryskett, cook, in Ireland, but he could not have been a child of Lodowick's, since he was a mature man in 1584–5.

St. Antholin, Budge Row — two months after her father's deposition in the Wrightington *vs.* Bryskett suit.[1]

I have run across two or three further references of no great importance, but of some interest.

Among the State Papers, Domestic Series, of the reign of Elizabeth is an undated slip [2] endorsed "A forfeiture of 200[li] for Lodouick Brisket," and bearing on its back the pencilled surmise, "Prob. 1590?" By this "Elizabeth by the grace of God &c." addresses "the Threr Chaunceler Barons and Chamberlaines of o[r] Exchecq[r]":

Wee let yow weete, that at the homble sute and in consideracon of the acceptable servicȩ done vnto vs by our welbeloued servant Lodo-wicke Brisket wee haue . . . graunted to him . . . the somͤe of Two hondred poundes Laufull English money w[ch] our pleasure ys, shalbe payed to him and his assignes out of any such gooddes wares or mer-chaundizes as ys or shalbe due as forefeited vnto vs by any of our Lawes or statutes and seisd to our vse by our sercher of our porte of London. . . .

The Hatfield Manuscripts yield a little more of a crop than Plomer has reaped from them in regard to Bryskett's imprisonment in Flanders and the negotiations for his exchange with the Jesuit Cardin. The exchange was not merely that of man for man; it was to be "Louis Brusquetus" and his companion for Cardin and his companion, and Hortensio Spinola. Spinola had apparently been held much longer than Bryskett, for a letter from Francesco Rizzo to Sir Robert Cecil, bearing the conjectural date of 1601, says that two years earlier petition for Spinola's release and offer of payment were rejected; lately, when he offered £250, he was told that Spinola's exchange with Mr. Bruschetto in Flanders was being treated; and now, since the matter drags and Spinola is in very bad health

1 Cf. Lodowick's letter (Plomer, *op. cit.*, p. 68) mentioning "a yonge child," evidently Elizabeth.
2 State Papers, Domestic, Elizabeth, 1581–90 (S. P. 12/235, no. 49).

and not likely to live long, he offers £300.[1] In January, 1602/03, Cardin wrote to Cecil,[2]

> For more than ten months in pursuance of your orders I have entreated the Archduke [and others] that Louis Brusquetus and his companion, who are prisoners in Flanders, might be exchanged for myself, my companion and Hortensio Spinola. This exchange we have now obtained with great difficulty, for Brusquetus was there held a man of great note and his ransom fixed at eight thousand French gold pieces.

He enumerated further difficulties that had arisen, such as the suggested exchange of Cardin for a Mr. Hawkins.

> So far as Spinola is concerned, you will confer upon him an unspeakable benefit by not letting him die in prison; for he is so ruined in his body, his nose eaten away, and otherwise sick, that . . . he seems on the point of death.

It is a cruel picture; and on his side Bryskett also was ill treated, because of an imprudent action of his own. Cardin heard of the latter fact through "Jeronimo Lopez and a brother of Lodivoco Brusquate." [3] Which brother — Henry, Michael, or Thomas — we do not know; but it may be the same one from whom a short note of March, 1602/03, endorsed "Bryskett's remembrance," appears in the Hatfield calendar: [4]

> It may please your Ladyship [5] to deal with Mr. Secretary to this effect, that either he will be pleased to perform his promise for the Jesuit Fernand Cardyne in case he be not exchanged for Mr. Hawkyns, or that Spinola and Aluori may be ransomed at a good rate and the money laid *in deposito* toward the ransom of my poor brother and Mr. Norton in case they be not released by the said Cardyne.

This is a curious commentary on Cardin's report of two months earlier that Bryskett had been released. Does its being addressed to "Your Ladyship" suggest that the

---

1 Hist. MSS. Comm., Cal. Hatfield MSS., part 14, p. 190 (39. 97).
2 *Ibid.*, p. 250 (187. 1).
3 Cardin's letter of 24 September, 1602, Plomer, pp. 71–72.
4 Hist. MSS. Comm., Cal. Hatfield MSS., part 14, p. 263 (92. 52).
5 Lady Cecil?

writer had tired of masculine delay and hoped for more from feminine influence? At any rate it shows Plomer wrong in his surmise that Lodowick was at home by the end of 1602.

Within three months of his brother's appeal to her Ladyship, however, as we learn from another newly discovered Chancery suit containing depositions by Lodowick,[1] he not only had been released but had reached London and made an attempt at settling down in Chelsea, just west of the estate which had been Sir Thomas More's. If he had hoped to end his life farming in peace by the river, he chose his neighbours unfortunately: for he became subtenant to one Nicholas Holborne who in his turn was tenant to the notorious Earl of Lincoln.

Lincoln's manor, described in this suit as the "chieffe howse, in Chelsey," and the Manor House, was the one which at the beginning of the century had belonged to Sir Thomas More.[2] It stood across the site of the present Beaufort Street, about two-thirds of the way between the Thames and the King's Road.[3] A description of it fourteen years after Bryskett had given up his tenancy under it calls it "the greatest house in Chelsea," with

two fore great courts adjoining, environed with brick walls, also a wharf lying in front, having a high brick tower on the east and west ends, and a high water tower standing upon the west corner of the wharf, and the watercourse belonging thereto. An orchard, a garden, having a peryment standing up in the middle, and a terrace on the north thereof, with a banquetting house at the east end of the terrace having a marble table in it. A great garden, dovecote close, containing five acres; the kitchen garden, brick barn close, containing ten acres.[4]

---

1 C 24/318 (30) and C 24/319 (18) in the Public Record Office, found by Dr. Sisson: the Earl of Lincoln, plaintiff, against N. Holborne, gent., defendant.
2 Alfred Beaver, *Memorials of Old Chelsea*, London, 1892, pp. 128–129.
3 L. C. C. *Survey of London, Parish of Chelsea*, part 2, p. 18, and Plate 22.
4 Close Rolls, 18 James, I, part 18, m. 38 (quoted by Beaver, *op. cit.*, p. 131).

After More's execution it had passed into the hands of William, later first Marquis of Winchester, who held it from 1536 to 1572, leaving it to his son John, the second Marquis. From 1576 to 1594 it belonged to Gregory Fienes, Lord Dacre, who had married the daughter of the Marquis's first wife.[1] Lady Dacre at her death just after her husband's in 1594 left the property to Lord Burghley, who was succeeded in it by his son Sir Robert Cecil, later Earl of Salisbury. It was Cecil who in 1599 sold the estate to Henry, Earl of Lincoln.[2]

The estate, lying between Milman Street and Church Street, the King's Road and the Thames, included various other lands in Chelsea and Kensington, one of them the ten-acre Brick Barn Close lying north of the King's Private Road and west of Park Walk.

Now William, first Marquis of Winchester, while he held the great house, had let part of his estate to Nicholas Holborne the elder (father of Bryskett's landlord) and Katheren his wife — had let him, explicitly,

one messuage, and certen landɛ meddowe and pasture, lyinge in Chelsey and Kensington . . . and one Messuage, called the psonage howse of Chelseye . . . twoe closes of pasture one called the psonadge Close wᶜʰ did belonge to the psonadge of Chelsey [3] lying on the West side of the Mannoʳ howse there, And the other called by the name of the brickbarne Close lyinge on the north side of the brick barne belonginge to the said Mannoʳ howse.[4]

---

1 Beaver, *op. cit.*, pp. 128–129.
2 Beaver, *op. cit.*, p. 130, says 1597/98; but the Cal. Dom. St. Pap., 1598–1601, p. 169, followed by Gibbs, *Peerage*, VII, 695 n., gives a letter of March 15, 1599; "The Earl of Lincoln has bought Chelsea of Mr. Secretary."
3 This does not refer to the site of the present rectory, which was given in 1566 to Robert Richardson (then Rector) by the Marquis of Winchester in exchange for what had before been the parsonage — the glebe being the land now bounded by the King's Road on the north, the Thames on the south, Milman Street on the east, and Dartrey Street on the west (L. C. C. *Survey*, pt. 2, p. 56).
4 Interrogatories *ex parte* Lincoln.

These exact terms are valuable to us as describing the property of which part was later held by Lodowick Bryskett.

In the time of the second Marquis the boundaries of the demised land varied somewhat. One year Holborne's cattle "did Come soe nere vnto the back side of the greate howse . . . that it was some annoyance thervnto." The Marquis therefore agreed with his tenant that Holborne's barn should be removed into the Little Parsonage Close. The plot of ground it had stood on was then enclosed in Winchester's estate and a stable built on it; at the same time a pale was set up from the west end of the brick barn down toward the river between the Parsonage Close and the great stable, whereby a little more of Holborne's land was taken up. All these encroachments on the demised property did not, however, amount to more than half an acre, and Holborne received compensation in money and in a little close, "a peece of ground of a greater quantitye lyinge fast by the Theames syde" which he caused "to be sowen wth early pees."

In general these matters seem to have settled themselves quite amicably, and the deponents are unanimous that the palings were valuable as keeping the horses in the great stables from trespassing in the Little Parsonage Close. The régimes of Dacre, Burghley, and Cecil also passed (for all we know) in peace. Nicholas and Katheren Holborne, dying, were succeeded in their tenancy by their son Nicholas the younger; and in 1599 the Earl of Lincoln bought the manor from Cecil.

This peer is one of the riddles of his time. He was a most eccentrically quarrelsome man; but his excuse may have been insanity.

For some reason he wanted to get rid of the younger Nicholas Holborne as tenant, to accomplish which end he tried to frighten off possible subtenants by declaring Holborne's lease void, and decreased the value of the demised property by trespassing on it in preposterous though original ways.

In 1599, in the very April after buying the manor, he began by having Holborne's servants frightened "from the ploweing of brickebarne Close pcell of the forsaid ferme," by the threat that if it were "sowen" it should be spoiled. A year later, in July, when the Brickbarn Close "was a moeing," he sent three servants "wth horses and Carte loden wth Rubbyshe" which they laid and scattered "in seu'all heapes vppon the lande & swathes of grasse then mowen of purpose to spoyle the grounde and grasse then Cut downe"; and "the next morneinge beinge a very wete morneinge," by the Earl's direction they overran "wth his Coatche and Coatche horses all the residue of the said grounde & grasse . . . then standinge & groweinge and thereby did spoyle the same." The next year there was more discussion as to whether the Earl had enclosed part of Holborne's "backe yeard demysed nowe or late Called the kitchin garden." One deposition *ex parte* Lincoln says that when his Lordship and Holborne met in March 1601/02 to have the matter arbitrated, Holborne found himself mistaken as to the precise extent of his lease. However that may be, this very kitchen garden proved a battle ground when Lodowick Bryskett entered the field.

Bryskett, newly released from his Flemish prison, became acquainted with Holborne at Midsummer of 1603, "in the tyme of the late great plague, . . . by occasion of taking at his hande the Lease of the [farmhouse], together wth a small close of iij acr of land adioyning to the same [apparently the Little Parsonage Close]." [1]

---

1 Bryskett's deposition.

When Bryskett took this house, Holborne told him of a "quill of water" belonging to it — "a pipe of leade or conditt of water wch did lye in the ground, and went crosse the greate Courte over agaynste the hall dore of the Manno^r howse, and so thorowe the wall betwene the said greate Courte and the yard or orchard" of Holborne. This was supposed to supply the farmhouse which Bryskett now took, but actually was out of commission, having been first taken up and replaced in the time of Cecil, and in Lincoln's time cut off entirely. This was done at the command of Sir Arthur Gorges, the Earl's son-in-law; the Earl himself disclaimed responsibility, and it is deposed that several times he told Holborne he might have it back when he liked. What spokes he may nevertheless have put in the way of Holborne's getting it, we may be over-suspicious to wonder; but at any rate when Bryskett took the house it had not this water, "the want whereof," he observed, "ͻaͦot but be very discomͦodious to any tenañt that shall hold or enioye the same."

Lincoln began his practices against Bryskett almost as soon as he took the place.[1] Lodowick, not knowing his man, began to build "a longe house wch he intended for a malting house, neare adioynynge to the wall of [the Earl of Lincoln's] great base Court": on the land he had rented from Holborne, "betwene two walls vizt the wall of the [Earl's] base Court, and the garden wall" of Holborne — now Bryskett's. Lincoln threatened to burn or pull down this new edifice, "and erected scaffoldͼ adioynenge to his owen wall and ꝑvided ingens or hookͼ" for the purpose. Indeed, "before [Bryskett] had finished it, ther was some part of it pluckt downe by vnknowen ꝑsons standing wthin the sayd base Court."

1 Stapleton's deposition in June, 1606, makes it "about three years ago," and it was in midsummer, 1603, that Bryskett became Holborne's tenant.

In the following year the disputed kitchen garden, "empaled betwene the backsyde of [Bryskett's, i. e. Holborne's] howse, and the great howse of the [Earl]," came into play. In the spring of 1604, when Lodowick had had the place for a year,

he hauing caused his backsyde to be digged, and sett, one part thereof wth cabbage plantes, and a part wth barley to make an experiment of the encrease by setting thereof: the [Earl] shortly after took downe the pale wch devyded the land, and his workemen tooke and caried away all the cabage plantes, and lett in cattel to spoile the barley then beginning to shoote eare, and in o⟨ne⟩ afternone consumed it wholy: and so left it open as long as [Bryskett] held the house, wch for this and other the lyke hard courses he was fayne to forgoe.

As for the adjoining "close of three acr" or Little Parsonage Close, Lincoln told him he should never make benefit of that, and prevented him by

not onely pasturing the same ground wth his owne horses and guelding℮, but layeng it open for all others to do the lyke: and drawing great heapes of earth and rubbish from out of the greate howse and layeng the same in the sayd close. Besyd℮ sondry other hard courses—

and here Lodowick's deposition must have become very vivid or impassioned, for the scribe almost consistently from now on wrote "me" instead of changing it into the third person, and had to go back and alter it afterwards, so that the effect is as if we could hear Bryskett's very voice — "purposely to weary [me, *changed to*] him, as by his owne word℮ dyvers tymes [to me] vttred did appeere." Bryskett therefore "finding him self greatly endamaged and fearing worse, was glad in fyne to resolve to departe from the howse, and to yeld it vp againe into [Holborne's] hand℮ at Ester last past" — Easter, 1605 — receiving monetary compensations from Holborne for the "empeachement" he had suffered.

An elderly yeoman of Chelsea commented briefly on Bryskett's tenancy that he "as yt seemed was soone weary of yt." Sir Robert Stapleton, the delightful old gentleman who appears to have succeeded him after these unfortunate two years, says with characteristic gentleness that Bryskett "was werye of the vnkind and hard courses used by [Lincoln] and that therfore he was willing to depart."

Sir Robert's gentleness did not save even him from the Earl. We cannot leave this adventurous bit of land without adding that his Lordship's practical jokes reached their climax upon this new tenant in Lent of 1605/06. Not satisfied with such minor afflictions as dumping more rubbish into the Little Parsonage Close, he negotiated with a dung-man in London, and then left for Lincolnshire just in time to save his lordly nose from what ensued:

ther was a dunge-bote or two [says Sir Robert] loden with very detestable ffilthye dunge (as he thinketh was ever seene) wch was brought and vnladen on the east and the west sides of the entering into the sayd house wherof one part was vnladen w^thin the highe water marke very neare vnto the two fountaynes w^ch [Sir Robert] had made for the pvision of his house [thus he, by the way, had solved the difficulty about a water supply for the farm], and some other part neare and vpon the west ende of [Lincoln's] wharffe ther so as if the wynde were ether in the East or westerly [he] and his family were incredibly anoyed wth the stinche beyonde beleeffe to the great daunger of their infection beside(, the dunge continewinge ther by the space of .12. dayes or theraboute(.

Evidently it seeped through the soil into the fountains near by, for another witness says that "at euery highe water the springe or Well wch did serve Sr Roberte(howse with water, was very muche annoyed and taynted with ill savours." Sir Robert "was therby enforced to fetche and borrow the greatest part of his vsefull waters abrode of his neighbours."

Bryskett apparently left the "village of palaces" for the City, since in November, 1605, when he deposed in Chancery *ex parte* Holborne, he was described as "of london

Esqr." [1] After this we lose sight of him except for what Plomer can tell us, and for a notice of him in his sister Lucrece's will of 1608, in which she leaves "to my brother Lodowick Briskett ffower yardes of black clothe of Twentye shillinge the yard" and "to my sister Briskett my brother Lodowicke wife a mournenge gowne of the like stuffe" as that which she has left to Sebastian's widow.

Beside the fresh material on Lodowick Bryskett himself which has come to light since Plomer's book came out, the public records supply a mass of interesting information on his widespread family connections, and allow us to see him not as an isolated figure but placed against a background of some detail.

[1] His age, curiously, is not given; a blank space has been left for it.

III. LODOWICK'S IMMEDIATE FAMILY

THE depositions of the Genoese merchant Anthony Bryskett, Lodowick's father, taken in November, 4-5 Philip
and Mary, in the Chancery suit of de Rochia *vs*. Wilford,
state his age as fifty-one. This would establish his year of
birth as 1506.[1] Apparently because he was granted letters
of denization in 1536, Plomer surmises that he came to
England about 1535. Plomer's saving phrase "or perhaps
even earlier" turns out to be abundantly justified, for
"The Reporte of the Searche of all the Straungers wythin
london and Southwerk and the liberties therof," taken in
November, 1571, enters him as follows:[2]

Genevia j.
　Anthonye Brisket Marchant borne in Genevia §　⎫
　came into this realme about xlviij yeres past §　⎬ parish churche
　　　　　　　　　　　　　　　　　　　　　　　⎭

This means that he must have come as early as 1523, when
he was still — even for the sixteenth century — hardly
more than a boy; and it increases the probability that he
married his wife Elizabeth after he came to England rather
than before. He also had a brother Francis, who in 1546
was going into Ireland as factor to Anselin Salvage — living up to the mercantile traditions of the family.[3]

1　C 24/45, Peter de Rochia vs. Elizabeth Wilford, widow, and Thomas Wil-
　ford. For this reference I am indebted to Dr. Sisson. This case throws no
　other light on Anthony Bryskett, beyond illustrating the affairs of the great
　merchants. The question in the case is whether Peter, in an account concern-
　ing his factorship for the Wilfords, was indebted to them for certain wares
　which he received at Viana "in the Realme of portingale in the p͡tℓ beyond
　the Seas," to sell for them, and whether he was bound to pay them any
　debts rising from his factorship in other places.
　　I have found no connection between the various Thomas Wilfords and the
　Wilfords who were related to Thomas Wrightington (see Chapter V).
2　P. R. O., S. P. 12/82. (State Papers, Domestic, Elizabeth.) It is unpaged,
　but he is entered under "Sainct Gabriell ffanchurch Parishe."
3　Calendar of Letters and Papers, Henry VIII, Vol. xx, part 2, no. 842, and
　Vol. xxi, part 1, no. 526.

Anthony appears from time to time among the Letters and Papers, Foreign and Domestic, of the Reign of Henry VIII. These notices are, however, of no particular interest except for the study of mercantile history.[1] Plomer also prints half a dozen of his Italian letters, but without translations. I do not know why he prints so few; many may be found in the Calendar of Foreign State Papers under Elizabeth.[2]

In 1574 Anthony died a very prosperous man, having more than made up for earlier reverses. His will[3] made his wife sole executrix, and his friends Vincent Guicciardine (who was also his son-in-law) and Benedict Spinola, both important merchants of the Italian group like himself, overseers. To his wife he left "all that my great howse, and all those londes and tenementȩ whiche I nowe haue" in St. Sythes Lane, and "my now mancõn or dwelling howse" in the parish of St. Gabriel Fenchurch, in which church his body was to be buried. His five sons were to share the lands and houses in Hackney. To his daughter Mary (afterward the wife of Edward Atkinson, merchant tailor) he left his nine tenements in the parish of St. Gabriel Fenchurch, excepting his mansion house. His other two daughters, Lucrece and Joan, are not mentioned in the will, presumably because they were already provided for by marriage. The terms of the will indicate the scale on which the family lived.

His wife Elizabeth did not survive him for many years; in 1579 Lodowick was drawn home from Ireland by "some grevous occasion of his owne . . . and that is the losse of his mother latelie deceased."[4]

---

1 See Cal. L. and P., Henry VIII, v, 601; xi, 565; xii, part 2, pp. 395-397; xx, part 1, nos. 747, 830, 1046, 1158; xx, part 2, nos. 660, 739, 842; xxi, no. 526.
2 Vols. iii, v, vi, vii, and x. He is also to be found among the State Papers of the Domestic Series. 3 Prerogative Court of Canterbury, 31 Martyn.
4 Plomer, op. cit., p. 11, quoting from the Irish State Papers. In the London

Sebastian, their eldest child, was born in 1536,[1] in the same year his father received letters of denization. Like Anthony he played a part in the secret service, and like the rest of his brothers had relations with the Cecils; in which connection it is interesting to note that either the family was divided in politics or else each served his own ends without troubling about factions, for his nephew James Guicciardine, of whom we shall hear more in a later chapter, was a secret agent of Essex's.

The little we know of Sebastian's private life sounds as if he were a responsible and affectionate person. He was a "speciall Acter" in the making of the deed by which his sister Lucrece's property was insured against her husband's extravagance. His will[2] has a tone that one likes. His body is to lie in the church of St. Gabriel Fenchurch, as near to his parents as convenient. To his wife Jane he leaves his six tenements in St. Sythes Lane, and the use and profit of 2,000 marks during her life, £500 of which she may dispose of as she likes at her death, though not before; he earnestly prays her to observe this, so that she will have enough during her widowhood. Then there are further bequests to his only child, his "sweete beloued daughter" Elizabeth, who was only twelve and a half at his death in 1592,[3] £50 apiece to his brothers Michael and Thomas — perhaps because they were the two youngest, or possibly because Henry and Lodowick, the elder two, were doing better financially; to his sisters, Lucrece Wrightington, "Joane Egleffeild," and Mary Atkinson, twenty nobles

---

Inquisitiones Post Mortem, II, 218, we find her in March, 1577, paying twenty pounds of pepper for a messuage in St. Sythes Lane, late in the tenure of Anthony Vivald.

1 Plomer, *op. cit.*, pp. 1, 86.
2 Prerogative Court of Canterbury, 63 Harrington.
3 *London Inquisitiones Post Mortem*, III, 60.

apiece to be bestowed on rings of that value "to weare for a remembraunce of me their lovinge brother"; and other bequests to friends and servants. Mr. Arden Waferer, the lawyer whom Lodowick visited in 1592 or 1593 on business of his own, is one of the overseers appointed.

His wife Jane one may guess had a head for business herself. In April, 1600, we find her making an indenture [1] with Robert Rookes of Norwich by which he sells her "All that messuage or teñte . . . sometyme called or knowne by the name of the Rose" in Denham, Buckinghamshire, "togeather with all houses edifys buyldinge barnes stables yarde backside orcharde gardens . . .," a cottage now occupied by a tanner, and "that Close or crofte of arrable lande . . . called Shawes conteyninge by estimacyon foure acres be yt more or lesse," another croft of two acres . . . called Hickman's croft, and a piece of meadow "called the moore." The reversion of all these premises and all Rookes's deeds about them are to be sold to Jane; and Rookes and his heirs, "& Johan nowe the wyfe of the said Robert Rookes" and anyone else having a claim to these lands shall no longer have it.

Her action sounds businesslike and venturesome; if she was inclined to be too venturesome, — the Rose sounds suspiciously like an inn, — there was the safeguarding clause in Sebastian's will. Her plan evidently was to sublet, for we find her making another indenture in 1607 [2] with Henry Gonner of London, yeoman, for the Rose, Shawes, and Hickman's Croft, now or late in the tenure of Elizabeth Bromely (or, in turn, *her* tenants), "in as large and ample manner as she the said Jane Bruskett or any of her fermors or vndertenante heretofore had held . . . the same."

1 Close Rolls, Chancery, 42 Eliz., part 28 (C 54/1672, 28).
2 *Ibid.*, 5 James, part 9 (C 54/1886, 9).

We know so much of Lucrece's daily life that she must have a separate chapter to herself. She seems to have been the eldest of Lodowick's sisters, and was born in 1540, four years after Sebastian.

Henry, probably the second son, if we may go by the order in which they are named in Anthony's will, must have lived a quiet and blameless life, or died young, to judge by his absence from the archives. I know no more of him than that he was joint heir with his four brothers in his father's will.

"Joane Egleffeild," whose existence is established by her brother Sebastian's will, was equally elusive for a time, but turns out to be interesting for an amusing coincidence: she was the wife of that Francis Eglefield of Little St. Bartholomew's, West Smithfield, with whom I have dealt in another paper as John Lyly's inconspicuous companion in the matter of hanging lines in the well-yard.[1] Joan had escaped my vigilance (and presumably Plomer's) the more easily because the Visitation of Essex [2] has accidentally made her the daughter of Anthony Brockett instead of Bryskett, and there really was an Anthony Brockett, though I believe he had no daughter Joan. She was Francis Eglefield's second wife. They had one son, Thomas. I surmise that she and perhaps Thomas died before Francis, since his will [3] made on January 23, 1606 (a year after the quarrel in the well-yard; is that why he, like Lyly, who also died in 1606, played no great part in that drama?), and proved on April 14, 1607, mentions neither her nor him,

---

1 See pp. 399–400 in article on Lyly in this book.
2 That of 1612 (Harl. Soc., XIII). It makes her wife of "Frauncis Eglesfilde of Estham, Esq." — where her sister Lucrece, by the way, held property (see Chapter V). The will of Francis Eaglefield of Little St. Bartholomew's asks that his body be buried in East Ham.
3 Prerogative Court of Canterbury, 31 Huddlestone. His half-brother Christopher's will is in 53 Harrington.

but leaves "All that the lease and terme of yeares which I haue of two howses or Tenementes with theire appurtenaunces scituate . . . in little Saint Bartholomewes neare West Smithfield London adioyninge to the Hospitall there in the well yarde" to the children of John and Bridget Atkinson[1] and to Mawdelin Challiner and Richard Gardiner.

Mary, the sister named last in Sebastian's will, was ten years younger than Lucrece, having been born in 1550 "or thereabouts."[2] If we are right in guessing that she was still a spinster at twenty-four, when her father died in 1574, at least she did not remain so. She married Edward Atkinson, a merchant tailor,[3] son of another Edward, also merchant tailor, and *his* wife Mary,[4] and had several children: Vincent, born in 1580, Elizabeth in 1585, Jeames in 1587, and a stillborn child in 1579/80.[5]

Edward Atkinson's brother John, citizen and grocer of London, brought suit against him in Chancery in September, 1586:[6] it alleged that whereas their father had died possessed of "Tenne Tenemtę and Gardenes" near the Tower of London in the parish of All Saints Barking, his wife Mary took letters of administration, and about September, 1585, assigned these tenements and gardens to

1 I have found no connection between these Atkinsons and the family of Mary and Edward.
2 C 24/277, 7 and 59 (P. R. O.). Mary Atkinson's deposition makes her fifty in February, 1599/1600.
3 C 24/277, 7 and 59, depositions of Edward and Mary Atkinson.
4 C 2 Eliz., A 4/19; John vs. Edward Atkinson.
5 *Register of St. Peter's, Cornhill*, pp. 22, 29, 31, and 127. (These Atkinson children are H. P. Vincent's discovery.) On p. 26 this register also records the christening on September 22, 1583, of Edward Atkinson, b. Sept. 18, son of Edward Atkinson, "purueior of the Queenes wines." This baby is yet another of Lodowick Bryskett's nephews.
6 P. R. O., C 2 Eliz., A 4/19. There are also among the Chancery depositions two sets in bundles C 24/303 and 304 belonging to a suit between Edward Atkinson, plaintiff, and William Scroggs, defendant.

John for the years then to come; by virtue of which John entered into possession of them by his farmers and tenants.

But lately John "by casuall meanes and mischaunce hath lost his said Indenture of lease and deede of assignemt out of his possession & the same by like mishapp are come to thands . . . of one Edwarde Atkinson" his brother — a wonderfully delicate avoidance of any hasty imputation! — who, having them, has contrived certain conveyances whereby he pretends title to the premises, affirming that their father Edward made these conveyances to him; and to give colour to his claim, Edward of late has wrongfully entered and taken possession of the premises himself. John, not having the leases in his own hands, cannot go to the common law against him; he therefore comes to Chancery and begs a subpoena against Edward.

Edward's answer is just what might be anticipated, that their father eleven or twelve years before his death granted "by worde" all his remaining years to come, and the original deed of lease, to the defendant; by virtue whereof the younger Edward entered and was possessed of the premises, taking the profits both during his father's lifetime and after his death; and he is keeping the original lease for the defence of his title, as he thinks he lawfully may.

Edward Atkinson appears less contentiously in the records of the Merchant Tailors' Company.[1] In 1607 King James invited them to give him a banquet, for which the preparations were sumptuous, the cost unprecedented in the history of the Company. Not to mention supplying vast quantities of food and drink, they appointed Committees to meet every day, and "Caters," Butlers, and "A Poet for a Speech," and took order for a window to be cut "for the King to look into the Hall," "Discreete Men

---

1 C. M. Clode, *Memorials of the Guild of Merchant Taylors*, London, 1870; and his *Early History of the Guild of Merchant Taylors*, London, 1888, Vols. I and II.

to look about the House," "The Brick Wall in the Garden
to be raised," and the vicinity "to be bewtified as much as
tyme will admytt." "Sir John Swynnerton," they record,
"is entreated to conferr with Mr. Benjamin Johnson the
Poet, aboute a speeche to be made to welcome his Majestie." Moreover, "notwithstanding Mr. Recorder's per-
suasion to invite ye Lord Mayor and Aldermen, yet it is
not thought fitt." Prince Henry, the King's eldest son,
however, was to be made free of the Company, and a garland put on his head.

The Master in Office was John Swynnerton the elder,
and his Wardens were Richard Wright, Andrew Osborne,
William Albany, and our friend Edward Atkinson, all men
of experience. Atkinson (who had been elected a Warden
in 1606) spent £16 7s. 6d. for hiring butlers. He had the
providing of the wine, for which the expenditure, as taken
from the Master's accounts, was £61 12s. 7d., covering
gasconie, canara, claret, rhennish, and others, besides many
gallons of "veniger," and also "cartage and portage of all
this wine," "a potle of white wine for the cooke," and "a
gymlett broken 12d." He also saw to borrowing the King's
plate for the occasion, and presented two bucks, apparently
as his own gift: ten shillings were paid "To 2 y^t brought
bucks from Mr Warden Atkinson."

Michael, Anthony Bryskett's fourth son, was admitted
to the Merchant Tailors' School in 1565 "at the request of
Mr. Mulcaster." [1] I have found no further trace of him
before 1580, when the Earl of Ormond, writing to Burghley, commended the bearer, Michael Bryskett, for his painful service in training the soldiers of Mr. John Zouche's
band. [2] Three years later Lord Justice Loftus asked Burgh-

---

1 C. J. Robinson, *Register of the Merchant Tailors' School,* i, 8. I owe this and
other items to Mr. H. P. Vincent.
2 Cal. St. Pap. Ireland, Eliz., ii, 225.

ley that the bearer, Mr. Michael Bryskett, might have confirmation of the constableship of Castle Maigne.[1] Lodowick, therefore, was not the only member of the family connected with Ireland; and in considering Michael's further affairs later we shall find more references to this connection.

Among the State Papers is an undated letter bearing the pencilled surmise of "1609":[2]

To the right honorable my singuler good Lorde the Erle of Salsbury Lo: Threr of England and one of his Ma^{ts}: most honorable priuie Counsell:

Righte Honorable and my singuler good Lorde, I am wth griefe inforst to importe vnto yor good Lo.^{pe} how my estate at this present standethe, wherin is to be noted Fortunes mutabillitie, or to speake more properly, (Gods visitacon) in afflictinge thos whome it pleaseth him to punnishe for their offences, emongest wch number I am one, by his permission, to the ouerthrowinge of my hole estate,

and here, like the man who admitted himself to be a miserable sinner but indignantly disowned having committed any miserable sins, he is abruptly deserted by his piety,

through the lewde dealinges of Yll disposed persons, that hathe gotten the same into their hands wthout intent of repayment, wherby I am so farre cast behinde hande, that I am not only driuen to hide my hedd, but likewise constrayned to ingage myself to others for supplyenge of thos ordinary occasions wch I am dayly inforst to vse. And forsomuche as I vnderstande that ther is at this instant an imployment of Souldiers into Ireland, I am therfore humbly to beseche yor good Lo:^{ps} honorable fauor towards me, for ye hauinge of a company of thos men, that are leuied here in London, or nerest therto, or if otherwise they be but for supply onely, that yet yo^u wilbe pleased to appoynt me for the conduction of sume of them, to thende I may by this imployment helpe to supporte ye time present, and by this meanes also to trye if happely some order may be taken wth my creditors for suche sumes as I doe owe vnto them:

---

[1] *Ibid.*, p. 470.

[2] St. Pap., James (S. P. 14/51 [5]). Plomer (p. 72, n.) refers to a letter of 1602/3 in which Michael asks to be employed as one of Cecil's servants or in charge of soldiers.

and so he takes his humble leave of "the onely Noble man vpon whome [his] hopes dependethe."

The sore straits in which we find him at this time explain something of his other actions, as we shall see presently.

Thomas, the youngest brother, twenty-three years younger than the eldest, Sebastian, and thirteen years Lodowick's junior,[1] appears from time to time in books on Shaksperian playhouses, because he had those rooms in Blackfriars from which Burbage made his theatre. Among the Loseley Manuscripts[2] is the indenture made on June 26, 1601, between Sir George More of Loseley and Cuthbert and Richard Burbage, selling them

all that messuage sellars romes wayes easiementes and commodities therevnto belongeinge nowe in the tenure and occupacionn of Thomas Brisket . . . beinge within the precynct of the late Blackfriars in London that is to say betwene the messuage romes and buyldinges of the saide Cuthbert and Richard Burbage on the east part, and the messuage romes and buyldinges of the saide Cuthbert and Richard Burbage and . . . George More whiche leadeth towards the glassehouse nowe in the tenure of Sir Jerom Bowes knight on the North parte and the messuages and yardes of [space] Fenton widowe now in the seuerall tenures ⟨lacuna⟩ . . . Clarke on the west part and the high-way that leadeth towards the messuage or mancion house of the right honourable George Lord Hunsdon Lord Chamberleyn. . . .[3]

This of course establishes Thomas as a resident of London, as does his deposition in the suit of Wrightington vs. Bryskett. But he did not confine his property to the City, for an indenture[4] of 42 Elizabeth, the year before the Burbage indenture, shows that in December he bought of Robert Okeman of Essex, yeoman, "all those his messuage howses landes tentę meadowes pastures feedingę woodę

1 C 24/277 (59). His deposition makes him forty years old in 1598/99.
2 Hist. MSS. Comm., VII, 659 b (MSS. of William More Molyneux, Esq., of Loseley Park, Guildford, Surrey).
3 No more appears at all pertinent for us. A considerable piece is torn from the middle of the indenture.
4 Close Rolls, Chancery, 42 Eliz., part 28 (C 54/1672, 28).

com̃ons rentę reũcyons remainders possessions & heredy-
tamentę whatsoeuᵣ . . . in the Towne townefeildę & Terri-
toryes of Stoken Pellham in the Countye of Hertforde."

The tone of his deposition in his sister's suit is not
pleasant; he sounds like a rather disagreeable and litigious
soul, and indeed in 1577 [1] Joseph Simonelli, "merchaunt
straunger," petitioned Walsingham, saying that one
Alexander Tybante had been about to take a house in
London by the means of Thomas Bryskett, and that since
Tybante was lately arrived in England and could not
speak the English tongue, Simonelli did his best to bring
the matter to a good effect; but since by some occasion
nothing was done therein, Tybante let the affair drop and
provided himself with a house elsewhere. Thomas Bryskett therefore soon sued Simonelli on a pretended contract
in Chancery; they were referred to the Common Law,
where a decree was given for Simonelli and against Bryskett, yet not without great trouble and cost to Simonelli.
Now, knowing Simonelli's intention of leaving England
soon about his urgent affairs, Bryskett had arrested him
again at the Common Law. Simonelli therefore begged,
since he had been only a friendly mediator between Bryskett and Tybante, and had had no benefit thereby, but on
the contrary had spent about £60 within three years on
that suit, that Bryskett be commanded to proceed no further against him. Of course we do not hear Thomas's side;
but what we do hear does not sound winning.

He also appears in the suit of Sir William More against
Cuthbert Burbage in 1601–02 over the Blackfriars lease.
In the Duke of Rutland's Manuscripts [2] he is called her
Majesty's purveyor.

---

1 Really this is only a surmise by whoever guesses the dates of the State Papers
(S. P. 12/127, 71).
2 Hist. MSS. Comm., Duke of Rutland, 1, 155, 1583.

These are all the Brysketts of Lodowick's generation in his immediate family. The *Alumni Cantabrigienses* names an Anthony Briskett who was governor of Montserrat about 1636 and was dead by 1654, leaving a son of the same name. If he was not a cousin, he may have been the son of Henry, Michael, or Thomas, of whose matrimonial affairs we know nothing.

There is also among the Domestic State Papers under James I [1] a letter, perhaps of 1603, from Charles Topcliffe to Cecil, written "At Mr Bryskette lodginge in Coldharb^r." Which of the brothers this was I have been unable to discover or to guess.

1 S. P. 14/5 (36).

IV. THE PAPER MILL AT HORTON

IF MICHAEL BRYSKETT was in evil case in 1609, he had not always had such financial difficulties. Like his father he seems to have had ups and downs. A suit in Chancery, and another in Star Chamber,[1] between him and one John Hellen throw light on his reverses and help to explain his desperate letter to Salisbury.

In 1597 or 1598 Michael, having money lying by him and wishing to have it employed to his benefit "(not by way of vsury for of that course he made some scruple in conscience but rather) by some honest sufficient man, who would trade wth it," asked his brother Thomas to help him to such a man. Thomas, having had former dealings with one John Turnor, and supposing him to be fit for the purpose, brought him and Michael acquainted, and by an agreement made in Michael's chamber "in Pawles Church-yard," with no witness except Thomas Bryskett, Michael gave Turnor at one time £100, and at another time £200, in Thomas's presence; this Turnor was to use in what stock or trade he should think most profitable, the increase to be equally divided between him and Michael. Afterwards Thomas heard Turnor confess that he had thus received of Michael at several times £400 and above "in the wholle."

Turnor must have been given to projects of this sort, for in July, 1597, he had borrowed from "John Hellen of Rearsburie" in Bucks, merchant tailor of London, £100 "vpon his owne bonde . . . to be imploied in a silke shopp"; if it were profitable, Hellen was to have "after the rate of that proffitt"; if not, Hellen was to bear part of the loss. Also Turnor had received £10 of Hellen "to lend vpon a skarlett cloke," and sundry other loans.

1 C 24/322 (14); St. Ch. 5, B3/24 and B45/9; cf. Requests 2/420/169, John Turner, weaver, vs. John Hellen, merchant tailor, 1603.

With Michael Bryskett's money, however, he turned to a different scheme. In March, 40 Elizabeth, 1598, he took a sixty-year lease of Edward Bulstrood [1] for a mill and grounds in Horton or Rasebury — "Collnett" or "Colt-net" mills, named for the river Colne apparently — and proceeded to lay out heavy sums in building. He hired one "Roberte Style of Wobourne in the County of Buck' Paper Make[r]" apparently as his foreman, for Style received money of him to pay the workmen for building, and by Turnor's appointment directed them in their work. But these buildings cost him more than he had received from Michael, for Style says he thinks about £800 was laid out in making a paper mill and a corn mill "and the dwellinge house adioyninge vnto them." [2] Accordingly he increased the debts he already owed to Hellen by borrowing £90 to be used in buildings.

These mills are of interest to us for two special reasons: first because little is known of 16th century paper-making in England, most paper at that time having been imported from abroad; and second, because these ill-fated mills in Horton must have been known, if only in a ruined condition by that time, to the young Milton thirty years later. It is a little curious that the Brysketts should have led us by two paths to Milton's doorstep in Horton; and that he may well have rambled by day past the relics of one brother's commercial misadventures, and by night have read, while browsing through his favourite Spenser, the other's elegies on dead Sidney.

1 C 2 Eliz., B 26/37. Bulstrood in 1572 had sued Edmond Drury and Mary Godfry for quiet possession of a messuage and water mill called Horton Mill on the eight-acre "mylle meade."
2 C 24/326 (30): Style was, at his examination *ex parte* Bryskett, on 6 December, 1605, of the parish of St. Giles without Cripplegate, free of the Company of Drapers, aged about fifty-two; at his examination *ex parte* Hellen in the following May (4 James) he was only fifty, and was "of Wobourne in Buck' Paper make[r]."

Whatever may have happened to the mills in later years, their success was not immediate. Style indeed says that ". . . he hath knowen some weeke foure pounde or thereaboute to be made of the pap myll towarde all charges, and he sayeth that wth good vsage so much money mighte have byn made of the same every seconde weeke/ & not much more/ as he thinketh. . . ." But whether this was less than Turnor had expected, or whether he had crippled himself by too great an initial outlay, the business fizzled out within two years and a half.

We have the story from Henry Heylyn of Burford in Oxfordshire, evidently John Hellen's solicitor.[1]

It begins with a tiny glimpse of romance. In October, 1598, he had made John Hellen's will, "then being in great extremitie of sicknes," and immediately after the will was written, John Hellen's *now wife* (*being then a widow and thereby appointed his executrix*) told Heylyn that John had committed a great part of his estate to Turnor's hands, to the value of "CC^{li}" or nearly. After writing the will John happily recovered, and married the widow. Several times he told Heylyn that Turnor was grown further into his debt, and that for his better security for the money Turnor had delivered to him the indenture of lease of the mills. Heylyn, understanding that he had only the *keeping* of the indenture, but no interest in the property, told Hellen that having the indenture would benefit him little, and advised him to take from Turnor an assignment of the lease. Soon after the end of the Trinity Term in 42 Elizabeth (1600), therefore, Turnor and John Hellen came to Henry Heylyn's chamber in Lyons Inn. After some discussion they decided that the lease should be assigned to Hellen for "CC^{li} pcell" of the debt, conditionally for redemption on

---

1 C 24/326 (30), deposition of Henry Heylyn; possibly a relative of John Hellen.

repayment of £200 in June, 1603, and Hellen gave Heylyn Turnor's original indenture so that he might draw up an assignment of it. This draft was delayed by Heylyn's being on the point of departure homeward into the country, but it was finally engrossed, and on the 28th of the next October (1600) signed, sealed, and delivered in the presence of Robert Veysey of Burford (Oxon.) and others.

At this time, and for a good while after, Hellen knew nothing of any debt by Turnor to Michael Bryskett.

At the same time Turnor sealed and gave Hellen an obligation of £400, in which his son Richard Turnor was mentioned as surety for his father. Richard was not then present, but his father promised that he should soon come to Heylyn's chamber and seal the bond. Accordingly during the same Michaelmas Term John and Richard Turnor came there together. In Heylyn's presence John told Richard that he had laid out a great deal of money about the paper mills, "And that howsoever in shew to the world he had caried himselfe in that busines yet he had therin vsed more money then his owne" and was therefore in Hellen's debt; that he had made over the lease with a condition to redeem it, and hoped he could; "but neu^{r}thelesse howsoeuer god should deale wth him yet said he, he was bound in Conscyence to secure [Hellen] of his money, he having so frindly lent it him. . . . And therewthall the said John Turnor and his said sonne falling both into teares the said John Turnor told his said sonne" that he should redeem the lease if possible; "but how soeuer said he yf I cannot redeeme it yet I must not inriche thee wth the good$_e$ of an other man," and asked Heylyn to tell Richard what had passed between him (Turnor) and John Hellen, and what was required of Richard to be done. Richard breaking into tears again, Turnor said "that he sought not to drawe him into bond for payment of his debt$_e$ but only to give bond wth him for his honest dealing wth the dẽft [Hellen], wch said he, yow may safely do vnleast yow thinke me a dishonest man"; whereupon Richard too sealed and delivered the bond.

In the meantime on the very day that the assignment of the lease was sealed, on October 28, Hellen "did by poll" lease the mills back to Turnor to hold during the time of mortgage. They agreed that the £200 for which the lease was mortgaged should be used as a stock for occupying and "setting on work" the mills and grounds; Turnor was to add so much more money to that as should make up a competent stock; and Hellen should have an allowance ratably after the clear yearly profit of the mills as recompense for his forbearance of that £200.

One would think that the encouragement of this fresh start might have given Turnor enough impetus to carry him to success. But it sounds as if he had either no head for business or else some fatal indolence, for again he failed to make anything of the mills. It was apparently at this time that he turned for help to a gentleman of Horton, one Edward Marshall. Having fallen into debt and having the mills still in his own hands,

he the sayd Turner fearinge to shew himselfe much a brode/ entreated [Marshall] (having the like millℓ not farr distant from him/) to make the best benefitt he might of the sayd paper Mill/ and of the stock wch the sayd Turner then had vpon it to the value of .20^{li}. or theraboutℓ/ wherupon this dep^t/ entered vpon it/ and imploying the sayd Mill and stock as well as he might, in the space of nyne weekℓ did make the sayd stock of 20^{li} be cleare to the sd John Turner six and fourty poundℓ or theraboutℓ meerly out of the sayd paper mill/.

He said that he did not know, however, what the corn mill did or would yield by the month or week, nor what the paper mill would yield "to continewe/ in an other mans handℓ, who should keepe a particular charge for it a lone."

This sounds more hopeful, and why it was not the beginning of better things I cannot say; except that if Marshall when he took over the mills found them stocked with only £20 worth of goods, one wonders what poor Turnor had done with the rest of the £200 with which Hellen so magnanimously furnished him in October. At all events he was in hiding for debts, and evidently not for his debts to Hellen, whose generous treatment of him is clear. Perhaps Michael Bryskett was the lurking hobgoblin.

In Hilary Term next (1600/01) John Hellen came to Heylyn and told him that Turnor was taking no steps to stock the mills, and that he doubted Turnor's estate was weak and he was in danger of losing not only his yearly profit but all that Turnor owed him besides.

Soon after in the same Hilary Term Turnor himself came and told Heylyn that he could no longer hold out in his occupying of the mills for want of money to stock them; that he feared to go abroad about his business for being arrested; that his estate was utterly sunken by means thereof; wishing often that he had never taken those works in hand. He said that if Hellen would now take the mills, he would surrender up the lease parole and put him in possession, for other means he had none, either to pay the hundred pounds he owed him or to yield him any yearly benefit for his £200.

Heylyn talked it over with John Hellen, who was fearful and unwilling to undertake the stocking and "setting on work," because of the charge and of his own unskilfulness; but he finally agreed to try it. In February, 1600/01, therefore, Turnor reassigned the property to Hellen, receiving back the bond of £100 he had forfeited; confessing that he owed him £300 and somewhat more.

For the unfortunate Turnor the next stage, as he had anticipated, was the Fleet. This was not till after he had reassigned the mills to Hellen; nor did Hellen, when he took that reassignment, know that he was about to break.

In the Fleet he was visited by Hellen, who for the first time of which we have record gave way to reproach: he "did seeme much to greeve that he ever intermeddled wth the same Milles very earnestly affirming that he had much hindred himselfe and ympayred his estate by them." Edward Marshall came to see him also and offered him £500 for the mills, with £10 a year during his life; but Turnor would not accept this offer, alleging "that they had stood him in much above 1000^{li}." He complained to Marshall, rather ungraciously, it would seem, that Hellen, contrary to his promise, was keeping him on a short allowance of maintenance while he lay in prison, and that Hellen's demands in his accounts were large and unjust.

One James Parke, a cloakmaker with whom Hellen was a partner in a cloak shop in London, was another of Turnor's visitors in prison. It is from him that we learn a little of Turnor's relations with Michael Bryskett,[1] whom we may surmise to be the creditor on whose account Turnor was in the Fleet: Turnor told Parke that he did not then owe Bryskett above some thirty pounds, for that he had paid back all he had borrowed from him except so much, and had allowed Bryskett after the rate of ten in the hundred interest for it. He said, moreover, that Michael, to make Turnor's debt the greater, charged him with allowance after £40 a year in the hundred under the name of profit for his usury.

Meanwhile Hellen in his turn had taken over those bewitched mills, only to prove his misgivings too well founded. He tried to let them out to someone else for

---

1 C 24/326 (30). Deposition of James Parke *ex parte* Hellen. He had been another creditor of Turnor's, having lent him thirty-five pounds out of the stock of his cloak shop, but Turnor had satisfied that debt.

rent, but was forced to occupy them himself for want of a farmer. And so he says in 1603 that since the reassignment in February, 1600/01, he

hath builded a new house called a ragge house something distant from the sd mills wch hath cost this def about ffiftie pownde & hath since repaired the sd mills in the wheeles hãmers & gudgyns & other pt℮ thereof at this defdt℮ charges bµt hath not new builte anie roome of the sd mills but hath [since that 11th February] new built the flood-gates belonging to the sd mills wch floodgates cost this def xx^{li} the build-inge or thereaboute And . . . he hath also ben inforced to provide other necessaries to furnishe the sd mills to this defdt℮ great charges.

Robert Style adds that Hellen made some new buildings besides repairing and finishing the former ones, "& also did certayne water worke in & vppon the same for the necessary vse & occupyinge of the sd myllns."

Hellen occupied them, says Style, two years with great loss. Perhaps because Marshall had run them with some success for Turnor, Hellen persuaded him to a partnership: Marshall dealt, he says, for nine or ten weeks with Hellen by way of partnership in the mills, and agreed to have so continued for divers years if both parties liked; or he that disliked was to give three months' warning. As soon as Marshall had been a week in this partnership, he perceived that Hellen had placed some such troublesome people therein with whom Marshall could not avoid intercourse, that he resolved not to continue. He would have broken off at once, but Hellen held him to the agreement (or part of it), and

drew [him] to allowe him his owne askinge for stuffe wch he brought in, to make paper of/ to allmost duble the value for wch this dep^t could have bought the like this dep^t rather resolving to breake off partener-shipp vpon so hard condicõns, then to endure the inconveience [*sic*] of those trouble-some and vnskillfuII people/.

Hellen, realizing that he was not cut out for this trade, after two fruitless years offered to let the paper mill to

Style. Style, having known the workings of it of old, and being, we may guess, better fitted for the business than the three speculators who had made such a mess of it, took it of him for his son Richard Style. This brings us to the time of his deposition in the Star Chamber, in 1603, when he deposed that he could not certainly say what benefit the corn mill had yielded him but that it yielded little profit "because it doth manie tymes want wo^rke," that he had not made over £45 profit of the paper mill; and that ever since entering it he had kept servants there for the most part — i. e. presumably someone to run the mill — and had furnished the same with all things needful so soon as he conveniently could, "one thinge after another."

Turnor ended his unhappy days before long, and Michael Bryskett turned his suit against Hellen, who, being himself a still more heavily unpaid creditor of the deceased, was thus ground between the upper and nether millstones. The upshot we do not know. But lawsuits are expensive, and whether Bryskett or his debtor was right as to the sums still owing, one partly sees why three years after these depositions he was writing so desperately to Salisbury.

V. THE HUSBANDS OF LUCRECE

LODOWICK'S eldest sister Lucrece, seven years his senior, contributes most to our knowledge of the family. In September, 1558,[1] at the age of eighteen, she married Vincent Guicciardine, twenty-two years her senior.[2] The frequent discrepancies of this sort, by the way, in the ages of husband and wife, explain why so many Elizabethan wives appear to have had such extraordinary vitality. More commonly than not, one would gather, a woman married twice, nor were third husbands rarely come by. The Wife of Bath appears to have set the fashion, rather than Henry VIII, who, one may fancy, was even something of a comfort to his male subjects.

Unlike his father-in-law Anthony Bryskett, Guicciardine seems never to have been naturalized, for after his death he was spoken of as "noe free denison." [3] He appears in the list of "Strangers in London Temp Eliz" of 1571 [4] as dwelling in the Tower Ward:

> vyncent Goodiergyne [*sic*] Italian m'chant
> he haith ij S^{r}uantes vīz Lewes Gady
> & Cristen de Short Italions they have
> byne here xxx^{ty} yeres
> } Italions/3/.

The servants had been with him for about half that time, for in a similar report of the same year [5] they are all listed in "Alhallowes Barkinge pishe":

---

1 *Allegations for Marriage Licences, issued by the Bishop of London, 1520–1610*, Harl. Soc., xxv, 19.
2 Req. 2, 97/38, Nicholas and Emma Backhouse *vs.* Vincent Guychardeyne and other defendants, 18 Eliz. Dr. Leslie Hotson very kindly referred me to this document. .
3 C 24/277 (59), interrogatory to Lucrece.
4 S. P. 12/84.
5 S. P. 12/82. Report of the Strangers in London.

Italians iij
> Vincent Goodgerdine a
> fflorentine a m'chant dwelling here
> this xxxty yeres & his two men s'uant℮
> Christian and Lewes dwellinge wth
> him this xvj yeres both fflorentynes

no church iij [1]

These reports usually mention wife and children. Probably Vincent's were not included, being of English birth. Lewes Gady we shall meet again, in sinister guise.

Guicciardine's coming to England is thus fixed as in 1541, eighteen years after his father-in-law's (cf. above, p. 269). This family of great Florentine merchants was widely scattered. There were a Jehan Baptist and Laurence who had a company in Antwerp.[2] Like Anthony Bryskett's, Vincent Guicciardine's affairs appear here and there among the papers of Henry VIII's and subsequent reigns. In 1557, for instance, we find three bonds restricting the amount of wares he might unpack and sell.[3] In 1543 [4] he, among several other Italian merchants, was to secure one Anthony Guidotti's debt to the king.

Again like Anthony Bryskett, Vincent held a good deal of real property. In a suit in the Court of Requests [5] in which he and others were defendants and Nicholas and Emma Backhouse were plaintiffs, he says that he had the lease of certain lands and tenements in East Ham made not to himself but to two other men "because ⟨   ⟩ would haue them assure yt over to this depon^t℮ wief ⟨   ⟩ tymes whan he should require them." Before the making

---

1 In 1577 the Bishop of Rochester, Thomas Walsingham, and Henry Cobham reported him as one of the six chief recusants of the diocese, together with William Roper, the son-in-law and biographer of Sir Thomas More:
"Vincent Guicchardyne of Lewsham, an Italian marchant, cometh to the churche verie seldome & hath not receiued the communion since he came to Lewsham, wch is almost two yeares." (*Catholic Record Society*, XXII, 11).
2 Letters and Papers, Henry VIII, vol. XVIII; see index, p. 468.
3 Cal. Dom. St. Pap., 1547–80, I, 90.
4 Letters and Papers, Henry VIII, vol. XVIII, part I, no. 208.
5 See p. 290, n. 2.

of the lease he did not at any time see and know all the parcels of ground contained in the lease, or the true value thereof — so he says himself, although another deponent, who adds Guicciardine's being a "straunger" as a reason for not having the lease made to himself, says that the lands leased were worth twenty pounds a year, and so much was certified to Guicciardine before the making of the lease.

Taking over property he had not even seen sounds as if he must have been used to dealing in real estate, and so much appears in his will. When he died in 1581, he asked to have his body laid "in the prishe Churche wherin I dwell withowte pompe," in which connection one remembers that ten years earlier he was described as of no church. He made bequests of money to his three daughters, Camilla (then about nineteen), Elizabeth, and Mary, on condition that they should not marry without Lucrece's consent. The rest of his property, except some bequests to servants, he left to Lucrece and to his twenty-one-year-old son James, whom he made joint executors. To Lucrece he left the leases of his house in Syding (Seething) Lane, that of the marsh ground at Streatham, that of the lands in Sydenham, and the lease "wch I houlde of ffraunces Backen in Eastham," who really *was* the future Verulam.[1] James's share was to be "all the gooddes wch I haue at fflorence" — which shows that the connection with his native land had remained unbroken — besides the following lands in this realm (England) which were bought with his money, but the instruments thereof made to his son upon trust: ten and a half acres of Plumstead Marsh in Kent "that was wonne" (reclaimed), the lands and tenements in "Hearithe" (Erith) bought of Thomas Barnes, and a certain part in the land "that shalbe recovered of

1 See below, Chapter V, p. 299 and n., and p. 304.

the breache at Herithe which I recken shall be "about seventy acres, in which part his son was invested by act of Parliament.

This rather high-sounding venture duly appears among the State Papers of Elizabeth's reign: [1] In May (?), 1563, one Jacobo Aconty addressed a petition to the Queen saying that the Thames has so overflowed its banks as to inundate the lands near Erith; he understands the means of preventing so serious a damage, but when the land has many owners they will rarely combine to bear the expense unless someone will take the risk. He cannot do it alone, but has friends who will help. (Vincent Guicciardine, as we know, was one of them; it sounds as if this were another of many examples which might be multiplied to show how the Italian group clung together.) Henry VIII, when the land near the Tower was flooded, offered half the land to be recovered to those who should recover it. Aconty therefore requests the same arrangement of Elizabeth. On June 24, 1563, Aconty had a license to take up workmen to amend Plumstead Marshes; in which venture also Guicciardine probably had a share, from his leaving his son part of the land there "that was wonne."

The legacy to James was conditional on his letting Lucrece use all those lands during her life. All his goods, plate, jewels, ready money, etc., were to be divided between his wife and son on the same condition; and James was to make Lucrece good assurance thereof within six months after his father's death. If he did not, he was to be deprived of his share and Lucrece was to enjoy the goods alone. This assurance, whether through negligence or through villainy, James failed to make; which neglect became the basis of a long quarrel between him and Lucrece's second husband, Thomas Wrightington.

[1] Cal. Dom. St. Pap., Eliz., VI, 538-539.

Thomas Wrightington was the son of Alexander Wrightington, who, with his wife Juliana, held premises in the parish of St. Bartholomew the Great, near West Smithfield. Thus they were neighbours to that Francis Eaglefield who married Joan Bryskett and lived on the other side of Duck Lane in the parish of St. Bartholomew the Less.

Thomas Wrightington's mother had three husbands in all. She was a Devonshire girl herself, Julian Shenn or Shine of Bradley.[1] Her first husband was Stephen Wilford[2] of Enfield in Middlesex, by whom she had John Wilford, at whose house in Enfield Thomas Wrightington and Lucrece were later to visit.[3] By Wrightington, her second husband, she had two sons, Thomas and George, and a daughter Barbara, who married a Thomas Denver or Denner of Bradninch in Devon. Barbara had a large brood of children, who thus were nephews and nieces of Thomas and Lucrece Wrightington: Edward, John, Thomas, Hugh, Winifred, Mary, Prudence, Gylian, Elizabeth, and Barbary. Julian Wrightington's third husband was also a Devonshire man, of Bradninch. He was Peter St. Hill, and their two children, Peter and Mary, seem to have been considerably younger than their half-brothers and sister. After the death of their parents it appears that they lived with Barbara (Wrightington) Denner and her husband Thomas.[4]

Not far from the time that our Thomas Wrightington married Lucrece (Bryskett) Guicciardine,[5] he was in difficulties about this younger sister, Mary St. Hill of Devon. In 1586 Humphrey Walronde the younger of Bradfeilde in

1 *Visitation of Devon*, Harl. Soc., VI, 249.
2 *Middlesex Pedigrees*, Harl. Soc., LXV, 35 (MS. Harl. 1551, fol. 21).
3 C 24/277 (7), deposition of Mary Atkinson.
4 C 2 Eliz., W 18/42; *Visitation of Essex, 1612*, Harl. Soc., XIII, 189.
5 By 1586.

Devon brought suit against him in Chancery: Peter St. Hill, he said, had treated with him, Walronde, about a marriage with Mary; gifts passed between them, and finally Mary "affyed & Contracted herself" to him "accordinge to the due Course of Lawe." After that, the contract becoming known to Thomas and George Wrighting-ton, they persuaded her "in most vngodlie sorte" to estrange herself from him, and even conveyed her "to A place to yo^{ur} saide Orator vnknowen." Walronde began suit in the ecclesiastical courts; whereon a conclusion was reached between the parties "touchinge the Assurance of the porcōn) of the said Marie . . . amountinge to fower hundred powndes" and for Walronde's assurance of a reasonable jointure; the Wrightingtons pretended consent, Thomas swearing on the Bible not to hinder the suit, and Walronde became bound to him in an obligation of 1,000 marks to relinquish all suit in the ecclesiastical courts.

Now, says his Bill in Chancery, after all these shows of good will Thomas and George Wrightington have again removed Mary to parts unknown to him; he consequently requests a subpoena.

All this sounds reasonable enough, if it was true; but the joint answer of Thomas and George Wrightington to Wal-ronde's "false and frivolous Bill" is very lively reading.

To begin with, they say that Walronde was *not* earnestly persuaded by Peter to arrange the marriage. On the contrary, as these defendants have been told by their brother-in-law Thomas Denner, in whose house Mary then was, and by Peter himself, Walronde "about Midsomer was twelvemonethes" was pretending suit to the daughter of one John Thomas, a near neighbour and special friend of Peter's. Accordingly Walronde came "vnloked for" to Denner's house, where Peter and Mary then abode (Mary having been committed to Denner's custody by John Wil-

ford, also half-brother to the St. Hills, and administrator
to their deceased father), and "dyd craftelie insynuate
himself" into Peter's company, pretending he had come
to see whether Peter too were a suitor to John Thomas's
daughter, and saying that, if so, he would relinquish his
own suit. Peter said he was not, so Walronde asked him to
come to John Thomas's house, and, in respect of his acquaintance with John Thomas, to further his (Walronde's)
suit. This Peter, to win friendship with Walronde's father,
who lived near the Denners, and because of Walronde's
earnest request, agreed to do. By that occasion Walronde
had frequent access to Peter, and used his pretended suit
to Thomas's daughter

as a most fraudulent meane to haue a colourable accesse to the Sister
[of Peter]; and most indyrectlie not respecting the Courtesye and en-
treteynement of the said Peter wth his readynes to pleasure him, attempted by his conninge pswacõns (affirminge that his ffather woulde
give him ffyfftie poundes lande by yere and suche lyke) to allure the
good lykinge of the said Marye verie seacreatlie towardℓ him wthout
the privitie of [Peter or the Denners], albeit they were then in the
howse wth her. And yet besides, dyd neverthelesse contynue his õpen
Suyte of Marryadge to the said John Thoñs his daughter.

So that Mary should not betray his secret suit to her
friends, he sought to persuade her that they were careless
of her preferment and purposely deferred her marriage to
keep her portion in their hands.

In all this he was so successful that Peter never suspected him, but still accompanied him to John Thomas's
till he had a full answer of denial there;

At wch verie tyme of deniall, [Walronde] retorninge home wth the said
Peter St Hill to the house of the said Thomas Denner dyd firste deliver
out on the same daye after his Retorne thether That he hadd that
verie tyme contracted himself seacretlie to the said Marye wthin one
Quarter of an hower after his then cominge to the same house not ac-
quayntinge . . . Peter . . . who was then wthin or neere about the
same house, nor the said Thoñs Denner nor his wief beinge at that

instant in the same howse lykewise, that he intended soe to doe, And
sithence that tyme hath also reported . . . That the said p^r tended
Contracte was hadd or made foure or fyve dayes or more before
thaunswere of deniall given him by . . . John Thomas. Wherby appeareth the said Complt ys not ashamed . . . to make knowen his
indyrect Dealinges therin.

It really sounds as if our Strephon were a rogue.

Thomas and George Wrightington, hearing all this,
thought Mary should withdraw from Walronde's access.
The young scapegrace therefore went to the ecclesiastical
court, which, finding the information of the defendants in
substance true, "and for the most pte confessed by the pl
himself," discharged the defendants.

Thomas and George then said that Walronde might
confer unhindered with Mary and see if she would have
him, if he would first be bound to Thomas that, if she would
not of her own free will, he should not attempt by suit on
any former supposed contract to call her or her name in
question. This must have been the conference at which
Wrightington swore on the Bible not to bias her. Wrightington sent her letters overseen and partly made by Walronde. She would not agree, and he tried to force her by
going to law — presumably by this suit in Chancery.

Walronde's replication, to the effect that this answer
contains "many fantasticall ymaginations shewinge the
malitious and vncheritable dispositions" of the defendants
toward him, trying "to blemishe the Complainaunte
Credit wth their fryvolous suggestions," says that after the
contract with Mary was first made, Peter and George both
liked it; and George in the County of Devon earnestly
many times moved Walronde's father to assure some living
to his son and Mary in consideration of the marriage to be
had between them — only one of several references which
suggest that the whole affair was rather a matter of money;

And lickewise the said Thomas Wrightington delte w[th] many of the Complainaunt℮ frend℮ in London to the licke effecte. . . . Neither is it licklie [he adds penetratingly] that the said Thomas Wrightington at that p[r]sent time would likewise become bounden vnto the Complainaunte in the some of one thousand pound℮ w[th] Condition in effecte tending to the purchasinge of c'teine land℮ [for Mary's jointure] if he had not ꝑfectlie knowen [from Mary] that she fully intendyd the performaunce of the said Contracte.

This leaves Walronde with the last word, though he has not explained his MacHeath-like actions. But the triumph must have been to the Wrightingtons. For Mary St. Hill married not Walronde but one Henry Martyn of Steeple Morden, Cambs., an alliance that cannot have displeased Peter St. Hill, since he himself married Elizabeth, daughter of Thomas Martin, Doctor of the Civil Law, also of Steeple Morden.[1]

Henry Martyn seems to have been a faithful friend to his brother-in-law Thomas Wrightington to the end of Wrightington's unpeaceful life, and was the sole executor of his pitiable will. It is good to know that this marriage turned out all that one could have wished: not that they merely prospered, in such terms as one guesses Walronde would have measured success, but that they stood by each other through reverses with more affection than the too unadvised, too sudden Walronde match seemed to promise.

Martyn when he died toward the end of 1619 [2] left his leases, including the manor and rectory of Steeple Morden, to Mary for her life, and after her death to their eldest son Thomas (perhaps named for Wrightington?), to whom Mary was to give £20 a year "so as" he "shall liue in any the vniuersities Cambridge or Oxford or . . . Grayes Inne either of the Temples or Lyncolnes Inne." Henry, the second son, was to practise as an attorney and live in any

1 *Visitation of Devon*, Harl. Soc., VI, 249.
2 Prerogative Court of Canterbury, 3 Soame (Henry Martyn's will).

of the Inns of Chancery; Richard, the youngest, was to be apprenticed to some trade in London. These two and the daughter, Elizabeth, received money bequests. Martyn stipulated that if his sons at any time hindered Mary's use of the leases or went to law against her, their own legacies were to be void. He ended by leaving all his money, plate, jewels, and household stuff to his wife *"for her Recompence for that she so freelie lovinglie and willingly yealded vp her Joynture which she had in all my freehould Landes whereso-euer which I soulde for the payment of my debtę."*

Wrightington [1] was, as his brother-in-law Martyn appears to have been, of the legal profession, having been admitted to Gray's Inn in October, 1588 — twelve years after Francis Bacon.[2] This was not till after his marriage with Lucrece, for he had apparently married her within five years of her first husband's death: on September 26, 1586, the Council appointed Lord Buckhurst and Lord Cobham to hear the complaint of William Waad, Clerk of the Council, who declared that Wrightington was going

---

1 The Ancient Deeds in the Public Record Office contain a bond (A. 6001) of Thomas Wrightington of London and William Mills of Gray's Inn to Thomas Marshe of Lincolns Inn for £400. It is dated 20 September, 29 Eliz. William Mill succeeded Marsh as clerk of the Star Chamber, a high office which Bacon sought in vain. The *Calendar of Hatfield MSS.*, part 13, p. 156 has a letter of 1578 that contains one delightful phrase; one would like to know definitely whether the reference is to our Wrightington. Vincent Skynner writes to Lord Burghley, "According to your L. pleasure I have attended on my L. of Essex to Cambridge, and delivered to Mr. Wright as your L. gave me in commandment, . . . betwixt whom and Writtington I found there had been *great and long stomaching* [italics mine] for the most part of these two years, and that the same was grown to such extremity that it behoved to have the same quieted speedily. For which cause chiefly I tarried one whole day at Cambridge, and have left them both in that good tune that they have each promised before me and given hands to other to forget all unkindnesses by-past, and return to the ancient love and amity that was at the beginning of their acquaintance in service about his Lordship."

2 *Register of Admissions to Gray's Inn.* Bacon was admitted on June 27, 1576, Wrightington on October 22, 1588.

"to molest" him at law over some "marish grownde" in East Ham, which Wrightington thought concerned him because he had married the widow of Guicciardine.[1]

Not a little of his and Lucrece's joint life and indeed of that of the whole Bryskett clan is to be learned from a suit in Chancery between him and Michael Bryskett about these very lands in East Ham and other bequests of Vincent Guicciardine.[2]

John Raymond, who was servant to Wrightington for several years before the Bryskett alliance as well as for nine years after, said at his examination *ex parte* Bryskett that before that intermarriage Thomas was "examiner under one m^r Marsh the Cleark to the high Court of Starchamber and kept 2. or 3. men under him." What his wealth was, Raymond could not say; but Mary Atkinson deposed on her brother's behalf that Wrightington was "generally reputed to be a man of verie litle welth before he maried the sd Lucresse," and Thomas Bryskett, who had a nasty tongue when he chose, added further that Wrightington "before & untill he maryed the sd Lucresse was but of mean sort and statiõ, and that he did owe mo^r then he was worth." Lucrece on the other hand had been "of great wealth and habilitie,"[3] possessed of those leases which we know her first husband had left her (see above, pp. 292–3). Half a dozen deponents, not all of them relatives of Lucrece, concur that the marriage improved Wrightington's worldly condition appreciably. Not only did he, as the custom was, take over the leases, but he was enabled by the marriage to take a long lease of a house in

---

1 Acts of Privy Council, xiv, 234.

2 C 24/277 (P. R. O.). The depositions *ex parte* Bryskett, for which I have used Mr. Vincent's transcript, are no. 7; those on Wrightington's behalf, no. 59. See also Wrightington's Bill of Complaint, 4 July, 1598, and Michael Bryskett's answer, October, 1598; and the Decree and Order Books in Chancery for 1598 and 1599.   3 Michael Bryskett's answer, C 2 Eliz.

St. Botolph's without Bishopsgate. Besides bringing him all this gear, Lucrece "demeaned her selfe both dutyfully & lovingly & verye respectyvelye toward hym as any woman might doe."

The property, however, was destined to be a source of trouble. It was handed over to Wrightington by Petola, whom Guicciardine had named an overseer in his will, and who had dealt for Vincent and Lucrece long before as their factor or clerk.[1] It may be that the leases were imperfect, for the interrogatory to Lucrece asks,

was not the lease wch yor Late husbande Lefte yo^u in Eastham Marshes a voide Lease by reason he had taken yt in his owne name beinge noe free denison And did not the plt therefore not onlye purchasse those yeares then to come of Mr Controller by vertue of his pattente of Concealm^{te} from the Quene but alsoe a newe Lease in Reu'cōn from M^r ffraunc℮ Bacoñ Esquier after the plt had Maried yo^u; [and] did not Mrs Duttoñ challenge yor Lease wch yor said Late husbande Left yo^u in Stretham in yor widdowhood for the wch yo^u paied xv^{li} a Yeare, And did not the plt purchase a newe Lease thereof Imediatlye after he had Maried yo^u and the Rente alsoe wch was Reserved therevppon.

Lucrece replies that one Mrs. Dutton claimed a lease of hers in Streatham "for wch this dept paid the yerly rent of fyftene pound℮ whervppon the sd Complt after his enter-mariage wth this dept did purchase a newe lease therof & allso the sd Rent of fiftene pound℮ reserved vppon the ould lease," but says that to her knowledge the lease of East Ham marshes was

ever reputed in the lief tyme of this dept℮ sd late husband a good lease & not a void lease as by the Article is intended But saithe that after the plt℮ mariage wth this dept the pltif obteyned a new lease in Revercon from M^r ffranc℮ Bakon of the sd Mershe Ground℮, and as the plit him self affirmed he gott a Confyrmacōn from Mr Controler for the yeres wch were then to come in this depts sd ould lease wch is more then this dept knoweth.

---

1 Wrightington vs. Guicciardine, C 2 Eliz., W 13/13 (1601).

This sounds reasonable enough, but trouble was breeding. According to Michael Bryskett's testimony Thomas behaved so extravagantly that within six or seven years of their marriage most of the wealth got by it was consumed; this, with specific actions like his going about to forfeit a lease in order to get it into his own hands, brought about the inevitable quarrel between him and his wife, in about 1592; and finally by the intervention of her relatives he was forced to make a deed of assignment to her.

The defendant Michael Bryskett's account of the affair will be as little to Wrightington's credit as any, but we may as well know the worst that can be said:

Lucrece, foreseeing poverty and resolving to recover what she might to support "her poore impaired credite and estate," and being helped therein by her eldest brother Sebastian (cf. p. 271), demanded a conveyance of such property as Wrightington stood possessed of; whereupon Wrightington, touched with remorse, as Michael thinks, but especially to eschew the disgrace Lucrece might have brought upon him by a public sentence in law undoing the marriage < *lacuna* >, agreed to assure the leases to some friend for her absolute use. It was proposed that he should convey them to Sebastian and to Thomas Darcy, who had married Lucrece's eldest daughter Camilla. After this agreement was reached but before the deed was actually sealed, Sebastian died (in the summer of 1592 [1]). Wrightington therefore made the conveyance to Thomas Darcy and to Michael Bryskett, and Lucrece accordingly used the rents and profits from her estate for many years to maintain herself and her family.

At the making of this deed Lodowick Bryskett, as we know (cf. p. 257), happened to be present, having come to Mr. Waferer's on business of his own; and being there,

1 Sebastian's will, Prerogative Court of Canterbury, 53 Harrington.

he acted as one of the witnesses, the others being Thomas Bryskett and Edward Atkinson.

In 1594 Thomas Darcy died,[1] leaving Michael as sole trustee, for a substitute was not appointed. During the years that followed, fresh trouble rose over the question of whether the tenants of the lands in question were to attorn to Lucrece and her trustees or not. In point of fact it seems that they did attorn, for the deponents are unanimous that it was Lucrece or some other by her appointment who received the rents. One Henry Jennings of Streatham deposed that he had been Lucrece's tenant for seventeen years and had always paid the rent to her or her assignees;

and dothe not rember that ever he paid his sd rent unto the pltif except yt were at one tyme at his offyce and then had an Acquittance for the reciept therof At wch tyme this dept thinketh [Wrightington] dyd receyve the sd Rent to the use of Lucresse his wief for that . . . he herd [Wrightington] saye that the Rentℓ for that land were his wives Rentℓ.

Joan Gosson, another Streatham tenant, deposes *ex parte* Bryskett that

she at one tyme comming to pay the sd Rent then dew mett wth the now complt m^r Thomas Wrightington, & told him that she had brought his Rent, who then willed this dept to pay the same to the sd Lucresse sayeing yt was none of his, it was his wifes: and sayth that the sd Lucresse hath likewise . . . Receiued the Rentℓ . . . : And sayth that she is fully pswaded that the sd Lucresse hath like wise pd or caused by her means to be pd such Rentℓ as she was to pay for the sd landℓ and tenemtℓ, . . . for that the sd Lucresse sometymes hath blamed this dept when she came late wth her sd rent sayeing to this effect vz How can I pay my Rent yf yo^u be so long till yo^u pay yours.

John Raymond, the Wrightingtons' servant for many years, says it was Lucrece who appointed him to sell "certain Coppes woode" when the underwoods were last cut

1 Prerogative Court of Canterbury, 35 Dixy.

at Streatham; she told him how much to sell them for, and received the money.

As time went on, however, Wrightington began to interfere in the receiving of the rents, possibly to establish a precedent for himself. Jennings tells us of one of several instances:

Abowte a weeke now past he . . . was sent for by Mrs Lucresse Wryghtington . . . vnto the Savoye in the Strand where she then laye to come & speake wth her abowte the payment of certen Rent wch he had then formerly payd vnto her . . . and wch he this Dept had not then readye to paye At wch tyme she tould this dept that when his said Rent was redy he should paye yt vnto her or vnto one Mr Harvy [this was Thomas Darcy's successor as Camilla's husband and Lucrece's son-in-law] in her absence to her vse . . . whervppon this dept tould her that his Landlord master Wrightington had bene to demand the sd Rent of him . . .

to which Lucrece and Harvey, at whose house she was, told him that Wrightington had nothing to do with the rent, and that if Jennings paid it to him he would have to pay it twice over.

As regards the *paying* of the rents, Wrightington had happened as a mere matter of convenience to keep a finger in the pie even when he was *receiving* none of the incoming profits. After he had made the assignment to her, Lucrece says, she or Michael

dyd ever receive the rent℮ due by the same leases And vppon the Recept therof this dept dyd vsually tell owte into a bagg the sume of fortye pound℮ for the Chefe Rent due at everye half yere to the sd Mr Baken & delyvered the same vnto hir sd husband to paye it over vnto the sd Mr Bakon for that this dept℮ said husband his Chamber was nere vnto the sd Mr Bakons lodging℮ in Grayes Inne

— which, by the way, establishes Bacon's identity, for no other of that name was a member of Gray's Inn at the time, and also at that time he was still "Mr.", not yet having received a title.

And vppon the payment therof [Wrightington] dyd usually delyver vnto this dept Mr Bakons Acquittances for the same wch Acquittances whether they were made in the pltif℮ name or in the Defdt℮ she cannot certenly saye for that she never loked further then to the subscripto of Mr Bakons name [a feminine sense for business, surely!], but thinketh that the pltif might & dyd take the same Acquittances in his owne name for that he would not haue yt knowne to Mr Bakon that he had mad⟨e⟩ anye Conveyance therof But saithe that after Mr Baken had sould his interest in the sd land℮ the now defdt received the sd Rent℮ & tooke Acquittanc℮ in his owne name.

Wrightington, as the interrogatories on his behalf were later to show, was trying to establish the fact that his assignment to Lucrece was in trust to her in case of her surviving him, and not to her immediate use and behoof. Perhaps it was with this in view as well as from wanting to turn an extra penny that he offered one Paul ¹ the lease of East Ham marshes for a fine of one hundred pounds, at the rent he had held it at before. Paul, as if to make assurance doubly sure, went to Lucrece about it. She replied that he might have what he wanted, but that she "would haue that hundreth pound℮ fyne to hir self." Afterwards she remonstrated with Thomas,

telling him that she marveled that he would offer to take the benefyt of the sd lease from this dept knowing that he had long before that tyme conveyed awaye his interest therin Nevertheles at the ernest entretye of the pltif and vppon his faithfull promis that he would repaye that money vnto this dept She this dept was contented that the pltif should procede in the bargen wth the sd Paule as he had begone & should receive of him the for sd hundreth pound℮.

That seems to be a score for Lucrece, to the effect that the trust was for her immediate use. But we have one for Wrightington to balance it. She deposes that when she had the coppice woods at Streatham cut and sold — which was about 1597, some four or five years after the conveyance was made — she,

_____
1 Probably either Sir Stephen Powle, who preserved letters by Lyly and Lodge, or his father.

not then knowing that the pltifͨ sd Conveyance was so absolute as in truthe it is, did acquainte the plaintif what she purposed to doe concerning the same woode and wᵗʰall requested him to bestowe the money wᶜʰ was made of the sale of that wood vppon hir . . . wᶜʰ the plaintif was contented to doe and so this dept had that money.

She apparently did not put it in quite this light without a rather searching examination, for what she said first bears a different emphasis and is entirely crossed out, her final statement being written overleaf. Surely, if as late as 1597 she still thought Thomas had some right to the rent, she could not very plausibly call his interpretation of the conveyance a "new pretended meaning."

But in 1597 things were gathering to a head. It looks as if Wrightington were trying to get the deed of assignment into his own hands, perhaps for fraudulent purposes. In this he appears to have found an ally in his servant John Denner. One wonders, by the way, whether this were not his nephew of that name (see p. 294); for it was not uncommon to employ relatives as servants (cf. Camilla Harvey's will, *infra*, pp. 348 ff.); and it seems as if such a servant might well be trusted in confidential business.

At all events, Michael Bryskett's servant Edward Elyott (alias Jennings) deposed that about three years past (i. e. about 1597)

one John Dennaʳ the sd Compltͨ servant whoe was then very familiaʳ wᵗh this dept dyd uppon a tyme request this dept to le⟨t⟩ him haue a sight of a certen writing wᶜh (as the sd Denneʳ said) was mad betwene the sd Complt and the sd deft mʳ Brisket saying that he would see but one worde in the same writing wherunto this dept aunswered saying that his mʳ did not kepe his writingͨ soe negligentlye as that he this dept could come by them and said more over that althoughe he could come at them yet he the said Dennar should not haue or see any of them . . . wherwᵗʰ the sd Denner seming to be satisfied depted But whether the sd John Denner dyd make the aforesaid motion unto this dept of his owne accord or by the comandement of the now Complt this dept saithe he dothe not knowe.

This sounds suspicious enough. Mary Atkinson tells us further that

uppon some falling owt of the sd plt & Lucresse at . . . m^r Wylford℈ howse at Enfeild [doubtless Wrightington's half-brother John Wilford] the p^lt came sodenly to london leaving his sd wyfe there And when he came whome to the sd ⟨house, *probably*⟩ w^thowt bishopsgate (as an auncient mayd servante of the sd Lucresse then told this dp^t wth teares) he the sd comp^lt had sent away a Chest wherein as she thought all her m^ris wryting℈ were And this dpt verely beliveth that the sd Comp^lte purpose therein was to have taken away the sd wryting from the sd lucresse for that she usually kept them in that chest but the sd lucresse at her coming whome . . . told the p^lt that he was deceyved of his expectacon for that she had disposed hir wryting℈ in a safer place.

In the same year came the culminating quarrel of the series. Did you not in Michaelmas term, asks the interrogatory to Lucrece,

tell the plt that yo^u woulde Dwell noe more wth him vnlesse he woulde geeve yo^u all the goods he had. And did yo^u not . . . Departe accordinglie and take wth yo^u a greate parte of the plt℈ good℈? . . . did not the plt intreate you dyvers tymes before to soiorne wth yor Children in Essex for a yeare or two vntill he mighte take some order for yor brother Atkinson's debtes wch he thoughte he coulde by noe meanes compasse and keepe howse alsoe by reason the debtes were soe greate for the wch the plt stood bounde wth him,

and did you call someone to witness that Wrightington offered you £100 a year for allowance while you were away?

These interrogatories presumably represent Wrightington's side of the affair, which in Lucrece's telling sounds rather different. She does admit to begin with that in Michaelmas term of 1597 he tried to break up housekeeping on account of debts to her brother-in-law Atkinson.[1] Wrightington's feelings on the subject she does not describe; of course it is not to her advantage to paint him with any. My own guess is that the prospect of a year

1 Cf. pp. 324–325.

or two free from domestic quarrels may have been rather
a relief. Lucrece's further description of the scene is lively,
yet to the inner ear a little pitiful. To begin with, she
denies the speeches imputed to her about refusing to live
with her husband unless he gave her all his goods. One
feels a rather pathetic futility in both question and answer.
It is the high vapourish language of a quarrel suddenly
condensed by the cold impact of "Did you, yea or no?"
Of course Wrightington has not reported her words exactly; he could scarcely have done so had he been taking
notes on them at the time; much less now that he is telling
his tale with irritation accumulated through two years.
Of course, too, she cannot remember what she said in a
temper, and hardly could be expected to recognize her own
hot speeches thus served up cold. Yet she proceeds in
amazing detail.

> But . . . abowte the tyme menconed . . . the now Complt moved
> this dept to break vp howse and to sudiorne wth Mrs Harvye one of this
> dept$\complement$ daughters wch this dept beinge vnwilling to doe tould the plit that
> she had rather lyve in her owne howse wth bredd & Cheese then to
> souiorne wth anye her Children wth far better fare.

"Bredd & Cheese!" How many times since has Lucrece
acted the little scene over to herself, glowing with indignation? For she seems to be of the emotional type readily
stirred to indignation or tears, and well equipped with
words to describe her wrongs. I have a sneaking wonder
whether she really made the bread and cheese antithesis
at the time or whether it occurred to her that night as she
was living over the scene in bed.

Meantime her husband replied

> that if there were no remedye she must be contented and thervppon
> this dept then towld him that she must then haue bedding & other
> thing$\complement$ necessary for hirself a man servant & a Maide servant and so
> wthin fewe dayes after this dept went vnto hir sd daughters howse and

caryed wth her certen bedding & other thing℮ for the furnishing of her chamber & for her necessary vse wth the plt℮ good lyking (as this dept then conceved) for she saithe that she made him acquainted wth yt and he semed not then to dislike therof.

Then, a little reluctantly, remembering perhaps the solemn oath she is on, she adds

that over & besides the things before menconed wher wth she acquainted the pltif she this dept being dryven to hir shift℮ to lyve owte of hir owne howse dyd carye wth hir [the best things, *struck out*] suche good℮ as she had in hir keping for hir mayntenaunce what nede soever she should stand in; [an inventory and evaluation she cannot give,] neither dothe she thinke hir sellf bound to declare in whose custodye the same good℮ are or to what place they were caryed.

The extorted confession is rather piteous. And so she went away to Camilla's, leaving Thomas to pay Atkinson's debts. As for the £100 allowance, she will not let that stand so: "certen leases," those made over to Michael and Darcy, being of the yearly value of £100, served for her maintenance — whether or not they might, since the making of the assignment, be described as an allowance.

More friction occurred during that year or the next in connection with the rent-paying. Mary Atkinson, deposing for her brother, Michael, says that at this time Michael

comeing whome to this d^{pt}℮ howse told this dep^t (as seeming to be much discontented therew^{t}h) that he had byn divrs tymes to have payd the cheefe rent then due for the sd m'she ground℮ . . . and amongst othr℮ . . . he named one m^r Ratclyffe sone to m^r Ratclyffe late Aldrman of London to whom he sayd he was appoynted to pay that Rent whereuppon this dep^t knowing that the p^{lt} was very greate w^{t}h broth^{r}s in Law of m^r Ratcliffes wil ⟨l⟩ed the dft to have speciall care of the payment of the sd Rent for that this dep^t dowbted sume hard measure therein yf yt were not p'vented and thereuppon the sd dft [Michael] went unto the sd m^r Ratclyffe who in the end receaved the sd Rent as the dft affi⟨rm⟩ed and at the same tyme the dft told this dp^t that he had learned yt owt that the p^{lt} had endevored to have had the sd lease forfayted and afterward as the dft told this dp^t he charged the p^{lt} w^{t}h yt who . . . did not denye yt but sayd that yf yt had byne forfyted he had taken order for [redeeming it].

Radcliffe's own deposition contains a rather obscure relation that may have some connection with the affair:

> That abowte two yeres now past [i.e. at the same time just mentioned by Mary Atkinson] there came unto this dept a gentleman who semed to be a frend of the sd Thomas Wrightingtons and requested this dept (as he thinketh from the sd Wrightington) that if anye dyd come to paye unto this dept or the sd Robert Tarbock anye Rent for the sd meadowe grownd℮ at Wolw℮h that then this dept & the sd Robert Tarbock should geue noe other acquittance for the receyte of suche Rent other than suche as should testifye the receyte therof from the sd Thomas Wrightington unto wᶜh motion this dept aunswered that he . . . would be glad to doe mʳ Wrightington anye pleasure that he might lawfullye doe But this dept saithe that to his nowe remembrance neither the sd Thomas Wrightington nor anye for him dyd at anye tyme practise wᵗh this dept for anye enterye to be made uppon the sd grownd℮ or for the doing of anye other Act for non payment of the sd Rent to the end that the sd Wrightington might purchase the same in his owne name.

In the last part of this there is not much change for Michael. The first part does sound as if Wrightington were trying to insure himself the name of the tax-payer on this property, to prove that the deed of assignment was really only to make Lucrece safe in case he died before her — not for her "immediate use and behoof."

Nor was Wrightington on his side without cause for anxiety about Michael's behaviour as trustee, we may gather from his Bill of Complaint which he brought before Lord Keeper Egerton on July 4, 1598.

The assignment that we know about had been made "by deede in truste" to Thomas Darcy and Michael Bryskett (as by the said deed now remaining in the hands of Michael may at full appear) — which conveyance was made "vppon meere truste and Confidence That yoʳ saide Oratoʳ shoulde duringe the Jointe lives of [Thomas and Lucrece] haue and enioye the said pʳmisses and the whole & entire benefitte & profitte of the said seu'all leasses to his owne vse & benefitte" during his life. Now, Darcy being dead, Michael, meaning to defraud Wrightington, has lately most unconscionably and contrary to the trust reposed in him conveyed, mortgaged for money borrowed, or otherwise entangled the various estates, interests, and terms of years in the premises, by secret conveyances or other encumbrances to certain persons unknown to Wrightington. He claims the rents and profits of these estates (and receives them) without Wrightington's consent, as if he were absolute owner, and similarly takes on him to pay most of the rents to the lessors; further, he now gives out that the assignment was made *bona fide* to him and Darcy, not upon trust; and threatens upon "Conceipte" taken against Wrightington to expel him out of the premises, to make sale of them, and to put the money in his own purse. Therefore, because Michael "is a man of little or noe livelyhood in landes or Tenemente," so that Wrightington fears that if he happens to die indebted the premises will subvert to the payment of his debts (whereof Wrightington has great reason to doubt, because he has lately heard Michael give out that if the world go not well with him he can serve in another country "wth a Culliver on his necke"), Wrightington begs a subpoena against his brother-in-law.

This subpoena was duly granted, but it produced an unusual effect on Michael, for the book of Decrees and Orders records on the 8th of July (four days after the Bill was brought),[1]

fforasmuch as Jo. Denner the pł srvaunt hath made oth That he hauinge served pcℓ vpon the defdt on Tuysday last to appeere in this Court at the pł suyte The said defdt therevpon in very owtragious mann^r vsed verye opprobryous and slanderous speaches against the pł not meete to

---

1 Decrees and Orders, 1598 A, p. 119.

be sett downe in wrytinge And beinge moved by the said Denner to forbeare those bad speaches . . . the said defdt therevpon bent his fyst towardℭ the said Denner Thretninge that he woulde stryck him and pay him him [*sic*] yf he did not hould his tonge or to that effect It is therefore ordered That an attachemt be awarded against the defd to answeere his sayd misdemeanoʳ or contempt.

This *may* have been righteous indignation on Michael's part, but it sounds much more like a score for Wrighting-ton. In spite of his blustering to Denner, however, Michael on the same day reported to the court that he could not answer directly to the bill for want of certain writings mentioned in it, which were in the country, and was therefore allowed till October.[1] October was more than half gone before the court recorded, "fforasmuch as the defdt apped & depted wᵗʰout Answeeringe therfor an attach is awarded against the defdt to the shreyf of Lon-don."[2] That was on the 18th; on the 28th we find that "he appeared in person for saving of his bond made to the shreef of London in that behalf/."[3]

Finally at the end of the month Michael made his answer: he describes Wrightington's poverty before marry-ing Lucrece (as we saw above), and the good estate in which Guicciardine left her, and of course the assignment to him and Darcy, which he said was for his sister's im-mediate use as an insurance against waste by Wrighting-ton. Now, he says, he finds the persons to be dead who should chiefly prove what was the original intention of the assignment, and knows that if Lucrece should later procure a divorce, still she could not be restored to such leases as had expired and been renewed in Wrightington's name. He therefore has devised to avoid and undo the grant made to him as aforesaid. For he fears that Wrightington, hav-ing now drawn his wife to live apart <with? (*lacuna*) >

1 Decrees and Orders, 1598 B, p. 124, and 1598 A, p. 154.
2 *Ibid.*, 1598 A, p. 206.   3 *Ibid.*, p. 248.

her own friends, will make a final end and waste of all that came to him by this marriage, and leave Lucrece in most miserable estate; for the effecting whereof Wrightington has concluded (as he himself has not spared to confess) with some of those that have the reversion of the premises to have the lease made to himself, having practised to forfeit the former lease. (As we know, Radcliffe at least knew nothing of any such practice by Wrightington.) Now Wrightington, finding himself prevented herein by Michael's care, pretends that the leases were granted to Michael only on trust.

As for the supposed encumbering of the leases by secret conveyances, Michael says that by Lucrece's direction and entreaty and her urgent necessity he mortgaged one of the leases, the sum being afterward duly repaid by Lucrece at the proper day. He says he is quite willing to convey the leases to anyone else Lucrece and the court think fit, but his own debts shall in no way impair the leases even if they remain in him.

Michael's reference to debts at this stage is interesting, since it was only a few months earlier that he had had enough extra money by him to lend large sums of his own accord to Turnor (cf. p. 28). And so in fact he continues that he thinks Wrightington really knows that he has enough to discharge his debts, which are few or none at all. Rather, he, Michael, has cause to fear that if the estates were in Wrightington's possession he would consume them away; for long since, when Lucrece demanded how he would deal by her if the property of her leases were in him, Thomas answered plainly that he should sell them to serve his own turn; which argues his unconscionably bad mind toward her by whom he was advanced.

Moreover, Wrightington at divers times has gone about to sell his office, purposing to get himself into Ireland and live there; so Michael says he has great cause to fear that if Wrightington could compass his desires, he would quickly leave Lucrece to the wide world to shift for herself.

Ireland again! It seems as if perhaps Lodowick Bryskett's numerous positions there, so unsatisfying to himself, held a far-off glamour for his relatives at home, if that unhappy land was the refuge to which Michael turned whenever his affairs in England grew desperate, and now Wrightington too hoped to find better things there for himself. But it was in this very month of October, 1598, when Lodowick's brother and brother-in-law were looking askance as two jealous terriers at each other's designs on Ireland, that the hideous rebellion there broke out in which Spenser's castle of Kilcolman was burnt, and he by one road with his family, Bryskett with his by another, fled to England.

Michael in his answer confessed to having the much disputed deed of assignment in his possession. This incidentally proves that whatever Wrightington's designs on it may have been, he had not stolen it. He said he needed a sight of the deed, so on November 25 Michael was ordered to bring it immediately into court.[1]

In the meantime his contempt in abusing John Denner who served the subpoena on him had been under consideration by Mr. Tyndall, one of the Masters in Chancery,[2] who on the 22nd of December reported him guilty; therefore it was ordered by his lordship that Michael "be fowrth wth Comitted to the p^{r}son of the ffleet for his said Contempt/."[3] Five days later, however, the Christmas season having possibly warmed the hearts of Sir Thomas Egerton and Bryskett and Wrightington, it was ordered by the Lord Keeper with the consent of both parties, being

1 Decrees and Orders, 1598 A, p. 402.
2 *Ibid.*, p. 417.   3 *Ibid.*, p. 419.

before him, that Michael's contempt be suspended till the beginning of the next term. In the meantime Mr. Lambard, one of the Masters, and Mr. Recorder of London were commissioned to hear the parties and witnesses, and see if they could end the matter; and Michael was ordered to bring them the deed of trust that Wrightington might peruse the names of the witnesses on it.[1]

In Hilary Term, when it opened, it may be that the matter of committing Michael to the Fleet for contempt of court was let slide; for an attempt at reconciliation was made. One Mr. Dr. Hutchinson met with Wrightington, Lucrece, and her daughter Camilla at Lincoln's Inn, in the chambers of the young barrister Thomas Ayloffe, who had married Lucrece's daughter Maria Guicciardine,[2] and was now conducting Lucrece's case. Hutchinson, who may have been a friend of the family — perhaps even he was the minister of some of them, since he was a Doctor of Divinity [3] — undertook the delicate task of mediating between Thomas and Lucrece Wrightington.

We have the account from Lucrece, in her depositions on both sides.

The immediate question to be settled was the satisfaction of Wrightington's demand for a new trustee in Michael Bryskett's place. Lucrece suggested her son-in-law Francis Harvey, Camilla's second husband; an arrangement that perhaps she thought appropriate because Darcy too had been Camilla's husband. Wrightington, however, objected that Harvey was "to Collericke a man."

Then said Dr. Hutchinson to Lucrece, "What say you to your son Ayloffe?"

"None better," returned Lucrece.

"Nay," said Wrightington, "Mr. Ayloffe is a lawyer."

1 *Ibid.*, p. 425.   2 See below, p. 355.
3 C 24/277 (7).

316 LODOWICK BRYSKETT AND HIS FAMILY

"He is so much the better hable to defend my cause," retorted his wife.

"And so after div⟨ers⟩ others were named," Wrighting-ton suggested Dr. Hutchinson himself.

"I thinke," said Lucrece, "that m^r Hutchinson will not be trobled w^{t}h yt."

"No sayd m^r Hutchenson I will not medle w^{t}h yt" — a wise decision on his part, one cannot help thinking; and so they reached no conclusion in that matter.

They also, however, discussed the terms of the deed. The interrogatories to Lucrece try to extort a confession that at that meeting she agreed that Wrightington's in-terpretation was the true one — that the property was merely insured to her use after his death if she survived him, not that it was for her own immediate use; and also that she came to the meeting resolved to be reconciled, and not to stand upon the deed. She and her daughter Camilla both deny all this. Wrightington appears to make one point, in that when Lucrece was asked whether Hutchin-son, at the earnest request of her and Camilla, did not en-treat Wrightington that she might have the disposition of the Bishopsgate house after his death, he then to have the rest of the leases, she refused to answer. Ordinarily her answers were untrammeled. In answering another inter-rogatory, however, she says she was willing for her hus-band, if he survived her, to use the house until his death, after which it should go to whomever she should have be-queathed it; but she was willing for him to let or sell the house for the term of two years from this conference.

Lucrece and Camilla retired into young Ayloffe's study, where, Camilla says, "Mr Do^r Hutchenson came in to them and fynding this dept℮ sd Mother weeping pswaded hir to come to some good end wth the pltif," but she does not tell what persuasions or suggestions he used.

The meeting accomplished nothing; so that in the following May the commission to Mr. Lambard and Mr. Recorder was renewed.[1]

In the February next (1599/1600) were examined those witnesses whose depositions we have been using.[2] The court tried to get at the exact meaning of Wrightington's much discussed deed of assignment; and — perhaps in case of failing a satisfactory conclusion in that matter — Wrightington's counsel also tried to minimize the benefit Wrightington had received by the marriage.

The latter point they try to make by showing how much Vincent Guicciardine's estate was dispersed, so that little came to Wrightington's hands. Briefly, the interrogatory *ex parte* Wrightington asks Lucrece whether she has not often said that her first husband left her and her son James Guicciardine a thousand pounds apiece, besides some household stuff and leases; and whether out of that two thousand pounds of their joint estate there was not spent "to Mr Nicholas Degozzi ffower hundred pound℮ by vertue of a bill of exchaunge sente vnto you";[3] to the partners of the breach at Erith (cf. pp. 292 f.) four hundred pounds; "ffor the ffunerall of yoʳ husbande two hundered

---

1 Decrees and Orders, 1598 A, p. 749.
2 At this time Lucrece was staying at Francis and Camilla Harvey's house in the Savoy.
3 The interrogatories to Camilla make this bill sent "from beyonde the Seas." De Gozzi was another important merchant of the Italian group, mention of whom appears at intervals throughout the Historical Manuscripts Commission Reports (see especially the calendar to the Hatfield papers). A long suit ran in Chancery between his sons Nicholas and Marino and his executor, Nicholas Di Menze, at about the same time as the Wrightington suits against the Bryskett family. The book of Chancery Reports for 1598 (vol. 2) contains a long "Cedule" of De Gozzi's accounts, which reveals dealings chiefly with other Italians, his far-flung debtors and creditors coming among other places from "Middleborrowe," "Hamborrowe," Venice, Antwerp, Naples, Genoa, Verona, "Bressa," and "Lyle"; but I do not find the name of Guicciardine among them — because, evidently, whatever scores there may have been had been wiped out before De Gozzi's death.

pound℮ . . . for the Marriage of yo[r] daughter Prowe two
hundered Markes[1] of yo[r] owne purse. . . . And howe
much of that estate left to yo[r] Sonne & yo[u] was Loste by
evell dett[rs] after yo[r] late husband℮ Deathe & neuer came
to the pl hand℮?"

Lucrece and her son answer unsatisfactorily. James
Guicciardine, whose estate we shall have occasion to consider separately, said he was not sure how much his estate
had amounted to, nor could he tell how much he had spent
without perusing his accounts. Well might he say so, as
we shall see. Lucrece for her part begins by quibbling dis-
gracefully. Asked if she has not said that her estate and
James's were a thousand pounds apiece — which surely
means *were* they not — she righteously disclaims having
discussed with anyone her son's portion under the will. I
imagine that she was glad of the ambiguous phraseology
in order to shelter James's somewhat doubtful dealings
since his father's death. She admits that her own portion
probably came to a thousand. She says, however, that she
never heard of the payment to Nicholas De Gozzi; that
although some money — she cannot estimate how much
— was paid to the partners of the breach at Erith, she has
always taken it to have been "Owte of thencrease &
profitt . . . of thestates," not out of the principal; that the
charges of her daughter Elizabeth Prowe's wedding she
had met by selling "certen drugg℮ and other things of
small moment" left her in addition to the thousand pounds
(which is still, note, intact); and that her late husband's
funeral cost about £150 (not the £200 of the interrogatory), but she does not know whether this came out of her
and James's estates or whether the deceased had left
enough besides to pay for it. As for "evell detters," she
knows only of "one Walthall a Merchant" by whom they

1 £133 6s. 8d.

lost £100. Thus she builds up very neatly the estate Wrightington has reduced so low.

With regard to the original meaning of the assignment, we are fortunate that the most able deposition is that of Lodowick himself. It has a sort of crispness of common sense, as in his observing, when asked what the intention of the deed was, that the deed itself could best testify to its own meaning; and possibly even a tinge — or a twinge, the Honourable Court may have thought it — of humour. Observe how dexterously he turns the tables on Wrightington. Did you know, asked the interrogatory, that the trust was to Lucrece *if* she should survive her husband? No, Lodowick answered pleasantly, I never heard of any other trust than "was plainly exp^rssed . . . and [I believe] in [my] Conscience that the sd Complt meant (as all honest men ought to doe) to pforme as muche as his dede purported." This has a charmingly neat urbanity. What more could Wrightington say?

In the meantime, where was this deed? Michael had long ago been ordered to bring it to court for Wrightington's perusal, and other witnesses like Lodowick also referred themselves to its terms. The answer appears in an order of the following March (1599/1600):[1] Forasmuch as the Lord Keeper was today informed by the plaintiff in the presence of the defendant that notwithstanding his order of December 27, 41 Elizabeth (i. e. 1598) suspending the defendant's punishment for "very haynous Contempte," so that Michael should be forward in ending the original dispute about the trust (to be settled by John Crooke, recorder of London, and Mr. Lambard) when it was ordered with Michael's liking that he should produce the deed to the Commissioners, nevertheless not only has Michael very contemptuously not produced the deed

1 Decrees and Orders, 1599 A, p. 374.

(though the commissioners have often required him to bring it), but to delude his Lordship's purpose of appeasing the controversy, as Michael has now confessed to his Lordship, he has conveyed away his interest in the deed to Francis Harvey since the same order awarded by his own assent, pretending thereby to prevent the commissioners' proceeding in the same cause: therefore the defendant Michael is to be committed to the Fleet to remain till he has satisfied the court in the matter.

Eleven days later, on April 8, the Lord Keeper ordered a subpoena awarded against Harvey to appear and bring the deed of trust into the court.[1]

Whether Harvey came I have found no record. But on "Jovis xxix die Maij" the Lord Keeper himself heard the matter in question at his house in the presence of "the councell learned on bothe ptes." [2] Learning that Dr. Hutchinson had already attempted a reconciliation, he ordered that rather than a public hearing should be had, all the parties in question should attend upon Hutchinson for an ending if possible, to which they all willingly assented; but should any variance arise whereby he could not end it, then his Lordship would be pleased to take such an indifferent course to terminate the affair that a perfect reconciliation might continue between the parties.

Since no further notices of the case appear, it seems as if Hutchinson's second labours must have been more happy than the first.

Even so, the eight-year-old quarrel was not really settled. We hear no more, to be sure, of Lucrece's disagreeing with her husband; even perhaps they were really reconciled, for after his death that surprising woman took over the quarrel which we now find ensuing between Wrightington and James Guicciardine.

1 Decrees and Orders, 1599 A, p. 384.   2 *Ibid.*, p. 577; 1599 B, p. 589.

There seem to have been proceedings on both sides, for in 1600 Guicciardine as plaintiff was adjudged to pay Wrightington as defendant "xiij^s iiij^d cost℮ for want of a bill," [1] while a year or two later we find Wrightington in his more familiar rôle of plaintiff. His Bill of Complaint to Sir Thomas Egerton (Lord Keeper) of February 10, 1601/02, tells the story, and illuminates further the difficulties between him and Lucrece. [2]

Vincent Guicciardine, he says, at his death left divers legacies of great value to his three daughters, Camilla, Elizabeth, and Mary, and some others; the rest of his estate he left to be divided between his wife Lucrece and his son James Guicciardine, *on condition* that within six months after his, Vincent's, death James should make Lucrece assurance of enjoying Vincent's lands in England which he had bought in James's name; in default of which James should be deprived of his share and Lucrece should have it in addition to her own. But James did not make Lucrece the required assurance; whereby Lucrece might lawfully enjoy all those lands for her life, and he was deprived of his right in them.

Afterwards, about eighteen or nineteen years ago (i. e. about 1583), Wrightington married Lucrece.

Now James, though he had not performed the condition, both before and after Lucrece's marriage with Wrightington not only intermeddled with the rest of the goods and chattels left Lucrece by his father and disposed a great part of them to his own use, but also, proposing to defraud his stepfather "of all the whole estate" of Lucrece, first by very undue practice obtained from her "a secreete graunte or deede of guifte vnder her hande and Seale" of all her estate left her by Vincent "wth an Antedate as a

1 Decrees and Orders, 1600 A, p. 166; 1600 B, p. 213.
2 Wrightington vs. Guicciardine, C 2 Eliz., W 13/13.

deede made in her wydowhoode"; then, at or near the same
time, James made two deeds of gift secretly as an executor
to Vincent, one to John Jobson, gent., deceased, the other
to his uncle, Lucrece's brother Thomas Bryskett, whereby
James granted Jobson and Thomas Bryskett all the estate
left by Vincent Guicciardine to him or Lucrece; all which
deeds are yet "deteigned" by James uncancelled, on pretence if Wrightington happens to outlive Lucrece to call
him in question for the whole estate, and "vtterly to defraud yor Lo^{ps} Orator of all the goode Debte Plate Jewells
howshold stuffe and money" due to Wrightington by his
marriage with Lucrece.

Notwithstanding all this, Wrightington, not knowing of
the deeds, "did still entertayne the said James in his howsse
& his servant Attending vppõn him very lovingly to yor
Orato^{rs} Chardge of ffyftye pounde a yeare at the Leaste,"
of which James made no recompense. Moreover, from
time to time James took out of his father's estate left in
charge of William Petola (cf. p. 301) divers great sums
amounting to a thousand pounds at least, which he dis-
bursed to his own proper use.

Afterward James had occasion to travel to Florence [1]
to one [blank] Guicciardine, his uncle, by whom he expected great advancement. Having spent all the money
he had received out of his father's estate or by the sale of
such land as his father had left him here in England, which
he had sold before his departure, and "feareing least his
said Vnckell would enter into some discourse w^{t}h him at
his cominge to him to vnderstand howe his ffather had
lefte him & what accompte he could make thereof And
doubting leaste his vnckell should conceave displeasure
towarde him if he could make him noe reasonable satis-
faccõn therein," James earnestly desired Wrightington to

1 Cf. Chapter VI.

make him an obligation purporting that Wrightington owed him £500. Wrightington, to help him avoid his uncle's displeasure, which might turn to his very great loss, did make, seal, and deliver such an obligation to James in about 29 Elizabeth, for the payment of £500 to James or his assigns, that he might show it to his uncle if necessary. Since then Wrightington has often required this to be redelivered and cancelled, but his stepson still keeps it, with intent apparently to abuse Wrightington's confidence reposed in him. And although James made him a release of this bond, he — James — has since by casual and indirect means got the release into his hands and suppresses it, intending to charge Wrightington with the bond.

Moreover, before this release and before James's departure beyond the seas, Wrightington had Petola draw up an estimate of how much money James had received of his father's estate, and what Wrightington and Lucrece had received, and balance it. By this estimate James was charged with much less than he was to be charged with, and Wrightington with much more. The Bill gives one example among several: whereas James spent at least £400 about the marsh lands from a certain "Breache of the Thames at Erithe," which was to be borne by James himself, because Lucrece never had any interest or assurance of those marsh lands, yet Petola in his notes charged James with but half of it, whereby Wrightington with no colour of just cause was charged with the other moiety.

Wrightington also bought from James half of the plate and household stuff left by Vincent Guicciardine, which James pretended should have been divided between his mother and him, as if the condition had never been broken. Thereupon James, having got as much as he could have if he had not broken the condition, ten or twelve years ago (about 1590, that is) made, sealed, and delivered a general release to Wrightington of all debts, duties, and demands whatsoever, from the beginning of the world to the date of that release. But that release and Petola's notes have by casual and indirect means come to James's hands too.

Now James very indirectly attempteth suit by bill in the court of Chancery, pretending to draw Wrightington in question *de novo* for the moiety of his father's estate, as if the condition were not broken and as if he had never received any part of it or made the release to Wrightington.

Still further, whereas one Lewys Gaddy, gent., a Florentine, sometime served Vincent Guicciardine as clerk here in England (cf. p. 290), and afterwards in the lifetime of Guicciardine departed the realm indebted to his master's estate to the sum of about £900 which he had collected from sundry debtors of Vincent's in England and concealed and spent to his own use, as plainly appears from Vincent Guicciardine's account books, James, having stayed at Florence many years at sundry times since his father's death and Lucrece's second marriage, where also Gaddy has been for years and is of great wealth and ability, has very secretly compounded with Gaddy for those debts since Wrightington married Lucrece, and has received satisfaction for all or most of them without rendering account for them to his stepfather, and detains the money to his own use.

As if this long score were not enough to show that poor Wrightington was not the only spendthrift in the family, we have yet one more item, and that one which explains the plaintiff's debts to Edward Atkinson, on account of which he wished to break off housekeeping and have his wife live with her daughters.

Whereas Wrightington while James was beyond the seas has at his request paid his proper debts as well by bills of exchange as otherwise to Edward Atkinson, amounting to at least fourscore pounds — whereof James secretly had promised to satisfy Wrightington — James since his last coming to England utterly refuses to make any such satisfaction.

Of what happened in this suit I have found no further trace. Wrightington himself was out of it four years later. He died in or before November, 1606, having been "sick of bodie" as early as April, and entirely broken in fortune. His pitiful will, but a few lines long, appointed his loving brother-in-law, "Henry Marten of Steeple Mourden," sole executor; whose only work was to satisfy £190 worth of debts, if his estate would perform the same.[1] Fifty pounds of this amount was due to Robert Prowe, whose wedding with Lucrece's daughter Elizabeth, we saw, cost two hundred marks.

So high had the battle raged between Lucrece and Wrightington, who, whichever side may have been right, does not appear as a welcome or gracious influence in the corporate Bryskett life, that one is hardly prepared to find Lucrece taking over her husband's case against her son James Guicciardine. Perhaps that accomplished young scoundrel, having once got her secret deed of gift as a weapon against Wrightington, was not willing to let slip an advantage even against his mother; we have seen that he was quite ready to make unscrupulous use of such opportunities. At any rate, in the very year of Wrightington's death we find an order in the suit of Lucrece Wright-

---

[1] Thomas Wrightington's will, Prerogative Court of Canterbury, 80 Stafforde. Mr. Eccles has given me a reference to the Subsidy Roll (E 179/146/369) for St. Botolph's, Bishopsgate, 1598, in which Thomas Wrightington is taxed upon £50. The mark "affid." shows that he had removed from the parish, as it does in this same Roll before the name of William Shakespeare, assessed on £5 under St. Helen's, Bishopsgate. In 1599 (146/394) Wrightington is listed again with a similar notation. Before the rift with his wife, he was ten times as rich as Shakespeare!

ington against "James Guiccherdyn" to the effect that "Ph'e Barrett made oathe for servinge A Subp^a on the defdt who hathe not appeared."

We learn of nothing more about how she sped, and quite possibly illness or age prevented her pursuing the matter, for the next year she made her will, which was proved in April, 1608.[1]

Apparently she had disposed of the disputed house in Bishopsgate, for her will describes her as "of the parishe of Saincte Marye Matfellon als White Chappell," and she asks to have her body lie in the church of St. Botolph's without Aldgate. Besides the fact that she had much more to leave, her will is strikingly different from her husband's, his brevity being the antithesis of her elaboration in enumerating separately each of those to whom she left identical bequests — even such ordinary matters as the four yards of black cloth or mourning gowns which she left to her brothers, sisters, and children. We are indebted to her, however, for a valuable list of her family. It seems as if her estate really had been much wasted away, whether by Wrightington, James Guicciardine, or her lawsuits, for, except much black cloth and a very little money, she has nothing to leave except the rents of her lease at Ham. It appears that she was living with her daughter Elizabeth, for it is to the Prowes alone that she bequeathes these rents — two years' to her daughter Prowe, £100 to Mary, a year's rent apiece to Onelia, Anne, Thomas, and William. All the rest of her goods remaining in Mr. and Mrs. Prowe's house or elsewhere she leaves to them.

1 Lucrece Wrightington, P. C. C., 34 Windebanck.

VI. THE CHILDREN OF LUCRECE

A. JAMES GUICCIARDINE

As WE read in Vincent Guicciardine's will, Lucrece had four children, James, Camilla, Elizabeth, and Mary. All three girls made such matches as their mother must have approved, Camilla marrying first Thomas Darcy and afterward Francis Harvey, both men well dowered with this world's goods; Mary, that Thomas Ayloffe who conducted Lucrece's case and in whose chambers Dr. Hutchinson tried to bring about a reconciliation; Elizabeth, the Robert Prowe to whom Wrightington died indebted, and whose house sheltered Lucrece's last years — and property. I find no record of James's having ever married.

It was just as well if that adventurous black sheep of the family remained single, and indeed he would hardly have known what to do with a wife during some of his years.

After his mother's death that suit must have dropped, but he followed it with one against Henry Martyn and Robert Prowe, small glimpses of which one can get in the Decrees and Orders in Chancery for 1608 and 1609. It really seems all the more that Wrightington and Lucrece must have made common cause against him in their lifetimes, since now he was bringing a joint suit against their respective executors. Nothing very intelligible comes out of the Decrees and Orders, but it was still, of course, a matter of property, and perhaps the sequel to Wrightington's account of the bond fraudulently got and held from him by his stepson, since James in 1608 pleaded a bond made for his benefit by Wrightington.[1]

Wrightington had said that he made this bond to help James out of a scrape when he went down to his uncle

---

[1] Decrees and Orders, 1608 B, p. 205.

Guicciardine in Florence. One would like to know whether the uncle — whom James really did go partly to see — served as a convenient blind even in the bosom of the family, or whether Wrightington knew his stepson's further purpose.

In Essex House in the Strand, says Lytton Strachey in *Elizabeth and Essex*,[1] Anthony Bacon sat directing a vast correspondence by which Essex was to beat the Cecils at their own game of controlling foreign affairs.

> Emissaries were sent out, at the Earl's expense, all over Europe, and letters poured in, from Scotland, France, Holland, Italy, Spain, Bohemia, with elaborate daily reports of the sayings of princes, the movements of armies, and the whole complex development of international intrigue. . . . The work grew and grew, and before long, such was the multiplicity of business, he had four young secretaries to help him, among whom were the ingenious Henry Wotton and the cynical Henry Cuffe.

And one of these hundreds of secret agents was our friend James Guicciardine.

Being a member of the Guicciardini and no doubt related to the statesman Francesco,[2] James had it in him by right to play the part required by this secret diplomacy.

---

1 Pp. 47–49. He says that Sir Thomas Bodley also came under Essex's influence. Bodley, like Francis Eaglefield, was another near neighbour of Lyly's in Little St. Bartholomew's.

2 So Plomer surmises, and obviously he is right. How close the relationship was, I do not know. Francesco had a brother Jacopo (F. Guicciardini, *Op. Inedit.*, vol. IX *passim*, and X, 140); his name might possibly account for our James's.

   As to Francesco Guicciardini's character, J. A. Symonds in an excellent and illuminating little article on his career (*Encyclopaedia Britannica*, eleventh edition), observes that he was a diplomat as that was understood in Italy: "to meet treachery with fraud; . . . to credit human nature with the basest motives, while the blackest crimes were contemplated with cold enthusiasm for their cleverness, was reckoned then the height of political sagacity. Guicciardini could play the game to perfection." He "hated the papacy with a deep and frozen bitterness, . . . declaring he had seen enough of sacerdotal abominations to make him a Lutheran." He had apparently "judged the tyranny of the Medici at its true worth. . . . Like Machiavelli, but on a

Our earliest letter from him was written in Florence in 1593 (?) before June.[1] Henry of Navarre — or Henry IV — had already won the battle of Ivry three years before, and was gradually conquering France from the Catholic League, which had the help of Spain. But now the balance of power in the royalist party had shifted to those who were Catholics first and royalists second and "too good Frenchmen to endure the domination of Spain,"[2] bringing about the situation described in James Guicciardine's letter — the rise of a third party besides the League and the Huguenots, which made Henry's staunchest Huguenot supporters see the advisability of his cutting the ground from under the League's feet by becoming a Catholic.[3]

Le Grand Duc, Monseigneur [wrote Guicciardine], [so esteems you that he thinks you should be]

averti d'un traité que prépare en France une partie des principaux seigneurs du Royaume, au cas que le roi persiste davantage en l'irré-solution de sa conversion tant nécessaire. Lequel traité tendra à un troisième parti, qui déjà se serait ensuivi, si le Grand Duc ne l'avait retardé avec l'espèrance de la dite conversion, laquelle avec beaucoup de raison son altesse pourrait espèrer se devoir ensuivre premier qu'à cette heure. . . . Sa Majesté [feels the step necessary to] son salut, celui du royaume, et de tant de bons cavaliers qui l'ont suivi sous cette espèr-ance [and who do not find it] raisonable d'obéir plus longuement à un roi non Catholique, avec perte de leurs maisons et de leurs vies.

France is weakening daily, and the Italian princes are losing hope in his power

---

lower level, Guicciardini was willing to 'roll stones' . . . for masters whom . . . he detested and despised. . . . Of a cold and worldly temperament, devoid of passion, blameless in his conduct as the father of a family, faithful as the servant of his papal patrons, ... the glaring discord between his opinions and his practice" would be contemptible were it not sinister.

1 Hist. MSS. Comm., Cal. Hatfield MSS., part 4, pp. 325–327. This is endorsed "Le Chevalier Guicciardin to ——." Might its recipient, who evidently had access to Henry of Navarre, have been Sir Henry Unton, who had gone to France from both Elizabeth and Essex House to watch the king? (Strachey, op. cit., p. 94).   2 Cambridge Modern History, III, 52.

3 Ibid., pp. 38, 52.

pour la conservation de leurs états. Ce troisième parti se va fabricant et s'ensuivra, comme vous verrez, bientôt, auquel se joindront la plus grand part des Français Catholiques qui n'ont ni veulent avoir adhérence ni participation avec la Ligue, et par ainsi ils trouveront lieu où se pouvait retirer en abandonnant le parti du Roi, comme ils désirent, grandement désespérés de son obstination. Les Princes Italiens, peu affectionnés à la Ligue, qui pour raison d'état et conscience ne peuvent entièrement s'unir avec le Roi [presumably on account of his Protestantism] auront plus d'avantage d'entrer en ce troisième parti que de vivre sous les périls auxquels l'ambiguité et irrésolution du Roi les a mis. Car avec eux concourreront le Pape et les autres Princes Catholiques, lesquels, sans doute, ayant plus de moyen de continuer la dépense de la guerre, seront beaucoup plus forts que n'est sa Majesté.

The King is plainly in a bad way,

Car, ayant eu toute la noblesse de France unie à soi, on lui a néanmoins sécouru Paris, avec une extrème gloire et félicité de ses ennemis . . . il a failli Rouen et perdu Caudebec, comme avec tant d'insolences publient ici ses ennemis . . .

These misfortunes had befallen Henry during the past two years. His tactics had been to isolate Paris. In April, 1591, Chartres surrendered to him. In July of that year he was reinforced by the arrival of Essex from England and troops also from Holland and Germany. In August he got Noyon and Picardy, and in November Essex and Biron laid siege to Rouen, the last important town held by the League in the north, but in January (1591/92) Parma came to the help of the League, and in April the King had to withdraw from Rouen.[1]

Therefore, continues Guicciardine, if he has made no more progress with all the Catholic nobility behind him,

il ne fera pas désormais grande chose, quand il sera privé d'un si fort bras, comme il sera par le moyen d'un troisième parti, lequel, avec cela lui étant ennemi, ce lui sera toujours double perte . . . il se juge qu'il est perdu, et le royaume ruiné, si, en bref, il ne prend l'expédient de cette con-

1 *Ibid.*, pp. 50-51.

version; car avec elle tout l'effort cesse avec lequel on cherche si ardem-
ment sa ruine. Et ne doit pas le Roi douter que déclarant sa voloént
disposée à se faire Catholique, le Pape ne soit pas pour l'embrasser et
recevoir, car encore qu'il semble autrement, il le fera. [If it has seemed
otherwise, it is because] par raison d'état, il est encore lui-même
obligé à ne se séparer d'Espagne, n'ayant pas assurance de pouvoir
avoir le Roi, ni le royaume de France Catholique.

Not infrequent observations like this last are illuminating as to the very mixed motives of the "religious" wars.
Among the extraordinarily interesting glimpses behind the
scenes which our young Guicciardine gives us are these
which show the great powers deeply concerned for or
against Henry IV's conversion, not because the Catholic
faith was the true or false, able or unable to save eternally
him and all who should follow his example, but because
that conversion was or was not for them politically expedi-
ent. This nephew of Lodowick Bryskett's, scoundrel
though he may have been, is not far behind his uncle in
drawing aside the curtain for us to look through into the
age he lived in.

Guicciardine continues that in the kingdom of Naples
4,000 foot are being raised for Provence; 5,000 Germans,
3,000 other Italians, and as many more forces as the Duke
of Savoy can raise are destined also for Provence, "qui
malaisement pourra cette fois résister à ce grand effort,
qui se fait par mer et par terre, pour la subjuger. D'où sa
Majesté peut consulter le péril auquel tomberont toutes
les autres provinces de Languedoc et Dauphiné," which
will suffer from the same effort; the King cannot help these
provinces much; no one will want to help the King while
he remains contumacious against the Catholic Church;
"car chacun en fait conscience et commence à connaître
que c'est volonté de Dieu qu'il ne puisse parvenir à subjuger les peuples Catholiques, étant d'autre religion."

The Grand Duke whom Guicciardine mentions, and to

whom he was Essex's emissary, was Ferdinand, Cardinal de' Medici, the "Grand Duke Ferdinand" of Browning's *The Statue and the Bust*, and son of that Cosimo whom Francesco Guicciardini in 1537 had helped to become Grand Duke of Tuscany; our James therefore held his post almost by a sort of inheritance, as well as by native ability. "Trained in affairs at the Roman Court, a patron of oriental learning, and a collector of antiques, he was an ideal ruler for Florence," [1] which needed just his combination of diplomacy and culture. Though his marriage with Christine of Lorraine put the Grand Duke in close connection with both the French crown and the house of Guise, he did not want the disintegration of France which would follow French dependence on Spain, so, like Queen Elizabeth, he was helping Henry of Navarre by secret contributions of money, and by actively contributing to his reconciliation with the Papacy and the house of Lorraine; and he played no insignificant part in the civil war in southern France, as one might perhaps surmise from the latter part of James Guicciardine's letter.

The latter wrote to Essex from Florence on 28 December/7 January, 1593/4, a note partly in cipher (indicated here by italics).[2]

"The disorders wherein I found my estate here by reason of my uncle's death, and shortly after some sickness," he says, have prevented his writing before; this incidentally confirms Wrightington's account (p. 322); "and so much the more as having lost my chiefest means and principal stay here, whom it pleased God to call to his mercy some weeks before my arrival, before he could receive the contentment of your letters."

1 *Ibid.*, p. 396.
2 Hist. MSS. Comm., Cal. Hatfield MSS., part 4, pp. 447–448. Most of the letters following appear from the calendar to be slightly condensed from the actual letters. The spelling has also suffered modernization.

This means he never had occasion to use the pretended obligation he had persuaded Wrightington to give him, and refused to give back.

He delivered, he goes on,

both your letter and the other to the party to whom they were directed. . . . *I find him resolutely bent to run one course and fortune with the French king, between whom and himself, so far as I can perceive, both by his own speech and enquiry of others, there seemeth to be very good intelligence.* He greatly desireth the *King's absolution*, with assured hope that *that once obtained*, the *Pope* would quickly after forsake *the alliance with Spain.*

The King appears to fear "*some hard conditions*, whereof these seem to be most important, and which *he will never be tied to, viz., to make peace with Spain, to leave the amity of our Queen, and to prosecute the Protestants.*"

Nothing else, he goes on, is happening here, except the preparation of shipping in the King's ports for the conducting of the Indian fleet, which we do not think here will be in Spain till the end of April. (This would be the Spanish treasure fleet from the West Indies.)

The party above-mentioned hath here a workman accounted by him singular in the tempering of armour, and is desirous you should make some trial of his cunning. And therefore willed me to write for your measure. . . .

About a month later James wrote again from Pisa: [1]

In Spain the long stay of their Indian fleet which is thought now for certain *cannot arrive before September* [and other lacks], *hath driven the King to very great difficulties. . . . In this extremity he is resolved to send presently to the fleet for one million and a half with what secrecy he can, lest it should be met by our English ships* [in the meantime borrowing from money left by the Archbishop of Toledo for other purposes].

A week later James was back in Florence,[2] writing that

1 *Ibid.*, p. 472 (February 1/11, 1593/94). Endorsed, "Part in cipher explained by E. Essex, from Guicciadrin."
2 *Ibid.*, p. 476 (February 8/18, 1593/94).

"opportunity [for correspondence?] falleth out very scant with me by reason of many troubles and suits at law."

> *In Rome* [he wrote] *the Spaniards do seek with all diligence and industry to hinder the King of France's absolution*, holding for an infallible consequence that if he be not *absolved he cannot be established peaceably king of France. The Pope fearing to displease either part, resteth doubtful what to do.* Howbeit it is thought that if he sees the *King prosper he will quietly incline that way, and already seemeth every day more and more desirous to receive him into the church. The best and speediest means to resolve this ambiguity in the Pope and to prevent the designs of his enemies* is thought here *for the King to march speedily with his power to Lyons* [for which resolution he advances reasons].

He apologizes for being tedious with his cipher in unimportant matters, saying he is forced to use it "for the more security" of his letters.

In October, 1595, he wrote a letter which might have some connection with the fact that he belonged to a family of great merchants: three months ago, he said, he sent a small piece of plush "which was made here *for the Duke* and *by him* delivered unto me to send unto your Lordship, . . . *as a gage of his love* towards your Lordship." [1]

In the meantime matters had been progressing in France. The object of the Third Party was, while keeping the crown in the royal house, to ensure its being worn by a Catholic. Part of their plan was a marriage between the Cardinal of Bourbon and the Spanish Infanta. "The scheme was revealed to Henry . . . by the interception of some correspondence, and decided him to take a course which some of his staunchest Huguenot advisers now began to regard as unavoidable." [2] In May, 1593, Henry wrote to the Archbishops asking for instruction in the Catholic faith; on the 25th of July he received absolution from the Archbishop of Bourges, and heard Mass at St.

1 *Ibid.*, part 5, p. 402.
2 *Cambridge Modern History*, III, p. 52.

Denis. This, although the League kept up hostilities for some time, avowedly in the interest of Spain, really ended the "War of Religion." Within eighteen months France and Spain were in open conflict [1] — just as, of course, England wished, a league between these two being dangerous to her. One sees why James, whose father was of "no church" (cf. p. 291), most of whose family were buried in the parish churches of their abode, and who was no true Guicciardine if religion meant much to him anyway, was so anxious for the King's conversion.

The matter duly finds its reflection in his correspondence. In November, 1595,[2] he writes to Essex from Florence after nearly a month's absence that everyone there is

altogether in peace and quietness, and become, as it were, idle spectators of others' actions abroad; and now especially attentive after French affairs and the effects of the King's rebenediction, which hitherto seem not to answer the general expectation and hope, Cambray being already lost and Marseilles standing in some doubtful terms. . . .

He continues about the relations between Spain and the Low Countries.

In December he wrote again,[3] having just got the Earl's letter of November with news of the success "of Zimenes his cause," which had come out just as he had expected. The Grand Duke had followed his own counsel in the matter rather than James's, "and my being not able to make, at any time, any direct answer to it, hath haply caused, if not my inclination, at least my diligence to be suspected." Obscure though this is in itself, it still gives us a little glooming light on the activities of James.

1 *Ibid.*, ch. 1. Elizabeth in virtuous indignation wrote lofty letters to Henry, but she sent Norris again with an English army to expel the Spaniards from Crozon (A. F. Pollard, *Political History of England*).
2 Hist. MSS. Comm., Cal. Hatfield MSS., part 5, p. 437.
3 *Ibid.*, pp. 502–403.

In the same letter we come back to the plush, and to an older friend: "The plush I sent unto your lordship in a chest of silks of Mr. Baptist Hicks, the mercer, to be consigned in London to Mr. Wrightington, who had orders from me to deliver it to your Lordship." If his tone was so lordly to his much abused stepfather, it cannot have helped soothe the friction between them.

In December/January, 1595/96,[1] affairs seem to have grown warm for him, for he wrote that in the last fortnight he had by the Duke's commandment kept out of sight in a retired place. This kept him from speech with "his Highness" but he delivered a letter to his Highness's secretary, reserving further business for a personal interview.

At the moment of writing he received intelligence from that quarter:

> The Turks' galleys' return to Constantinople hath greatly rejoiced the ministers of Spain. . . . The Pope sendeth into Hungary his nephew with 10,000 foot . . . so that this war of Hungary giveth of all other least disturbance to Spain, who maketh rather his benefit thereof, the Turk being so engaged there as he cannot attend him . . . The King of Spain [in spite of heavy losses by tempest], yet doth . . . still threaten, and make new provision for another invasion.

Of this impending invasion more was to be heard. Guicciardine wrote again five days later,[2] in regard to some private business (to which he gives us only insufficient clues) and said he had heard that the Cardinal in the Low Countries was hard bestead for want of money. Italy was using all diligence to send some, but feared he must "be first in great extremity, and perhaps the soldiers in a mutiny. The King's ministers in these difficulties do deal with the Lisbon merchants to supply their wants, but do hope for little help." Then he continues with the fleet which Philip hoped was to make a more successful Armada:

1 *Ibid.*, pp. 506–507.   2 *Ibid.*, p. 510.

The Adelantado's fleet is yet in the port of Ferrol, and hath had commission to disembark their soldiers and lodge them . . . not intending, it should seem, to try their fortune any more this winter after the late blow they have received. . . .

They now report that the English and Flemings begin to arm anew; against which they will have enough to do to defend themselves. Actually it was not till June that Essex went to Cadiz to destroy the Spanish fleet.

The King [this would mean Philip, not Henry] is out in interest almost a million every year, and his yearly expenses otherwise importeth two millions, which is more than his revenues unpawned amount unto, so that his affairs seem to be in evil terms.

On the same day James wrote again,[1] both by the Duke's command and because he wanted to

for mine own discharge, being part of my negociation at my late being in England. The matter is concerning the corn . . . to be brought into this State, for which the Queen had granted her passport for their passage through her narrow seas; which passport . . . she hath called back, to the great loss and prejudice of such as are interested in it, and indignity (as he esteemeth it) to himself, affirming that if he had not most confidently relied upon her Majesty's promise, the ship should not have passed that way. . .

The Queen's alleged reasons are the same as those objected before she granted the passport, in spite of which she did grant it. She need not fear the corn's coming into the enemy's hands, and

if her Majesty had need for her own country she might have had plenty, without staying of this . . . I assure you I never knew him more moved for anything than he is now for this, and I greatly fear, if her Majesty hold still this determination to stay the corn, it will not only be an occasion to break off all matters of correspondence between them, but also cause her subjects and their ships to be neither welcome nor yet secure within his State.

This last gathers special force when one remembers the hordes of young Englishmen who were travelling to Italy

1 *Ibid.*, pp. 510-511.

every year and becoming "diavoli incarnati." One is tempted to draw a parallel with modern times for the effect of international economics on the tourist's status abroad.

When next he wrote, on April 24 / May 4, 1596,[1] he had received a letter from Essex and accordingly gone straightway to "your lordship's friend," to whom he imparted Essex's compliments and some other particulars in the Earl's letter. They had a long conference, in the course of which the unnamed gentleman "*delivered freely* and with some *vehemency his opinion*, which with great earnestness *he willed me to signify unto* your lordship; and . . . *caused a secretary to set it down in writing*"; which Guicciardine encloses.

He adds a postscript: "If you do determine to *present the Duke with* anything from *thence, there will be nothing so acceptable unto him as some dogs of that country or Ireland* that were *fair* and *fierce for the wild boar.*"

The enclosure [2] is of particular interest in view of that year's events:

It cannot be that the King of Spain intends an enterprise in England, for he has dismissed six of the twelve galleons which Piero de Veglia brought from Naples, and they have allowed the galleon of the marquis Spinola, Genoese, . . . to leave Calais. The common opinion is that they intend to transport Spaniards to Ireland to aid that rebel earl. [This of course means Tyrone. All this time, it will be remembered, Lodowick Bryskett was holding office in Ireland.] Also that if it were true that the Irish rebel only on account of religion, measures might be taken to get rid of this continual vexation, with good certainty that the Catholics should not conspire against the Queen on that plea. And, doubtless, the affairs of Rome are altered since the absolution of the King of France; the suggestions of the enemies of that King and the Queen being recognized to have been for matters of state and to ruin these kingdoms, and not for zeal for religion.

---

1 *Ibid.*, part 6, p. 154 (40. 59).
2 *Ibid.*, p. 155. It is written in Italian.

A second paper bearing the same date as this and the letter, and probably enclosed at the same time, continues on the same theme: [1]

The King of Spain has neither vessels nor means nor preparations sufficient to make an enterprise against England, but alleges such an enterprise in order to keep the Queen in suspicion and prevent her sending forces against Havana and the Indies. Her Majesty and her wise Council know how, with little expense, to make England secure. The King cannot attempt that enterprise without great and manifest preparation; and in Ireland I should think that affairs might, with clemency, be arranged. Meanwhile her Majesty has only to turn her forces elsewhere; because to take Havana and stop the King's fleet of the Indies would, as the cutting of Sampson's hair left him helpless, [is there also a reminiscence here of singeing King Philip's beard?] leave that great monarch without means or credit wherewith to save himself, much less to harm others. It is therefore necessary not to be alarmed by Spanish demonstrations; and first of all to succour Cales, [which will be easy]. In Bluet too the Spaniards might be left, so as to keep them engaged in several places. . . . If Havana were England's everything would go to the Queen, who would not only be able to compete with Spain but to overthrow it.

He concludes with suggestions about a possible enterprise against Havana.

Less than two months after this was written, Essex had set out for Cadiz, sent by Elizabeth with Lord Howard to forestall Spanish help to the simmering Irish rebellion. In late June they reached Cadiz Bay, destroyed the Spanish fleet, and took the town with all its riches and strength. The honours of the sea-fight were to Raleigh; it was Essex who led the assault on the city and came home a popular hero, only to meet sudden coldness in Elizabeth.[2]

Guicciardine in October acknowledges [3] receipt of writings from Essex, and of the honourable present which

1 *Ibid.*, pp. 155–156, also in Italian; cf. Essex's *Opinions concerning an imminent Spanish invasion*, November, 1596.
2 *Elizabeth and Essex*, pp. 97–106.
3 Hist. MSS. Comm., Cal. Hatfield MSS., part 6, p. 454 (45. 108).

coming from his lordship he could not well refuse, unde-served though it was.

His next epistle,[1] written just less than two months later, in December, 1596, gives us a tiny glimpse of ad-ventures beside which his lawsuits and family feuds, on whose account perhaps he had just been home, must have seemed tame indeed:

With more haste than good speed I find my going into England, how secret soever I thought to have kept it, was by some Englishmen that met me on the way openly published in Florence, and by that means notice thereof given into the Inquisition, from whence I had long since received a precept not to return into England without leave; and now, as I hear, they have in my absence framed a process against me and already laid wait for me. I had at Venice advertisements given me not to come into Florence by any means, but not knowing from whence they came, I imagined it to be but a practice of my adversaries to keep me from thence; but at my arrival in Florence, I found the intelligence I received in Venice was sent me by the Duke of Florence's order, by whose direction likewise I did retire myself presently into a place of more safety, where I do yet remain, doubtful what will become of this matter, for that in causes of this nature the authority of these princes doth very little avail, and therefore [they] do not willingly interpose themselves to make trial thereof. I have not as yet spoken with the Duke, so as I cannot advertise your lordship of matters as I would.

[P. S.] — I beseech your lordship let this matter be kept secret, and if you send any letters unto me, that they may be delivered to Hicks the mercer [by whom he had sent the plush] and the superscription made, "to Lewis Caddi" [that ex-factor who had cheated Vincent Guicciardine and with whom James had later made up, probably for the sake of receiving Caddi's debts instead of letting Wrightington have them].

In March, 1596/97, James sent Essex a note[2] of no spe-cial interest, not even telling how he had sped with regard to the Inquisition — whose clutches, however, he evidently avoided. A few days after, he wrote again [3] on behalf of

1 *Ibid.*, p. 518 (47. 40, in cipher; 47. 39 is a decipher of the same letter).
2 *Ibid.*, part 7, p. 95.
3 *Ibid.*, p. 109 (39. 45).

the captain of the *St. John Baptist*, who wanted her Majesty's passport for the Narrow Seas, and added, "This day I do write unto your lordship at large." One would like to think this referred to his escape from the Inquisition, but more probably it only alludes to a longer letter written the same day (March 22) in three pages of cipher.[1]

The Spaniards having fresh in memory the great blow received at Cadiz [i. e. Essex's expedition of the preceding summer] which . . . would have been the utter ruin of his [*sic*] greatness if the English had held it; or if they had stayed but some few days [to] have intercepted the Indian fleet [both of which suggestions had been Essex's idea also at the time, but had been negatived by the Council of War[2]] they had at least clipt his feathers, as manifestly appeareth by this that, howbeit his fleet came safely into Spain, yet he was forced by his loss at Cadiz and other expenses above his revenues to retain particular men's monies [which has so hurt his credit that he can borrow from nobody in Naples, Genoa, or Milan]; the Spaniards, I say, do fear nothing so much as the power of the Queen's navy, as they evidently shewed by sending out in so unseasonable a time . . . the late fleet of the Adelantado of Castile,[3] besides the expense of keeping their soldiers in pay this winter without employing them to any use.

He continues with a description of Philip's evil case from the Moors, and in the Low Countries and elsewhere. "In sum, all these great preparations and stirring which they would have the world believe to be intended for an invasion, is thought to be only to defend themselves from the Queen's power. . . ." They are especially weakened by the firm league between England and France, and are therefore themselves trying to negotiate a peace with France, "which if they intended sincerely, and that there might grow a general and sure peace through Christendom, it were a thing . . . by all means to be procured," but they only want to disunite their enemies. "They seek

1 *Ibid.*, pp. 109–111 (39. 43, 44).
2 *Elizabeth and Essex*, p. 104.
3 The unsuccessful Armada to Ireland in 1596, scattered by a gale (*Elizabeth and Essex*, p. 137).

in Scotland to get themselves favour and . . . to declare
the King [i. e. of France] excommunicate and uncapable
of Government. . . ." It behooves England therefore to
forestall their practices, especially the negotiations for
truce between France and Spain, and by invasion to drive
them to seek peace.

In May Guicciardine sent Mr. Henry Ardier with com-
munications by word of mouth,[1] perhaps too private to
write, and a fortnight later a note in cipher [2] which remains
very obscure even in the interpretation of the Historical
Manuscripts Commission, since it is full of undeciphered
symbols such as ᴕ and X.

Guicciardine's desire for an active offensive policy was
gratified almost at once. The Spaniards [3] had for some
months been preparing a fleet in Ferrol and Corunna for
an unknown destination, which preparations Guicciardine
had taken to be merely defensive. But at home it was
thought better to forestall the danger by sending Essex in
the summer of 1597 to attack the Adelantado's fleet as it
lay in Ferrol. He started in the early summer, but was
driven back into Plymouth by a huge storm.

In August he set out again, this time on his most ill-
fated Islands Voyage. Thinking the Spanish fleet had in
the meantime left Ferrol to meet and convoy the treasure
fleet from the Indies, Essex waited for it at Fayal, where
a quarrel between him and Raleigh led to their missing the
treasure fleet. Meanwhile the other Spanish fleet had been
in Ferrol all the time. While Essex and Raleigh were safe
out of the way at the Azores, the Adelantado made a sally
towards England, but his ships were scattered by the wind
near Scilly and returned to Ferrol. Essex, having bungled

1 Cal. Hatfield MSS., part 7, p. 204.
2 *Ibid.*, pp. 547–548 (52. 12).
3 *Elizabeth and Essex*, pp. 127, 132–146.

his whole expedition and left the English coasts unguarded, went home to Elizabeth's rage.

As for Guicciardine in the meantime, our next notice of him is in a letter from that young secretary of Essex's whom Strachey calls "the cynical Henry Cuffe," who was in Florence in October, 1597:[1]

"From Rome we hear weekly of the Pope's extraordinary pains . . . in . . . praying devoutly for that peace betwixt the two great monarchs which neither himself (simple though he be) nor any other prince in Italy doth much desire," Cuffe writes, justifying Strachey's adjective and referring to the peace between Spain and France of which half Europe was afraid.

My first coming . . . being signified by Mr. Guicciardin to the Grand Duke, he sent me a kind message, promising all possible favours, and willed me, if I were desirous, to bring me to him. I returned answer to Mr. Guicciardin, that if it pleased his highness to use my service in sending anything into England I would presently give attendance; otherwise if it were but to kiss his hand, I would, if he thought fit, expect some time when I might acquaint him with some matter of consequence from home. . . .

James had his own affairs at this time to trouble him, as he wrote to Essex in midwinter from Pisa:[2]

I have of late . . . myself been so troubled with tedious suits as to have no leisure for other things. I have now come to an end of them [little did he know! — this being only January of 1597/8, over a year before Wrightington even brought suit in Chancery against Michael Bryskett, in the quarrel preceding that of Wrightington vs. Guicciardine] but upon so hard conditions that I know not whether to count it

---

1 Hist. MSS. Comm., Cal. Hatfield MSS., part 7, pp. 423–424 (55. 106). An account of the examination of John Berington, who "served the King of Spain, and received a pay of him in the Low Countries" (Ibid., part 6, pp. 419–421), mentions his having met at Florence "with Mr. James Guychardin who lent him 5 crowns."
2 Cal. Hatfield MSS., part 7, p. 548 (58. 74).

good or bad fortune. . . . Owing to my agreement with my adversaries they give me now some intermission; yet I assure myself the sore is only salved up, and fear it will break out yet more dangerously; and have determined to leave these parts and come to England.

He did not return for nearly a year, at least. We meet him again in March [1] through another of Henry Cuffe's letters home from Florence:

> Upon the young gentleman's coming here S. A. [Son Altesse?] had some large conference with Mr. Guicciardin, and afterwards by his secretary sent a note of some intelligence for his Lordship. From Spain he is advertised that the Adelantado is making forth eight ships of war for the 'waifting' home of the treasure from the Terceras. [This was what Essex had supposed him to be doing the summer before.] . . . The young gentleman was brought to S. A. by Mr. Guicciardine. His entertainment was very good; his charges borne at Pisa; and at his departure he was presented with a chain of gold.

In July/August Cuffe wrote again, still to another of Essex's young secretaries,[2] that on his parting, the Grand Duke, wishing "to continue a strict intelligence from time to time with his Lordship [i. e. Essex]," sent "Cavalier Guicciardine, who is his agent here," to talk with him.

In December (1598) James wrote Essex the last of these letters that we have: [3]

> His highness here still continuing his demands in behalf of these Portingals who he avoweth for his subjects, saying that the continual molestation they receive by our ships . . . will force them to leave off their traffic, to the great hindrance of his said Highness's custom, whereby he shall be in the end constrained to expel either the one or the other [wishes your lordship to find some remedy for their safety].

A year later this able young man was at home, deposing *ex parte* Bryskett in his stepfather's suit, and soon to be involved in further suits of his own, as we have seen. Whether anyone succeeded him in Florence I do not know. One of the Domestic State Papers (Elizabeth) [4] lists the

1 *Ibid.*, part 8, p. 76.   2 *Ibid.*, part 14, p. 63.
3 *Ibid.*, part 8, p. 493.   4 S. P. 12/283 (72).

"Intelligencers imployed abroade this yeare *1601*" by the rival government service, Cecil's, and includes this entry:

florence   Mr Wilson an English. Gentl: imploied for florence. he hath
        allowance of [   ] And hath receaued at his depart-
        ure — li 30–0–0

Whether this was exactly Guicciardine's office and so approximately his salary I do not know.

A later notice of him is in the Hatfield MSS. (Cal., part 12, p. 140) in two notes from Thomas Windebanck: one to Cecil, saying he has a letter written by the Queen with her own hand, for Guicciardine, which he is keeping for Mr. Vice Chamberlain to deliver; and the other to Sir John Stanhope, on the following day (5 May, 1602). As in the note to Cecil, he says he has this letter, which the Queen

willed me . . . as far as I could understand her (being in walking), to deliver . . . to your Honour, and that you should send for Signor Guicciardin to deliver him this included letter, and to let him know how welcome his coming hither hath been to her Majesty, who hath always had in good reputing both his name and himself, and generally hath esteemed well of the gentlemen of Italy. I beseech you, if perhaps I mistake her Majesty's meaning of sending this letter to yourself, to send it to Mr. Secretary with this my letter.

A rather delicious picture, this, of the poor gentleman not daring to interrupt that always dread Sovereign to make sure that he had understood her directions!

B. CAMILLA DARCY

Lodowick Bryskett's three nieces, Lucrece's daughters Camilla, Elizabeth, and Mary, with their descendants, provide a notable family tree.

Camilla, as we know, married first that Thomas Darcy who until his early death was Lucrece's trustee with Michael Bryskett.

He belonged to a family which had held lands in Essex for many generations; it was from his great-great-grand-father that Tolleshunt Darcy where he and Camilla lived had its surname.[1] This family came from the same stock as the family of Darcy, Earls of Holderness — the Norman de Areci living at the time of the Conquest.[2]

These Essex families were wonderfully interwoven. For instance our Thomas Darcy's maternal grandfather was Sir Eustace Sulyard, who was also the maternal grand-father of the Thomas Ayloffe who married Camilla's younger sister Maria; thus the two sisters married second cousins. Our Thomas's father was another Thomas Darcy, who had been Sheriff of Essex in 1580.[3] It was he who built the present bridge over the moat at Tolleshunt Darcy Hall,[4] where his son and Camilla lived. He died in 1586–87.[5]

His son died less than ten years later, at the age of thirty-three. His short married life with Camilla had pro-duced five daughters who would, one thinks, have been a satisfaction to him had he lived — Margaret, Mary, Elizabeth, Bridget, and Frances — as well as three sons who died without issue, two of them young.[6]

We have a notice of his death from the Gawdy papers.[7] Young Philip Gawdy of Clifford's Inn writes to his brother "From my Lord of Shrewsbury's house," "My brother Darcye at Tolson is deade, and hath left his wyfe 400*l.* a year and much wealthe besydes; the land to descend to his three daughters."

---

1 Morant, *Essex*, II, 139–140.
2 *Ibid.*, I, 396.   3 *Ibid.*, I, 397.
4 *Transactions of the Essex Archaeological Society*, IX, 364–365.
5 *Ibid.*, I, 397.
6 Morant, *Essex*, II, 140; I, 396–397.
7 Hist. MSS. Comm., VII, 522*a*. MSS. of G. E. Frere, Esq., of Roydon Hall, Norfolk. (See *Ibid.*, p. 518*b*, for Philip Gawdy).

This sounds as if Gawdy had married a sister of Darcy, who had several. His summary account of Darcy's bequests is nearly correct, though he has the number of daughters wrong. Darcy left[1] Camilla "my Manno^r Howse called Tollishunt Darcie Hall" and all his lands for her natural life, his lands to be divided among as many of his daughters as survived her. This sounds as if the three boys had already died.

After his death Camilla married Harvey, whom we have met before in the course of the Wrightington-Bryskett suit. While her mother was losing money and peace of mind in many quarrels, Camilla was becoming yearly more prosperous. Her second husband was Francis Harvey of Witham, "wher he lyeth buryed he was Pentioner to Q. Eliz."[2] He and Camilla had only one child, Elizabeth, the darling of her father's heart.

It was beside Mary Nevell, his first wife, that he was to be buried,[3] when he died in 1602. Camilla, his executrix, was to "cause a faire white Marble or Touche Stone Table-wise twoe yeard$_e$ longe and three ffoote broade to be sett wth Pillers three foote highe over the grave or Vaulte where I shall lye wth my former wieffe;" it was to cost twenty pounds, and more if needful. He left sums varying from five to forty shillings to the poor of sixteen parishes with which he was connected.

To Camilla, his "deere and welbeloued wief," he left all such goods as he had had by her which had been Thomas Darcy's, and the wardship of her five Darcy children, Margaret, Mary, Elizabeth, Bridget, and Frances, which he had "by hir Ma^{tc} graunte vnder hir Broade Seale." To her also he left his manors of Drayton and

1 Prerogative Court of Canterbury, 75 Dixy, Thomas Darcy's will.
2 *Visitation of Essex, 1612*, Harl. Soc., XIII, 215.
3 Harvey's will, P. C. C., 40 Montague.

Bringhurst and "the Sheepes close" in Leicestershire
during her life, after which they were to go to his "onlye
daughter and heire Elizabeth Harvie and hir heires for-
ever," unless she died without issue before she was twenty-
one or married, "wch God forbidde." For this little girl's
godly, virtuous, and good education and better advancement he left the very large sum of two thousand pounds,
"wch I haue in good goulde lyenge in my Closett in Cres-
singe Temple," to be used toward "good and comelie En-
duemente and for hir advauncemente as shalbe meete and
fittinge for A Gentlewoman and for the betteringe of hir
estate;" in using which he reposed great confidence in his
wife and overseers, "desieringe them to haue a tender and
speciall care over hir herein and alsoe for hir p^{r}ferment
in marriadge." This he stresses, when he appoints his
overseers, "desiringe them of all loves to haue due care
of the bestowinge of my said daughter to a fitte gentleman."

This tenderness for his ewe lamb, a gracious thing to
find among much litigiousness and avarice, was not to be
rewarded in the way he had hoped; for even before her
mother Camilla, less than four years later Elizabeth had
died.[1]

He made bequests also to his nephew and servant,
Robert Vasey, and to his sister Ursula, Robert's mother,
provided maintenance for life, secured against Camilla's
making default in paying it.

Camilla, the second time a widow before her mother,
survived Francis Harvey only till 1606. Her very long
and elaborate will is as good a commentary as I know on
their manner of life. She may have been the show-member

[1] Camilla's will, P. C. C., 58 Stafforde. During her widowhood she had engaged
in at least one lawsuit (appearing in Chancery Reports, Vol. vi) against
Thomas Smith and other defendants, in 3 James.

of the Bryskett and Guicciardine clan, but I think her standards of living cannot have been far from typical.

She was evidently the *grande dame* of her neighbourhood, as one might expect from her two excellent marriages. On the day of her funeral five pounds was to be given to the poor who resorted to it; and to the poor of Tolleshunt Darcy, "to whome I haue hitherto allowed a weekly releife not lyke to be contynued after my decease," ten pounds within three months of her death. Although desiring no vain pomp at her funeral, she left mourning apparel to a long list of kindred and friends.

It now transpires that she had not yet fulfilled Francis Harvey's detailed request about his tombstone. She therefore asked her executors to "take a speciall care to provide" one, and left twenty-five pounds for it — an improvement on Francis's twenty; and explained that she had not deferred getting it from forgetfulness or neglect, but "vppon a purpose to haue pformed yt with some addicōn of my owne kindnes yf god had spared me life."

She provided for her servants, one of whom was "Elizabeth Prowe my Servaunte and Neece" — daughter therefore of Elizabeth Guicciardine about whose marriage with Robert Prowe Lucrece had spent two hundred marks, made by selling certain drugs which she had in the house (cf. p. 318). One may surmise from this that Elizabeth's marriage was less of a financial success than Camilla's; and that within the family too Camilla acted the Lady Bountiful. Her husband's relations with his sister Ursula Vasey and her son suggest that the same thing obtained on his side. She left Elizabeth, Jr., a dowry of fifty pounds, and if she died unmarried it was to be given to "Cicilla Prowe my neece and goddaughter," or after her to her surviving sisters. To their mother, Elizabeth (Guicciardine) Prowe, she bequeathed her "blacke taffatye gowne and kyrtle," and money; to her sister Mary (Guicciardine) Ayloffe, money too, and "alsoe my damaske petticoate trimmed with three silver laces and fringed with my kirtle bodies and sleues of blacke stitched satten"; and to Mary Ayloffe's children Guicciardine and Mildred [1] £ 20 apiece for "Cheines of goulde."

Among other bequests we find this:

Item if mr Thomas Wrightington [who did not die apparently till a few months later in 1606 than Camilla] Will and doe release to my Executo^{rs} his interest . . . he hath to one Crimson satten bedd with furniture of Curtaines and Guilt . . . giuen into my possession by my saide mother accordinge as the saide $\overline{mr}$ Wrightington hath heretofore made offer to doe Then I will that twentye poundes be giuen and payd in liew therof to . . . my saide moth^r And if such release be made then . . . I doe . . . bequeath to my most deare and approued frind the Ladie Mildred Maxey the saide Crimson satten bedd;

if the release be not made, thirty pounds shall be spent on some other bed or whatever may be most pleasing to Lady Maxey.

The Maxeys to whom this bed was left — Lady Mildred and her husband Sir Henry — further exemplify the entangling alliances of these families. Sir Henry was a stepgrandson of Eustace Sulyard whom we have noticed as grandfather of both Thomas Darcy and Thomas Ayloffe; at the same time, Sir Henry's grandmother having married three times, he was also the step-grandson of Thomas Ayloffe's paternal grandfather, William Ayloffe of Great Braxted.

It is diverting that we are able to trace a little further the history of the crimson satin bed. Wrightington died so soon after his stepdaughter Camilla that perhaps he had no time to relinquish his claim as she had suggested. Accordingly, the matter fell into the hands of his executor, Henry Martyn, and a further development of the Guic-

1 Sic; but I find no other record of her. Does it mean Camilla? Cf. p. 356.

ciardine *vs.* Martyn and Prowe case is an order in Chancery
on the 17th May, 1608:[1]

Forasmuch as . . . it appeared that [a certain bond in question]
was made by one Wrightington who married the plaintiff's mother
with the condition amongst other things that she should dispose of all
such goods and chattels psonell as she upon her sepacion brought to
the house of one Robert Prowe and she having as it was now alleged
brought thither a satten bedd with the furniture [and?] given to the
same to the Ladie Maxey The said Martin as executor to the said
Wrightington has Comensed suite at the Comon lawe against . . . S^r
Henry Maxey and recovered xxxj^s x^d for the saide bedde It is therefore ordered that a subpoena be awarded against the defts to bring
the sd bond into this court and to show cause wherfor the same
should not be put in suit against the executor of Wrightington, etc.

In other words, one could not even inherit a bed peaceably
in that litigious family!

Probably Camilla had better fortune with her other bequests. Much of her will is devoted to providing for the
four little heiresses, her Darcy children, Mary, Elizabeth,
Bridget, and Frances — the eldest, Margaret, having already been married to Thomas, son and heir of Sir Anthony Browne.[2]

For these small grandnieces of Lodowick Bryskett she
made provision by asking her brother James Guicciardine
— now home for good, apparently, from Italy — and her
brother-in-law Thomas Ayloffe to keep house in "Tolsount
Hall my nowe mansion howse" for them until the elder
two, Mary and Elizabeth, should either be bestowed in
marriage or reach the age of twenty-one, at which age they
should dispose of themselves for their habitation as they
pleased. The scale of this household one may estimate
from the fact that Mary and Elizabeth were to allow their
uncles a hundred pounds — fifty from the portion of each

1 Decrees and Orders, 1608 B, p. 774.
2 Camilla's will, and the *Visitation of Essex, 1612*, Harl. Soc., XIII, 187.

— for the housekeeping. By this means all four girls might "remayne and cohabit together with my . . . saide twoe brothers," who she hoped would, with her sister Mary Ayloffe (Thomas's wife) continue the children in "that good nurture and education I haue hitherto to my greate Comforte trayned them in." After the house was dissolved, she consigned the younger two, Bridget and Frances, to Lady Maxey and Mary Ayloffe.

She made careful provision also for her husband's "Syster Veasey," and for numerous servants, and left specifically several household articles — to her mother Lucrece (who lived two years more) "the silver porrenger and maudlyn pott I doe ordinaryly vse"; to Lady Maxey (besides the disputed crimson satin bed) "one downe bedd ordinarily lying in the Chamber Called my Ladye Darcyes Chamb^r"; to her daughter Margaret Browne "my beddsteed and beddinge alsoe the hanginge and other furniture in the newe Gallery Chamber Also my litle Chamber bason and ewer of silver," and so on.

Camilla especially charged her daughters to be well advised touching their marriages, and "proceede not to any marriage without the Councells directions and Consente of their lovinge kinsman Sr Henry Maxey and their Lovinge vnkles" James Guicciardine and Thomas Ayloffe. The matter may well have seemed imminent, since the four were respectively nineteen, eighteen, fifteen, and fourteen; and Margaret, already married, was twenty-one.[1] To ensure their well-being, she stipulated that they should not receive their portions of five hundred pounds apiece, unless they married as these advisers wished.

All four did marry: Mary, Christopher Nevell, third son of Edward, Lord Abergavenny; Elizabeth, Sir Henry Mildmay; Bridget, Sir George Fenner; and Frances the

1 See Morant, *Essex*, I, 397–398.

secretary of state to Charles I, Sir Henry Vane himself,[1] thus making Lodowick Bryskett great-great uncle to Sir Harry Vane the younger; and so very circuitously bringing us round to Milton once more. Three knights and the son of a peer, one feels, would have satisfied Camilla well enough to put us out of fear lest any of the children lost their legacies.

True to form, however, they did become involved in litigation. Their father Thomas had been the eldest son of a large family, so that they inherited their grandfather's estates away from their uncles and aunts. One of these, Thomas Darcy's younger brother Eustace, the very next summer after Camilla's death was suing James Guicciardine (doubtless in his capacity of guardian), Thomas and Margaret (Darcy) Browne, Elizabeth, Mary, Bridget, and Frances Darcy, and Thomas Ayloffe being "of Councell wth the def[ts]," in regard to some of their lands.[2] Those mentioned are pleasantly named — the field called "the ffattinge ffeilde or spare pasture," and "the grounde called High feilde, bradfeilde, Goosecrofte, hoamemeade, Bridges house lande: and Spoonere ffeilde."

One has a glimpse of the workings of the household that Camilla left in the depositions by a tenant's wife. About three weeks after Camilla's death she went at Ayloffe's summons to Tolleshunt Hall to confer about her tenancy; but — she answers the assumption of the interrogatory — *he* never came to *her*, nor did she ever give him any fee for his advice — one catches the tone of "I hope I know my place better." On going to the Hall she found Ayloffe, Sir Anthony Browne (father of Margaret's husband), and some others. After some conference about the farms in question they told the woman, Mrs. Chaplin, that "her

1 *Ibid.*, 396–397.
2 Wards Deps. 30. (I am indebted for this reference to Dr. Hotson.)

leases were nought & nothinge worth in regard that M^{ris} Harvye was dead," and Ayloffe told her that unless she would take them anew, she should not have them, "for y^t there was an other belowe in ye hall y^t would take ye same." Thus cornered, she did take them for a year from the following Michaelmas (Camilla having died by July). Either, however, she in turn sublet to one Wyles, or else something went wrong with her lease and he succeeded her; for the interrogatory asks, Did you not drive Wyles's sheep and cattle from the fields (Goosecroft, Homemead, etc.)? Did you not know then that Wyles had hired the fields? Have you not since last Michaelmas kept possession of the manor house which you held in farm of the said coheirs, and "did not you in pson, stryve, wrestle, wth the saide Wyles, to keepe the saide Wyles from out the saide mancõn house?" She answers that after Michaelmas her husband had some bullocks in the fields in question for a few days, which were presently impounded; and she did keep in the house after Michaelmas, but "did never wrastle" with Wyles nor seek to keep him out. However, "shee haueinge a pannell and a grate [?] in ye kitchen of the said howse did goe into ye said kitchen to fetch the same and therevppon the said Wyldes did pull her forth & willed his servant to throwe her pannell after her."

C. Elizabeth Prowe

Elizabeth, as we know, married Robert Prowe at some time after Vincent Guicciardine's death. It must in fact have been very soon after, since the registers of St. Botolph Bishopsgate (where the Wrightingtons also lived) record on the 28th November, 1583,[1] "Camella, daughter of Robt. Prowe." They must have moved, for no more of

1 *Register of St. Botolph's, Bishopsgate*, transcribed by A. W. C. Hallen, 1889.

their children appear in this register. We know, however, that there were more, since Camilla Harvey in her will mentions Elizabeth Prowe, her servant and niece, and her god-daughter Cicilla, while Lucrece, who lived with the Prowes after her separation from Wrightington, made bequests to Onelia, Anne, Thomas, and William — those children for whom Camilla had not already provided.

Beyond this I know only that Robert Prowe, Lucrece's son-in-law, appears in several Chancery suits, including one against Sir Anthony Browne (the father-in-law of Thomas Darcy's eldest daughter, for these suits were nothing if not family affairs) and one against James Guicciardine, in which Wrightington's executor Henry Martyn was Prowe's co-defendant.

D. Mary Ayloffe

Mary, like Camilla, married into a large and important Essex family whose ramifications may be seen in the appended family tree. Her husband, whom in 1599 we find so demurely acting as counsel for his mother-in-law and lending his chambers for Dr. Hutchinson's ministrations of peace, had not always been a model of behaviour. The Lincoln's Inn Black Books [1] reveal that in 1588 he was put out of commons and fined £6 13s. 4d. for assaulting and beating one of the butlers. Not sufficiently chastened, in June he assaulted an utter-barrister's servant, and was therefore expelled. In November, however, he was readmitted upon his humble submission, and in January, 1593/94, was called to the bar. This cheering record was culminated by knighthood in 1603.[2]

Thomas was the younger son of William Ayloffe, Justice of the Queen's Bench, who was doubly connected with

1 II, 7.   2 Morant, *Essex*, I, 70.

Thomas Darcy's maternal grandfather, Eustace Sulyard: William's father had married as his second wife the widow of Eustace Sulyard, and William himself married his step-sister, Eustace's daughter. Of his several children only two concern us: his heir, William, who like Thomas was knighted on the 11th May, 1603, and was made baronet nine years later; and Thomas, who married Mary Guicciardine.[1]

Thomas Ayloffe's career at the bar — and in this transitory life — closed in 1614, no doubt to the loss of his widespread family, who had had the benefit of his professional services. His will,[2] made four years earlier, shows that he was accustomed to live on a large scale, but had prospered less consistently than his brothers-in-law Darcy and Harvey:

> And toucheinge that smale estate god hath blessed me with I haue thought fitt partely in regarde of some debtę I owe which I knowe I am bounde in Conscience and vppon perrill of my soul to satisfie [he says a trifle too piously], partely in Consideracõn of my want of meanes otherwise to provide for my poore innocent and frendles daughterę to appoint my howse and landse in Alvely to be soulde for the better provision of my saide daughterę, [payment of debts, and advancement] of my well deserveinge wyfe with my hopefull and good sonne Gwichardin Ayloffe.

The wife Mary and the son Guicciardine were each to have one third of the proceeds, the other to be divided among his three daughters (also bearing names familiar to us), "Camilla Lucresse and Jane Ayloffe." Camilla Harvey's will also mentions a Mildred.[3]

---

1 See Morant, *Essex*, and the *Visitation of Essex*, Harl. Soc., XIII.
2 P. C. C., 17 Rudd.
3 I suspect this of being a mistake for Camilla. One of the most interesting features of this family tree is the handing down of names from generation to generation. Elizabeth is too common to help us much by its recurrences, but Camillas and Guicciardines in particular burgeoning on remote limbs make one feel that the essential family sap flowed far.

This establishes what family he had. His lands, we know from the will, were in Alveley (because as a younger son he had not succeeded to the holdings in Braxted Magna) and he also had leases in the Minories without Aldgate.

His eldest daughter, Camilla, married Edward Wentworth of Bocking, and had Guicciardine and Camilla. Here came another doubling up of the family, for her first cousin, Thomas, son of William Ayloffe of Braxted Magna, married Edward Wentworth's sister Elizabeth. One of their grandchildren was also named Guicciardine.[1]

A few minutes' contemplation of the Ayloffe family tree will enlarge one's view of the Bryskett connections. Some of them were important in their several generations. The Duke of Sutherland's manuscripts[2] include a series of letters from Guicciardine Ayloffe that run parallel to Pepys and are nearly if not quite as interesting. But by that time much water had flowed under London Bridge since Lodowick Bryskett was laid to rest.

What we have learnt about him — that he had a wrangling brother-in-law, or a nephew by marriage who beat the butler — will not alter the course of history. Yet it is

---

1 Essex Archaeological Society, *Transactions*, new series, III, 222, and Harl. Soc., XIII, 519.

2 Hist. MSS. Comm., Report on the MSS. of the Duke of Sutherland at Trentham, Co. Stafford. In Vol. v Guicciardine Ayloffe's very interesting correspondence runs from 1652 to 1661, besides some undated letters. The MSS. of Lord Kenyon at Gredington Hall, Salop (Hist. MSS. Comm., Report 14, App. IV), have a series from Guicciardine Ayloffe to Roger Kenyon between 1663 and 1671, and from 1671 on a further series from Guicciardine Wentworth to Roger Kenyon. I have not had access to the manuscripts, and therefore do not know whether it was possibly the same young man writing both sets of letters, having perhaps for reasons of inheritance altered his surname for another one in the family, or whether the letters are really the work of two kinsmen. This would be readily ascertained by comparing the handwritings and the seals of arms. The letters signed Guicciardine Ayloffe are numbered 230, 239, 249, 254, 287, 291, etc., in Lord Kenyon's collection, and no. 299 (as well as various subsequent ones) is from Guicciardine Wentworth.

good to find his twig in a well-ramified date-bearing family tree. There is an intrinsic if not great value in being able to set Sidney's companion and Spenser's friend against a family background of some detail; in surmising the scale on which they were accustomed to live at home and the work which they did abroad. We are glad to see what we have not seen before, that Italian family of great solidarity — a crushing weight poor Wrightington must have found it — acting *en masse*. If they were rather hard on outsiders who did not fit in, they seem to have warmly embraced those who did; and from Lucrece's time on it may be reckoned no less a Guicciardine than a Bryskett clan.

NOTES TO APPENDIX I

THIS map is made from a plan of the estate in about 1595, from the Hatfield MSS. (L. C. C. Survey, Plate 21), Kip's *View* in 1699 (*ibid.*, Plate 22 and page 25), James Hamilton's survey in 1664 (*ibid.*, Plate 1), plans in King's MS. (transcript, pp. 207 and 209, in Chelsea Public Library), and Alfred Beaver's sketch map of Chelsea in 1625.

The gravest hiatus is not knowing when the manor stables or barns were moved from the position of c. 1595 here shown and Gorges' house built partly on their site. One would like to know this because it appears that Bryskett's house must have been on or near this site.

A rival claimant is the site of Lindsey House, nearer the river. I am not able to settle this rivalry, but present the material for decision:

(1) The Holbornes held of Winchester and later of Lincoln two messuages: the Parsonage House, and the Farm House near the S. W. side of the manor itself, this farm being served by the "quill of water." (See Beaver, *op. cit.*, p. 147.)

(2) Bryskett and later Stapleton rented "the farm" from Holborne. This might be taken to mean that they did *not* rent the Parsonage.

(3) The Parsonage, however, I have not identified. Dr. King in his MS. survey (transcript) says on p. 169 that it "stood where Mr. Priests or Mrs. Dowells stands . . . whence Mr. Priests Close is called Parsonage Close to this day." His maps on pp. 207 and 209 show that Mr. Priest's was what had been Gorges', and Mrs. Dowell's stood close to the southwest corner of Lindsey House. His uncertainty prevents our eliminating either of these as the farm.

(4) The Lindsey House claim rests on Mr. Davies's proof in *Chelsea Old Church*, ch. 9, that the house occupying this site had been termed "the farm." On p. 156 he cites a warrant in the State Papers Domestic (1671, Entry Book 34, fol. 81) for a grant of "the Farme House in Chelsea and the wharf there";

and on p. 157, a deed entered at the Middlesex Registry (1717, Bk. IV, no. 24) reciting an indenture of 1671 in which the Earl of Lindsey leases

All that messuage or tenement with the appurtenances commonly . . . known by the name of the Farm House in Chelsea aforesaid, and also all that the wharf which lieth along by the Thames and extendeth to the full breadth of the said messuage or tenement on the south side thereof.

This appears to place the farm along the waterfront. Moreover, he proves the continuity of its history from the fact of its enjoying the right of common. (L. C. C. Survey, II, 37.)

If the predecessor of Lindsey House were Stapleton's, the dung-boat story is more effective, since the house was very near to the river and one can easily see that the fountains would have been tainted.

(5) Nevertheless the site of Gorges House was not far either — only halfway up Milman Street — and the evidence in favour of it seems to me even stronger:

(a) Both the Parsonage and the Farm proper may loosely have been called "the farm"; such must have been their use; and Stapleton speaks of "the rest of [Holborne's] farm" besides what Stapleton had rented. His and Bryskett's house may therefore possibly have been the Parsonage; at any rate it was not necessarily *the* only farm.

(b) The "quill of water" serving Bryskett's house, we are told,

did lye in the ground, and went crosse the greate Courte overagaynste the hall dore of the Mannor howse, and so thorowe the wall betwene the saide greate Courte and the yard or orchard of [Holborne].

(c) Part of the ground containing the stables of the great house had been demised to Holborne with the house and Little Parsonage close. It would go more naturally with Gorges House than with Lindsey House; and moreover Holborne describes the Earl's new brick barn as being on part of one of the yards that are on the backside of the demised messuage; at that time the Little Parsonage Close lay open "before the doores of the two stables now in the . . .

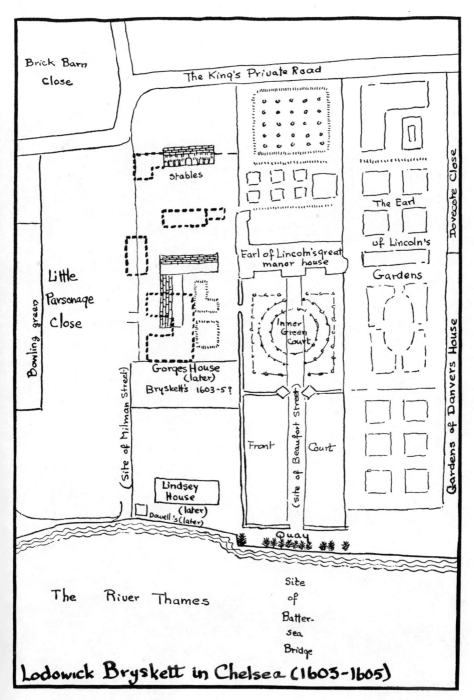

Lodowick Bryskett in Chelsea (1603-1605)

MAP SHOWING BRYSKETT'S HOUSE AND ORCHARD IN CHELSEA

possession of the now Earle of Lincolne." These stable yards cannot be described as being at the backside of Lindsey House.

(*d*) One matter in dispute is the brick wall which replaces the pales between the back green court and stableyard of the Earl, and the Little Parsonage Close. This again would not affect Lindsey House.

(*e*) What goes farthest to convince me is that Lodowick Bryskett says that his back yard is called the kitchen garden, and is "empaled betwene the backsyde of the sayd howse, and the great howse." The back yard of Lindsey House would hardly answer to this description. Davies (ch. 6, p. 117) clinches this argument:

Also the great kitchen yard or garden on the west side of the house and of the said great garden with all the buildings on the south end of the same and with the brick barn and stable on the north side; which yard extendeth to the back yard and buildings belonging to the said late dwelling house of Sir Arthur Gorges on the south and to the stable yard and close there on the west and to a plot of ground lying next the highway on the north and to the said great yard on the east.

APPENDIX II

THE LODGE FAMILY

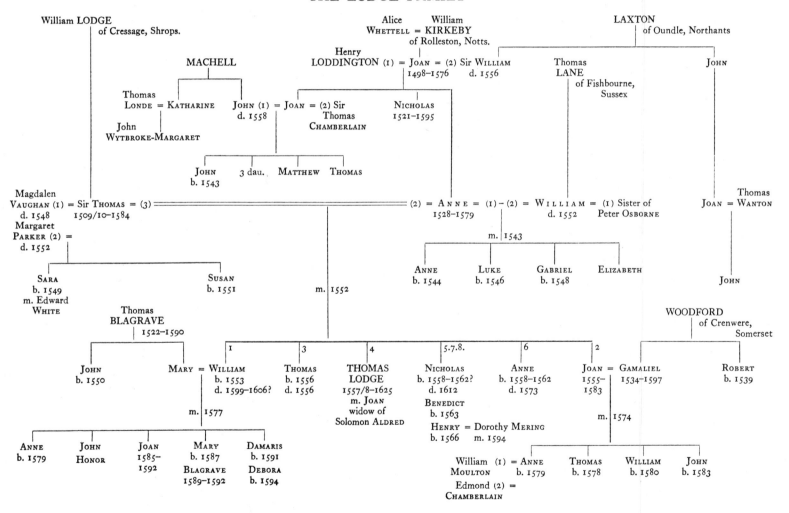

BRYSKETT–GUICCIARDINE

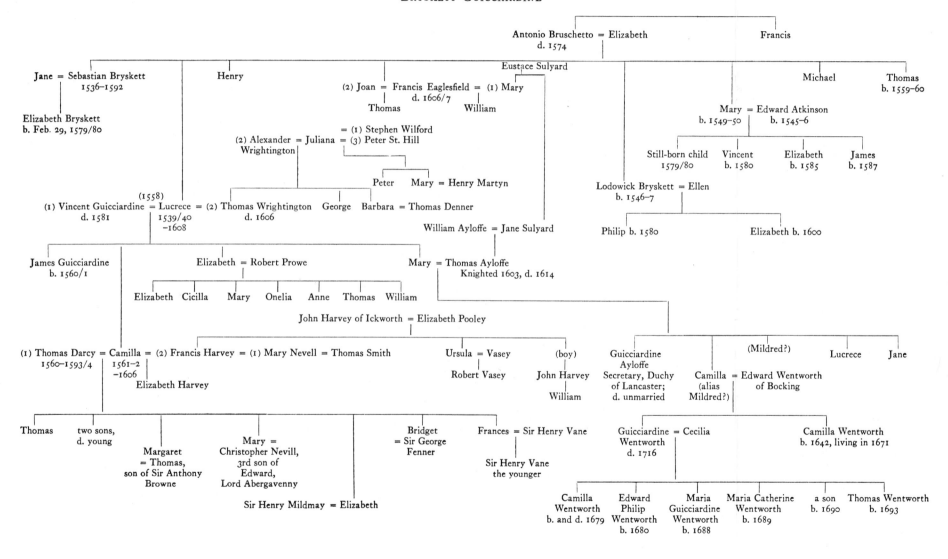

JOHN LYLY AT ST. BARTHOLOMEW'S
OR
MUCH ADO ABOUT WASHING
By DEBORAH JONES

CONTENTS

JOHN LYLY AT ST. BARTHOLOMEW'S

OR

MUCH ADO ABOUT WASHING

I. THE QUARREL IN THE WELL–YARD

Hᴏᴡ now, you proud fool, you proud ass, wilt thou put by the hanging of our line here? Come out of thy doors if thou darest, thou lunatic coxcomb, come out of thy doors; if thou cuttest my line I will cut thy coxcomb!"

It is not always that a servant coming with a message runs into so lively a conversation as that which William Elger found raging at Thomas Cotton's gate on Thursday the 19th of September, 1605,[1] when he arrived on some errand for his master.

To be more accurate, Elger arrived a moment before it began. Blocking his approach to Cotton's gate hung a clothesline strung across between the porches of Mr. Denman's and Mr. Squire's, two neighbouring houses, in such a way that he had to duck underneath; and hanging out her clothes on it was Mistress Frances Collier, who lived in one of the adjacent houses. Sara, wife of Francis Denman, Mrs. Collier's next door neighbour, was at her own door; Thomas Cotton, whose gate was so barricaded, came to his in annoyance and said to Mrs. Collier, "I marvell you will hange vp yoʳ lyne here, if it were her lyne [point-

---

[1] All dates are given Old Style. [The preliminary work upon this document was done by Miss Jones, Miss Rosemary White, and Mrs. Judith Randall in collaboration. *Ed.*]

ing to Sara Denman in her door] as it is yo^{rs} I would cutt it downe."

For the hanging of lines was a sore subject with Cotton, as with other inhabitants of the same well-yard, whom we shall meet. A little earlier that day when Frances Collier's line went up, he had sent her a message of protest, and at the beginning of the same month of September he had said he would get an order from the Governors of the Hospital whose tenants they were that no more clothes should be hung in the well-yard, and soon after had sent orders to this effect by his servant to Mrs. Denman and Mrs. Collier. They had protested that they should keep on drying their clothes as they were wont to do. To Mrs. Collier he was rather more gracious than to Sara, offering her his garden for the purpose, only to hear that she would not lose her right of divers years past in the well-yard "to goe into another bodies garden for the drienge of her clothes."

Now Francis Denman, attorney-at-law, was standing in his hall window on the 19th of September and overheard the conversation of his wife Sara, Mrs. Collier, and Cotton, as it increased in warmth. Cotton's gratuitous rudeness to Sara fired his quick Elizabethan temper, and "grieved at [Cotton's] showing more special malice to him and his wife then to the other neighbors," he ran down into the yard with some of the "vndecent and vnseemly speeches" which Elger heard. Denman reports his own speeches as:

Be better advized Cotton & give not so much leave to rage for what ragingly & rashely is begunne will challenge shame before it be halfe done, That o^r lynes & especially myne should now be more offensive to thee then it hath heretofore ben, wch for nyne yeares & vpward℮ ever since my comming hither hath hunge in the self same mann^{er} as now this doth wthout anie excep͂con to me or mine, & considering thine owne clothes hath also in the self same mann^{er} ben often here hanged & others also, it may be woundered at what should move thee now to be so much oversene.

To this Cotton answered that he knew Denman better
now, and what was done before was but by his courtesy;
and said "in a scorning & disdainefull manner,"

you are now knowne to well what you are . . . as if he had knowne
this def [had ben] to be a contemptible pson & of lewd & bad disposicon.

Denman, much provoked, answered,

What dost thou knowe me to be, thou knowest me to be no waie inferior to thy self & I must tell thee that thy insolent pride doth to much
mislead thee wch God graunt it draw not vpon thee that Lunacie or
frensie wch by report thou hast ben heretofore to much troubled withall,
& I haue heard some say that Pride was then thought to be the cause
thereof . . . & therefore it behoveth thee now to looke better into thy
self & to learne to know thy self aright, wch once learned thou shalt be
the better able to iudge of others.

Cotton, "seeming to be much enflamed wth choller &
splene," swore that next time Denman's clothes were out,
he would cut down the line before his face to spite him the
more. Denman said that if he did, it would be enough to
make him try to beat Cotton from the line and break his
coxcomb; "therefore doe not vrge me to farre." Cotton
"smiling in derision, vsed these worde Alas silley fellow
what art thou able to doe, thou canst scold, & that is all."
Denman answered that he dared do all that Cotton dared;
and they parted.

Cotton's smile of derision is otherwise interpreted by
Elger, who attributes to him "a mylde and temperate
manner." He describes Denman's shot about lunacy more
vividly:

Thou has ben lunatick, & yt is now full moone, & fall of the leafe,
thou art lunatick againe & lyttell lesse then madd, otherwise thou durst
not Cutt the lyne. . . . And if thou Cuttest yt, I will cutt thy Lunatick
Coxcombe.

If by any chance there was more in it than sheer insult,
it was a cruel thrust; but though Cotton had evidently a

passionate temper, I have found no other suggestions of this nature.

If Elger is to be believed, Cotton, "saying his worde were noe slander, vsed some other mylde speeches vnto him and soe turned aboute & went into his howse."

That evening, being Thursday, Cotton's wife Elinor fell into difficult labour, a week too early, and on Friday night was delivered of a child.

This quarrel took place in the well-yard or close of St. Bartholomew's in West Smithfield, among certain tenants of the Hospital; for Bart's then as now secured part of its revenue by leasing tenements and land. This well-yard, as it appears from maps and plans of the early seventeenth century, was on the site of part of the present Hospital itself, which in the past three hundred odd years has naturally swallowed up its surrounding "messuages and tenements." As nearly as I can tell from comparing the 1617 map with a modern one,[1] the well-yard must have taken up part of the ground now the great square in the midst of the Hospital. This probability is the more attractive because in the square is a fountain which one would like to think the lineal descendant of that well where Mrs. Collier, Mrs. Denman, and others dried their clothes.

There were many more tenants in the close [2] or well-yard than are to concern us. Our immediate interest centres round Cotton, the Denmans, the Colliers, and Beatrice

1 Sir J. D'Arcy Power, *St. Bartholomew's Hospital.*
2 Not to be confused with the present Bartholomew Close, which was the close of the priory of St. Bartholomew the Great, across the street (Duck Lane, or Duke Street, now part of Little Britain) from the Hospital. Our close, so called often in the Hospital records, is the close in the parish of St. Bartholomew the Less, which church stands within the precincts of the Hospital. Perhaps to avoid confusion with the priory close, the Star Chamber case with which we are concerned always uses the term "well-yard." The most casual inspection of the Hospital Ledgers and Journals shows the two terms to be synonymous.

Lyly, wife of a certain John Lyly not unknown to fame as
the author of *Euphues*, a handful of court comedies, some
pamphlets, and other works characteristic of his age.

It is pleasant to know exactly where Lyly was living in
1605 (about a year before his death in November, 1606),
and the certainty comes from a Star Chamber suit in the
Public Record Office, listed as Star Chamber Proceedings
8, 93/8: a handful of neat depositions lapped about with
crumpled and slightly mutilated parchments bearing most
of the corresponding interrogatories, and the Bill and
Answers. The Bill of Complaint is brought by Thomas
Cotton, Gent., against "ffrauncis Denman and Sara his
wyfe, Thomas Collyer and ffrauncis his wyfe, John Randall [the constable], William Hewys [Denman's man-
servant], Mary [Andrews] the maide S^{r}vaunt of the said
ffraunc$_e$ Denman John Lylley Beatrix his wife," and the
subject is the hanging of clothes lines in the well-yard.
There are examinations of every defendant except Lyly,
and also depositions of William Elger, servant to Mr. Rod-
man or Redman, of Great Shelford, Cambs.; Elizabeth
Colborn, wife of a shoemaker in St. Sepulchre's; and
Richard Hunter, citizen and draper, aged 29.[1]

For the quarrel did not end with the "hott words" between Cotton and Denman.

Of course those speeches were food for the gossip of
the neighbourhood. On that same day young Richard
Hunter, a draper, from his mother's house opposite the
Colliers' heard them and Collier's mother and Mrs. Martin
talking it over as they sat at Collier's door. Mrs. Martin
wished a good end were made in the matter; Collier said
if it were *his* line and Cotton cut it, "he woulde talke wth
him whersoeu^r he mett him."

1 Star Chamber 8, 126/10 is a countersuit by Francis Denman of Thavies Inn
vs. Thomas Cotton, student in Gray's Inn, his wife Ellen, his servant Robert
Fryette and others, on the same affray.

Denman, fearful of what might come of the affair, spoke to Randall the constable, who in turn went to Cotton and asked him the cause of the falling out. Cotton answered unsatisfactorily, by Randall's account: he "aunswerd in Conclucõn after manie idle excuses . . . that in deed he Could not of late indure or abide the sighte of anie Clothes newe washed to be hanged ther," and that he would cut the next line hung there. The interrogatory to Randall throws light on Cotton's point of view:[1] it expresses a wish that the Denmans and Colliers would hang their lines less often and so that "Comers to and fro the same [gate] might pase without stopping vnder the Clothes or put- tinge them bye"; but would hange them "at tymes Con- venient in the Vacacõn time and when there was no Daunger of infeccõn." According to this also, Randall rather tactlessly proclaimed that all the rest of the inhab- itants of the well-yard, "yea and all the dwellers in Duck- lane also mighte hange there." Randall says he asked Cotton to keep the peace until he had at least spoken to the Governors. This the constable apparently did, for Denman says that they sent for him and Cotton, and Randall more explicitly says that

the next daye then following wᶜʰ was the xxᵗʰ daye of September . . . (he) made the whole matter knowen unto suche of the Gov'noʳˢ as he found then in the Courte house adioyninge to the said Courte yeard a place Where some of them doe usuallie meete uppon satterdayes & mundayes, and . . . desired them to be pleased to Call bothe parties before them, and soe in hearinge them to decide the Controv'sie be- twixte them for feare of mischeif that might insue;

whereupon the Governors sent for Cotton to appear the next Monday at about eight, "wᶜʰ albeit he had notice

---

1 Randall says that Goodwife Man (perhaps Johane Manne) told him Cotton would be glad to have him end the controversy, but Cotton showed no such mind.

thereof did not come but absented himselfe as this defendant nowe thinketh to an evill purpose."[1]

As a matter of fact Cotton did not cut the very next line
hung there, perhaps because he was saving his spleen for
the Denmans, sparing even Beatrice Lyly, who was already in his black books: Cotton says in the Bill that he

did frō tyme to tyme in gentle and neighbo^rlie sorte intreate and pswade
wth the said ffrauncis Denman and Sara his wyfe, Thomas Collyer and
ffrauncis his wyfe, *John Lillye and Bettresse his wyfe* . . . to desiste and
forbeare to vse the said Annoyaunce. (Italics mine.)

Beatrice Lyly deposes that she

dyd cause her servantę to hange vp twoe lynes from the sd mr Denmans
Porche to mr Squyers poarche the xxvj^th & xxvij^th dayes of September
being thursdaye & frydaye [i. e. just a week after the high words in the
yard] . . . for that then her next neighbor dyd builde against her
Garrettę & stopp vp the lightes therof, so as she this def could not
hange her clothes in the same Garrettę as she was woont to doe before:
. . . saying further, that when she this def first caused her sd lynes to
be hanged in the sd wellyard she . . . dyd not know or vnderstand of
the varyances betwixt the sd pl' and mr Denman And this def sayth
that Mary M^ris Denmans mayde dyd helpe this def^ts mayde to sett &
propp vp this def^ts sd lyne . . . & that care was then vsed, for the
leavinge of A great space for passeng^ers to come to & from the howse of
the sd Cpl^t.

I do not know what the Denmans did about their washing for the next ten days after the quarrel. Possibly Sara
skipped one week to let things blow over a little. In any
case, on Saturday, the 28th of September, as she was leaving London with Frances Collier to spend Sunday in the
country, she left word with Mary Andrews her servant to
hang out the clothes as usual on Monday — to "wash vp
her bucking clothes & to hang them vp to drie in the sd
yard." By way of precaution Denman told Randall that

[1] The Hospital Journals make no mention of this; they have no entries between
3 August, 1605, when Randall was sworn constable, and 11 January, 1605–06.

this was to be done. Randall promised to be there, but
told Denman to keep out of the way.

Accordingly, on Monday morning at seven, before her
mistress's return, Mary hung up the line from Denman's
porch to Squire's, ten or twelve feet from Cotton's gate,
and left it hanging empty while she went to do the
washing. The interrogatories set to the defendants show
Cotton felt that the line hung so early, and left empty at
that, was hung for a challenge rather than for use; but
Mary deposes that being a new line it had been washed in
lye, not to stain the linen, and had to be up early to dry.
The interrogatory further inquires: Why was it hung only
from your master Denman's post to Mr. Squire's, not from
Squire's to the well "as you were woonte to doe: Since as
greate or a greater pte of the Lyne was Left at yor Masters
Porche folded vpp then that pt of the Lyne was that was
honge vpp from yor saide ⟨Mas . . . orche⟩ to Mr Squierss
Porche./" But for that too Mary has a quite simple answer, that in the first place there was *not* much of the line
left over, and moreover she had

an intencōn at the same tyme to hange [another] an olde lyne from the
sd Mr Squyers post to the well and had so donne, if the weather had
served & the styrr not bin.

(This other line, not being newly washed in lye, had no
need to go up so early.)

To Cotton's excited mind, however, everything was being done on purpose to spite him. When Sara Denman and
Frances Collier came home from the country at about
nine, attended by the Denmans' manservant Hewysh, the
line was hanging empty as Mary had left it. Soon after,[1]
however, Cotton came out of his house — let us hear the
tale from Beatrice Lyly as our most interesting witness:

[1] Denman and E. Colborn say at about nine; Sara and Hewysh about ten;
   Beatrice Lyly and Mary Andrews about eleven.

[She] dyd see the sd Comp^t [Cotton] about eleven of the clocke on the sd laste daye of September come home to his sd howse in the sd well yard. & allso she dyd see the sd Compl^t all allone wth his dagger drawne in a wrathfull and despightfull manner stricke at M^{ris} Denmans Lyne hanging in the sd well yarde wth ppose to cutt Downe the same lyne, wch when he sawe he could not doe, then dyd he the sd pl [Mr Cotton] bringe fourth a lowe stoole & a naked knief into the same wellyarde, & stood vppõ the sd stoole & wth the same knyef dyd cutt the sd lyne, there beinge then no resistance, nor anye Companye eyther in the sd mr Denmans Porche or in the sd wellyarde at the tyme of the so cuttinge of the sd Lyne.

The Denmans' Mary, who was washing clothes in their backyard, heard someone knock at Denman's door and call to her, "Mary Mr Cotton hath cutt yor lyne, looke to ytt." She went out to the well-yard, saw the cut line, "& a stoole & a naked knyef in [Mr Cottens] the p^{lts} hande̜"; as Beatrice had said, no one was with him nor in Denman's porch.

Sara, presently coming to her house door and seeing the line down, sent Hewysh for Randall and for Mr. Shaw, one of the Masters of the Hospital, to see what Cotton had done. He not being at home, she sent Hewysh for her husband, "he y^{en} being wth his worke folke̜ aboute his building in St Sepulchers pish." Then she went to tell the Colliers next door, who came back with her, according to her deposition; though Collier may have lingered behind the two ladies, for he says he met Denman in the well-yard at about ten. This is quite possible, for St. Sepulchre's is so near the well-yard that Hewysh by hurrying might have got him there in the time it took Sara to go and tell the tale to her next neighbours; especially if, as seems probable, she and Frances wasted time in exclamations.

At all events, Denman met Collier and told him that the line was cut and Sara had many clothes to dry (cf. p. 371) and nowhere else to dry them, and he would have his line hung up again. He then despatched Hewysh once more for the absent Randall, and with Collier joined their wives in his porch, where Collier "being then in [his] Cloke staied leaninge there againe a post for no purpose at all but looking vpon the sd lyne as it lay cutt in the ground." Denman said he would tie the line up again, to which Collier answered, "If you will do it, do it quickly." Denman accordingly directed Mary to do so. At this point Hewysh came back with the report that Randall was still to seek. Denman answered, "God graunt he doe cõm to prevent Mr Cottons mischeif, yet I hope it will not be so bad as it semeth he intendeth by the preparacõn of wepons," and shortly afterwards sent Hewysh into the house.

While Mary was hanging up the line again, Robert Fryett, Cotton's servant, came through the yard to his master's house. "Yo^r master hath cutt our lyne once," Mary remarked; "I hope he will not doe it againe"; to which Fryett returned, "yes by God it shalbe cutt againe presently." To this Sara retorted from her porch, "Your master hath cutt my lyne a bott℮ on him lett him now come forth & hange himself by it if he will."

To Cotton inside his gate it must have seemed (and did seem, we know from the Bill and Interrogatories) that the little crowd had collected definitely against him, instead of half from curiosity as to what was up and what would happen next. Of course the defendants depose unanimously that such was their innocent motive; until Collier, seeing Cotton come to the wicket of his gate with a long gauntlet up above his left elbow and a rapier drawn in his right hand, stayed to see what he was going to do with them.

Beatrice Lyly too, from the vantage ground of her chamber window, spied this alarming sight:

And this def dyd at the same tyme beinge in her sd Chamber wyndow
. . . see the now Cplt w^thin his gate wth his rapyer drawen in his hand
& wepons standinge by him w^thin the same gate And this def thincking
that mr Denmans lyne would presently be cutt downe agayne & fearing
that theruppō some quarrell & affraye would instantly happō betwixt
the sd pl' and mr Denmā abowt the same dyd goe downe owt of her
chamber into the sd wellyard to call for helpe to keepe the peace w^ch
she feared would p^rsently be broken betwixt the sd pl' & mr denman.
And when she this def came fourth at her doore she chaunced there to
meet wth mr doctor Covert & one mr Lowman sometyme an Attorney
of this ho C^rte w^thout having any wepō or weapons abowt them or eyther
of them, to whome this def^t then sayd. Gentlemen I hope god hath
sent yo^w hither as Angles [sic] to keepe the peace & to prevent blood-
shed, & shewed vnto them mr Cotton the pl' then standing w^thin his
gate wth wepons by him, & allso she then shewed vnto them the sd mr
Denman & mr Collyer then standing weponed as aforesd in the sd mr
Denmans porche. And the sd mr doctor Covert then lookg towardę
mr Cottons gate sayd, Looke m^ris Lylly yonder . . . is mr Cotton &
wepons by him, owt of doubt some mischief is pretended. And w^thall
the sd mr doctor Covert & mr Lowman went into this def^te howse
saying that they would staye there to see the peace kept. And this def
herself went vnto the sd mr Denman & mr Collyer being in the sd mr
Denmans porche & sayd vnto them ffor goddes sake take heed what
yo^w doe, one of yo^w (meaninge mr Denman) hath a wief & gotten goodes,
& the other allso a wief & charge of children, & in an affraye yo^w may
aswell receyve a mischief as doe yt & then in what cases shall yor
wyeffę bee and w^thall this def then told them that 2 gentlemen meaning
mr doctor Covert & mr Lowman would come & staye to see the kę
peace kept Wherunto the sd mr denman answered sayinge. M^ris Lyllie
wee (meanyng himself and mr Collyer) intende not anye vyolence but
onely doe purpose to keepe the lyne from being cutt. & I pray yo^w lett
the twoe gentlemen meaning mr Doctor Covert & mr Lowman staye.[1]
And theruppō this def went into her sd howse.

No sooner had she gone than Denman and Sara (who
says she saw Cotton standing within his wicket, hose un-
trussed,[2] with gauntlet and rapier) heard him order Robert

1 The sense is ambiguous here, but the other depositions make it clear that he
  meant "stay away," not "stay to help."
2 For convenience and flexibility, on the same principle that one would roll up
  one's sleeves for violent exertion. Miss Mary Forster Martin tells me that an
  instance is to be found in Stow.

Fryett to cut the line again. Out came Fryett with a
brown bill [1] (a "blackebill" by Collier's account [2]) and
began to hack at the line, — two or three blows, Mrs. Collier deposes, — the line being tied somewhat high.

Denman immediately flew out with his pikestaff (a
small knotted staff varying from six to nine feet, if we may
believe all the witnesses, who combine to admit that it had
a little pike in the end), "wch before for the most pte was
sett to stand behinde this defte porch dore," and which at
Collier's and Sara's advice he had picked up when they
saw Cotton's state of preparedness. Denman rushed
down upon Fryett and struck at his bill to turn it from the
line. Fryett "did . . . make a full blow at [Denman's]
head"; Denman tried in vain to parry with his staff, which
by the force of the blow was "driven vpon his owne head."
At the same very instant, before Denman had recovered
from the blow, Cotton ran at Denman from his wicket
with drawn rapier, thrusting at his head with it, and struck
off his hat. Fryett also making for Denman, Thomas
Collier, seeing his danger, threw off his cloak, drew the
short dagger which he usually wore, ran in amongst them,
and bore off another blow which Fryett struck at Denman's head, "wch blowe if this def had not taken wth his
sd sword this def verily beleveth the sd Mr Denman had
ben slaine thereby." [3] He and Denman between them were
too much for Cotton and Fryett, whom they beat back to
Cotton's wicket, Denman in self-defence hitting Cotton
on the side of the head.

Just as they got back to the wicket, Hewysh, who had
heard the fray from inside Denman's house, ran out with

1 E. Colborn calls it "an olde short rustye Bill."
2 Collier says this was at about eleven.
3 Collier is rather graphic about his own part in the play — and so, by-the-bye,
  is his wife, to whom plainly he was the centre of the affair.

drawn sword and dagger, and began hacking at Cotton's and Fryett's weapons as they thrust them out at the wicket,[1] until Denman ordered him back.

All this while Sara Denman and Frances Collier, who had come down from the porch into the yard, much frightened by the affray, "did runne vp & downe the sd well yarde not knowing what to do to appease it." Sara says that she and

M[ris] Collier were so much afrighted & amazed that they did runne vp & downe the sd welleyard & intreated [their husband(e] & cried owt to the now Comp[t] & his man asking them what they meant to doe . . . but did no other matter at that time then desired that their husband(e would com̃ away & were owt of that companie.

They deny having said it would make no difference if Cotton were knocked on the head. Surely, however, they must have cried out the Elizabethan equivalent of "Give it to him! Knock his block off!" which would have conveyed substantially the same impression to Cotton himself. The fact of their husbands' coming off victorious is perhaps a testimonial to the success of their incitements, for Cotton had no such encouragement. His poor wife Elinor, hardly over a week delivered, came and stood anxiously inside the gate, and Cotton says a naked dagger[2]

1 Such is the order of events according to the depositions of Denman, Sara, Collier, Frances, and Beatrice Lyly — all of them defendants. But E. Colborn says that they all assaulted Fryett as he was about to cut the line, forced him inside the gate (where Cotton still was), and thrust their weapons through after him. Collier says he and Denman did not come within eight feet of the wicket.

2 Bill: "but by god(e provydence the same happened to fall flatt and not to sticke in the pointe, whereby althoughe it tooke not that effecte as it was mente, yett it did sore bruise and hurte her to her then greate terro[r] and daunger and her yett Contynuall griefe. And some other of the said Riottous psons then also bent theyr weopens agaynst her wth the pointes close to her brest, threatninge and endevoringe to mischeefe her; wherew[th] she was soe extremelie affrighted that therby she fell sodenlie sicke and therof languished to the pill of her lyfe."

was thrown which struck her on the breast; a fact which the defendants consistently deny.

As soon as he could for the clashing and hacking of weapons at his gate Cotton clapped his wicket to; immediately Beatrice Lyly saw him "stoupe & open the lowe[r] bolt of his great gate w[ch] he dyd then flinge open, & that being done, she did also see the sd mr Cotton & his man ffryett well weponed come fourth agayne into the sd well-yarde."

Sara was too much frightened to notice what happened next, but Denman knew: as he was standing "a pretty way" from the gate and from his man Hewysh and Collier, Cotton ran at him with drawn rapier and struck at him; after him with sword and dagger came Fryett, whom Hewysh engaged. Denman defended himself against Cotton with his staff alone, the blows of which were "borne of alofte by one Dennys[1] (then one of the sd Comp[ts] [Cotton's] companie as this deft beleveth)." Denman being "in great hazard to haue ben spoiled by the sd Comp[1]," Collier came to the rescue with his short sword, whereupon Dennys struck Collier.[2] Presumably it was this diversion of Dennys's help from Cotton that gave Denman a better chance, for now the blows of his staff broke Cotton's rapier. Cotton, whether in disgust or in a sort of desperation, flung the useless hilts at Denman,[3] and ran from him — unpursued, according to Denman and Collier, though

1 A shoemaker.
2 Collier's account is that Dennys came up to him with a long pikestaff and willed him to keep the peace or he would knock him down; whereon Collier retired.
3 Sara too remembers this fact. She must have been watching her husband and no one else, for she remembers little that does not immediately concern him. Frances Collier too seems to have been watching her own husband. She says that at the time of Cotton's and Fryett's second emergence he was standing a pretty way from the wicket, she thinks to keep Fryett from coming out to hurt Denman. This unconscious self-revelation of Sara and Frances throws a pleasant light on an otherwise ungracious story.

Elizabeth Colborn says that Denman pursued him so violently with the staff that he had to fly back, and that if he had not been rescued by "one x͂pofer" (Christopher) Dennys, she thinks he would have been beaten or slain. (Of course it would not be easy for an excited onlooker to know exactly the order of events, or tell what happened after and what before the rapier broke.) Denman perhaps in relief turned to the people present, with his back to Cotton. Suddenly the people cried out to him to look about or he would be slain. He turned just in time to see Cotton coming at his back with a dagger. Denman laid his hand on his own, but did not draw it, for Cotton stopped.

It was apparently at this point that the tardy constable Randall appeared at last; not such long last as it seems, by the way, for the riot must have taken considerably less time than does the telling of it.

It is hard to know just when the several other people present arrived — whether before or after the constable. After Cotton and Fryett had assaulted Denman, Sara says, two gentlemen — evidently Beatrice Lyly's "Angles," Lowman and Covert — ran down out of Lyly's house, unarmed, one in a gown, the other in a cloak. Frances Collier says that about the time Randall came, she saw one Mr. Barton in the yard, "he dwelling in that Courte," with rapier drawn, also to keep the peace. Randall is interrogated as to the presence of one Thomlinson, whom he says he does not know.

Randall explains his apparent tardiness. Having promised Denman to be on hand when the washing went up,

accordinglie the mondaie in the morninge beinge the laste daye of September laste, this defendant was aboute eight or nyne of the Clocke in the said well yeard, who seeinge the lyne hange up, & noe Clothes theron, & noe Companie then in the yeard, or in the said ffrauncis denmans porche, wher the lyinge in ambushe was supposed to be [i. e., by the Bill], and the morninge beinge Clowdie & like to rayne as this def[t] then thoughte, had the lesse Care to staye ther, who havinge some busines that daie at the Guyldehall in london went thether and staid ther aboute some two howres, in w[ch] space the lyne was Cut . . . the wife of the said ffrancis denman, . . . not knowinge what to doe wth her Clothes, her servaunt[e] beinge readie to hange them owte & the daie beinge Cleered up, she thought (as she said) that if she should Cause her servaunt[e] to hange up the lyne againe, that the said Complaynant wouldbe as wilfull as he had before alreadie ben, and therfore she sente her man to this defendant[e] howse; [Denman sent for him again, and] lefte worde wth this def[ts] servant[e] that the said ffrancis denman woulde intreate this def[t] assone as he did Come in, to Come . . . who aboute ten or eleven of the Clocke being Come home, & understandinge what message the said ffrancis denman had sent him, he this def[t] goinge toward[e] the said Cowrte yeard, and by the waye beinge tolde that the said Complaynant & others and the said ffrancis denman were in fightinge, he hastened thether.

He arrived with his neighbour, John Greene, at the end of the fray, ordered Denman to lay aside his staff and knife and go into the house, which he did, and told Collier to put up his sword. Hewysh too went in with his weapons and saw no more.

Then Randall turned to Cotton, who he says was standing about two yards from his gate, weaponless, but "rayling & reviling at the sd M[r] Dẽman calling him base companyõ," during all the time that Randall said to him, "ffryend Cottñ are yo[u] nott ashamed to make such a styrre here?" and the like words.

He then charged Cotton and Fryett to go into the house and keep the peace. When they had gone, Randall turned to the people assembled and told them to "depte in peace to their seu'all dwellinges." He had no sooner spoken these words than some of the people cried, "M[r] Constable Looke abowt, & w[th] that this def turned his face toward[e] M[r] Cottons gate . . . and ther he this def sawe ffryett M[r] Cottons man w[th] A Glayue in his hande w[th]out his masters gate strycking, at what or at whome this def^t cannott certẽly say."

What he was striking at [1] we have from Mrs. Colborn: he

came sodeynly out at the gate wth a Rusty forrest bill or such like weapon in his hand (it being a weapon wch this deponent had not before sene in all the said affray) And stroke one blowe therwith to haue Cutt the lyne. saying haue we had all this stirr for a lyne and standҽ yt vp still wthowt Cutting?

Randall went and took hold of Fryett's glaive, charging him to keep the peace. The servant refused to give up his weapon, whereupon Mr. Lowman, one of Mrs. Lyly's two gentlemen, came and asked him if he were mad not to obey the constable, and helped Randall to wrest away the glaive, "or els great mischief had byn done by the sd ffryett to the sd M^r Dẽmã." Simultaneously Cotton came out of his gate again and told Fryett that Randall was the constable, and then Fryett "(though before that tyme the sd ffryett knewe this def^t to be the constable)" gave up his weapon; after which Randall dispersed the company and took away the glaive with him.

The whole of this affray must actually have been the work of a very few minutes; it is easy to see why deponents who looked on from a little distance describe it much more briefly and less clearly as one short and muddled assault of the assembled Denman-Collier group on Fryett, with damage to his would-be rescuer, Cotton.

The accounts of the combatants — Cotton's in the Bill and the defendants' in their answers and examinations — really agree better in making it a double battle: first the emergence of Fryett to cut the line, and the beating back of him (or him and Cotton) within the wicket; second,

1 Collier says Fryett came out with "a long gleive" and offered to strike at Denman.

the raid of Cotton and Fryett, in which Dennys took part
and Cotton's rapier got broken; with the ultimate arrival
of Randall. They agree reasonably well in the outline in
spite of opposing points of view, the consequent different
emphasis, and certain divergences in fact: for example,
whether Cotton came out after Fryett the first time,
whether the defendants tried to force their way inside the
wicket, whether a dagger was thrown at Elinor. As to
some of these details we have lost the testimony of a witness the tone of whose other depositions makes one think
he would have spoken impartially: Richard Hunter, the
twenty-nine-year-old draper, coming into the well-yard
for his eleven o'clock dinner at his mother's house opposite
Collier's, saw only part of the quarrel, "for that this
depo^ts mother then locked him this depon^t in her howse
& wolde not suffer him to goe forth," so that he did not
see so much "as otherwise he shoulde haue donne."

II. THE ROOT OF THE QUARREL

MANY such dead quarrels put us rather in the position of Old Caspar with regard to the Battle of Blenheim: we may or may not share his certainty about the famous victory, but we are very sure we do not know what 'twas all about.

The Cotton-Denman quarrel is an exception. There was more in it than mere neighbourly irritation. It is true that Cotton had a special reason for not liking the entrance to his house blocked, a reason which may even have given him a certain prestige with the honourable Court of Star Chamber: as he says at the beginning of his Bill,

for the space of these ffortye yeares last past and vpwardes the Office of makinge of all yor Maties process℮ of yor Highnes most honorable Courte of Starre Chamber hath bene and yette is kepte in the House where yor Ma^{ts} said Subiect nowe dwelleth . . . yor Ma^{ts} said Subiect℮ father being yor Maties nowe Officer of the said Office.

But the real significance is this: Cotton must have been desperately afraid of the smallpox and the plague.

He was not, poor man, afraid without reason. To begin with, there must always have been a certain amount of danger from living so near a neighbour to the House of the Poor in West Smithfield [1] in those pre-antiseptic days when among the more esteemed precautions against infection were amulets of arsenic worn about the neck, and pomanders to smell, made

after this sort that ensueth. . . . Take of the flowers of red *Roses*, of *Violets*, of *Buglos*, of each halfe a little handfull, of the thrée *Sanders*, of each a *Dramme*; of the rootes of *Angelica*, *Gentian*, and *Zedoary*, of

---

1 Henry VIII desired that the Hospital, re-established by him, should be called by this name. Happily the old title of St. Bartholomew's Hospital clung instead (Sir Norman Moore, *History of St. Bartholomew's Hospital*, London, 1918, II, 159 ff.).

each foure scruples; of white *Encens, Cloues, Nutmegs, Calamus, Aromaticus,* of each a dram, . . . of *Ladaum* infused in *Rose-water* one ounce, mixe all these together in *Rose-water* wherein the *Gum Dragacanth* hath béene infused, and with a little of *Rose-vinegar* make a paste, of which you may forme certaine rounde Pomanders, to weare about your necke, and smell vnto continually.[1]

But his more immediate reason for distress appears from the Bill of Complaint and the examinations. For those two dread diseases had gone about the well-yard of Little St. Bartholomew's and taken their toll in the months before the quarrel came to a head. In early May [2] Lyly's daughter Elizabeth [3] died of what was reported to be the plague, although Beatrice Lyly [4] says that "her daughters Phisicion was of opynion that yt was not the plague wherof she died: And thoughe this def[t] dyd then feare yt was the plague, yet nowe she is pswaded yt was not, bycause nonne other of her howse were infected." In August (about Bartholomew-tide, Beatrice says) a girl in Collier's house had the smallpox "in some smale measure." But the smallpox was first and most, Sara Denman deposes, in Cotton's own house, which was visited at St. James' tide, on 25 July. We learn of no one's death from it, but as he saw it spread from his house to Collier's, and week after week pushed his way past the drying clothes not only of the Colliers but of "suche as M[ris] Collyer washeth to," [5] he may well have been seized with panic; have offered his

1 Thomas Lodge, *Treatise of the Plague*, Hunterian Club, IV, 23.
2 Denman; Collier says at Easter or Trinity.
3 Feuillerat's genealogical table in *John Lyly* (Cambridge, 1910) gives us her Christian name.
4 Much of her examination is crossed out and rewritten, possibly because, asked to depose about the death of her child so short a time before, she could not give a very coherent account. There is occasionally the matter of tragedy in these formal documents.
5 The interrogatory to Beatrice Lyly, Randall, and Mary Andrews asks whether while the smallpox was at Collier's all this linen did not hang across Cotton's gate? And the Bill says there is no getting to Cotton's gate "w[th]out daunger of the vapour of infectious Clothes."

own garden to the Colliers — for it was of a fair size and stretched well away from his house, with apparently a wall between;[1] and, that neighbourly offer refused, have given way to his choleric temper as we have seen; falling at last into a sort of *folie de persécution*, that self-consciousness and awkwardness of a person at odds with those about him, testified to by his perpetual certainty that they were talking about him and laying plans to trap him, which is as pitiful as irritating and as irritating as natural.[2]

The question about hanging the clothes there was not a new one in 1605; nor was this the first disagreement in that neighbourhood. If Denman was "given much to Contentiõ, stryfe, and disturbance wth his Neighb[ors], and of a buisie Spiritt," he was not the only contentious or unwelcome person in or about the well-yard, as occasional notices in the Hospital Journals witness. In 1592, for instance, "John Randoll plum̃er & others Inhabytauntẹ of Ducklane complayned agaynste xpian the wife of Richard Scoefeild Tailor to be a slaunderer & disturber of her neighbors whoe they suppose to be a Comõon Harlott." In 1599 our Cotton had a controversy with his subtenant, Mr. Hunt, about the taking down of a shed which Hunt had set up. In the same year Denman, who had then been there but three years, complained in writing against William Allen the constable for "certaine oppression of the inhabitauntẹ w[th]in the close:" it is perhaps noteworthy that he was on better terms with the later constable, Randall, with whom Cotton, who had had Randall for a subtenant, was on worse.

There had been matters of hygiene also. In 1598 we find William Allen complaining that a common vault be-

1 Plans 2 and 8, Plan Book.
2 Cf. the interrogatories, which ask what the defendants were saying about him as they sat in the porch.

longing to the poor of this house "lately syncketh into his well in his yard." In 1602 "certaine of the Inhabitaunt͏e w^thin the Close complayned of the Annoyaunce they receave by the sisters of this howse in brynginge of the stynckinge wate^rs and plasters out of the ward͏e of the poore into the close to the great annoyance of them. . . . It is ordered that the same shalbe" examined by the Governors next Saturday and some workmen called for redress if convenient.

In September, 1592, Dr. Doiley was annoyed by

diu'se of the poore Inhabitaunt͏e w^thin the Close whoe hange there beddinge & beastly Ragg͏e vppon the Rayles before his dore And by some of the Systers whoe have often emptied [slops] vnder his Chamber wyndowe. And in that allsoe some of Smythfeild doe washe there buckes w^thin the close at vnreasonable tymes.

It was therefore ordered that the porter should give them notice, "And that if he fynde any of there clothes hanginge there after he cast them to the grownd." [1]

The last clause is a foretaste of Cotton's wrath thirteen years later. Dr. Doiley cannot have been satisfied, for in two years he complained again that some of the inhabitants of the precinct

have accesse at vnreasonable howers to the well w^thin the Courte & doe washe & beate theire Buck͏e to the greate dysquyett of certayne psons of greate worshipp wch lye in his howse: It is therfore ordered That from henceforthe the Inhabitaunt͏e wch dwell w^thin ye Court wheare the well is shall washe & beate theire Buck͏e before theire owne dores & not at the same well;

those not dwelling in the well-yard were not to be allowed in at all henceforth to wash clothes.

This is a definite enough decree about the actual washing; but either the inhabitants slipped back during the years that followed, or, more probably, took "washing"

1 These difficulties are in Journal 3.

literally as not to include "drying," [1] for the depositions concur that drying in the yard was a time-honoured custom. The interrogatories rather trickily ask how long Denman has been there, and whether lines ever hung across Cotton's gate from Squire's present house to Denman's *before his coming*; the natural answer to which would play into Cotton's hands by being "no," since Denman's house was new when he took it; [2] but Randall evades the pitfall by saying that before Denman's coming he knew the lines tied from where Squire now lives to the house where one Taylor lived, where Denman's house now stands. This crossing of lines and drying of clothes is the due and right of the inhabitants, he thinks, "yet so as the goodwills & consentę of the owners of the postes where the sd Lynes were tyed were allwayes had . . . & neuer denyed that this def ever hard of." Lines had been hung from the well-posts to the door-posts of Squire's house without leave of any of the dwellers there, as long as he had known the yard, at least thirty years past. He never knew of the Governors' forbidding the hanging of clothes in the yard, "vnles yt were the vncleane & filthye clothes of the poore diseased people w^th^in the sd hospitall" (perhaps an allusion to the Doiley affair), but ever since he had known the yard the Governors "dyd . . . allowe & like" the clothes to be dried there.

Mrs. Hunter's imprisonment of her son during the fray might be taken to argue that he was likely to go to extremes of combativeness, or merely that he was of an obedient disposition. At all events he brings a Lady-from-Philadelphia tone of common sense to the heated controversy, saying that ever since he can remember (and we know he was twenty-nine) clothes have been dried

1 Denman's Mary, as we have seen, did her washing in the back yard.
2 Journal 3.

there, the lines commonly hung from Squire's door to
Denman's across Cotton's gate, and usually upheld with
a pole, "that a man maye goe easely vnder, And when
they hang clothes vpõ the same lyne there is Comonlie a
space left wthout Clothes against the saide Compl^{ts} gate
for the better passage of people to and fro."

Cotton says it was "vpon a sufferaunce of Neighb^{or}-
hood" that the lines were hung. He tries to establish the
point that not only he but even the present defendants
have found the line in the yard inconvenient in times past;
and he adumbrates an old quarrel among them: Beatrice
is asked whether the Denmans ever fell out with her or
John Lyly, or any of the other neighbours, to which she
replies

that some vnkyndenes & fallinge owt hathe heretofore happned betwixt m^{ris} Denman & this def & that mr Denman her husband dyd
reconcile those differenc̨ betwixt his wief & this def^{t}. And this def^{t}
further sayth that there hath likewise byn some fallinge owt betwixt
the sd Mr Denman & some of his other neighbors. but in such fallinge
out she sayth that the sd mr denman hath not doone any wrong to
his neighbo^{rs} that euer she hard of but hath rathe^{r} pceeded of some
good that the sd mr Denman intended toward̨ the gen'all good of the
pishe where he dwelleth.

This corresponds closely to the testimony of the Denmans
and Colliers. Frances says that about four years ago there
was a little unkindness between her and Sara, but they
were shortly friends again and have not fallen out since.

Collier and his wife are asked whether, when they were
falling out with the Denmans, they were forbidden to
hang lines at the Denmans' porch, and where they hung
them. They answer that they were never forbidden to tie
lines as supposed, but that once three or four years ago
Frances and Sara consented to dry their clothes in the
fields for a while, "vntill they founde the inconvenience
therof."

The interrogatory to Denman and his wife also asks whether they have forbidden one Mrs. Doiley or her servants to tie a clothesline to their porch, and inquires searchingly whether this was because the Masters of the Hospital had forbidden any lines and clothes in the wellyard. They deny remembrance of any such episode, and in general the defendants say they have never heard the hanging of lines forbidden (except of noisome clothes about sixteen years ago).

If they had not, however, they soon did. What His Majesty's Honourable Court of Star Chamber decided that winter remains a mystery, since the Star Chamber decrees (with rare exceptions [1]) are lost, but the practical point was settled by the Governors the following August, 1606: [2]

In presence of Sir John Spencer knight p^rsydent S^r Thō: Lowe knight Mr Baron Sotherton Sr Thomas Smythe knight Mr Collymor Threr [3] Mr John Newman Mr Woer Mr Juxson Mr Varnon Mr Johnson Mr Shawe M^r ffoxe Mr Woodford & Mr Twyste:
This day the matter of controversy fo^r & concerninge the hanginge of clothes vppon lynes in the Well close betweene Mr Thomas Cotton Mr Eagleffeilde & others of the one pte And M^r ffrauncis Denman Mr Thomas Collya^r and others of the other pte inhabytantℓ in the said close hath bene considered by this Court And the said ptyes beinge seu'ally hard, It is ordered that noe psone or psons shall hange vp any lynes for there clothes in the said Close called the well Close vntill this Court doe give order for the same And in the meane tyme all the said ptyes to be contented.

One of the defendants at least (though an inactive one) must have been contented, being nearly out of reach of neighbourly brawls; for John Lyly died two months later, in November, 1606. One question that confronts us is his

---

1 A few have been preserved in the *Proceedings*. Many decisions of the Court have, of course, been recorded in the Acts of the Privy Council.
2 Journal 3, p. 274.
3 Treasurer.

part in the whole affair. He cannot have had as little share as he seems to, or Cotton would hardly have included him among the defendants in the Bill; but alone among the defendants Lyly makes no answer. This would be a grave breach, amounting to contempt. Dr. Sisson therefore suggests that his not answering may throw light on his physical condition at the time, showing that his death was preceded by at least a year's illness so serious as to set him apart from the brawls below his windows.

III. THE TOPOGRAPHY OF ST. BARTHOLOMEW'S

THE court poet had nearly lived out his patchwork life, gay, disappointing, brilliant, and sorrowful. Behind the drama of enchantment, wit, and compliment which he had woven to charm Elizabeth and her court, it is curious to watch the homelier drama in the midst of which he lived familiarly, and which for anything we know never kindled a line of his poetry: tragi-comedy of wash-lines, travail, windows darkened by new building, plague, death.

One of the most interesting parts of this case is tracing the topography of Little St. Bartholomew's. The maps preserved in the Plan Book at the Hospital are wonderfully explicit, and correct and supplement each other so well that from them I have been able to make the accompanying plans with something like certainty as to the general relation of the various places marked; only I make no claim to accurate proportion. I am the less concerned about this because all the maps I have used disagree among themselves, so that it would not be possible to be right in every detail according to them all. I have done what I could to reconcile their differences, taking my general proportions from Ogilby's map of 1677. It is also true that since the maps may belong to different dates (and the one reproduced from Bart's Plan Book by way of Sir Norman Moore's *History* is of 1617, twelve years later than our case), almost any given house in the plan may not in fact have been standing in the year which interests us. This in particular might account for the "galiri to drie cloths in:" is that possibly the next development of our quarrel?

Nevertheless, I think we run an excellent chance of being at least very nearly right in our identification of most of the houses. The ones I have marked in italics I know to be accurate, having them from the contemporary maps; the conjectural I have printed in block capitals, even when, as in the case of Cotton's house, the conjecture amounts to a certainty.

Cotton's is almost impossible to mistake because a plan in the Plan Book of St. Bartholomew's Hospital marks "Mr. Cotton Garden," to which the house we have indicated as his apparently belongs. The only other one which could go with it is the little one behind with its back to Duck Lane, which would not be confronted at the distance of ten or twelve feet by lines in the well-yard itself. It had "a little Courte betweene the outter Gate and" the house. Careful examination of the 1617 map shows what seems to be a wall at a little space from the house, adjoining the entry to Duck Lane.

The Cottons — our Thomas, and his father Bartholomew, and his grandfather Thomas — appear at frequent intervals through the Journals, in entries usually connected with real estate, for they held and sublet numerous leases, e. g. in "the comõn m'she of hackney," and Duck Lane, as well as in the Close itself. In 1588 Bartholomew Cotton had a lease for Mrs. Hone's house and part of the garden adjoining. In 1595 we find him getting a new lease of house and garden and the "fysshe room," but not the vaults under the fish room, which are to be used as the Governors think meet; besides paying fine and rent, he is to make a brick wall from the fish room to the pale of his garden. In the following July he is to have the vaults newly made under the fish room added to his lease except the doors, windows, and stairs, which are reserved to "this house" (Bart's), "wth the painthowse thereof." His outlay must have been heavy, for the next February he was granted more time to pay his fine.

His son, our Thomas, in 1598 sued for the lease of cer-

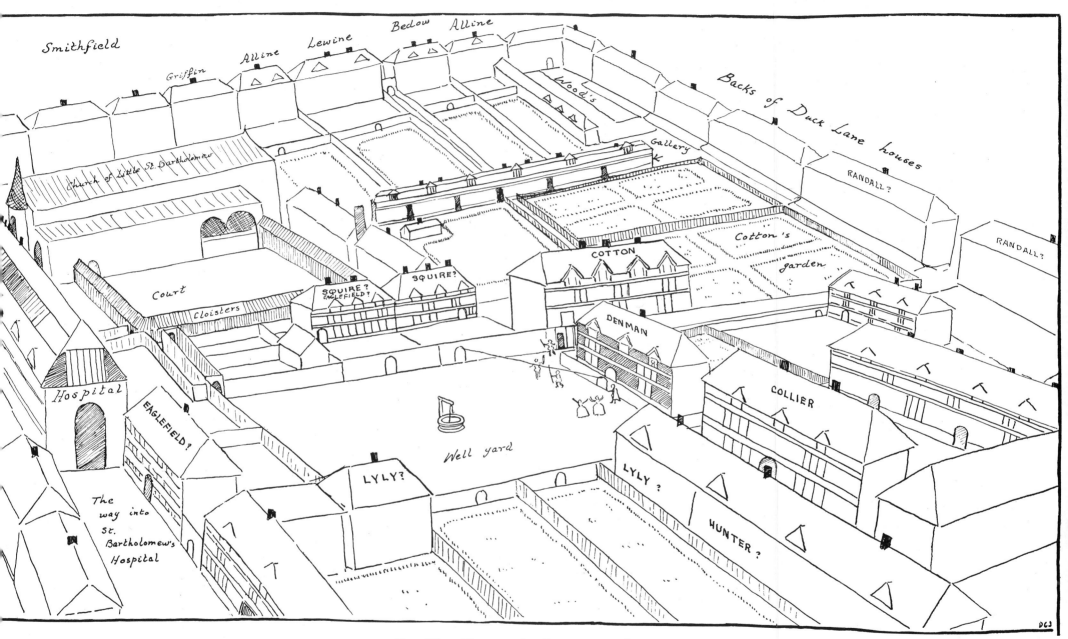

THE WELL-YARD AT ST. BARTHOLOMEW'S

tain tenements in Little St. Bartholomew's, of which the court decided to make no grant as yet, but hereafter to let the property to whomever "they shall thinke meate." One wonders whether this decision had anything to do with the fact that Randall appears to have wanted the lease of part of the same property. On the other hand, when in 1600 one Boxall (an appropriately-named carpenter) and John Shaw offered to build on tenements in Duck Lane if they might have the leases, it was ordered that Thomas Cotton should be heard first in the matter, having some time yet to come in his leases.

In July, 1601, Thomas Cotton was granted a piece of yard to be divided from the other part of the same yard (late in the tenure of one Hill), which said yard to be severed as aforesaid was to contain from the late erected chimney of the tenement in the tenure of John Randall to the wall at the south end of the tenement, thirty-three feet long from north to south and eighteen feet wide from east to west. Further details are given about the new building which Cotton was to set up in it, which would be of interest to us, were it not that a year and a half later in January, 1602–03, Cotton, perhaps finding the expenses heavier than he had anticipated, refused the grant and asked to be discharged from it. We know from the Ledger (1605) that his yearly rent was comparatively heavy — six pounds. The family interest in real estate seems to have survived in a Bartholomew Cotton, whom we should surmise to be our Thomas's son, who in 1632 sued for renewing the lease of his messuage in the Hospital Close.

It is hard to be sure where Randall was living at the time of the quarrel. In 1587 he had been "guider of the spitall house of highegate," where he was granted "vj d a weeke weekelie" for keeping a blind woman.[1] By six years

---

[1] These details, like the preceding, are from the Journals, particularly no. 3.

later he was one of the "Inhabytaunte of Ducklane" who complained against the Scoefields. In connection with his Duck Lane tenement we find possible light on the difficulties plainly existing between him and Cotton — who, it will be remembered, accuses him of partiality to the Denman faction. For in July, 1595, he, being then undertenant to Cotton for the house he lived in in Duck Lane, asked to have the lease of it himself, but was referred to wait till Cotton's were nearly expired. In November he tried again and was again put off, this time to wait for two years, till the expiration of Cotton's lease. In 1595 he was granted the rooms next adjoining his house in Duck Lane. Finally in March, 1600, he was to be granted a lease of his own for the house he lived in, with part of the garden belonging to the tenement next adjoining, and also *the entry next him, leading into Duck Lane*, which Thomas Cotton now held. This narrows him down to one of the two houses, one on each side of the little entry which ran from the well-yard past Cotton's into Duck Lane. In 1603 he was to have his lease new made to him with the yard now inclosed as it had been severed and divided — perhaps half of that garden of which Cotton had planned to use half.

All this seems fairly definite; and his telling Cotton that he and all the people in Duck Lane might hang their clothes in the well-yard if they wanted sounds as if that were where he lived in 1605. My only misgiving on the subject comes from the fact that the list of rents received by the Hospital from Michaelmas 1604 to Michaelmas 1605 includes Randall's for property not in Duck Lane but "w^{th}in the Close" and in St. Nicholas Fleshshambles.[1]

1 Ledger 3, 1605, account of "Marten Levellen Receyvou^r." Randall paid £4–6–8; for St. Nicholas Fleshshambles his yearly rent was 3/4. (Several attempts seem to have been made to reproduce the proper Welsh pronunci-

Moreover, the name next before his in the list — if juxta-position mean anything — is that of "John Greane," whom Randall speaks of as his neighbour who accompan-ied him when he came at the end of the quarrel. If again — as is quite doubtful — juxtaposition is significant, Ran-dall and Green would be near neighbours to Griffin, whose house we know from the Plan Book was on the north or Smithfield side of the Close. On the other hand, it is al-ways possible that a house on the corner of the entry to Duck Lane from the well-yard might have been counted as "within the close."[1]

Denman's house I conceive to be the one opposite Cotton's across the little passage to Duck Lane.[2] This would make Collier's the large one next, a theory corrob-orated by the Journal, which calls it "the Greater howse" and "the Greater Teñt." One feels the more certain of Denman's house for the description of it in the Journal: "the newehowse late builded wth the garden plott lyinge on the back pte thereof beinge wthin the well yard of the said hosp^{ll}."[3] The joint answer of the Denmans and Col-liers says similarly, "there is a yarde Comonlye called the well yarde or Coo^{rte} yarde adioyninge to the same teñte [i. e. Denman's] and there are divers other teñtes adioyn-inge to the same yarde." The garden behind the house,

---

ation by phonetic spelling: besides the more conventional "Lewellen" to be found, for example, in Journal 4, p. 205, we find in the same Journal on p. 179 the rendering "fflewellen," obviously the same as Shakespeare's "Fluellen.")

1 There is also the possibility that Randall's tenement within the Close was one which he sublet to someone else. But this does not explain why no rent for his Duck Lane tenement is listed.

2 We cannot take Denman's to be one of the small houses on the other side of Cotton's, because neither is next to a house that could be called the Great House.

3 Journal 3, p. 170, gives the terms of Denman's rent: "the yerly rent of xj^{li} xiij^s iiij^d And the fyne of C^{li} to be paied viz l^{li} at the Insealinge to be bounde to all repacõns."

plainly shown in the 1617 map, is where Mary was washing at the time the line was cut. The only other details we can glean about the house are that its hall windows commanded the corner between Denman's, Cotton's, and Squire's; that it had a porch with posts, or at least with one, and perhaps also a gate in front,[1] which would imply a wall; that it was near enough to the fields (Smithfield?) for clothes to be taken out there to dry, though not conveniently. We know too that Denman, who was an attorney at the common law, had "his worke folk aboute his building in St Sepulchers pish," a few minutes' walk away. The rent, the Ledger tells us, was £6 13s. 4d.

John Collier, Thomas's father, paid the rent for their messuage until his death in 1593. In 1590 he was granted for 3s. 4d. a year a piece of void ground at the north end of his house toward the "Colehouse," that "serveth to noe purpose." (Of this coalhouse I find no trace.) Beginning with 1594 it was Thomas who paid — or did not pay — his rent of £4 a year: in 1603 he is listed as half a year in arrears, 40s., and in 1605 as three-quarters of the year, £3, at the time when rents were due.[2] He seems not to have persisted in delinquency. Other business of his turns up from time to time in the Journals, and it is interesting to find that in 1613, after his death (less than ten years after our quarrel), his widow Frances, who for some reason had let the house go, sued for a new lease of her late house in the Close, "since in the tenure of her brother Hone,"[3] and received in March, 1615, a lease of "the Greater Teñt," where she lately lived; which as late as 1636 we find her renewing for twenty-one years from its expiration.

A line from Denman's cutting off the approach to Cot-

1 Interrogatory 11 to Beatrice speaks of her going to Denman's *gate*.
2 Ledger 3.   3 Journal 4.

ton's as described must have been tied at the other end to one of the two small houses next to Cotton's, which will be Squire's. It is impossible to tell which; the first from Cotton's may seem more natural as being the nearer, but on the other hand Squire's house had "a stable haylofte & other Roomes thereby," a description which, from our 1617 map, seems more suited to the second from Cotton's. Even that gives the clothesline a length of probably little over thirty feet, not an inordinate length.

Thomas Squire had succeeded his father William, lately dead in May, 1590, as Clerk of the Hospital.[1] In 1602 he was granted to occupy "the Teñte wth the roomes there-vnto belonginge wch he now holdeth nexte adioyninge to the Court howse" without rent while he remained clerk. This sounds as if he lived next to the court house, but per-haps it merely means that the "roomes" were next to it, for his own house appears to have been the court house itself: Randall and his interrogatory speak of it as the house where the Governors keep their courts, where Squire now lives, and the joint answer of Randall and Beatrice is still more specific:

If infectious Clothes had bene there hanged the danger thereof would have bene so much unto the said ffrancis denman & his familie yea & to such of the Gouo^{rs} as doe usually repayre unto the Ct house in the said well yard That neyther the Goũno^{rs} nor the said ffrancis denman would have indured it: the lynes being tyed from the said ffrancis den-man his dore unto a poste at the dore where the Governo^{rs} entreth in to the said Cõt house.

Beyond that, we know merely that the neighbours were also accustomed to tie lines from Squire's to the well, a distance apparently rather more than from his post to Denman's:[2]

1 Journal 3.
2 Cf. the interrogatory to Mary Andrews given on p. 372, implying that from Denman's post to the well was farther than from Denman's to Squire's.

not greatly illuminating, since we do not know just where in the yard the well was.

The matter of the Courts is a tiny puzzle. Dr. Doiley in 1592 asked to have his house built a story higher, because he was somewhat restrained from his hall, which was lately used for the "Cowrt howse" for the causes of this house.[1] Possibly we are to infer that the Governors held their court at Doiley's then, and later at Squire's.

This was that same Doiley who grew so choleric over the "beastly Ragge" on his railings and the bucks washed at "vnreasonable tymes." Besides his tenement in Little St. Bartholomew's he held of the Hospital the messuage of the Antelope in Holborn, which he left to his son Michael who travelled overseas.[2] The entries in the Journal show that he died between 15 January and 12 March, 1602–03. Readers of *John Inglesant* and all other lovers of Serenus de Cressy (Hugh Cressy) will hear with interest that this Dr. Doiley was his maternal grandfather.[3] Doiley himself was a man of some note in his time.

In our immediate concern with Lyly we are interested in this extract from Sir Norman Moore,[4] who presumably did not know Lyly lived at St. Bartholomew's:

Doyley was of Magdalen College, Oxford, where he graduated B.A July 24, 1564, and M.B. in 1571. . . . Sir Philip Sidney, John Lyly the Euphuist, Richard Hakluyt, and John Thorie of Christ Church were all at Oxford with Doyley, and were probably known to him, as he shared their taste for the Spanish language and literature.

One likes to think of the two old Oxonians, moving as they did round different centres, exchanging the time of day in the well-yard and perhaps talking over matters like this

1 Journal 3, p. 106. It was too expensive to be done that year because they were enlarging the sweat-house.
2 Journal 3.
3 Sir Norman Moore, *op. cit.*, II, 448–449; pp. 442–449 give a résumé of Dr. Doiley's career.   4 *Op. cit.*, p. 443.

common interest of theirs; although one feels safer in the surmise that they exchanged views on homelier matters such as the hanging of lines, which we know concerned them both. Unfortunately Doiley, dying in 1602, could not know that the matter was settled in a way he would have approved.

The other people's houses marked in the plan, and the various other topographical details, I have taken chiefly from the Plan Book of the Hospital.

Walter Lowman, one of Beatrice's two rescuing "Angles," lived in Giltspur Street.[1] He seems to have troubled the governors with few requests; in 1592 he asked permission for recourse to a well in Myter Alley.

Mrs. Martin, whom Richard Hunter overheard gossiping with the Colliers on the 19th of September, is probably the wife of Thomas Martin, formerly a subtenant of Cotton's, who since 1602 had himself held the lease for his tenement in the Close.[2]

It will be remembered that on seeing her line cut, Sara first sent Hewysh flying for Randall and for Mr. Shaw, one of the Governors. He held some land and at least two houses in the parish, one the house just north of Mr. Kerton's house, and several gardens, one between Dr. Frier's three gardens and on the way from Christ's Hospital to St. Bartholomew's. There was also the John Shaw who wished to lease and build on three tenements in Duck Lane, "wth the backsyde & shedd in the same," then held by Cotton: I do not know whether he was the same man.

The Mr. Eaglefield who in the Governors' decision about clotheslines appears to have been on Cotton's side cannot have been a litigious person, or otherwise troublesome to the Hospital; in the Journals I have found mention only of the lease of one *Richard* Eaglefield (1601); but if he was

1 Ledger 3, 1601. 2 Journal 3.

closely concerned with the clotheslines, he is more likely
to be that "ffrauncis Eagleffeild" whom Ledger 3 lists as
"w^{th}in the Close," and who married Lodowick Bryskett's
sister Joan.[1]

Mrs. Hunter, the cautious mother who shut up her son
during the brawl, lived opposite the Colliers. I imagine
her to belong in the second from the end of the row of
(apparently) three small houses, two of which are opposite
the Great Tenement.[2]

For two reasons I do not give her the end house abutting
on the Court itself: in the first place, when she shut up her
son she quite cut off his view of events in the yard; and in
the second, I suspect that we must attribute to this unpre-
tentious little end dwelling the honour of housing Lyly
himself.

For Lyly's house in the well-yard of Little St. Bartholomew's, according to Beatrice's evidence, is to fulfil several
requirements: it must command a view of Denman's porch
and of Cotton's dooryard, which Beatrice could watch
from her chamber window, and also from her door, where
she stood when Dr. Covert pointed out Cotton's panoply,
which she had already discovered for herself. Also it must
have been built against or very close to its next neighbour,
since that neighbour "dyd builde against her Garrett[e] &
stopp vp the lightes therof."

The only other houses possibly fulfilling these requirements would be either one of the two little dwellings next

---

1 See my article on Bryskett, p. 273.
2 Her husband John, and after his death her son Richard, his mother, and her
  second husband George Mowse were sued next year by the Lord Mayor and
  the other governors of the hospital, for wrongfully holding the brewhouse and
  bakehouse of the priory of Great St. Bartholomew's, in Newgate (see accompanying map), and the gatehouse in Newgate Market abutting directly on
  Warwick Lane, and pretending that their lease was descended from a grant by
  Henry VIII made to persons unknown to the plaintiffs (Repertory, pp. 119 ff.;
  Journal 3). Some of the documents remain in the P.R.O.

Cotton's, the other of which we have already given to Squire, and the end house in the block of houses diagonally across the well-yard from Cotton's. It is hard to be sure whether Squire's next neighbour could have seen inside Cotton's wicket: I do not think he could without a periscope. That would eliminate either of these two little houses. Against the other possibility, Cotton's diagonal, I can advance nothing except that, being at a greater distance, it would command a less detailed view. That is not to say much, because the well-yard was roughly only sixty by thirty-five feet,[1] so that even the diagonal view would be fairly near. Yet the details Beatrice was able to see, such as Cotton's stooping down *inside* his great gate and unfastening the bolt, would require her to be both high up and close.[2] This seems to favour the nearer house, opposite the Colliers.

It is disappointing that although we can narrow down Lyly's exact dwelling so closely, we can find no trace of the terms on which he held it. I have searched the Hospital Ledgers in vain. In the long lists of those who paid rent and those who were in arrears, his name simply does not appear. I suppose this means that he was undertenant to somebody else, perhaps one of those who, like Mr. Shaw, William Allen, William Bowecher, Frauncis Adkyns, Thomas Doiley, and others, held two or more messuages within the Close.[3] Other subtenants sued from time to time to have the leases on expiration made out to themselves; Lyly apparently did not. Professor Bond, who knew from the Register of Little St. Bartholomew that

1 Plan 2, Plan Book (1617).
2 The little building which I have taken to be one of Squire's outbuildings could not have housed a family of the size of Lyly's; nor could it have been Lyly's, inasmuch as it is not built against its next neighbour.
3 Ledger 3, 1605, and Plan 8, Plan Book.

Lyly lived within the precincts because some of his children were baptized there, also discovered that in the Subsidy Rolls for 1598 and the two following years Lyly was assessed eight shillings on property of the value of £3 in the parish of St. Bartholomew the Less.[1]

Mr. Eccles tells me that in these assessments the property of Thomas Bodley, Esquire (as yet untitled), was valued at £100 and Dr. Doiley's at £10, while the £5 men included Francis Denman, gent., Thomas Cotton, gent., and Thomas Collyer, lawyer — a nice distinction!

We know that in 1605 Lyly had lived in the parish of Little St. Bartholomew's for some time, both because his numerous children's births had been registered there since 1596,[2] and because Beatrice's memory of the place goes back before Denman's coming: she says that Denman has been there for eight years or so, "& that before such tyme as the sd mr denman came to dwell there . . . Lynes were tyed and clothes hunge theron from one neighbors howse to another."

There is one other small, fairly acute point. The much damaged eleventh interrogatory to Beatrice (consisting about one-third of lacunae) asks among other things, "⟨Did you say⟩ Collier was your Flesshe Bloud and Boane ⟨   ⟩"? To which she deposes, "Neyther dyd she . . . saye that the sd Mr Collyer was her fleshe, blood & bone & that she must & would helpe him or anye wordɇ to the like effecte."

Negative as it is, this must imply that she and Collier *were* related by blood; they cannot have been brother and sister, because her maiden name was Browne,[3] but they may have been cousins. This might account for Frances

---

1 R.W. Bond, *Complete Works of John Lyly*, 1, 72.
2 *Ibid.*, 1, 66.
3 Feuillerat, *John Lyly*, genealogical table.

Collier's presence [1] at the making of Beatrice's second husband's will.

It is not without family interest to know the ages of Lyly's young brood in the September of our quarrel.[2] Robert Browne Lyly was fifteen and a half, Bridget twelve and a half, Jane between five and nine, John five, Frances (was she named for Mrs. Collier?) two and a half, and Thomas eight months. (An older John, who had died, would have been nine.) We do not know the age of Elizabeth, whom they had just lost in May.[3]

It is nearly unimaginable that this little tribe of urchins were completely out of the way during the brawl. Even if Beatrice took Mrs. Hunter's precaution of locking them up, we know their windows overlooked the whole scene. Nothing very definite is said about them, but Cotton may have had a wary eye on their possible evidence, to judge by the twelfth interrogatory to Beatrice: Have you been advised by some to take heed you did not make your daughters perjured in swearing that Cotton was out of his gate with rapier drawn at the beginning of the affray, at Robert Fryett's coming to cut the line and being driven back? And did you answer that rather than it should go on Cotton's side, your daughters should swear?

She answers, with some dignity, that she

was not advisd by anye boddy to take heede that she dyd not make her daughters piured in swearinge of anye suche matter as in this Intē is mencened . . . . And . . . doth from her sowle & conscyence vtterlye deteste & abhorre to make eyther any of her daughters or any other boddy . . . whatsoeu' to Comytt the detestable synne of piurye.

There is a certain quaintness in the reflection that unless Lyly had older daughters whom no one has yet dis-

1 Feuillerat, *op. cit.*, p. 566 n.
2 Feuillerat, *op. cit.*, genealogical table.
3 Bond (1, 76) says we have no record of her baptism.

covered, the ages of these possibly perjured damsels ranged
from two to twelve.

As we know, Lyly was buried in 1606, on 30 November.[1]
Beatrice remarried — a Thomas Staunton of Little St. Bartholomew's, who died in 1617.[2] I have found no trace of
him in the Hospital records: perhaps like Lyly he was subtenant to somebody else. His will says that he held "two
howses or Tenementes with theire appurtenaunces scituate
. . . in little Saint Bartholomewes . . . adioyninge to the
Hospitall there in the well yarde."

This lawsuit does not bring forth any important new
facts concerning Lyly's career, but it confirms Bond's discovery [3] that he must have been living within the precincts
of the Hospital, and allows us to go beyond this in making
a fairly approximate guess at the actual house — an unusual closeness of information. And it tells us a little more
about his daughter Elizabeth's death in 1605. For lovers
of London antiquities in general (and of Bart's in particular), and for those interested in seeing the daily effects of
the epidemics, as well as for all who for various reasons of
their own are interested in John Lyly, its most valuable
contribution is its picture of the neighbourhood he lived
in: not truly at its best, but certainly off its guard and not
posed for the camera.

1 Bond (1, 76), citing the Register of Little St. Bartholomew's.
2 Feuillerat, *op. cit.*, p. 566 n.
3 Bond, 1, 44, 72.

APPENDIX

PLANS OF ST. BARTHOLOMEW'S

THE information to be found in this Star Chamber suit is verified and largely added to from the Journals, Repertory, Ledgers, and Plan Book of Saint Bartholomew's Hospital, a complete set of records beautifully kept in accordance with the Order for the Hospital printed in 1552, a copy of which is to be seen in the British Museum. The maps which I have used from the Plan Book are:

No. 2. 1617 map of the Hospital, from Smithfield to the wall by Christ's Hospital.

No. 3. Smithfield and Hosier Lane.

No. 4. St. Nicholas Fleshshambles, St. Martins, and By-rames Court.

No. 5. From the "Street without Britten Gate" to the Wall, and from "Docke Lane" to Kirten's and Shaw's.

No. 6. Shoreditch, Chick Lane.

No. 7. Christ's Hospital, the Walk from it to St. Bartholomew's, and the gardens, houses, etc., between these and Rosemary Lane.

No. 8. The Smithfield and Duck Lane corner of Little St. Bartholomew's; showing Cotton's garden.

No. 9. The space between Newgate Street and the reach of Wall between Christ's Hospital and Bart's.

The last plan in the Plan Book: from the Wall to just south of the well-yard, and from Duck Lane on the east to Kerton's and Rosemary Lane on the west.

Some of these maps are conventionalized, e. g., turning an acute or obtuse angle into a right, or straightening a line, perhaps for the sake of symmetry and neatness; others make an attempt at reproducing the actual shape. As a result it is impossible to be consistent with them all. In making the accompanying plans, I have also drawn on the following:

Ogilby's Map, published in 1677. (1894; Br. Mus., S. 235 [13].)

Mitton, G. E. (ed.), *Maps of Old London*. A. and C. Black. London, 1908. (Br. Mus., Maps 27.b.38.)

The Cittie of London. 1640. (Br. Mus., Maps 184.G.2 [1].)

Wyld, J., *London in 1549*. Published 1849. (Br. Mus., 3518 [2].)

Plan of Newgate Market, 1755. (Br. Mus., 3495 [10].)

Map of the Hospital as it is at present, in D'Arcy Power's *St. Bartholomew's Hospital*.

Ledger 3 (St. Bartholomew's Hospital) gives the following list of names of those paying rent "wth in the close" from Michaelmas, 1604, to Michaelmas, 1605. Even that is not a complete list of adult male residents; Thomas Cotton is not included (apparently because his father was paying the rent), nor one Barton who, Frances Collier says, lived in the yard, nor Lyly himself. Of course this is a list not of those who may have been there as subtenants, but of those paying rent directly to the Hospital:

Thomas Raynshaw, Henry ffary, Augustyne Bullocke, Willm Bowecher (entered twice), Willm Allen (twice), ffrauncis Eaglefeild, Joseph ffenton, Humfry Healy, Thomas Medley, John Welles, Thomas Baker, Ralphe Bradshawe, Willyam Gryffen, John Greane, John Randoll (£4 6s. 8d.), George Allthropp (twice), ffrauncys Adkyns (three times), Johane Manne, John Hunte, George Bowman (?), Roger Mascall, John Lynge, John Trott, Thomas Marten, Edward Hawkins, Thomas Berry, Mary Barrs, Bartholomewe Cotton (£6), ffrauncis Denman (£6 13s. 4d.), Margarett Carewe, Thomas Collya^r (£4), Thomas Doyley (twice; one at £4, one at 20s.), ffrauncis Snellinge, Mary Crofte, Nycholas Scattlyffe, Mathewe Johnson, Maryan Delaunder, Thomas ffanshawe, Thomas Squyer (£5), Sr Thomas Bodley, knight, Myles Hayward, Robarte Goninge, Scysley Popley, Daniell Hilles, Willm Hunter, Willm Digge, John Sare, John Pallmer, Henry Asheley, Thomas Wardegate.

It is a particular pleasure to express my thanks to Mr. Hayes and Mr. Cross at St. Bartholomew's Hospital, who, acting for the Governors, gave me access to their remarkable set of records; and who, during the week in which I was practically quartered upon them, treated me with the kindest of hospitality.

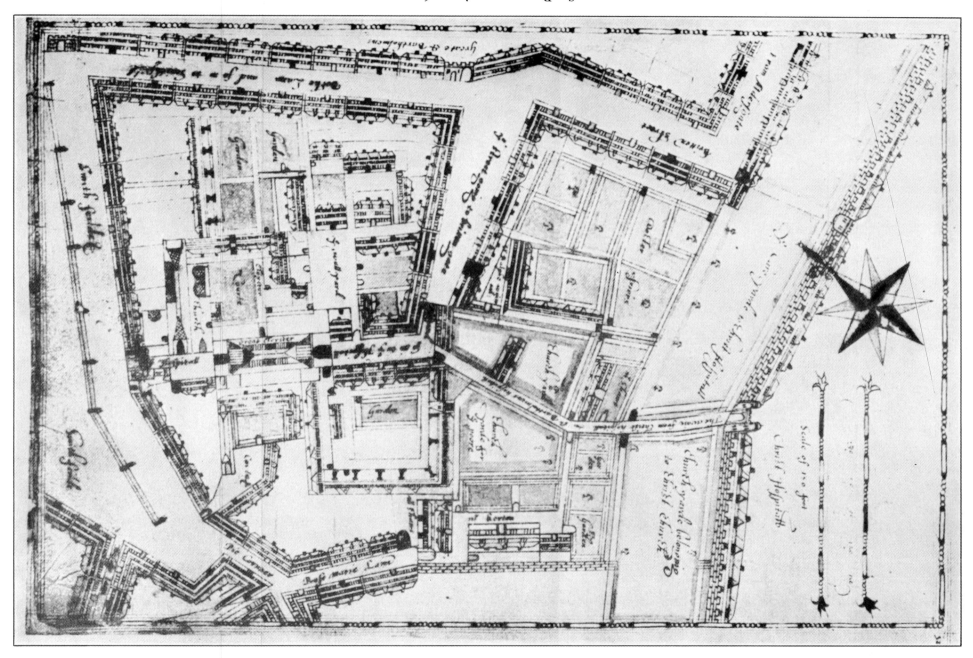

St. Bartholomew's in 1617

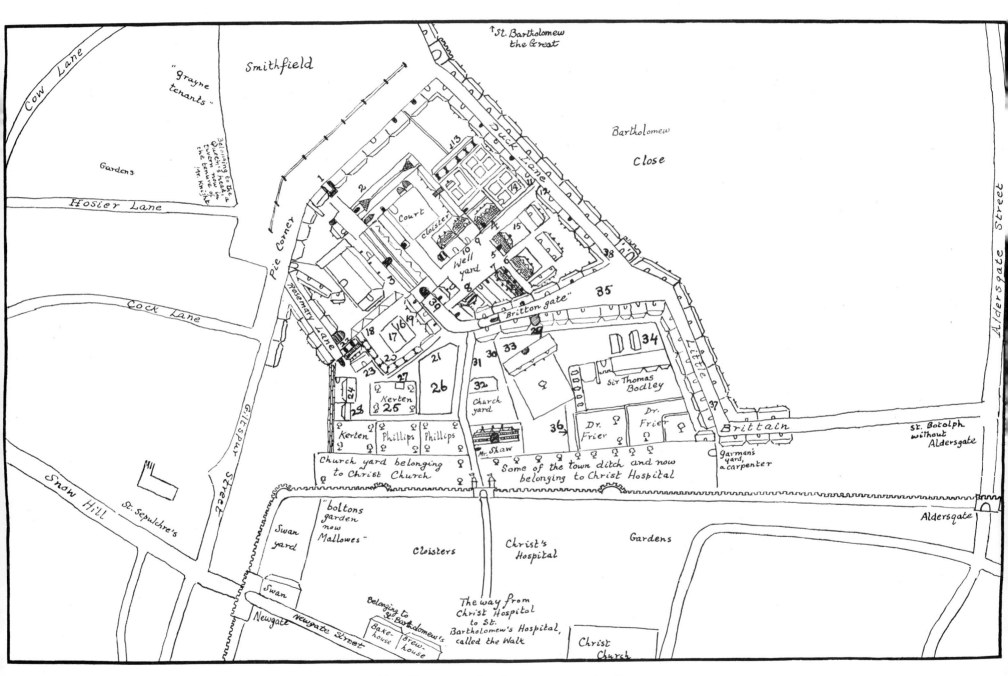

THE PARISH OF ST. BARTHOLOMEW THE LESS

Key to Plan of Parish [1]

1. *Henry VIII gate*
2. *Church of St. Bartholomew the Less*
3. *St. Bartholomew's Hospital*
4. Cotton's House
5. Denman's House
6. Collier's House
7. Lyly's House?
8. Lyly's House?
9. Squire's House?
10. Squire's House?
11. Randall's House?
12. Randall's House? (Perhaps more probable, as it has more ground.)
13. "*Y^e openn parte for A gallerie*" (Plan 8)
14. *Cotton's garden* (Plan 8)
15. *Denman's Back Yard*
16. *Matron's garden* (Last Plan)
17. "*Grene Court for the poore*" (Last Plan)
18. "*The way to the washous*" (Last Plan)
19. "*The waie to the church yarde*" (Last Plan)
20. "*the galiri to drie cloths in*" (Last Plan)
21. "*and A way to picorner in tymes paste*" (Last Plan)
22. *Mr. Shaw's* (Plan 2)
23. *Kerton's Court and House* (Plan 7)
24. *Kerton's house* (another one) (Plan 7 and Last Plan)
25. "*Mr Kertons Garden som tym an Orchard*" (Last Plan)
26. "*The Hospital church yard for the burying of the poor that dieth*" (Last Plan)
27. "*cotch hous*" (Last Plan)
28. *A tenement*
29. "*Sr Thomas Bodlye to Rosmarie Lanne*" (Last Plan)
30. "*A parte of the Church yarde and nowe demised to Sr Thomas Bodlye*" (Last Plan)
31. *Church yard, Little St. Bartholomew's*
32. *St. Nicholas Chapel*
33. *Sir Ralph Winwood*
34. "*Jengkins yarde*"
35. "*ye street going to britton gate*" (Plan 2. The Last Plan calls it "*the streete Called pettiefrance.*")
36. "*the Towne Ditche, & so to Aldersgate by the Masters of Coobretheren*" (Last Plan)
37. *The Pelican* (In Ogilby's Map, Br. Mus.)
38. *Blue Anchor Inn.* (*Ibid.*)
39. Francis Eaglefield's house?

---

1 Unless otherwise specified, plans referred to are in the Plan Book at the Hospital.

SIR GEORGE BUC,
MASTER OF THE REVELS
By MARK ECCLES

CONTENTS

SIR GEORGE BUC,
MASTER OF THE REVELS

WHEN Shakespeare wrote a play, he had to reckon with three sorts of people beside himself: his audience, his actors, and the censor. On the reef of the last, plays like *Sir Thomas More* were wrecked, while others sailed forward only after more or less extensive repairs. To trace the effect of the censorship upon Elizabethan drama requires a very careful handling of clues, and before attempting inference so delicate it may be well to learn as much as we can about the minds of the men who exercised the censorship, the Masters of the Revels.

The Revels Office records have been admirably studied by scholars from Malone and Chalmers to Chambers and Feuillerat, but we have known very little about the Masters themselves. Since we have to deal at so many points with their actions, we should like to know what kind of persons they were, in order to interpret their official acts and records less by the light of conjecture and more through some understanding of their individual characteristics.

The three Masters who for almost a century ruled in succession over their little kingdom each extended its domain. Edmund Tyllney, who became Master in 1579, first obtained the right to read and license all plays before they could be performed, an outgrowth from his original function of rehearsing and correcting plays for the Court. Sir George Buc secured the further privilege of examining plays before they could be printed. Sir Henry Herbert, Master for fifty years from 1623, endeavored to make himself censor for all new publications, and brought the Revels Office to the height of its power. Each has therefore an important place historically, but Buc is the most interesting of the three as an individual, because he tells us most about himself.

He had more experience of authorship than either of the other Masters, though Tyllney published in 1568 *A Briefe and Pleasant Discourse of Duties in Marriage called The Flower of Friendshippe*, an imaginary conversation in an Italian garden which fully lives up to the adjectives in its title. As a poet Buc is known only by occasional verses such as his quatorzain to Watson in 1582 and a Latin poem on the Armada, and by his pastoral, Δαφνις Πολυστεφανος. He wrote an interesting description of arts and sciences in London, *The Third Universitie of England*, and he left in manuscript *The History of the Life and Reigne of Richard the Third*. It was published in 1646, in 1647, and in Bishop Kennett's *Compleat History* in 1706 and 1719, being chosen to accompany the histories of Milton, Daniel, Bacon, Habington, and Sir Thomas More. This work made Buc well known to the eighteenth century, which discovered much about him that the nineteenth century forgot.[1] The *History* grew out of a chapter in *The Baron, or Magazin of Honour*, generally supposed to have been lost, but identified by Dr. Bald with a manuscript volume in private hands.[2] It is very likely that other manuscripts will eventually be identified as Buc's.

The Baron further gave rise to his 'particular commentarie' on the Art of Revels, which has not been found. On a shelf of the same library in Limbo rests his 'particular treatise' on poets and poetry.[3] That this discussed con-

1 *Biographia Britannica*, ed. 1748, II, 1005; ed. 1780, II, 676; George Chalmers, *An Apology for the Believers in the Shakespeare Papers* (1797), p. 488.
2 R. C. Bald, *Times Literary Supplement*, March 17, 1927.
3 Stowe, *Annals*, ed. 1615, sigg. Oooo 1ᵛ, 3ᵛ.

A
PLEASANT
CONCEYTED CO-
medie of *George a Greene*, the Pinner
of VVakefield. ε

Written by . . . . a minister, who a[ ]
[ ]y pined[ ]el in it himself. Teste W. Shakespe[ ]

As it was sundry times acted by the seruants of the right
Honourable the Earle of Sussex.

Ed. July 5 4[ ]y[ ]4 y[ ]y pley was need by Lo. G[ ]as[ ]

Imprinted at London by Simon Stafford,
for Cuthbert Burby: And are to be sold at his shop
neere the Royall Exchange. 1599.

BUC'S ORDINARY HAND: ON THE TITLE-PAGE OF *George a Green*,
CITING THE TESTIMONY OF SHAKESPEARE

temporary work is clear from Camden's remark concerning the epitaph on Sidney in St. Paul's, 'most happily imitated out of the French' of Du Bellay, 'as it was noted by Sir *George Buc*, in his *Poetica*.'[1] Here Buc is in advance of modern scholarship, for the latest editor of Ralegh remains unaware of any source for the corresponding stanza of Ralegh's fine elegy on Sidney, and indeed conjectures that the epitaph derives from Ralegh, instead of the other way about.[2] Buc's Revels Books have also vanished, with their entries that would date Shakespeare's later plays and illumine dark places in dramatic history and authorship.

Since the censor constituted one influence on the formation of a play's printed text, the question of Buc's attitude and practices touches upon the history of most of the Jacobean plays before 1622. Buc enters also into a number of other problems, such as the Revels Accounts for 1611–12 and the authorship of *Locrine* and *George-a-Green*. These are not matters that can be discussed thoroughly and at the same time briefly, and the present chapter must be content to lead up to them. It does not pretend to do anything more than the preliminary work of offering a biographical background that can be relied on.

1 *Remains concerning Britain*, ed. 1605, sig. g 3ᵛ. This may be added, together with *Sydney Papers*, I, 109, to the list of works quoting the epitaph given by Rollins, *The Phoenix Nest* (1931), pp. 128–129.
2 Agnes M. C. Latham, *The Poems of Sir Walter Ralegh* (1929), p. 137.

I. POET AND COURTIER

'Our biographers,' says Chalmers in 1797, 'have raised, rather than gratified, curiosity in respect to Sir George Bucke.' The best illustration of this was to come ninety years later in Bullen's article in the *D. N. B.*, which requires mention only because succeeding writers have in the main taken their facts from it. The various errors there introduced hardly surpass those in Sir Sidney Lee's article on Tyllney, except perhaps the innocent assumption that for two years people brought plays for a lunatic to license ('Twill not be seen in him there; there the men are as mad as he'). The omissions are only natural, considering that the writer was clearly unacquainted with the chief biographical accounts of his subject (in the *Biographia Britannica* and Chalmers' *Apology*), and that he did not think it necessary to read any of Buc's works. Though no one has made more than occasional explorations into these, they are full of information as to Buc's personal history and form by far our best source of knowledge as to his mind and character.

We are not here concerned with Buc's origin and the circumstances of his career in themselves, but because only by knowing something of them can we possibly put ourselves in his place as he censored a play. His account of 'The Ancientry of Buck' is characteristic of his feeling for the history of England as a living thing. Like the audience at an Elizabethan chronicle-play, he summoned the pageant of his ancestors. First of the line came Walter de Buck, 'a Cadet of the hous of Flanders,' 'who had that surname of great antiquity from the Castell de Buck in Lisle,' and who commanded troops sent by the Duke of Brabant to aid King John. Rewarded with lands in York-

shire and Northamptonshire, he settled in the former
county and married his son to the heiress of Joscelin de
Buck, of the ancient family of 'Buck of Bucton, in the
Wapentake of Buccross.' In Edward I's time Sir John
Buck of Harthill 'maryed a Strelley, and was so constant
in his love, that (although she dyed in his best age) he
vowed never more to mary, and becam a knight of the
Rhodes, his Armes are yet to be seene in the ruines of the
Hospitall of S. Jones nere Smethfeld' — the home of the
Revels Office until 1608. Another Sir John, whom a follower of Effingham would recall with pride, was committed
to the Tower 'for his too much forwardnes & hardines in
the Charging a fleet of Spaniardes w'hout the leave of his
commander in cheef the erl of Arundale L. Admirall.' His
son Laurence was slain at Agincourt. But most of all Buc
remembered his great-grandfather Sir John, Comptroller
of the Household to Richard III, who 'for his service to
the House of Yorke, especially at Bosworth, lost his head
at Leicester.' [1]

Now began that connection with the Howards to which
Buc, like Tyllney before him, owed the Mastership. His
grandfather Robert and the other children of 'that unfortunate Bucke . . . who withered with the White Rose,'

were brought into the south parts by Thomas Duke of Norfolk, wher
ever since we have remayned . . . for those children beeing orphans
were left in miserable Estate by the Attainder of their Father; but the
Duke bestowed two Daughters in marriage. . . . The sonnes were one
a Souldier, the other a Courtyer and the third a preist; afterward the

---

1 *Cotton MS. Tiberius E.* x, ff. 121ff.; *History of Richard the Third*, ed. 1646,
pp. 67–69. Anthony à Wood, whose system of shorthand was clearly not in-
fallible, writes that 'he lost his Hand' (*Ath. Oxon.*, 1, 38). His wife was of a
famous Yorkshire family — Margaret, daughter of Henry Saville (*Harl. Soc.*,
XLI, 123). Though the pedigree from Walter has many gaps, Buc has not
tried to fill them in from imagination, but has depended on documentary
authority and the evidence of arms.

Duke placed Robert Buck the eldest sonne at Mellford-hall in Suffolke, a rich and pleasante seat and by his favour hee marryed into the families of Higham and of Cotton . . . one of the Daughters of this Bucke Married to Fredericke Tillney of Shelley hall, a gentleman of a very ancient house and his nearest kinsman by the Duchesse his Mothers side.

Robert Buck of Long Melford [1] married Joan, daughter of Clement Heigham of Giffords, from whom Swinburne was also descended. Clement's wife was Joan Cotton of Landwade, Cambs.,[2] and thus Buc could claim distant kinship with his friend Sir Robert Cotton, as well as with Sir Clement Heigham, Chief Baron of the Exchequer and Speaker of the House under Mary. How well Sir George kept up family connections is evidenced by one of the sheets of his *History*, which bears the address of a letter to his 'loving kinsman m^r Thomas Heigha*m* esquier at S^t. Edmund*es* Bury.'

It should be noticed that Buc was not the nephew of Edmund Tyllney. The error originated with Malone, and though Chalmers set forth the relationship clearly and correctly,[3] Lee in the *D.N.B.* ignored his evidence and all later writers have done the same. The relationship was not one by blood (except very remotely [4]), but by marriage: Sir George's aunt, Margaret Buck, had married Frary or Frederick, first cousin to Edmund Tyllney. The chief connection between the two Masters of the Revels was that both followed the fortunes of the Lord Admiral. Instead of 'securing the reversion for his nephew,' Tyllney

1 Cf. *Stowe Charter* 248; *Suffolk in 1524*, p. 30.
2 W. C. Metcalfe, *Visitations of Suffolk* (Exeter, 1882), p. 22.
3 *Apology*, p. 492 n.; cf. Malone, *Shakspeare*, I, ii, 45 n.; *Variorum*, III, 57. Lee's statement, that Buc's mother 'seems to have been Tilney's sister,' is no nearer truth than the remarkable conclusion drawn from it by A. W. Upton, *P.M.L.A.*, XLIV, 1048: 'he seems to have married his position along with the daughter of Tylney' — who had no children. See the pedigree at p. 506.
4 Buc's ancestors had intermarried with the Tylneys in the 14th or 15th century (*History*, p. 68).

appears as Buc's 'adversary' and makes no mention of him in his will.

In an interesting paragraph preserved in manuscript, but not in the printed *History*, Sir George tells us that 'these Bucks were all souldiers': for his grandfather followed Norfolk and was with him at Flodden, his father served King Henry at the siege of Boulogne and Somerset at the battle of Musselburgh, 'et nos militauimus et Bella vidimus; G:B:.'[1] He writes of his grandfather as 'an ancient & wise & veritable gentilman, who was brought vp from a child by this most noble erl Thomas, & was euer w'th him vntyll his old age [& was] well acquainted w'th all his actions & his fortunes.' From him he has the true story of how the future victor of Flodden saved his life in 1485 only by lying hid in the house of a friend till his wounds were healed, and by what answer to King Henry he won his pardon.[2] This is a source unknown to the biographers of the Howards.[3]

Robert of Melford Hall had seven children: 'John their eldest who was a preist in the tyme of K.H.8 and since and dyed vnmarried'; Robert, Sir George's father; George; Edmond and Clement, who died when children; Margaret, wife of Frederick Tylney and later of John Smith; and Elizabeth, wife of George Raye of Derston. The authorities are Robert Buck in the Cambridgeshire Visitation of 1575, and the deposition in 1602 of 'George Buck of Longe Melford in the County of Suff gent aged 80. and odd yeares.'[4] Chambers inquires whether the gentleman of

1 *Egerton MS.* 2216, f. 165ᵛ; *Malone MS.* 1, f. 169ᵛ.
2 *Cotton MS. Tiber. E.* x, f. 110ᵛ; *Egerton MS.* 2216, f. 153.
3 E. M. Richardson, *The Lion and the Rose* (1922); Brenan and Statham, *The House of Howard* (1907).
4 *Harl. Soc.*, XLI, 123, from *Harl. MS.* 1534, f. 131 (the Buc arms are also in *Harl. MS.* 2198); P.R.O., C 24/299/13.

the Chapel who retired in 1603 was Sir George, but like
the historians of the Chapel Royal he had not observed
that the list of liveries bestowed at the funeral of Queen
Mary includes among 'Thordynary of the Chappell,' just
before Richard Edwardes, the name of George Bucke.[1]
This uncle lived to receive mourning for Elizabeth, and
died in 1605 at Long Melford, still calling himself in his
will a gentleman of the Chapel.[2] He had been a musician
in many reigns, for at the Dissolution George Buck, gent.,
and Richard Stephen, gentleman of the Chapel, secured
many manors and woodlands in Suffolk and elsewhere.[3]
It is not impossible that he was the George Bucke who became free of the Stationers' Company in 1560, by purchase
instead of by service, and appears for a few years only, not
as a printer but as publisher of a translation by Jasper
Heywood and of one by Golding.[4] In May 1567, he took
out letters of administration for the estate of his brother
John, rector of Snargate, Kent,[5] and of Ripe, Sussex.
George married a London mercer's daughter, Elizabeth
Bramston,[6] whose nephew John was to become Lord Chief
Justice.

Buc's father lived in 1575 at Ely. The visitation calls
his wife 'Elizebeth d. of pettle of Brandon fferry,' which
Chalmers has turned into 'Peter Lee of Brandon-ferry.' [7]
Her daughter by a former husband, Joan Nun, married
Henry Blaxton, master of Chichester school in 1570–71
and Chancellor of the Cathedral from 1572 to his death in

---

1 L. C. 2/4 (2); *The Elizabethan Stage*, I, 96; E. F. Rimbault, *The Old Cheque
Book of the Chapel Royal, Camden Soc.*, p. 6.
2 H. C. de Lafontaine, *The King's Musick*, p. 44; P.C.C., 3 Hayes.
3 Copinger, *Suffolk Records*, v, 31; *Letters and Papers, 1546*, pt. ii, p. 248
Deputy Keeper of the Public Records, 10th Report, p. 267; Edward Jones, *Index
to Records*, I (1793), sig. M.
4 Arber, *Transcripts*, I, 159, 197, 210; Hazlitt, *Hand-Book*, p. 543.
5 Presented by Queen Mary in 1553: Rymer, *Foedera*, xv, 350.
6 *Harl. Soc.*, I, 56; XIII, 157; XIV, 641.   7 *Apology*, p. 488

1606. Dr. Blaxton deposes in behalf of Buc in 1602 that he 'hath knowne him from his childhoode, for he was in his yonger yeares skoller unto this deponent and boorded with him in his house in Northamptonshire at Higham Ferrers.' This must have been between Blaxton's graduation from Cambridge in 1564–5 and his coming to Chichester in 1570. Buc in the preface to his *Eclog* quotes charters of Athelstan, Edmund, Edwy, Edwin, and Bishop Brighthelm (godfather of Brighton), which he has seen at Chichester Cathedral 'by the fauour of the reuerend D. Hen. Blaxton Chauncellor.'[1]

Robert Buck sold his house at Ely and followed Blaxton to Chichester, where he died in January 1579–80. He left his Chichester house to his wife and after her death to his second son, Robert. To George, the eldest, he gave his copyholds at Ely with the goods and implements therein, and he bequeathed a yearly charity to the poor of Trinity parish, Ely. The witnesses were Blaxton, named executor (with Mr. Roger Drewe of Chichester as overseer), Buc's mother, and Richard Juxon, Register to the Bishop of Chichester (and father to Charles II's Archbishop of Canterbury).[2]

Previous biographers have known nothing of Buc's life before he was elected to Parliament in 1593, except for his sonnet to Watson in 1582. He must have written this sonnet before he was a year old according to the reckoning of Corser, who very explicitly informs us that Buc was

---

1 Sig. B3ᵛ; Venn, *Alumni Cantabrigienses*. It was Buc's nephew Henry Blaxton who wrote affectionate Latin letters from Cambridge to his old master at Westminster, Camden, asking when he had a fever for 'Castilionem tuum . . . cum Poetis Italicis' (*Camdeni Epistolae*, pp. 44, 344). He has a funeral song on Sidney in the *Academiae Cantabrigiensis Lachrymae*, p. 53. Another nephew, Joshua, wrote verses to Elizabeth as a Westminster scholar in 1597, and acted in both *Labyrinthus* and *Leander* at Trinity in 1602–03 (*Royal MS*. xii A. 41; F. S. Boas, *University Drama in the Tudor Age*, pp. 399, 401).

2 P. C. C., 1 Arundell, made January 10, proved January 23.

twenty-three in 1605. This age he invented to fit in with his theory that Buc was the 'G.B.' who wrote *The Famous History of St. George* after the Restoration, and even after he was convinced of the absurdity of this ascription he did not like to abandon so precise a date.[1] Since Buc gave his age as thirty-nine on September 15, 1602,[2] he was born in 1562 or more probably 1563.

After beginning his education under his brother-in-law at Higham Ferrers, Buc very likely continued it as a scholar at Chichester Cathedral. Blaxton became master of the school there in 1570, and on December 10, 1578, I find the name of the schoolmaster at Chichester given as George Buck.[3] Unless this was his uncle, the gentleman of the Chapel (who, however, is not mentioned in Robert's will, or otherwise heard of in Sussex), young George was now far enough along at least to assist in the teaching. It would have been natural for him to go on to Cambridge, but there is no direct evidence that he did so. Hunter supposed that he was of Trinity Hall, because he writes of the Master, Dr. Henry Harvey, Dean of the Arches, 'whom I being a young Scholler knew.'[4] But Harvey was also a prebendary of Ely, and Buc might have known him at either place. Sir George's younger brother Robert is called in 1598 'Cantabrigiensis,' and the Venns have included him in *Alumni Cantabrigienses* on this ground; but since he was of Ely, it seems rather more probable that this description refers to his native county.

Even Buc's study of the law has escaped his biographers, though he himself tells us of it. In *The Third University of England* he writes of Thavies Inn that 'at my first com-

1 *Chetham Soc.*, LXXI, 172; *Bibliotheca Heberiana*, pt. xi, no. 98; *N. and Q.*, II (1850), 38, 73.
2 P. R. O., C 142/267/107.
3 *Victoria History of Sussex*, II, 407.
4 Stowe, *Annals*, ed. 1615, sig. Nnnn 4ᵛ.

ming to London, I was admitted for probation, into that good house'; and to the Middle Temple he wishes all honor and prosperity 'for my particular obligation, hauing beene sometimes a fellow, and student (or to confesse a truth) a trewand in that most honourable Colledge.'[1] He had probably left the study of law in the meantime, for a number of years seem to have passed between his first coming to London, by 1580, and his admission to the Middle Temple, on April 16, 1585, not from Thavies, but from New Inn. The regularity with which he was fined for absence from readings for the next two years fully bears him out as to his truancy.[2]

Buc's sureties on entrance were Samuel Barrow and Samuel Elmer, the latter the son and heir of Bishop Aylmer of London, the former of Philip Barrow, probably the physician and author.[3] Why they took an interest in Buc was at first sight not apparent, but the question was answered when I found from the manuscript of the *History* that whereas in the printed editions one of Sir John Buck's daughters married the 'Heire of Buck' (p. 69), Buc wrote 'of Bures,' an old Suffolk family through which they were akin. Joan Buck's dowry was the manor of Moryeves, with lands in Groton, Melford, and elsewhere; her daughter was a nun who after the Dissolution married a former monk of Walden Abbey; and their daughter Judith became the wife of Bishop Aylmer. Other cousins of Buc were Henry Barrow, the founder of Congregationalism, and his sister Anne the wife of Sir Charles Cornwallis, who, we shall see, kept up the cousinship. Strype informs us that he owned manuscript 'Collections Historical and Genealogical' written by Buc, which mention that from matches with Bures

1 *Idem*, sigg. Nnnn 3, 2.
2 C. T. Martin, *Minutes of Parliament of the Middle Temple*, I, 276, 280-290.
3 *D.N.B.*; *Alumni Cantabrigienses*; G. C. Williamson, *George, Third Earl of Cumberland*, p. 8; J. J. Howard, *The Visitation of Suffolke*, I, 259.

'sprang many Noble and eminent Families of the Mordaunts, Barrows, Bacons, Bucks, Gawdies, Tilneys . . . Aylmers . . . &c.'[1]

There were far more fascinating things to do in Elizabethan London than to study law, and one of them was to write poetry. Already in 1582 'G. Bucke' had contributed to Ἑκατομπαθια 'A Quatorzain in the Commendation of Master Thomas Watson and of his mistress, for whom he wrote this Booke of Passionat Sonnetes.' The sonnet is Italian in form, and begins, 'The starr's, which did at *Petrarch's* byrthday raigne/ Were fixt againe at thy nativity.' At this time Buc, who cannot have been long in London, was probably at Thavies Inn, where Matthew Roydon, who first appears as a poet in this volume, was also a student in 1581–2.[2] Peele was another who praised Watson in verse, and Lyly, then at the height of his fame, sent a letter 'to the Authour his friend.' The patron of both Watson and Lyly was the Earl of Oxford, who, as we shall see, 'vouchsafed' Buc 'his familiar acquaintance.'

It seems possible that Buc may be referred to four years later in Webbe's *Discourse of English Poetrie*. Webbe, having mentioned Oxford and other poets at Court, desires pardon 'of the learned company of Gentlemen Schollers, and students of the Universities, and Innes of Courte, yf I omitte theyr severall commendations in this place, which I knowe a great number of them have worthily deserved, in many rare devises, and singuler inventions of Poetrie'; and after praising Whetstone and Mundy (then Oxford's 'servant') he adds, 'With these I may place Iohn Graunge, Knyght, Wylmott, Darrell, F.C. F.K. G.B. and many other, whose names come not nowe to my remem-

---

1 *Life of Aylmer*, p. 174; Chauncey R. Burr, *Bures of Suffolk* (New York, 1926).
2 G. C. Moore Smith, *Mod. Lang. Rev.*, IX (1914), 97.

braunce.'[1] Buc as an Inn-of-Court man certainly belonged to the class of which Webbe is speaking, though the
initials are not rare enough to be quite conclusive.

A still more interesting question is the identity of the
'G. B. Cantabrigiensis' who was Greene's most faithful
friend in the writing of complimentary verses to his prose
works: English verses, signed only 'G.B.,' to the second
part of *Mamillia* (S.R. 1583); Latin verses to *Alcida* (S.R.
1588), entitled 'carmen Enkomiastikon,' by 'G. B. Cant.,'
and to *Ciceronis Amor* (1589), by 'G. B. Cantabrigiensis.'
Malone in a manuscript note on Ritson in the British
Museum gave these verses to Buc, and it is true that
the last set immediately follows one by his friend Watson;
but since Buc is not known to have been at Cambridge
I suggest that they belong to William Boston, who was
of Greene's own college, St. John's,[2] and who has verses,
'In Sacrosancta Ogerii Bellehachii Normanni Bvcolica,
Carmen Εγκωμιαστικον,' in 1583, signed 'Gulielmus Boston: *Cantabrigiensis*.'[3] In the same way Hunter assigned to Buc the 'carmen Asclepiadum Gliconicum' by
'G. B. Cantabridg.' on *The First Week* of Sylvester, which
in 1605 came just before the verses of Samuel Daniel, in
1611 and later editions before those of Ben Jonson.

Definite information as to Buc's next few years is not
easy to gather. Since the Queen suggested him in 1595 for

1 Ed. Arber, pp. 35-36. Haslewood, *British Bibliographer*, II (1812), 619, believed that Webbe was referring to the G. B. whose *Shippe of Safeguarde* was
published in 1569, although this was Barnabe Googe, whom Webbe had mentioned already. Professor Gregory Smith, in *Elizabethan Critical Essays*, I, 412,
suggested either Buc or 'M. Bewe,' and Professor Rollins conjectured a
'George Bewe?', on the basis of the 'M.[aster] Bew' who appears in the 1576
edition only of *The Paradise of Dainty Devices* (ed. 1927, p. xliii).

2 Cf. *Alumni Cantabrigienses*. Dr. Dee in a letter to Cotton in 1596 sends commendations to Master and Mistress Boston (Ellis, *Original Letters of Eminent
Literary Men*, Camden Soc., p. 88).

3 Bellehache, *Sacrosancta Bucolica Elizabeth Britanniae, Franciae, et Hibernie
Reginae Dicata*, London, 1583.

French Secretary, it occurred to me that he had probably spent part of his time in France. It was satisfactory, therefore, to find the following record of him among the Declared Accounts of the Treasurer of the Chamber:[1]

To *George Bucke* gen*tleman* vppon a warr*ant* signed by m^r Secr*etary* walsingham dated at the Courte xxj^{mo} Aprilis 1587 for bringing a packett of *lett*res for her ma^{tes} affayres out of ffraunce from Sr Edwarde Stafforde knighte her highnes Amb^r residente there to the Courte at Grenew^{ch} xiij^{li}vj^{s}viij^d.

His reward thus came to twenty marks. Stafford had written Walsyngham on April 4, in a postscript: 'Pray let my servant George be sent over as soon as you may. The poor fellow hath waited a great while.'[2] If this was Buc, Stafford lost no time in giving him despatches to carry back again from Paris; but as a gentleman Buc would probably have been called by his surname. In his later works he showed himself particularly fond of quoting French historians, and he even wrote a couple of verses in French, like Lodge. On his arrival at Court he had the opportunity of seeing Du Bartas, who had also crossed to England in April with letters from Henry of Navarre.

As a follower of Howard of Effingham, Buc was in the thick of things in 1588. He not only served against the Armada but celebrated the triumph with verses in Latin entitled 'The Battle of the Black Eagle of Austria and the White Lion of Norfolk, or the Victory of the Most Illustrious Worthy *Charles Howard* . . . under the Divine Auspices of our *Diana* . . .':

> . . . Congrediuntur in Oceano, *Leo* fortis et *Ales*
> Pugnant inque Vicem laniant, sparguntur ad auras,
> Percussi fluctus tonitru, coelum omne remugit,
> Fulmina dira volant, passim certatur vtrinque

1 Pipe Rolls, E 351/542, f. 94^v.
2 *S. P. Foreign, 1587–88*, p. 272.

Marte, diu dubio, dum pectore saucivs *Ales*
Hic fugit, Insequitur trepidum Velocior Ille;
Mergitur Hostis atrox, Victorque revertitur Albus
Numina laudantur, quorum haec Nomine gesta.

Richard Robinson preserved these in his *Archippus* as
'Certeyne Verses given me by one Mr Buck a gent*leman*
of my Lord Admiralles to be annexed vnto' the Latin account of Emanuel van Meteren which Robinson presented
in 1589 to the Lord Admiral.[1] That this poem has not
been noticed before is owing to the very miscellaneous
character of Robinson's manuscript.

Buc's service had evidently won him the confidence of
Effingham, for he was elected member for Gatton, Surrey,
in the Parliaments which sat from February to April 1593,
and from October 1597 until the following February.
Gatton was a borough of six houses, for which Howard had
secured the return of Edmund Tyllney in the Parliament
of 1572–83.[2] Norton, co-author of *Gorboduc*, represented
it in Elizabeth's first Parliament. Burghley in 1584 commanded the election of young Francis Bacon, and in 1597
he placed his secretary Michael Hicks as Buc's colleague.
In later fame Gatton was second only to Old Sarum; but
it is still more remarkable as offering in 1553 the first recorded instance of a woman electing a member of Parliament (Dame Elizabeth Copley, daughter of Justice Shelley

1 'Georgius Buck' has fifteen verses, to which Robinson adds others by himself
and by Theodore Beza: *Royal MS.* 18 A lxvi, f. 21. *Archippus*, first written out
on Queen's Day, 1589, and last on August 23, 1602, to offer Elizabeth, was
finally presented to James. The Admiral was kind enough to reward Robinson for this, for one of his books of psalms, and for a history of the Cadiz adventure, 'liberally gratifying my good will: dyverse Knightes of yᵉ sayde
Cadiz Voyage bestowed vpon mee allso bothe theyʳ frendly benevolence for
the same Copyes, and furthered mee in perfecting the Originall for my future
benefit amongst others.' Buc may have helped the poverty-stricken author in
this work also, called *An English Quid for a Spanish Quo*; cf. Williamson,
George, Third Earl of Cumberland, p. 26.
2 *Members of Parliament* (1878); Manning and Bray, *Surrey*, II, 233.

and grandmother of the poet Southwell), and of a minor as member — for she elected her son.[1]

The Admiral in 1595 wrote the following letter to Cecil, recommending Buc for either French Secretary or Clerk of the Signet:[2]

Sir I did vnderstand this day by M^r Jo Stanhope that her M talkyng w^t him of Mr Niccasious that is called vnto Gods mercy and of the offyses that he had wyche wer two. her M^e sayd ther weer dyveres suttores for the*m* and named sum. but of her selfe she sayd that they weer other mens servants. and asked wher m^r Buk was showyng of her self A grasious disposision to do him good and to thynke him fyte for on of thos plases as sure he is. I know not how you ar alredy ingaged for any other by your promys yf you be not I shall thynk my selfe in this as I am in all thynges much beholdyng vnto you yf he may have your favor in it. for I know for the French tonge he Cane dow it very well to serve her M^e and yf you may w^{t}out the preiudis of your word to any. to moue her M^e in my name for him. I did stay as long as I could to have downe it my selfe. but am forsed now to yous your frendshyp [yf you may], otherwyse yf it plaese you to acquaynte Mr Stanhope w^t my letter that he may youse my name vnto her M^e and that I had wrytten to him in it. I wyll dow the lyk for him in anythyng he shall requyer me. The gentleman hathe ben A long Atendant and hathe by his graet desier to serve her M^e lost somm other service that myght hapely and to his good falne vnto him. he deservethe well and Canne dow well, and so dow I wyshe you ever as to my selfe   fro*m* Chelse This 28 of Ap.

your most Afecsionat trew frend,

Howard.

Since there was never any lack of suitors at the Court, that the Queen should thus spontaneously suggest yet another one is proof of a genuine liking for Buc, which must have weighed the scale finally in his favor when it came to securing her promise of the Mastership of the Revels.

1 *D.N.B.*, 'Sir Thomas Copley'; E. Porritt, *The Unreformed House of Commons*, I, 97, 223, 376; Merewether and Stephens, *History of the Boroughs*, III, 1646.
2 From the original, calendared in *Hatfield MSS.*, v, 189. For permission to print in full this letter and two more written by Buc, I am indebted to the courtesy of the Marquis of Salisbury.

Chambers remarks that this letter was written after the death of Nicasius Yetsweirt,[1] and so it was, but it was at least eight years after. For I find in the Signet Office Docquet that on August 6, 1587, his son Charles, Clerk of the Signet, was granted valuable leases 'w^thowt fyne in considerac*i*on of the longe and faithfull service of Nicasius Yetswert Esquier deceased.' 'Master Nicasius,' who had served Thomas Cromwell and was already Clerk of the Signet under Edward VI, is mentioned by Ascham as present at the Windsor dinner which led to the writing of *The Schoolmaster*; and he has complimentary verses to Googe's *Art of Husbandry*. Norden in 1593 speaks of him as buried at Sunbury, Middlesex.[2] The Admiral, there-fore, evidently meant to refer not to Nicasius but to his son Charles, who succeeded him in both his offices, and whose widow wrote Cecil the next day to protect his monopoly for law-books against the revolt of the Sta-tioners' Company. As it turned out, no new Clerk of the Signet was appointed; and Buc's rivals for the French secretaryship offered strong arguments. Edward Jones, for example, wrote Cecil on April 14 that he was favored by the Lord Keeper, Essex, Buckhurst, and Fortescue, and offered to show his thankfulness with £300; it was only in a postscript that he mentioned his qualifications. He was known as 'a great translator of books' and 'a special man of language,' and he called both Cecil and Sir John Stanhope to witness that 'her Ma of her selfe named me for secretary for the French tonge.'[3] The office went to Thomas Edmondes as his only reward for spend-ing all his estate as the Queen's agent at the court of

1 *Eliz. Stage*, I, 98.
2 *Speculum Britanniae*, p. 40; cf. Hunter, *Add. MS.* 24480.
3 *S.P.D. Eliz.* 251/114; Chambers, *Review of English Studies*, I (1925), 76–77; cf. *Lansdowne MS.* 77, no. 47.

Henry IV, and he was employed not as secretary but as envoy and later ambassador.[1]

Next year Buc attended the Admiral on the Cadiz Voyage. The first official news of the English triumph was carried to the Queen by her Clerk of the Council, Sir Anthony Ashley; a fortnight later, 'master *George Bucke* was dispatched by the lords Generals to her Maiestie, to make relation of that which had passed in the armie since the fleetes departure from the Bay of Cadiz.'[2] The most careful historian of this expedition, Sir Julian Corbett, by a natural confusion calls the messenger 'Buck, the provost-marshal';[3] but that officer was Sir John Buck, who was knighted at Cadiz and founded a family at Hamby Grange, Lincolnshire. Slyngisbie in his *Relation* writes that Sir Arthur Savage was sent to report the proposed attempt on the Azores, and Master George Buck the generals' change of mind.[4] Fortunately we have Buc's own account of the matter, which shows that it was just the other way about.[5]

Buc tells Sir Robert Cotton how the Lords Generals read to him their joint letter to the Queen, and first Essex, then Effingham, showed him their private letters to Elizabeth, Burghley, and Cecil, before sealing them. The generals made their report in the form of instructions addressed to Buc, relating the burning of Faro and that

(as you knowe) a Strong northerly wynd took vs and forced vs to hale of seas. wee are nowe 80: leagues from the Cape St Vincent towards the Ilands of the *Assores* and now Callinge a second Counsayle we are aduised by alle men to goe for the Iland*es*, for there wee shalle releeve

---

1 *S.P.D. Eliz.* 257/86, 262/38. Rymer (*Foedera*, XVI, 290) makes him secretary 'pro Lingua Graeca' instead of 'pro Lingua Gallica.'
2 Stowe's *Annals*, ed. 1615, sig. Ttt3^v.
3 *The Successors of Drake*, p. 123.
4 *Navy Records Soc.*, XX (1902), 91, followed by E. P. Cheyney, *A History of England from the Defeat of the Armada to the Death of Elizabeth*, II, 81.
5 *Cotton MS. Otho E.* IX, ff. 343–350; cf. Edwards, *Life of Ralegh*, II, 137.

our men wth water: and fresh vittayles we shalle ly for the Carak*es* and West Indian fleet: and never want wynd to Carry vs into England when our army shalle not be in Case to stay out any longer Besides we are advertised that there are at those Island*es* a fleete of 25 men of warre of the Spanyar⟨ds⟩ of w^{ch} (if wee meett them) we shale (by *Gods* grace) geue as good an account as of the fleet of Armados Gallions Levantiscas & others wch w⟨e⟩ found at Cadiz.

Buc was to pray the Lords of the Council 'to bee our good Angells and to deale with us as they would be dealt wth if they were in our places.' He wisely took care to be ready for Elizabeth's questioning: 'Then I desired theire lo:^{pes} advise how I should answere the Queene if her Matie should aske mee why the fleet watered not at *Faro*,' a critical question to which Essex framed his reply. 'The erl of Essex also willed mee that as soone as I was landed at Plymouth I should take order wth the magistrat*es* and officers there that none of the ould band*es* of Souldiers should be discharged,' but that they might be 'employed in some enterpryse of importance vppon the Enemyes Coast*es* at home for Dunkerke, Newport, Calays, &cc. . . . Thus farr th erl of Essex his charge giuen & comitted to me at my taking leaue of his Lp abourd ye Du repuls,' on July 24.[1] Here Buc's narrative has been burnt away, and from the account in Stowe it is possible that he did not finally leave the fleet till it was off Corunna. At Greenwich Elizabeth summoned him into the drawing chamber and willed him to make a new report of what had happened at Cadiz, which she was pleased to hear him tell several times over.

If we wish to hear the very story Buc told to Elizabeth of 'the winning, sacking, and burning of the famous towne of Cadiz,' we have only to turn to the pages of Stowe's *Annals*. The account printed there is always referred to

1 Corbett conjectured July 23, but cf. *Hatfield MSS.*, vi, 282; see also pp. 285, 292 f., 310 f.

simply as Stowe, but he of course did not write it. He introduces it as 'An Abstract of the expedition to Cadiz 1596. drawne out of Commentaries written at large thereof, by a Gentleman who was in the voyage.' This gentleman has never been identified, but I think it can be demonstrated that he was Buc. In the first place, the author is clearly a follower of the Admiral, whose actions he describes much more explicitly than those of Essex or of Ralegh. 'Master *George Bucke*' appears by name on two separate occasions, whereas Slyngisbie mentions him only once and most of the other relations not at all. What particularly led me to suspect Buc as the author, however, was observing that the expedition is spoken of as 'we' up to the moment when Buc left for England, and that after this the final paragraph has only 'they.' For evidence to clinch the matter we may turn to the passage which parallels that quoted above, from 'a Strong northerly wynd' to '25 men of warre.' This reappears in Stowe almost verbatim, taken straight from the instructions which the Lords Generals put in Buc's hands, and not otherwise accessible.

Buc, then, furnished Stowe with an eyewitness's account of the Cadiz expedition, just as on the following page his close friend Segar contributed a journal of Shrewsbury's embassy to Henry IV. That he was on friendly terms with the old chronicler we know from his *History*, where he adduces information given him by Stowe '*viva voce.*' He had good reason for not letting his name appear as author of the Cadiz relation, since the Government had refused license to print any account of the voyage except the Admiral's own. Even the excellent *Discourse* by Dr. Marbecke, who was physician to the Admiral, after being announced by Hakluyt in his title-page and preface and actually printed off, had to be left out of the published

work. As Hakluyt edited Marbecke, so Stowe has probably cut from Buc's narrative some of its interesting detail
and personal character, but occasional touches of humor
remain. The Admiral, for example, received letters '(from
his olde acquaintance, since 1588.) the duke of *Medina
Sidonia*,' and when the Spanish galleys lay too close he
commanded them 'to depart from thence and go further
off; which commaundement they obeyed as readily, as if
the Admirall of Spaine hadde sent it.' As for the famous
shower of knighthoods at Cadiz, 'Stow dryly remarks'
(to quote Corbett) that 'after dinner they made a great
many knights, euen all almost that did deserue it, or affect
it, or not neglect and refuse it (as some did:).' Buc tells
how he marched into Cadiz among the 'gentleman ad-
uenturers, & men of qualitie' following Effingham, and
next morning saw Fort St. Philip yield to the red ensign
of England. He was able to converse with '*Signior Fan-
tonio*, the rich Florentine,' who 'affirmed to me in his
house in Cadiz' that the Spaniards themselves fired two
of the Twelve Apostles (galleons) and that their whole loss
was at least twenty millions of ducats. He tells us that the
library of books in the Bishop's palace at Faro was valued
at a thousand marks: the books which Essex in 1600 presented to the Bodleian. Buc's narrative should be added
to the sources for the Cadiz voyage of which Corbett gives
a critical review, unaccountably omitting Stowe. Buc was
not one to let the deeds of a Howard sleep in forgetfulness,
though it is only after three centuries of eclipse that we
have chanced to rediscover either the verses in which he
celebrated the defeat of the Armada, or the abstract of his
Commentaries on the winning of Cadiz.

We now come to the interesting riddle of Lyly's first
letter in regard to the Revels, written to Cecil on December 22, 1597:

Offic*es* in Reuersion are forestalld, in possession ingrost, & that of y*ᵉ* Reuell*es* countenaunced vpon Buck, wherin the Justic of an oyre shewes his affection to yᵉ Keper, & partialty, to yᵉ sheppard, a feint[1] fauor.

Lyly's editor offers three different explanations of this sentence, but two of them drag in an 'ogre' instead of 'oyre' and the third explains the word as 'oyer and terminer.' The *O.E.D.*, however, gives 'oire' as a 16th-century form of 'eyre,' and mentions the office of 'Justice in eyre of all his Majesty's forests,' held in 1622 by Buckingham. The only example it cites of an *o*-form (from Ascham's *Schoolmaster*) is misplaced under 'oyer' meaning 'oyer and terminer': 'Seing so worthie a Iustice of an Oyre hath the present ouersight of that whole chace,' where the reference is to Burghley as Chancellor of Cambridge. A further instance is found in Buc's tribute to Effingham, among his other dignities 'Lord Chiefe Justice in *Oyer* of the better part of this Kingdome.'[2] The word, then, has nothing to do with 'oyer and terminer.' Lyly uses the exact form in Ascham, and the same figure of a forest, suggested by 'Buck.' Since the interlined words imply that what goes before is ironical, the shepherd may mean Lyly himself, as a poet; the keeper (contrasted with 'Buck'), Tyllney, as Master — someone, at least, who has recommended Lyly for the reversion; and the justice, Effingham or Burghley. Any number of other interpretations are equally possible.

Lyly's letter, though it has been taken to mean that Buc

1 R. W. Bond (*Lyly*, 1, 68) read this word as 'french' or possibly 'fienet,' and Chambers (*Eliz. Stage*, 1, 96) printed 'french,' but a careful examination of the original confirms Feuillerat's 'feint' (*S.P.D. Eliz.* 265/61; *John Lyly*, p. 555). The last three words are interlined as an afterthought.

2 *History*, sig. K2. Manuscript copies have 'eyre,' 'Eyre' (*Egerton MS.* 2216, f. 162; *Malone MS.* 1, f. 166; *Add. MS.* 27422). 'Justice in oyer,' 'of Oire,' occur in *Hatfield MSS.*, vi, 304; xv, 256; and in the Pipe Rolls, 'Justice of Euoyer beyonde Trente' (E 351/543, f. 105ᵛ).

had actually received an appointment, shows only that he had secured some sort of promise. No patent was issued him under Elizabeth,[1] and from a letter of his it appears that he was not yet sure of the office. He wrote Cecil on June 1, 1599:[2]

Sir)
  I understood by a very hon. freind of mine not many moonths since that you were very well affected to myn old long sute, & y^t of y^r own most hon. disposition offered to move ye Q. in my behalf. Although I came not then to acknowledge how much I was bound to y^r H. for this great fauour (as knowing in myne own conscience the litle woorth of my pore thanks) yet I humbly entreated my most noble L. myne old L. m^r [3] to give you his kindest thanks for it. & ever since [till yesterday] I reckned myself in the same state of y^r hono. good fauour: till yesterday y^t I heard y^t you had given y^r goodwill to another, & besides had persuaded one of my cheefest hono. freinds to be sollicitour for him. I am very sory for this alienation of y^r hon. fauour yet consydering my interest therin accrued out of frank-almoigne onely & y^t y^{r}fore I can claime no estate but during pleasure, yet I hoped as other pore true tenants doo, not to be turned out so long as I performed my honest dutyes: wch charitable fauour I doo heer most instantly begg of y^r ho: & also y^t you (in whome I haue had so good hope) would not bee the meanes y^t any part of that Swoord should so much hurt mee, wherwth I hoped alwayes to bee defended: Especially in a cause so iust, & so reasonable as this, & myne onely sute, wherof my whole estate, & fortune dooth & hath depended this XI yeres: & thus therfore hoping of y^r ho. fauorable good meanes, (wch if I may hold or recover I wilbee as thankfull as my pore talent of witt, or fortunes or other best meanes will yeeld) & humbly craving pardone for this boldness I tak my leaue most humbly. 1. June.
                Most humbly at y^r honours commandement
                                                    G. Buck

  The full text of the letter gives information that was absent from the abstract in the *Calendar*, which stopped short before coming to 'myne onely sute.' It is curious that Lyly also first aimed his courses at the Revels in 1588,

1 Feuillerat, *Documents relating to the Office of the Revels in the Time of Queen Elizabeth* (*Materialien*, xxi), p. 439.
2 Manuscripts at Hatfield, 70/73 (cf. *Calendar*, ix, 190).
3 'Lord and master,' the Admiral.

so that in length of service there was nothing to choose between the two suitors. It has been conjectured that 'Perhaps Buc did not pay, as was usual, for his appointment to the Revels Office which was given to him as being of the household of Howard,'[1] but the only evidence for this is Buc's mention of 'frank-almoigne,' and it now becomes clear that this refers not to the reversion but to Cecil's favor. It is significant that Buc offers to be 'thankful,' a well understood phrase; but the best way to win Cecil's support was to show a record of experience in faithful service to the Crown.

The following entry shows that Buc was already an occasional servant of the Queen, and employed at some time during this year to carry despatches. It occurs in the Declared Accounts for the year ending in November 1599, under 'Riding charges':[2]

George Bucke gentleman Esquire of her Maiesties bodyie extraordenarie vppon one bill x^{li}.

The amount bears witness that Buc's journey had been one of more than ordinary length or importance.

According to a leading authority, 'In 1597 the reversion of the Mastership was secured by Tilney for his nephew, Sir George Buc, who thereafter served as deputy.'[3] The truth is that further evidence will be necessary before we have the right to say when Buc began to share in the work of the Revels: whether before he received his patent of reversion in 1603, or immediately thereafter, or not until 1606, when his first license is recorded in the Stationers'

---

1 Frank Marcham, *The King's Office of the Revels, 1610–1622* (London, 1925), p. 3.
2 Pipe Rolls, E 351/543, f. 45^v.
3 J. Q. Adams, *The Dramatic Records of Sir Henry Herbert*, p. 7, and *A Life of William Shakespeare*, p. 503. Dr. Tannenbaum has erected upon this a baseless argument as to the date of *More* ('*The Booke of Sir Thomas Moore*,' p. 18; cf. Sisson, *Modern Language Review*, XXIII [1928], 234).

Register. There is one piece of evidence for Buc's having served in Elizabeth's reign: Herbert's relicensing in 1624 of '*Jugurth, King of Numidia,* formerly allowed by Sir George Bucke.'[1] *Jugurth* was paid for by Henslowe on February 9, 1600–01;[2] but it may have come before Buc for allowance or reallowance later, or Herbert may have been mistaken, since the copy formerly allowed had been burnt. Tyllney is hardly likely to have given up his licensing fees to Buc, and Buc had no allowance from the government until 1611, retrospective to 1608.

He is the less likely to have entered the Revels so early as 1601 since in that year we find him actively engaged on a diplomatic mission to Flanders. Cecil wrote on August 19:

> You shall vnderstand that her Matie in respect of yor discretion hath made Choyce to imploy you to visite Sr *Francys Vere,* who lyeth now at *Midleborough* being lately Come from *Ostend,* sore hurt as also to deale w^th *Count Maurice* and wth the States of *Zeland*. . .

He was to consult with Vere as to whether Ostend could still be held against the Spaniards, and if not, to feel him out by degrees as to whether there might not be some means 'to drowne the towne or aboue althing*es* to destroy the haven,' first discovering by conversation with others whether this was practicable. Buc writes that 'at my takinge leave at Windsore' the Queen gave him charge what to say, 'and vsed some sharper Word*es* to stirre vp the remissnes or Couldnesse (as her Matie suspected) of the prince and of the States' for the relief of Ostend. He carried letters also to Sir Robert Drury and to Sir Robert Sydney, who, in his answer, 'having told mr Bucke, as much as I know myself,' passes over the news 'becaus I wil not doe any wrong to his descours.' Vere writes that

1 Chalmers, *Supplemental Apology,* p. 218; cf. p. 203.
2 *Henslowe's Diary,* I, 118.

'vpon his aryvall I fownd my self sensibly to gather strength, wch I doe impute to ye excedinge Comfort I receved by her Maties notable demonstrac*i*on to the worlde of her most gratious Care of me by sendinge this Gentleman. . . .' Buc had waited until the arrival of the Prince, 'And I thinke,' says Vere, 'that his stay to speake with him hath bene to very good purpose for the setting vs on worke.'

The Queen had bidden Buc to congratulate Prince Maurice on his recent victory and 'to desire him to impart vnto you what is purposed . . . and what himself Conceaveth of the place.' Buc reports that in the Castle at 'Campuere' (Ter Veeren) and in the Abbey at Middleburgh 'he gave me very good satisfaction in all thing*es* in like maner. & was also confident that the enemy should nev^r wyn Ostend.' The principal persons of the States gave him audience in their council chamber in the Abbey, and 'took such care of this message as they presently supplied' all that was lacking at Ostend 'very roially.' Buc's language is exactly echoed by Cecil in a letter of September 4.[1] The negotiations, like his letters of credence from Elizabeth, were in French. They ended as happily for the envoy as for his mistress, for after 'my leave taken I had presented to mee deux toneaux de vin de Gascoyne by the secretarie of ye states & a fowre pointed diamond of S^r Fr. Vere.'[2]

Soon after Buc sailed from Flushing on August 26, there rose 'so great storms as no ship was able to put out of the haven.' At length, however, he reached England and found the Queen at Reading, where on September 1 he

1 *Hatfield MSS.*, xi, 381.
2 Buc's account of his mission is in *Cotton MS. Galba D.* xii, f. 330. The draft of his instructions, incomplete and much corrected by Cecil, occurs also in S. P. 84/61, f. 238, followed by letters mentioning Buc from Prince Maurice, the States, and the English envoy and captains.

received twenty pounds for carrying despatches to and from Vere. Since he had already on August 18 been paid a like sum in advance for his mission to the United States and Prince Maurice, he received in all forty pounds, a very exceptional reward.[1]

At this very time news arrived that Biron was coming as ambassador, and Biron himself landed at Dover on the first of September. The embassy was so unexpected that Elizabeth had set out from Windsor on progress, and London was deserted. Cecil sent Buc post-haste with letters to arrange for Biron's escort into Hampshire by as many English nobles as could be suddenly assembled. On the road Buc met and summoned Lord Grey of Wilton; in London he bore Cecil's orders to the Lord Treasurer's, then to Clerkenwell to the Earl of Cumberland at one o'clock in the morning. At nine he took horse again for Hackney, probably with a message to Lord Zouch. An agent of Cecil's, who was bidden to entrust Buc with a further business to despatch, had to enquire for him at all these places, at Westminster, and at his lodging in the Old Bailey.[2] It was this embassy to England that Chapman tried to bring on the stage in *The Conspiracy of Byron* seven years later, when Buc was censor.

1 E 351/543, f. 70.
2 *Hatfield MSS.*, xi, 379 ff.; *A.P.C.*; Williamson, *George, Third Earl of Cumberland*, p. 245 (the Earl's midnight interview was not with Buckhurst, who was then in the country, but with Buc).

II. GRIFFINS' TALONS

One of the most interesting questions connected with Buc is the authenticity of the inscription in his hand in Dr. Rosenbach's copy of *Locrine*, stating that the play was written by his cousin Charles Tilney. As a preparation for discussing this problem elsewhere, we may turn to the similarly contested inscription to Lord Chancellor Ellesmere in a copy of Buc's *Eclog*, published in 1605. Collier gives the verses in facsimile in his catalogue of the Earl of Ellesmere's library: [1]

> Great & graue Lord) my mind hath longed long
> In any thankfull maner to declare
> By act or woord, or were it in a song,
> How great to you my obligations are
> Who did so nobly & so timely pluck
> from Griffins talons Your destressed Buck.

Dr. Tannenbaum has denied the genuineness of these lines, declaring: 'That the penmanship is not George Buc's is apparent at a glance; that the inscription is a forgery is beyond the shadow of a doubt; that Collier was the forger may, in the light of what we know concerning him and his methods, be taken for granted.' [2] These remarkable pronouncements will have to be taken for granted if they are to be taken at all, for they are certainly not borne out by the evidence. It is apparent at a glance that the verses are not in Buc's informal English hand, but Dr. Tannenbaum omits to mention his formal Italian hand, seen in the dedication of his *History*, which has been available in fac-

---

1 *A Catalogue, Bibliographical and Critical, of Early English Literature, forming a Portion of the Library at Bridgewater House* (London, 1837), p. 41; reprinted, not in facsimile, in his *Bibliographical and Critical Account of the Rarest Books in the English Language* (London, 1865), I, 95. Dr. Greg furnishes a more accurate reproduction in *The Library*, December, 1931, Plate V.
2 *Shakspere Forgeries in the Revels Accounts* (New York, 1928), p. 56

simile since 1925.[1] The arguments used to support the second assertion are thoroughly unreliable, as Dr. Greg has shown,[2] since Dr. Tannenbaum has fallen into the trap of trusting to Collier's inaccurate tracing instead of examining even a photograph of the original. The 'convincing evidences of identity' which he finds with the Revels Accounts can hardly convince anyone who is willing to examine the letters closely and to rely not on imagination but on what is actually before the eyes. Finally, Dr. Tannenbaum notes as especially significant the date 1837, and it is quite true that we ought to inquire very closely into any document first brought to light by Collier about that time. This does not apply, however, to Buc's verses, for Collier was not the first to publish them. They had already been printed in full by the Reverend William Beloe in his *Anecdotes of Literature* [3] in 1812. 'Though the expert bibliotist usually conducts his investigation without any regard to such external circumstances as the history of the document,'[4] yet an expert's decision which is squarely contradicted by the history of the document does not inspire confidence in bibliotics.

Those acquainted with the simple fact that Buc wrote a formal as well as an informal hand are likely to agree with Dr. Greg that there is no reason to doubt that the inscription is genuine.[5] But the final evidence that Buc wrote it comes in the 'Griffins talons,' a heraldic allusion characteristic of Buc, which Collier could not be expected to understand. He did his best with it by drawing the natural inference that Buc was referring to 'a person of the name of Griffin, who possibly had been his adversary in a chan-

1 Marcham, *The King's Office of the Revels, 1610–1622.*
2 *Review of English Studies*, v (1929), 350–351.
3 VI, 112.
4 Tannenbaum, *Shakspere Forgeries*, p. 61.
5 *English Literary Autographs*, Part I (1925), no. xxx.

cery suit which Lord Ellesmere decided in favour of Sir George Buck.' The key to the inscription is in a Chancery case discovered by Dr. Sisson, in which Buc is plaintiff against Emery and Thomas Tylney, cousins of Edmund. And what are the arms of Tylney? Argent a chevron gules between three griffins' heads erased, beaked or, with three griffins for the crest.[1]

The head of the Tylney family was Philip of Shelley Hall in Suffolk, where he had once entertained his kins-woman the Queen. When he died in March, 1601–2, his Suffolk manors went to his uncle Emery, who, being seventy-four, left the management of the estate to his son Thomas.[2] Philip held lands in Lincolnshire, however, which he had inherited not from the Tylneys but from his mother, Buc's aunt Margaret. Having survived her first husband, Frederick Tylney, and a second, John Smith of Cavendish, Suffolk, and of Boston, she died on November 2, 1597.[3] Upon Philip's death, Buc secured an inqui-

1 To be seen on Edmund Tyllney's tomb at Streatham (Manning and Bray, *Surrey*, III, 391), on the choir stalls of Shelley Church, near Hadleigh, and most elaborately at Shelley Hall, in stone, brick, and oak chimney-panels (*Proc. Suff. Inst. of Archaeol.* VI [1883], 321, VIII [1885], 203; Copinger, *Manors of Suffolk*, VI, 79; *Collectanea Topographica et Genealogica*, III [1836], 64, 70).

2 Emery Tylney wrote for Foxe (*Acts and Monuments*, ed. 1838, V, 626) an enthusiastic account of George Wishart, with whom he had lived as a boy at Cambridge in 1543 (*Alum. Cant.*). He has been suggested as the author of *A Song of the Lordes Supper*, published in 1550 with 'Finis quot E. T.' (Hazlitt, *Hand-Book*; *D.N.B.*, 'Edmund Tilney'). See also F. A. Inderwick, *Calendar of the Inner Temple Records*, I, 190, and J. C. Jeaffreson, *Middlesex County Records*, I, 203. Thomas, who succeeded him on his death in 1606, was the executor of Edmund who signed the Revels accounts for 1610. He was Sheriff of Suffolk in 1611, as Philip had been in 1591.

3 Inquisition post mortem, taken at Boston in 1598 but discharged by Buc on May 23, 1604 (C 142/409/12). The inquisition upon Philip is endorsed, 'Mᵣ Bucke hath paid Mᵣ Barfoote for the retorne of this office' (C 142/267/107). The lands included the manor of Skidbrooke, held of Peregrine Lord Willoughby and in 1602 of his son, with meadows in South Somercote and Saltfleet Haven; land at Lichfield Horn on the west of the water in Skirbeck, held of Thomas Lord Burghley; and a mansion with two gardens and two orchards on the west of the water in Boston, held of the town. This was re-

sition finding himself heir to the Lincolnshire lands as next-of-kin to Margaret, from whom Philip derived his title. Thomas Tylney, however, claimed that Philip had devised the lands to him by will. Buc accordingly brought suit in 1602, the question at issue being whether or not Philip had left a will.

Buc's witnesses give a curious account of the deathbed of this Elizabethan squire, whose only son Charles Tylney, 'antiqua generis claritate, vnica spes familiae,' [1] and possible pioneer with Marlowe of the blank-verse drama, had suffered a traitor's death as a conspirator. There was one witness from each of the learned professions: Edmond Coleman of Furnival's Inn, Philip's law agent for many years and undersheriff during his master's shrievalty; Thomas Moswell, a Hadleigh physician; and Dr. George Meriton, Rector of Hadleigh. Meriton as a fellow of Queen's had acted in *Laelia* (the Cambridge play which perhaps helped to suggest *Twelfth Night*) and may have been its part-author. He had also acted in Bacon's device which Essex gave before Elizabeth in 1595. An epigram of Weever's praises him and George Montaigne for both these entertainments. Nashe in 1592 had written of 'two rare yong men, M. *Meriton* and another,' who in reading the philosophy lecture at Cambridge 'haue surmounted all former mediocritie, and wonne themselues an euerlasting good name in the Vniuersitie.' [2] In the *D.N.B.* (to which none of this was known) may be read how he later became Dean of Peterborough and York, Chaplain to

---

ferred to as Mesnam's house, from the former owner, but when Buc leased it out in 1619–20 it was 'to bee called by the name of Greenpooles' — which suggests that Buc could relish the flavor of a name, probably reviving an old one.

1 Camden, *Annales*, ed. 1615, sig. Fff 5.
2 *Works*, ed. McKerrow, I, 313; cf. John Weever, *Epigrammes* (1599), iv, 19; *Laelia*, ed. Moore Smith (1910); *Eliz. Stage*, III, 212; IV, 375.

Queen Anne, and grandfather to 'certainly the meanest *Dramatick* writer ever *England* produc'd' and to an excellent Yorkshire humorist. The deposition gives us his age, thirty-seven on October 14, 1602.

On the last day of Philip's life, Coleman and Moswell testify, seeing him 'weaker indeede then yt seemed m^r Tilney thought himselff,' they urged him to make his will. He said he would before two days, but 'shifted yt off w^{t}h odd answeares saying that was no tyme to make a will' and 'that yt was fittest to talk of such a matter when a man was in p*er*fect health.' Coleman drew up the preamble of a will and read it to him, but on Moswell's suggesting that it was customary to remember the church and the poor first in a will, he broke out:

> What do you meane? my Will? I tell you I would not make my will for ten thousand pound*es.* What? would you have me overthrow my house for ever? do not you know that they are poore beggerly and miserable adding also that he had in his head great matters, great p*er*sonages, great contentions, quarrel*es,* and debat*es,* and greater reasons then this dep*onent* had any to alledge agaynst him.

When Meriton came and asked if he had disposed of his estate, he 'gave indyrect & imp*er*tinent answeares taking hold [& playing wth the doble vnderstanding]' of 'dispose.' Meriton testifies that on being urged more seriously, he said 'he might heerafter do yt tyme ynough.' On Meriton pressing him to do it at that instant, and continuing his earnestness, Master Tylney told him 'that he vsed him like Job. & sayd he wold lay a wager he wold lyve as long' as Meriton. The rector suggested to the recalcitrant that if he were left alone with Coleman he would perhaps make his will. Tylney said, 'Perhaps.' But after leaving them together, on his return Meriton found no likelihood of any will being made. Tylney, seeing that the rector was about to continue his persuasions, said, 'Do you love me, Coleman?' 'Ay, sir,' said he. 'Then,' said the squire, 'as thou lovest mee let mee heere no more of this mocion.' Within four hours more he was dead.[1]

Buc, with his wide acquaintance among learned lawyers, could choose the best of counsel: Coke himself, then Attorney General, James Walrond, Autumn Reader of the Middle Temple in 1601, and Francis Moore of the same society, counsel to the University of Oxford and 'one of the ablest lawyers of his day' (*D.N.B.*). A twelvemonth after Tylney's death, the Lord Chancellor heard the case and gave his decree. Emery Tylney had disclaimed having any title; Thomas had produced no witnesses, but at the hearing the Chancellor as a favor examined the same three 'credible and substantial witnesses' *viva voce* on the defendant's interrogatories. Instead of proving that Philip had intended the 'scribled papers' as his will, 'contrarywise' the witnesses testified that they had never heard of the papers till they were found in Philip's study after his death. Though the will purported to leave the lands to Philip's executors during Emery's life, then to Thomas for life, it named no executors, nor was it subscribed by any witnesses. Since the papers were so 'fowly blotted defaced and enterlyned' that no perfect sense or construction could be collected from them, the Chancellor decided that he could not accept them as a will. Accordingly, he decreed that Buc, the common-law heir, should quietly enjoy the lands unless the defendant could show better evidence or recover at common law.[2]

---

1 'The xijth of Marche,' records his neighbor Adam Winthrop of Groton, 'Mr. Philip Tilney Esquire Died.' It was with 'Mr. Dr. Meriton' that Winthrop arranged his resignation as Auditor of Trinity College, Cambridge, dining with him in Hadleigh: *Winthrop Papers* (*Massachusetts Historical Soc.*, 1929), I, 65, 75, 103.

2 Depositions, C 24/299/13; Decrees and Orders 1602A, ff. 78, 180, 281, 397, 510, 511, 608, 672; 1602B, ff. 76, 106, 206, 304, 399, 533, 542, 543, 713; 1603A, ff. 505, 742, 748; 1603B, ff. 366, 466, 475.

By this legal victory Buc secured a landed property and a suddenly increased income; in the nick of time, for had he been an impoverished loser, James would probably neither have knighted him nor granted him the reversion of the Revels. Indeed, in May 1603 a patent was granted to Edward Glascock, a young courtier of Castle Heding- ham, Essex, who was a barrister of Gray's Inn and M.A. of both Universities. He had married the daughter of Chief Justice Catlyn, and since she was the widow of Sir John Spencer of Althorpe, he had influential connections in Lord Chamberlain Hunsdon and Lord Chancellor Eger- ton, while his stepson Robert Spencer was reputed the richest man in England. But his patent for the Revels reversion is marked 'stayed,' no doubt through the influ- ence of Buc's patrons, Cecil and the Howards. Glascock died on September 2, 1604, and in the same year, in a Chancery suit brought by Sir Thomas Gardiner (son of Shakespeare's adversary) against Edward Glascock the elder, the father is quoted as saying that his late son Ed- ward 'was in great busines at the Court' but had impover- ished and 'coosened him, by receaving the rent*es*' in his father's stead.[1]

Buc's patent passed on June 23, 1603, and with it a commission giving him the same wide powers entrusted to Tyllney in 1581.[2] At Elizabeth's funeral 'Mr George Bucke Esqr for the bodie' was allowed mourning to the amount of nine yards for himself and six for his servants.[3] Lyly, also an Esquire for the Body, was given only seven and four yards. Under James, Buc became a Gentleman of the Privy Chamber. Like most of the other chief offi-

---

1 *Harl. Soc.*, xiv, 576; Baker, *Northampton*, i, 109; T. Wright, *Essex*, ii, 286; *Alumni Cantabrigienses*; Feuillerat, *Materialien*, xxi, 439; C 24/312/36.
2 *Patent Roll*, 1 Jas. I, pt. 24, mm. 25, 31; cf. *Eliz. Stage*, i, 99.
3 L. C. 2/4(4), a reference which has superseded that given for the same docu- ment in *Eliz. Stage*, i, 96.

cers of the Crown, he was caught in the King's miraculous draught and knighted in the royal garden at Whitehall on July 23.[1]

The 'Griffins talons,' however, were reluctant to unclasp. In May 1603, James Segar (written also Sugar) made affidavit that Thomas Tylney had broken the decree (served by Buc's footboy), and an attachment was ordered for contempt. Twelve months passed before he responded, stating that he had written Buc for further time because the 'terrors Courtrolles and writinges' were not yet ready and 'because he thought yt not convenient to sende them by sutch a youthe as was sente vnto him for the same.' He has warned the tenants to be careful how they pay rent to Buc, lest they should happen to pay it twice, for he has 'some hope to recover the landes againe.'[2]

The next suit tells us more about Buc himself. Two days after receiving the Revels reversion, he filed a bill in Chancery against John Petty, who had served Philip Tylney 'euen from his Childhood' and had long been Tylney's confidential clerk. Three months after his master's death, says the bill, Petty came to Buc and 'did muche insynuate and thruste him self into your saide Orato^rs famyliaritie,' affirming that he knew so much about Buc's right to the lands that without his help Buc should never recover them, and 'vowinge withall that no man in Englande could doe him that good but he.' Buc, 'Consideringe in howe many daungers he stoode' and that the suit could not be speedily ended without evidences which Petty possessed, especially a deed from Margaret conveying all her Lincolnshire lands to Buc, in the end agreed to reward Petty for his information and aid. The clerk demanded a bond assuring him certain closes in

1 Nichols, *Progresses of James*, I, 215.
2 D. & O. 1602A, ff. 608, 672; C 24/308/84.

Boston, when they should be won by his means. As soon
as he had extracted this bond from Buc, he went to 'olde
Emerye Tilney' and by threatening to 'marre all their
matters' got a hundred-pound reward for promising to
help the Tylneys and 'not to Cleave or adhere' to Buc.
He then kept carefully out of the way until Buc 'by his
owne meanes and industrie had recouered the saide landes,'
upon which he bobbed up and demanded his reward.
When Buc answered that he thought the other would not
for shame demand it, Petty with much threatening replied
that he would not only sue on the bond but that he could
and would overthrow all Buc's title and decree. Accordingly, he goes about to slander Buc and impair his title by
'secreete Complottinge*s* and Cunnynge devises' with
Buc's adversaries. The most interesting statement in the
bill was interlined afterwards: that Petty at the sealing of
the bond told how

> Thomas Tilney and one Edmond Tilney M^r of the Revells had com-
> plotted & agreed together howe & vpon what Considerac*i*on the said
> Edmond Tilney should take vpon him to be execut o^r of the said
> Phillip[s] Tilneys supposed last will & testam^t

Edmund plainly had energy enough for the Revels Office
and to spare when he could consider taking on the further
responsibility of a contested executorship, by no means a
bed of roses.

After a perfunctory and unconvincing first answer,
Petty tried in a further answer to avoid the issue of his own
non-performance and to say everything he could against
Buc and his right to the land. Happening to meet one day
at the Temple, his story goes, Buc marveled that Petty
would be so much against him over the land, invited him to
his lodging and to dine and sup with him, and promised
that he would so prefer Petty about the Court that the
best man in Suffolk should be glad to seek unto him for his

favor and friendship. The canny clerk insisted on the
more solid reward of land, secured by a bond, in return for
which he promised to help only Buc and, unless forced by
oath, not to acknowledge what he knew on the contrary
part — for if he had, he declares, he could have done Buc
far more harm than the value of the reward. Thus se-
duced by Buc's fair promises, 'fayned & grounded wholie
vppon Subtiltie,' he lost the friendship of the Tylneys,
'by whome he was in verie great likelihode to haue bin
advanced aboue Three Hundred poundes,' as well as his
chance of recovering household stuff which he claims he
had bought from Philip. To prove 'how extremlie the
said Philip Tylney abhored' Buc, he offers to show a copy
of a letter (answering a spiteful letter from Buc about
January, 1600–01) which he carried for his master to King
Street, Westminster (the scene of Spenser's death), where
Buc then lodged — 'at a Taylors howse,' he adds with
malicious relish, 'being an alehowse.' His master told
Petty that he wished to exclude Buc from ever having any
part of his lands, but feared that after his death Buc
would come in with some counterfeit or forged deed as
from his aunt. For this there was no remedy but to sell the
lands, which he planned to do. Philip also related that
Buc 'told one Edmonde Tylney Esquire [then] [1] Master
of the office of the Revells that the said Margaret Smythe
hadd giuen him the said Complainante all her landes after
her death or after the death of the said Philip.' Upon this
he wrote and visited his mother (now about eighty) to
persuade her not to do so, whereupon 'she vseing manie
sharpe speaches of the said Complainante in sheweinge her
dislike of him . . . quothe she doth he so report . . . I never
promised him anie parte thereof and for his lustines wheras
I purpossed to giue him a hundred poundes after my death

1 Deleted as an error.

he shall not haue one penie.' On an altar tomb in Shelley
Church this lady lies in state, not as a mere Smith but as
Dame Margaret Tylney. Beside her Boston estate, she
was lady of the three manors of Haverhill.[1] Her husband's
first wife was 'Anne daughter of William Britton of London'[2] — which accounts for one of the sisters, whose fortunes Grosart could not trace, of Nicholas Breton.

Walking in Paul's once, Petty says, Buc offered that if
he would give up the bond he should have a sixth part of
Margaret's personal goods, which he might help to recover; Petty answered him 'that now his turne was serued
he would shift of gladlie this deffendant wth so smalle a
matter.' Further to show Buc's 'vnthankfullnes toward*es*
alle men' Petty says he has heard that Buc promised
Thomas Smith, who knew the law and who was Margaret's
stepson, fifty pounds for his counsel if successful, but after
winning told him 'he ought him nothing nor nothing would
paie,' and only offered him something by way of benevolence. Smith says 'that his Resolute purpose is to sue'
Buc on the promise, 'for that otherwise he never thinketh
to haue penie of him.'[3]

Of the witnesses Buc produced to make good his account
of the affair, the first was his former opponent, Emery
Tylney. The old man indignantly tells how Petty used
many plausible words, promising never to help Buc, and
saying that his service would do the Tylneys a thousand
marks', or pounds', worth of good; he even 'pretended
∧$^{\&\ still\ doth}$ for mariage wth one of this dep^{tes} daughters.'
Emery faithfully paid the hundred pounds, but how well
Petty has kept his word the sequel shows. George Pype

---

1 Copinger, *Manors of Suffolk*, v, 241.
2 Metcalfe, *Visitations of Suffolk*, p. 65.
3 Smith entered the Middle Temple in 1572–3 (*Minutes of Parliament of the
   Middle Temple*, 1, 192). He made an affidavit in this case, not extant, but
   mentioned in D. & O. 1604A, f. 487.

of Barnards Inn testifies that Buc sent him to remind Petty of his part of the bargain, who merely answered, 'what wittnes hath Sʳ George Bucke to that?'

William Segar, who as deputy to Buc licensed *Troilus* and several other plays in 1608–09, was clearly the herald and writer, apparently praised also by Meres among the chief English painters of the time.[1] The depositions in this case show that he was one of Buc's closest friends, and make unnecessary Chambers' tentative conjecture[2] that his status was that of an 'assessor' such as those whom the Archbishop and the Lord Mayor were authorized to appoint in 1589 (there is no evidence that they ever did). Buc's brother-in-law, 'Mʳ francis Heydon preacher *p*arson of Brodwater in Sussex,' tells how in June 1602 he witnessed the sealing of the bond at Buc's lodging in the Old Bailey 'at the house of wᵐ Segar now Garter.'[3] 'W: Segar Garter principall King of Armes' (as he signs himself in a triumphant hand, having just succeeded in displacing Dethick for the second time) remembers that Petty often resorted to his house, 'for that he had borne the Compˡᵗ in hand that he would do him speciall helpe,' and that Buc 'did very much beleeve him' and in the end yielded to seal a bond '(thoughe this depᵗ *p*erswaded him to the Contrary).' Petty first demanded a bond of a thousand pounds, then fell to five hundred, and at last three hundred. After

1 Meres in *Palladis Tamia* heads his list of limners with Hilliard and of painters with '*William* and *Francis Segar*, brethren.' I do not find the identification made either in lives of the herald or dictionaries of artists, but it seems very probable, considering that a herald showed his chief skill in painting, and that the name of Garter's father was also Francis.
2 *Eliz. Stage*, I, 319.
3 Lord Grey noted at the time of Biron's embassy that 'Mr. Buck is lodged at an herald's house in the Old Baily,' and in a letter to Cotton in 1605 Buc gave the same address. Segar, September 13, 1604, stated his age as fifty or thereabouts, so that he must have been Garter till close on eighty. Heydon was fifty-one, and fifty-five when he deposed in another suit in 1608 at 'Brighthelmston' (Requests 2/441). Cf. KB 29/228 (Hil. 35 Eliz.) and 230, m. 41*d*.

the sealing he desired to go apart with Buc into his study, where it was expected that he would reveal the important secrets he had promised. But after a quarter of an hour he took his leave, and Segar, seeing Buc 'to looke somethinge [solemn] sadly vpon the matter asked him if the def^t had discovered vnto him any such thing*es* as he looked for/ no by my troth (quoth the Comp^{lt}) he hath told me nothinge more then I knew before I feare he will cosen me.' He never kept his promise to come again when he had more time, nor did anything for Buc except write 'certen frivolous letters importinge that he would assuredly bee p^{r}sent at the hearing . . . if he could possibly recover his health'; but Heydon has seen him in Westminster Hall attending upon Buc's adversaries, aiding the Tylneys because of the bond he got underhand from them.

If Buc had anything to do with the Revels at this time, his duties must have been much interrupted. The case dragged on from 1603 to 1604–5, when Petty, who had failed to bring in the bond, was returned by the sheriff of Lincolnshire as not to be found in his bailiwick, and a commission of rebellion issued against him; and even to 1605–6, when in January he was given two days to produce his witnesses, and in May peremptorily ordered to do so, followed by an order that the testimony should be considered closed. It is a safe conclusion that Buc won, for he died possessed of 'the Shuftes' in Boston, the lands in question.[1]

Not only had Buc to follow the suit against Petty, as a defence against the latter's common-law action on the

---

1 Pleadings, C 2 Jas. I/B 21/49; depositions, C 24/309/10; orders, D. & O. 1603A, ff. 149, 465, 819, 827, 1012; 1603B, ff. 142, 542, 548, 639; 1604A, ff. 487, 502; 1604B, f. 541; 1605B, ff. 388, 574, 629. 'Farther Shuftes' and hither or 'Heather Shuftes,' late belonging to the Guild of Corpus Christi, were hard by 'le Eight hundreth ffen.' The name posed even the faithful historian, Pishey Thompson (*History of Boston*, p. 257). Buc leased the first to a John Pishey.

bond, but at the same time he was suing in Chancery to stay a certain William Becher's execution against him as surety for William Higate. Higate had bought silk from Becher and paid him with a statute for two hundred pounds in 22 Eliz., the year in which Buc succeeded his father, though as he was still under age his signature would hardly have been legally binding. Higate was in 1580 even younger, being only sixteen, the son of Thomas Higate or Heygate, field marshal general of the army before St. Quentin in 1557 and provost marshal in Scotland. William later served with Leicester in the Low Countries, while his brother Thomas was provost marshal general under Essex at Cadiz and died in 1616.[1] He left a son Thomas, probably the Thomas Heygate who in that year has verses before William Browne's *Britannia's Pastorals*.

William Becher was a prominent financier of the day who had been bankrupt, convicted of transporting corn, and thrice outlawed, and who in June 1604 was described by an indignant plaintiff as now prisoner in the Fleet, 'where yt should seeme he purposeth to make his habitacion and vexe disturbe and molest many of yor Ma^{tes} Loyall and good subiect*es* w^{t}h vniust sutes w^{t}hout takinge any course to paie his debt*es*.'[2] The pleadings in *Buc v. Becher* have not been found, but on reading Becher's answer the Lord Chancellor was inclined to agree with Buc and stayed the execution (1604–5). A year later he ordered the examination of witnesses in the country by Sir Henry and Sir Thomas Beaumont and two other knights of Leicestershire.[3]

1 Nichols, *Leicester*, IV, 628; *S. P. Spanish, 1580–86*, p. 556; *Harl. Soc.*, LXV, 87.
2 Requests 2/332, *Stephen Ridlesden esq. v. William Becher and John Quarles*.
3 D. & O. 1604A, ff. 454, 483; 1604B, ff. 504, 537; 1605A, f. 92; 1605B, ff. 88, 388, 536.

III. DAPHNIS

In the spring of 1605 Buc went once more to Spain with
the Lord Admiral, but this time to celebrate the new-made
peace. The embassy was in Spain from April 15 to the end
of June, and each gentleman was presented to the King
and Queen, 'every one after other bowing himselfe in
obeysance and kissing the skirt of Her Highnesse kirtle'.
Buc was one of the twenty-six English knights, richly clad
in black velvet, who with captains and gentlemen and their
servants made up a train of over six hundred — six hundred heretics, wrote Góngora in satiric verse, on whom
Spain was wasting a million in jewels and revels and wine.
The masks and revels must have furnished Buc material
for his commentary on the art. At Corunna, where the English celebrated the feast of St. George, the Spaniards presented a mask of the Judgement of Paris, followed by
barriers in which the English joined. The Duke of Lerma
entertained them in his patio, after a splendid banquet to
music never ceasing, with a comedy by de los Rios' company, possibly one of the two hundred and twenty already
written by Lope. At Court in Valladolid 'the King himself
was an Actor' in the mimic battle of canes, and the Duke
of Alva and other nobles in the 'desperate hunting of the
Bull.' Conspicuous in the final 'mask of enchantment'
was the little Infanta,[1] enthroned on a chariot as on a gal-
ley, under a roof of stars like the vault of heaven; and with
pavans and galliards and the ancient Spanish torch-dance
the embassy ended — except for the return journey, on
which the English lamented their lodgings in mountain
villages among bears and wolves.

In 'Sʳ Charles Cornwallis his Negotiation as Liedger

1 Anne of Austria, then aged four, later Louis XIII's queen.

Embassador for Spayne' we find a letter to Buc, written from Valladolid about September 1605.[1] The ambassador signs himself 'Yo[r] assured loving freind & Ally,' an allusion explained when he writes, 'I thanke you much for yo[r] kinde Care of my poore wife yo[r] kinswoman.' This was Anne Barrow (widow of Sir Ralph Shelton, not Skelton as in the *D.N.B.*), who was descended from Sir John Buck. Cornwallis had been slighted in a matter of precedence by Nottingham, whom he wrote on September 2 to 'have in memorie that himselfe was borne onely M[r]: *Charles Howard*, as I was borne *Charles Cornwalyes*.'[2] Hence his remark to Buc that God and time have 'made Paules Steeple knowne to bee but a Steeple, & poore White-Chappell a Church though low & little, yet in his measure, not vnfitt for the vse it is put vnto.' He assures 'Worthy S[r]: George,' however, that he would have written long before 'if I could have effected anie thing to the content of you & those other of my good freinds whome you mencioned in yo[r] l̄r̄e.' The most distinguished of these was probably Charles Blount, Earl of Devonshire, and it is interesting to learn of Buc's friendship with that scholarly nobleman. Cornwallis writes:

> I pray Commend my humble service to my lo: of Deuonshire & when the booke hee desireth shall bee finished I will by Gods grace conveigh it safely vnto his Lo[pp] to whome I shall neuer want a desire to performe anie acceptable service.
>
> I heare nothing here of anie booke written of the enterteynem[t]: giuen to my lo: Ad: Hee came, hee was here, hee is gone; & soe is his memorie saue onely in the shopps of this Cittie where the Spanish Gallantes will as they say continue it yet for a yeare or two.

Buc was evidently eager to see the official Spanish account of the embassy, which was in fact written by Antonio de

---

1 *Harleian MS.* 1875, f. 115[v].
2 *Idem*, f. 89[v].

Herrera, 'Chief Chronicler of the Indies' and author of
The General History of America.

In the same year Buc published his Δαφνις Πολυστεφανος,
*An Eclog treating of Crownes, and of Garlandes, and to whom
of right they appertaine.* The most amusing thing about
this poem is the *D.N.B.*'s description of it as 'an explanation of the nature and properties of trees.' [1] The one tree
which it does explain is the family tree of the kings of England, the 'Genest Plant.' In fifty-seven stanzas of fluent
but undistinguished verse 'Silenus the Prophet of the
Shepheards' reviews at the request of 'Damaetus a Wood-
man' the whole line of Plantagenets. He considers 'The
greatest *Britanne* King' Henry II, under whom Madoc
discovered America and who by searching out Arthur's
tomb in Avalon redeemed him 'from the iniurious imputation of a fabulous *Heros.*' In gratitude to James, however,
he explains that Apollo has reserved the chief garland for
his favorite Daphnis, king and poet.

Buc writes that he began the poem 'long since, but then
the end was *in nubibus.*' He has clearly shown it to many
friends, since he answers their criticisms. Sir Walter Buc
comes into the poem under King John, with a reference to
Camden and Holinshed for the story of his winning of Ely.
A hymn and two Latin epigrams follow the eclogue. James
probably enjoyed the flattery and the serried marginal
notes referring to authors from Lycophron to Hakluyt.
Buc's poem is more arrayed with learning even than his
History. Anyone might write verse, but not even Ben
Jonson — to whom there is a reference in the margin —
could document it more impressively.

An unnoticed Chaucer allusion occurs in the preface,[2]

---

1 Bullen appears to have formed his idea of the poem entirely from Corser, who
  happens to quote a few verses on trees (*Chetham Soc.*, LXXI, 167).
2 Sig. B 4.

where Buc is supporting the union of Britain under one crown by arguments drawn from medieval authors and even from so recent a book as *Toxophilus*:

Whereupon (to note also by the way) some thinke that the word *Anglia* was sometimes vsed for the whole Isle, and which *Ion Lidgate* disertly asseuereth in King *Arthurs* complaint in these words, *Great Britain now called England*: and so doth *Geffrey Chaucer* in the *Franklins* tale (viz.) *In England, that Clepid was Britain*: And Ranulfus Cestrensis a grauer Authour. . . . [Higden in the *Polychronicon*].

The quotation from Lydgate is not from Arthur's lament in *The Falls of Princes*, and Buc seems to be quoting a *King Arthur's Complaint* which, so far as I can learn, is no longer known.

Buc's inscription in the copy of Δαφνις which he presented to Ellesmere has been discussed time and again since it was first printed in 1812, and we have seen something of the controversy it has provoked. It is surprising, therefore, that no one has ever mentioned a similar presentation copy in the British Museum, inscribed by Buc to the Earl of Northampton.[1] The hand is the same carefully printed Italian which he used when addressing Ellesmere and later Arundel, and once again we have the very forms of the individual letters which Dr. Tannenbaum in his haste pronounced 'impossible' and 'absurd.' The inscription provides still another warning as to the rashness of branding a piece of writing as a forgery without taking the trouble to compare it with every possible example of the hand in question.

Before he presented his pastoral to Northampton, Buc very carefully corrected the text with his pen, adding parentheses here, a diaeresis there, changing 'Hertford' to 'Hereford,' 'datus' to 'datur,' and paying special attention

1 The Grenville copy, G. 11553. See facsimile.

to double letters, exactly as he did also when going over the 1611–12 Revels Accounts. All these changes correspond to the list of 'Faults escaped in the Printing' which occurs in other copies. In the same brown ink used for these corrections and for the inscription to Northampton, the legend on the chart of Plantagenet descent, 'I.W.S. delineauit. Ioan. Woutneel excud. 1602,' has the date altered to '1605.' The same change is made in other copies of the poem, and it may indicate, as Collier suggested, that Buc like Cecil and many more had taken care to be ready for the rising sun.

Among other gift copies of the *Eclog* Buc sent one to Sir Edward Coke. When the Chief Justice's private catalogue of his library turned up a few years ago, it was found that the only English poets he possessed were Chaucer, Spenser, Daniel, a presentation manuscript of *Nosce Teipsum*, and 'A book of English verses, *inter alia* of Garland's.' The Librarian of Holkham naturally lamented its disappearance, writing, 'This might have contained something unique.' [1] It seems quite safe, however, to identify it with Buc's *Eclog treating of Crowns, and of Garlands*, especially since it was to Coke that Buc later presented his manuscript of *The Third University of England*.

Buc was above all things a lover of the Middle Ages and a scholar, and it is natural to find him associating with the other men of learning who formed the Antiquarian Society. One of the Cotton manuscripts preserves notes headed 'Constabularius Anglie. Justitiarius Anglie.' and signed 'G. Buc.' [2] They are written on the back of one of eight discourses on the High Constable of England, another of which bears the date November 27, 1602. The custom of

1 C. W. James, *Chief Justice Coke* (1929), p. 314; *The Library*, March, 1931, p. 442.
2 *Titus C.* 1, f. 35ᵛ, printed by the editors of Hearne's *Collection of Curious Discourses* in 1773 (II, 88).

Illustrissimo viro, D. Henrico
Howard, baroni de Marnhill,
Comiti de Northampton, V. portu-
um custodi, Connestabulario
castri de Dover, a regis matis
S. consilijs. &cc. . . . . F.V.

Sit quamvis gravibus felix obnoxia VIRTVS,
INVICTAM SOLAM tu tamen esse doces.

G. BUC.

BUC'S ITALIAN HAND: A NEW EXAMPLE

the Society was to choose a subject on which each member prepared an essay, and one might naturally assume that Buc was a member and read his paper on that date. A citation from Selden, however, who was born only in 1584, shows that Buc must have given Cotton these notes (from medieval chronicles) some years after the King's suppression of the Society in 1604.

On the eve of his Spanish voyage — for the date March 24, 1605, cannot here mean 1605-6 — Buc, though having 'many businesses & more then I can finish before I go,' yet took time to fulfill Cotton's request for 'my employment*es* in matters of estate.' To this we owe the full reports of his mission from Cadiz and that to Sir Francis Vere, and he speaks of these as only samples, no doubt the most important. He prays 'Good Sr Robert' to make friendly use of them, for one of them (evidently the one on Prince Maurice and the States) contains secrets which only discreet persons should see. 'If my small library,' he writes, 'may stand you or y^r studies in any stead you shall not fynd the dore shutt against you'; and at his return he hopes to be 'better acquainted wth y^r rich library.'[1]

In the 1600 edition of *Britannia* Camden spoke highly of Buc and thanked him for much historical information, citing his name also in the margin for the account of Walter Buc and the description of Morpeth.[2] To the 1607 edition Buc contributed Latin verses expressing the wish that Camden, the phoenix of the age, having described Britain so vividly and faithfully, would next write the deeds of the British heroes: the work which Camden's scholar Ben Jonson planned to write and which Fuller carried out. Buc entitled his verses, 'Ad amicum suum Guilelmum Camdenum Georgij Buc Equitis aurati Reg. Sp. C. Hepta-

[1] *Cotton MS. Julius C.* iii, f. 47 (which Bullen in the *D.N.B.* interprets as 'Julius Caesar iii.'!)   [2] Sigg. C5, Aaa2^v.

stichon,' expanded by Chambers as 'Regiorum Spectacu-
lorum Curatoris.' ¹ This does not quite warrant us in concluding that Tyllney had probably ceased to perform his
duties between June 29, 1607 and the publication of the
Britannia; ² for in his 1605 *Eclog* Buc had already described himself as 'R. Sp. C.', though Tyllney had not yet
retired. Camden in 1607 does not call him Master (as
Malone stated) but only 'Eques auratus & à regijs spec-
taculis,' which is ambiguous. There is no evidence, indeed,
that Tyllney ever wholly gave up the charge of the Revels,
for he drew up a 'writinge touching his Office' about 1607
and he continued to render the accounts; ³ but Buc was at
least managing the office by 1608. Whether Tyllney allowed him part or all of the licensing of plays for the stage
does not appear.

1 *Eliz. Stage*, I, 104.
2 V. C. Gildersleeve, *Government Regulation in the Elizabethan Drama*, p. 63.
3 *Eliz. Stage*, I, 99–103.

IV. THE KING'S OFFICE OF THE REVELS

The function which we know Buc did perform during Tyllney's mastership was one entirely new to the Revels Office: that of licensing plays for the press. The first instance of this was a special case, Sharpham's *Fleire*, entered on the Stationers' Register May 13, 1606, with a proviso that the publishers must 'bringe good aucthoritie and licence' for its printing. By November 21, when it was transferred, it had been authorized not only by the wardens and a clerical licenser but by Buc.[1] During 1607, when more plays were entered than in any other year, Tyllney licensed one and Buc eighteen (including *King Lear*); during 1608, Buc licensed eleven and his deputy another. It looks rather as though Buc's having to wait until Tyllney should make way for him stirred him to broach a fresh source of income in this important new privilege. It was evidently he who secured it, perhaps through the influence of the Lord Admiral and his cousin Suffolk, Lord Chamberlain. The move was a good one from the point of view of the Government, since instead of the responsibility being divided among various licensers, it would now be centered upon a single office, already familiar with the plays.

From 1607 until 1615 every play licensed bore the signature of Buc or his deputy except one: 'A Yorkshire Tragedy written by Wylliam Shakespere allowed by Master Wilson,' May 2, 1608.[2] Pavier, the publisher responsible for this anomaly, probably did not break the general rule without a reason. The reason may have been that Buc, with his fuller information and his devotion to

1 *Eliz. Stage*, III, 169, 490.
2 Arber, III, 377. Buc sometimes licensed masks of Jonson and Daniel, but not civic pageants or Inns-of-Court masks.

accuracy, was less likely than the clerical licenser to pass
over the ascription to Shakespeare. Either he refused to
do so, or Pavier did not run the risk of trying him. 'The
booke of Pericles' and 'A booke Called Anthony and Cleopatra,' entered by Blount on May 20, were licensed in the
proper way by Buc.[1] The evasion in the case of *A Yorkshire Tragedy* makes it seem probable, therefore, that the
ascription to Shakespeare (which has led to such wild
theories as Fleay's gift of it to Edmond Shakespeare) was
a mere publisher's fiction.

The clearest case in which a distinction is drawn between licensing for the stage and licensing for the press is
that of the *Biron* plays in 1608, the censorship of which
provoked a strong letter of remonstrance from Chapman,
'the poore subject of your office for the present.'[2] Buc's
name does not appear, but it was he who finally licensed
the plays for the press, and Chapman refers to his corre-
spondent as a man of learning. Chapman considers him
very unreasonable not to pass for the press what the Privy
Council thrice allowed for presentment; but there was
certainly reason in Buc's objection that he ought to be
shown the copy which the Council had approved (and
which Chapman specifically mentions that Buc had not
seen) before he could license the new copy submitted to
him. Apparently he had been lenient enough to allow the
play for performance, marking for omission a few lines
which the disobedient Children of the Blackfriars spoke
in spite of him, and he had thus been involved in the storm

---

1 Arber, III, 378. Professor Oliphant, in *Shakespeare and his Fellow Dramatists*
(1929), II, 144, thinks that Shakespeare's *Antony and Cleopatra* might be
much later than this entry because 'we cannot say positively that this "book"
was a play.' Fortunately we can say it positively, for Buc, of course, licensed
only plays.

2 *Athenaeum*, 1901, I, 433; reprinted by Fowell and Palmer, *Censorship in England*, p. 59, and in part by E. M. Albright, *Dramatic Publication in England*,
p. 162.

which the play caused. The French Ambassador protested so vigorously that Salisbury (who himself has several long speeches in the *Conspiracy*, though not named in the printed text) ordered the imprisonment of author and players and the closing of all the theaters.[1] Had this continued, Buc would have had to go whistle for a living, and it is not surprising that after this warning he should be careful to see that the version printed was authorized. As one who was Elizabeth's messenger in arranging for Biron's embassy in 1601, he might indeed have objected to the accuracy of the scene at Elizabeth's court and of her speeches; the important cuts, however, must have been ordered by the Council. It has been assumed that Buc made them, but clearly such scenes as that which particularly offended the Ambassador when acted cannot have been left in the copy which the Council approved. Buc may have originally done somewhat more censoring than the 'two or three lines' Chapman mentions, but the letter does not suggest much more, and its protest is aimed not at any alteration by Buc but at his doubts about licensing the play at all. The whole letter is so haughty that one wonders whether Chapman ever sent it. It was not likely to lead to what actually happened, Buc's licensing the play. This, however, he seems to have been ready to do provided he were shown the allowed copy, and he was probably satisfied either by this precaution or possibly by the guarantee of Suffolk as Lord Chamberlain. One can hardly speak of 'a long delay' in granting the license, since the interval between performance in April and the entry on June 5 was unusually short.

It has seemed somewhat strange that in one season only Buc should turn over to Segar seven plays to license for the press: one entered in the Stationers' Register October 4,

1 *Eliz. Stage*, II, 53; III, 257.

1608, followed by two with Buc's license, then *Troilus and
Cressida* and five more entered under Segar's hand between
January 26 and March 10, after which no plays were entered until in the autumn of 1610 Buc reappears, licensing
Epicœne and *The Alchemist*. This might be partly explained by the fact that most of Segar's licenses occur during the Master's busiest time, that of the winter revels,
and that Buc had his hands especially full because it was
the first year of establishing the Revels Office in new quarters. But the chief reason for Buc's long silence of two
years after October 1608 was illness, as we learn from a
letter to Salisbury which has not before been noticed: [1]

> May it pleas y^r *lordshi*p &cc'. Wheras Sr Charles Howard Knight
> beeing bound by statute, & (wch is aboue all bonds) by his woord, &
> many deep & solemne othes & protestations to pay to mee xx.ɫi p*er*
> an*num* during my life, & vpon such   , & consyderacion as hee him-
> self long sought, & much desired. of wch anuity (notwthhstanding y^e
> premisses) hee for the space of almost 4. yeeres hath paid mee but 14.ɫi
> & odd mony. (besides xx.ɫi.wch with overmuch entreaty, & importun-
> ityes I gott of the Lady his wife: so that now he oweth me 40.ɫi. & hath
> made me spend as much as half the debt cometh too in run*n*ing & ryding
> & sending vp & down after him & for the most p*a*rt by his own appoint-
> ments, & all in vayne. making no conscience either to pay his due dett,
> or to releeue mee wth myne own, & especially in this tyme of my long
> sicknesse & adversity. So that I know not how to come by the mony
> (for I am most vnwilling to arrest him, or to extend his land for the
> honour, wch I beare to the name, wch he beareth.) & therefore I am en-
> forced to appeale to y^r most hon^{ble} fauour, humbly praying y^r L^p (my
> ancient honorable good L.) y^t you wilbee pleased to take such order in
> the Exchequer y^t I may haue my mony payd me out of such fees or
> pensions as hee receyveth ther at those vsuall feasts. & I shalbee bound
> to pray for y^r L^{ps} continuall helth & prosperity, & ever remeyn
> 29. Sept*ember*   Most humble at y^r lordships com*m*andment
>   1609.   G. Buc.

Sir Charles was the Admiral's younger son and successor
as Earl of Nottingham, and he showed himself even more
graceless to Tyllney than to Buc.

1 MSS. at Hatfield, 127/165.

Heywood writes in his *Apology for Actors* of the former palace at St. John's, belonging to the Revels, 'where our Court playes haue beene in late daies yearely rehersed, perfected, and corrected.'[1] When St. John's was granted in 1607 to the King's young cousin Aubigny on his marriage, and Jonson left his roof for that of another patron, the Revels likewise removed from the Priory of the Whitecross Knights to the Priory of the Whitefriars. The Master's office, by March 10, 1607-8, was next to the Whitefriars playhouse,[2] but these quarters were only temporary. Buc now had to rent, 'at a high & dear rate,' a house large enough not only for the office and for his lodging, but for the Revels wardrobe and storehouse; and he got no allowance for his charges until, after Tyllney's death, he presented a petition on July 1, 1611. Before he sent this, Buc cut out two interesting personal paragraphs, praying Salisbury

honorably to consyder y[t] this office is the onely reward of my long, chargeable & faithfull service doon in court & abroad; by land & by sea; in warr & in peace for the space of wellneere 30. yeeres: & is the best meanes of my living,

and hoping favor 'for her sacred sake, who would haue doon mee right, & now raigneth in glory.'[3]

Since each officer under him had £15 a year for lodging, Buc asked for the Master's customary 'treble (or at least double) allowance.' Salisbury accordingly allowed him £30 a year, payable from Allhallows, 1608 (not Michaelmas, as Chambers makes it by momentary confusion with the next warrant).[4] By November 1608, then, Buc was

---

1 Sig. E 1[v].
2 *New Shak. Soc. Trans.*, 1888, p. 275.
3 *Harl. MS.* 6850, f. 258; the letter actually sent is in *S.P.D. Jas.* 65/2, printed by Chalmers, *Apology*, p. 490.
4 *Eliz. Stage*, I, 103. The statement there that Buc protested the amount, and that Salisbury probably turned a deaf ear, is inference only, for in his letter to

certainly responsible for the office, though Tyllney drew beside his salary an allowance of £20 for a house and £15 for the Revels chamber and wardrobe, 'notw^{t}standing y^t hee was not at the charge of hyring of any house: & besides had 100 li for his better reco*m*pense.'[1] The house Buc found for the office was on St. Peter's Hill between Paul's Wharf and Paul's Chain, in the neighborhood of the ghostly old house in *Little Dorrit*. It was conveniently near to the King's Men at the Blackfriars and to the Wardrobe, and it was just across the way from his friends the heralds at the College of Arms.

A later lawsuit, which mentions Ambrose Randolph as the owner, gives a key to the history of this Revels Office. Ambrose was son of Thomas Randolph, Elizabeth's ambassador to Scotland and Russia. Stow describes his dwelling on St. Peter's Hill as 'a large House of antient Building, sometime belonging to the Abbot of St. *Mary* in *York*, and was his abiding House when he came to London.'[2] It was divided into two large residences, of which Buc's office belonged to the ambassador's widow, Ursula Randolph, and after her death in 1617-18 to Ambrose.[3] The other part had been the dwelling of the redoubtable Mistress Julian Penn, who about 1590 had let it out furnished to the Earl of Oxford. Thomas Churchyard gave his bond for the rent, which resulted in the old poet's taking sanctuary while Mistress Penn was reminding Oxford of the Day of Judgement. From 1592 to 1612 the house

---

Salisbury's secretary Buc does not quarrel with the amount. The further £20 was granted him on December 19, 1612, retrospective to Michaelmas 1610 (Cunningham, *Shak. Soc.*, VII, xxii).

1 *Harl. MS.* 6850, f. 258.
2 *Survey of London*, ed. 1720, I, 225.
3 E. A. Fry, *London Inquis. P.M.*, III, 147; *Harl. Soc. Reg.* XL, 267, 270; XLI, 207, 224, 230. One of the scraps on which Buc wrote his *History* is a letter signed 'Ambrose' (Marcham, p. 16); the surname, burnt away, can now be restored as 'Randolph,' since the letter is in his hand.

belonged to her son Sir Michael Hicks, Buc's colleague in the 1597 Parliament.[1]

From 'his Maiesties Office of the Reuels, vpon Saint *Peters* hill,' August 24, 1612, Buc dedicated his account of London as *The Third Universitie of England*.[2] Edmond Howes tells of his fortune in securing this work, which Buc had given and dedicated to Chief Justice Coke,

to be disposed at his Lordshippes pleasure, whereof I hauing aduertisement, became an humble sutor to his lordshippe, that I might haue it to print with the rest, whereunto his Lordshippe very fauourably condescended, and forthwith delivered it vnto mee, with speciall commendation, and approbation, as of a worke worthy the publique Light, and to that purpose gaue his honourable allowance vnder his owne hand.

The treatise is a little book in itself, and well justifies the statement on its titlepage: 'Gathered faithfully out of the best Histories, Chronicles, Records, and Archiues.' Buc has himself pursued the studies he prescribes for heralds: 'they must search old roles & scrowles and peruse authentike records, archiues, olde Charters, euidences, & such like.'[3] After tracing the history of each of the learned foundations of London, especially the schools of divinity and of law, he writes a brief chapter of each of the arts recommended by 'Conte Baldessar,' arts though not academical, yet fit for a gentleman: horsemanship, the science of defence, the arts of shooting and of swimming, poetry and music, dancing, painting, heraldry, and the art of revels.

It is a fact not generally known, but clearly established by the historian of the Temple, that it was following Buc's suggestion in this work that the Middle Temple adopted

1 Mrs. William Hicks Beach, *A Cotswold Family*, p. 71; B. M. Ward, *The Seventeenth Earl of Oxford*, p. 301.
2 Stowe, *Annals*, ed. Howes, 1615; ed. Mundy, 1631.
3 Ed. 1615, sig. Ooo03.

the ensign of the Holy Lamb which it still bears.¹ Buc
mentions having seen it 'enlumined' as a symbol of the
Knights Templars in an ancient MS. book 'belonging
to the right honourable, and most learned noble Gentleman, the Lord *William Howard of Naworth*' — Scott's
'Belted Will.' Of the other ensign of the Templars, two
knights on one horse, he writes that 'I myself haue knowne
a gallant Gentleman yet liuing' who rescued a noble
knight by carrying him on his horse, and he translates a
similar passage from Ariosto, because Haryngton, though
an excellent translator, has 'discosted from the Author.'
In his *History* also he Englishes a stanza from 'the Divine
Ariosto,' 'translated by me long befor' Haryngton's *Orlando* appeared.²

    As is natural considering his friendship with Segar, Buc
is an ardent admirer of the art of painting, 'an Art not
now accounted ingenuous or fit for a Gentleman,' but
which he defends against those who account it base and
mechanical. He cites as witnesses in its favor Aristotle,
Castiglione, Pliny, Gregorio de Alfaro, and Alexander
Neapolitanus 'in his booke of *Geniall* dayes.' His cham-
pionship does not include painting of the face, on which
subject he translates an epigram of Lucilius, not from the
Latin but from Greek. Particularly interesting are the
projects for the improvement of London in which he recom-
mends the richer merchants to bequeath their wealth
rather than let it 'bee ryotously consumed by acolastes ³
and ungracious heyres': to free the walls from tenements
and gardens, and bring a river or fresh current into the

1 J. B. Williamson, *History of the Temple*, p. 371, and *Genealogist*, N. S. xxxvi, 118.
2 *Cotton Tiberius E.* x, f. 82.
3 The *O.E.D.* records only one instance of this word for a prodigal, in the form 'acolaust,' 1633. It was familiar in the Latin plays of *Acolastus*. The verb 'to discost,' above, is not given in the figurative sense until about 1677.

town ditch; 'to enlarge the cumbersome and dangerous straites of the royall and most publique wayes'; 'to make a faire Piazza, or Market place within London, such as is and ought to be in euery good cittie' — which shows the influence of Italy, and probably of his journey to Spain; and many other such plots ('whereof I haue a iolly Catalogue').[1] His stately Latin verses in praise of the metropolis, like Dunbar's ballade, reveal the true lover of London.

As Master, Buc with his four personal servants attended at Court from Allhallows till the beginning of Lent, and at other times whenever embassies or other special events gave occasion for shows or triumphs. In the Revels Accounts for 1611–12, *The Tempest* and *The Winter Night's Tale* head the list of 'Plays & Inventions' which he had chosen, reformed, and rehearsed before they were acted at Court. Next year he had the King's Men give the same two again, and such others as *Much Ado about Nothing*, *The Moor of Venice*, 'Cardenno,' 'The Hotspur,' and 'Sir John ffalstafe.'[2] He received an allowance of £16 this winter in lieu of lodgings at the Court, which was especially crowded for the marriage of Princess Elizabeth to the Palsgrave.[3] During these years Buc was licensing, as well as producing at Court, plays by Shakespeare and Jonson, Webster and Tourneur, Beaumont and Fletcher. As to the sort of corrections he made, we have a few hints in the manuscripts of such plays as *The Second Maiden's Tragedy* and *Sir John Van Olden Barnavelt*.

The first of these Buc himself christened, finding it without a name when he licensed it on October 31, 1611. Of the various changes in the manuscript, Dr. Greg in his Malone Society edition has shown that only a few can safely be assigned to the censor's hand, the surest being

1 Ed. 1615, sig. Nnnn 5ᵛ. 2 *Eliz. Stage*, IV, 177–180.
3 *Eliz. Stage*, I, 103.

those against which Buc has put a cross in the margin. There has been no satisfactory discussion of the censor's reasons for his alterations, or of how far he actually deleted oaths.[1] These questions can be treated only in connection with the other plays of the time and especially with the censorship of *Barnavelt*, which has been still less understood.

The Privy Council, in June 1617, wrote requiring Buc upon his peril to suffer no performances of an intended play concerning the late Marquis d'Ancre, assassinated two months earlier in France.[2] When Sir John van Oldenbarnevelt was executed on May 13, 1619, a hostile pamphleteer in *The Golden Legend of the New St. John* compared him with d'Ancre as an ambitious conspirator against his native land, and Fletcher and Massinger promptly put him into a play.[3] Instead of refusing the play because of its subject, Buc undertook to correct it, though the manuscript does not bear his license. The play was forbidden by the Bishop of London, but eventually allowed and acted before large crowds.[4]

In the absence of Buc's office books we have only a few records of his acts as Master, but enough to show the authority he enjoyed over the world of players and entertainers. He gave a license on September 6, 1610, 'to shew a strange Lion, brought to doo strange thing*es*) as turning an oxe to be rosted.'[5]   For a license to erect a new play-

---

1 Cf. Gildersleeve, p. 109; Fowell and Palmer, p. 62; E. M. Albright, pp. 122, 190.

2 *Malone Soc. Collections*, I, 279; *Acts of the Privy Council, 1616–17*, p. 267.

3 *The Tragedy of Sir John Van Olden Barnavelt*, ed. W. P. Frijlinck (Amsterdam, 1922).

4 Fleay, followed by Greg and others, supposed that 'my Lo: of London' was the Lord Mayor, but gave no instance of this unprecedented use of the phrase which regularly refers to a bishop. Chambers takes it without question as the Bishop (*William Shakespeare*, I, 110, 115).

5 *S.P.D. Jas.* 57/45.

house in the Whitefriars he received £20 on July 13, 1613, probably from Rossiter or Henslowe.¹ It suggests a certain financial talent to have extracted such a sum from either of them, for a fee such as no other Master seems to have secured, and especially for a playhouse which so far as we know was never built. He may have allowed Rossiter to transfer the license to his Blackfriars venture of 1615. Heming, Burbage, and all the other actors in London on March 29 of that year were summoned before the Council for playing in Lent despite the command of the Lord Chamberlain signified to them by the Master of the Revels. In 1616–17, however, and in 1618–19, the rule was relaxed and they were allowed to play on paying Buc for a dispensation.²

In July 1615, Buc wrote that he had consented to the formation of John Daniel's company called the Youths of Her Majesty's Royal Chamber of Bristol, approved by the King through the Queen's mediation in behalf of Samuel Daniel. He also reminded the Lord Chamberlain's secretary that the Revels officers had received no wages since December 1613.³ In one of the stray notes preserved in the MS. of his *History* he complains that Robert Kirkham, Clerk of the Signet, has secured a warrant for twice the amount properly due his late father (Edward Kirkham, Yeoman of the Revels). Among other notes is one to a 'mᵣ Later for so I hear youᵘ ar ca⟨lled⟩,' who has used contemptuously someone bearing Buc's license, which insolent wrong to the King's authority he is commanded to amend.⁴

1 Adams, *Dramatic Records of Sir Henry Herbert*, p. 42.
2 *A.P.C. 1615–16*, p. 86; Adams, p. 48.
3 Not '13 Dec.' as in the *D.N.B.*: *S.P.D.Jas.* 81/12. Buc's letter of course had nothing to do with the licensing authority granted Samuel Daniel in 1603–4, as Miss Albright supposes (p. 51). Her date for the patent, and that of Chambers (*Mal. Soc. Coll.*, I, 279; *Eliz. Stage*, II, 68), are corrected by Chambers' text of the patent.
4 Marcham, *The King's Office of the Revels*, pp. 45, 42.

It was probably from seeing Buc's name on the license that the town clerk of Bristol called a company which acted there in the summer of 1618 'Sir George Bucks players.' Professor Murray suggests that it was a Children of the King's Revels company, and it may have been one of those that played at Leicester the same year.[1] *Twelfth Night* and *The Winter's Tale* were acted at Court that Easter. The following year '*Pirrocles, Prince of Tyre,*' lasting till two in the morning, was played at Whitehall before the Marquis de la Tremouille.[2]

At the age of fifty-five Buc contemplated marriage, as we learn from a letter of Ambrose Randolph to his father-in-law Thomas Wilson on April 5, 1618:

Sir, my wife and I beinge lately with my cosen Edmond Mewtys his wife, wee had there by chance some speach of s^r George Bucke and my cosen Elizabeth howe fittly they would be matched together, the one desiring a maide of good yers the other an oulde knight. This I take to be the occasion of my vncles writing to me, to which I have answred that I think the knight may easily be perswaded to like my cosen with a thousand pounds, for so he hath tould me of some other of less merit then she, and that I doubte not but s^r Geo: will be glad of so good an offer: but of his humorous and shie proseeding I saide nothinge only I haue let him knowe howe willinge and glad I shall be not only to further the matter but allso to effecte it or any other thing in my powere.[3]

Wilson was Keeper of the Records at Whitehall, and on marrying his only daughter Dorothy, Randolph was joined with him in the office. It was about this time that Wilson sent Fulke Greville, for Sidney's sake, a copy of the translation of Montemayor's *Diana* which he had made on his travels in 1596 and dedicated to Southampton.[4] From the

1 J. T. Murray, *English Dramatic Companies*, II, 12, 218, 312–313.
2 Chambers, *William Shakespeare*, II, 346.
3 *S.P.D.Jas.* 97/8. The *Calendar* has concealed it by indexing the page as 553 instead of 533. The one-line summary there printed mistakes Elizabeth for a daughter of Wilson.
4 Printed in *Revue Hispanique*, L (1920), 367.

mention of the wife of Edmond Meautis, 'cosen Elizabeth' may be identified as Mrs. Wilson's niece Elizabeth, daughter of Thomas Meautis of West Ham and sister of Edmond and of Sir Thomas Meautis, Bacon's secretary and successor at Gorhambury. Instead of becoming my lady and a rich widow, she married John Claxton, a Suffolk squire and kinsman of Buc.[1] Sir George's 'humorous and shie proseeding' becomes very comprehensible when one discovers Mrs. Dorothy Randolph's relentless ardor in the making of marriages. She carried on a remarkable correspondence with another Meautis cousin, the mother of Sir Frederick (later Lord) Cornwallis, for whom she sought a bride among at least eleven various young women, not to mention the eleven daughters of the Earl of Bridgewater (remembered for *Comus*, but whom she disposes of as merely 'some of the nobility, which I harkened not to, becaus I think you desire not to match with them'). She sends Mr. Randolph to view the candidates, and on the portion of each she gives the current quotations, 'for,' she writes, 'I doe most ernestly desire to se him maried.'[2] Sir George would have liked to continue his family name, but his desire for actual marriage may have been less earnest than his hope of causing some consternation and change of heart among his heirs.

For his only brother was outlawed, an exile from the realm. The first hint of this comes from another overlooked letter in the *State Papers*, which he wrote to Sir Thomas Studder on November 16, 1615.[3] Studder is an elusive person, but we learn from Edmondes' despatches

---

1 *Harl. Soc.* XIII, 247; LXI, 195.
2 [Lord Braybrooke], *Private Correspondence of Lady Jane Cornwallis*; 3 *N. and Q.* i, 483.
3 *S.P.D. Jas.* 83/36. The *Calendar* erroneously assigns to the Admiral what Buc says of 'one great Howard more yᵗ bears office in the state' — Suffolk, Lord Treasurer.

that he was a follower of Sir Francis Vere and became Sergeant Major of the English Regiment in the Archduke's service, said to be recruited by Catesby to be in readiness for the Gunpowder Plot. Immediately afterwards Studder headed a faction against its Colonel, Lord Arundell of Wardour, which ended in a mutiny and the cashiering of all the chief officers. His close connection with the Jesuits is supported by the statement of Anthony Greenway *alias* Tilney on entering the English College at Rome in 1606 that he owed his conversion partly to Studder.[1]

Sir Thomas, it appears, had desired Buc to mediate with the Howards for help in redressing wrongs received 'in those p*artes*,' not specified. Buc replies, 'I reco*m*mended your sute to my L. Admirall, & that is all that I can doo,' for though Suffolk 'is I hope my very good L.,' Buc does not wish to stretch his credit by soliciting any such suits. Though he delivered the enclosed packet to the Countess of Suffolk, he now fears that its contents were offensive to the King or State, since the messenger was imprisoned and he was ordered to send the King Studder's other letters. Therefore, though he signs himself 'y^r very loving frend,' he bids Studder send any further intelligence to those who are authorized to deal in such matters, 'of wch number I ⟨am⟩ none now' (implying that he once was — apparently, a collector of foreign news). 'But as concerning my brother,' he writes,

I doo not desire y^t you should tak⟨e⟩ paynes to reconcile vs: he hath followed his own wayward w⟨ill and⟩ taken a course vtterly disagreable to me, & hatefull to the state of England, & so hath foolishly & vnaturally divorced himself from me & his other frend*es* & he hath banished himself from his natiue country.

---

1 *Stowe MS.* 168; *Harl. MS.* 1875, ff. 396, 512; H. Foley, *Records of the English Province, S. J.*, 1, 466.

This letter suggests at once that Buc's brother was a Catholic, and the *Douay Diaries* confirm the conjecture. Robert Buck came from Rheims and entered the College at Douai on October 1, 1598, was baptized as 'Cantabrigiensis,' and in 1600 tonsured and ordained as 'Eliensis.' On August 6, 1600, 'profectus est Insulas D. Robertus Burquus, sacerdos, ibi in quadam ecclesia in ejusdem civitatis suburbiis victurus, ad aliquod incertum tempus, data ei aliqua competenti conditione.' Two days later, 'reversus est Insulis D. Robertus Burquus, spe sua frustratus, et ita studia hic prosequitur in statu quo prius.' [1] In 1612 he entered the Society of Jesus and in the year following his brother's letter came over upon the mission to England, where he remained many years.[2] We shall meet him again after Sir George's death.

1 *First and Second Diaries of the English College, Douay*, pp. 17, 283; *Third Douay Diary, Catholic Record Soc.* x, 3, 4, 15–18, 28. The 'Burquus' is probably a misreading; the earliest entry gives 'Buck.'
2 Foley, *Records of the English Province, S. J.*, VII, pt. i, 101, who states that the records date his birth in 1573, either in Suffolk or Gloucestershire. The latter at least must be an error, for the Gloucestershire Bucks were quite a different family; 'Glocestrensis' may have been read for 'Ciscestrensis.' Buck is also in a 1602 list of priests 'that now be in England, and presently to come' thither (Foley, II, 141).

V. RICHARD THE THIRD

The great work of Buc's last years was his *History of the Life and Reigne of Richard the Third*. This was published in 1646 by George Buck, Esquire, whose name also occurs in several MSS. of the *History*. Who he was, and how he posed as the author of the book, will appear later. Sir George's original manuscript, most of it in his own hand, is *Cotton Tiberius E.* x, a rough draft continually canceled and rewritten, and partly burnt in the Cotton Library fire of 1731.[1] It contains much that is omitted or sophisticated in the printed editions.

Buc is original in his sturdy defence of the character of Richard, whose annals were written under his Tudor enemies. He had denied the orthodox view as early as 1605 in his *Eclogue*. Sir William Cornwallis, at some time before his death in 1614, wrote a *Praise of Richard the Third*, but he ends, 'Yet for all this know, I hold this but a Paradox.' Horace Walpole in his *Historic Doubts* took up the case where Buc had left it, and Sir Clements Markham has argued it with equal vigor, though all these authors write as advocates rather than judicial historians. Buc made an advance over former writers by his use of the Chronicle of Croyland, and of an important letter to Norfolk, no longer known, which he saw 'in the magnificent Cabinet of *Thomas* Earl of Arundel and Surrey' — to whom, as head of the house of Howard, he dedicated his work. The Earl was the famous patron of Bacon and collector of the Arundel Marbles, 'the Father of Vertu in England.'

The *History* is a scholarly performance, well buttressed

---

1 Not, as Chalmers and Bullen conjectured, in a fire of Buc's books. Beside the negative evidence of Smith's catalogue in 1696, the recent damage is specifically mentioned by Casley in 1734 (*Catalogue of the MSS. of the King's Library*, p. 314).

from public records in the Tower and in 'the chappell of the Convertites in Chancery lane' (now the Record Office). Here we must confine ourselves to its biographical interest. After a tribute to the 'heroicall Howard' of 1588 and of the taking of Cadiz, 'I speak not by hearsay but ex certa scientia et visu proprio,' he adds, 'for I followed him in those & in other expeditions'; 'I was both a spectator & an actor in them.' [1] With the same loyal enthusiasm which he shows for the Admiral, he calls Elizabeth 'the best Queen that ⟨ever⟩ was [for she was a kingly queen & a masculine dame],' so far exceeding those much-renowned Amazons, Hippolyte, Semiramis, Thomyris, and the rest, 'as that they wer but May-ladyes' in comparison of her. Such were her noble acts and arduous achievements in themselves, 'as that the poets & Romanzers shall haue no Need to study for any new devises or delightfull & artificiall Inventions to sett them forth or to embellish the⟨ir⟩ poesyes.' [2]

Buc's praise is not that of an author in need of a patron, but comes spontaneously whenever he has occasion to mention someone he admires, as in *The Third Universitie* he writes that the old Temple 'now is called *Southampton* house, and was neuer in a more noble, or more worthy Patrons handes, then at this instant it is.' [3] In the *History* he speaks of Pembroke as 'my most honorable good Lord' (as Lord Chamberlain), and '(in a word) a true heroicall gentilman,' who has a brother Sir Philip as near to him in noble disposition and virtues as in blood.[4] Of the seventeenth Earl of Oxford, who in his youth was so promising a patron of poets, he writes that

1 *Tiber. E.* x, f. 118ᵛ; cf. f. 116ᵛ; omitted in 1646.
2 *Idem*, f. 134ᵛ; all but the first six words are cut in ed. 1646, p. 77.
3 Stowe, *Annals*, ed. 1615, sig. Mmmm 6ᵛ.
4 Elsewhere he mentions having common ancestors with the Herberts in the Staveleys, whence also Blount and Parr: *Tiber. E.* x, ff. 26, 121.

certaynly the erl was a ⟨   ⟩ magnificent & [a very] learned & religious ⟨   ⟩ man & so [much] worthy every way, as I haue heard some graue & ⟨d⟩iscret [&] honorable *p*ersons (who knew the erl from his y⟨outh⟩ & could very well iudge of th hopefullnes & tow⟨ard⟩lynes of young men) say & affirme [that] he was much more like to raise & [to] acquire [& to establish] a new erldome then to [des] decay & [to] [loose] wast & loose an old erldome. yet this erldome was . . . [& (in a word) he was a⟨   ⟩in deed as in name *Vere nobilis* for he was w⟨   ⟩ & truly noble, & a most noble Vere. & I spea⟨k⟩ bu⟨t⟩ what I know, [for he vouch-safed me] haueing [the honor] had the honor of his familiar ac⟨quaint-ance⟩].[1]

Oxford's friend Lord Lumley (suggested, without good evidence, as the author of the *Art of English Poesy*) described to Buc in conversation the barbarous execution of the Countess of Salisbury in 1541; and for the death of John, Earl of Oxford, in 1512, Buc cites as authority 'Dominus de *Arundell, viva voce.*' Regarding Richard's personal appearance he writes that Stowe 'hath acknowledged *vivâ voce* that he had spoken with some ancient men, who from their owne sight and knowledge affirmed he was of bodily shape comely enough, onely of low stature, which is all the deformity they proportion so monstrously.'[2] For the use of their libraries he particularly thanks his 'better-booked frends,' Camden, 'the good herald m^r Brook,' and above all Cotton. An amusing echo of his Spanish experience is heard in his remark that the Spaniards are politic, close, and wary, and 'wyll giue many gudgeons to Tramontane Travaylers.'[3]

Arguing in favor of the Don Sebastian who had been written of by Chettle and Dekker and who was later to appear in Massinger's *Believe as You List*, Buc quotes the evidence of a Venetian ambassador to England, a wise and grave gentleman 'of the Senatorious order.' Having been

1 *Idem*, f. 210; omitted from ed. 1646, p. 105.
2 Ed. 1646, pp. 143, 105, 79.
3 *Tiber.* E. x, ff. 4, 185.

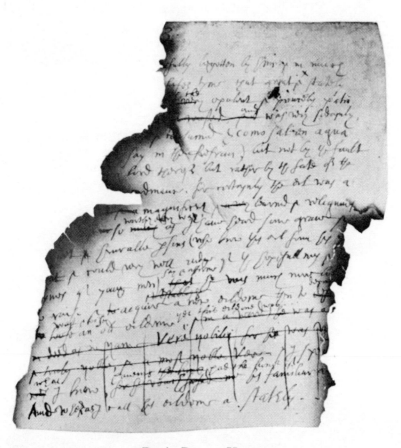

BUC'S ROUGH HAND:
COMMENTS ON THE SEVENTEENTH EARL OF OXFORD

RICHARD THE THIRD 477

one of the commissioners who personally examined the fugitive at Venice, he affirmed and solemnly declared that he and all the others, after a thorough investigation, were clear and very confident that here was indeed the true Sebastian. This 'embassadour ligeir for the Signory of Venice' is called by Buc Lorenzo Justiniano, the name having reached him orally. The person intended is evidently Zorzi or Giorgio Giustinian, who during his residence in England from 1606 to 1608 took the Florentine Secretary and the French Ambassador and his wife to see a performance of *Pericles*.[1]

'Hic legatus,' Buc notes in the margin,[2] 'haec Domino Baroni Darcey retulit'; and the date '162.' just above, possibly the year in which Lord Darcy in turn told Buc, may indicate that he continued to add to the *History* after drafting his dedication in 1619. A letter to Cotton, 'from the Kinges office of the Revells 10. March 1620,' shows that he was already engaged on another project; for he explains that 'my noble L. Darcy hath bene ernest wth me to deliuer him some matters concerning the great men of the realm in former tyme.' He mentions having met Cotton's uncle in Paul's, where 'wee sat vpon one of the new benches, & talked of sundry matters & of newes,' and of a manuscript which Sir Robert had borrowed on promise to keep it safe in his own possession, but which he had let go out of his hands and could not return when Buc wished to consult it for the work he was writing. Sir George compares his own carefulness in returning books, and confesses that he was much disturbed, because the manuscript belonged to the Lord Admiral. He characteristically prays Cotton to 'consider this y^t I haue alwayes bene carefull to hold my credit wth good men & cheefly so good & so great

1 Chambers, *William Shakespeare*, II, 335.
2 Ed. 1646, p. 98.

men as my ancient & most noble good L. the L. Noting*ham*
for otherwis if the book had bene myn, I would not haue
pressed the having of it. & you know that my pore library
is open to you at y^r pleasur. & I wyll doo you any curtesy
service or hono^r y^t I can.' [1] If his notes on 'the great men
of the realm' were ever finished, they have not been
traced.

The play-lists [2] which Buc occasionally used with other
waste paper for the manuscript of his *History* are dated by
Chambers about 1619–20. They cannot be later than 1621.
The lists furnish us with the titles of five or six plays not
otherwise known, the earliest mention of *The Two Noble
Kinsmen* and other plays, and the latest of '*Titus, and
vespatian.*' 'A very unexpected entry,' Sir Edmund Chambers called this in 1925, justly remarking that 'the name
can hardly have clung to *Titus Andronicus.*' [3] It is therefore difficult to agree with the opposite statement that the
entry 'gives some confirmation to the view that the titles
are equivalent.' [4] A theory originally built upon such in-
substantial foundations, and which has to explain away
the testimony of Henslowe and the thousand years that
separate Vespasian from Andronicus, can hardly stand
against this fresh evidence that the two plays were quite
distinct.

As to whether any of the lists are in Buc's hand (about
which Mr. Marcham was undecided),[5] it seems clear that
the first two are in a more clerkly hand and the third in a
much bolder one. What Buc has done is to add to '⟨The⟩
Maior of Quinborough' the title more familiar to him, 'or

1 *Julius C.* III, f. 49.
2 Reproduced in collotype by Marcham, *The King's Office of the Revels, 1610–
1622.*
3 *Review of English Studies*, I (1925), 483.
4 *William Shakespeare*, I, 319.
5 *Review of English Studies*, II (1926), 95.

Hengist K. of Kent,' and to 'The History of Philaster,'
'⟨ or Love Lies a bleeding.' Outside the play-lists (which
include another fragment mentioning *Falstaff*), Buc's
handwriting begins in Mr. Marcham's facsimiles with the
dedication (p. 22) and is evident in all the notes that follow. It has not been pointed out that of the eleven known
plays in the first two lists, nine are plays of the King's
Men, and another a printed Cambridge play which they
would be free to act. The remaining play, '*The Tradgedy
of Jeronimo*,' Sir Edmund Chambers identified with *The
Spanish Tragedy*, which he thought would at this time be
a Palsgrave's play; but I do not see why it should not be
the play which the piratic Children of the Chapel turned
into '*Jeronimo* in decimo sexto.' [1] Whether this was *The
Spanish Tragedy* or 1 *Jeronimo*, it was a King's play. The
King's Men, therefore, may have furnished Buc with a
selection of such of their plays as they considered would
best please the Court. It is interesting to observe that the
choice included *Hamlet*, *The Winter's Tale*, *The Two Noble
Kinsmen*, *The Fox* alone of Jonson's, and that deleted,
and four of Beaumont and Fletcher's.

In the final year of Buc's Mastership the usual tug-of-
war with the Exchequer became more desperate than ever.
Three Revels petitions to Lord Treasurer Cranfield and a
long letter from Buc are preserved among the *Sackville
MSS.* at Knole.[2] The Master, officers, and servitors of the
Revels beseech payment of £500 remaining due on a privy
seal of £700 granted by the King upon 'most earnest sute'
to pay their wages and fees for the first two of six years in

---

1 Webster, *Induction to the Malcontent*. Sir Edmund himself now grants that *The
Spanish Tragedy* was not the exclusive property of the Admiral's Men (*Eliz.
Stage*, II, 210; III, 396), since Burbage played in it (*William Shakespeare*, I, 148).
2 I am indebted to the courtesy of Lord Sackville for permission to examine
them. They are mentioned in *Hist. MSS. Comm.*, IV, 316, but are now being
more fully calendared. The letter is no. 884, the petitions nos. 5008, 5402, 5742.

arrears. A similar petition from the workmen only, dated November 11, 1621, declares that the work 'was performed six yeres past, now begon vpon the Seaventh,' and that the £200 paid already 'being devided amongst soe many did but little pleasure. . . . And now the time comeing on for more service, inrespect the Branches & wire rodd*es* are much-decayed, they are not able to perform the same.' Buc writes, in a letter received by Cranfield on December 17, 'of a strange, & of a Rare kind of offence' which happened on the 3d of the month. Receiving order for a second £200 on the old privy seal, and seeing that there was no hope of more at present, he went to the Exchequer and presented his order to Sir Francis Egioke,

& forth w\(^t\)h there was 200. li in gold & siluer layd vpon the boord, & the w\(^c\)h to tell for me (as they pretended ther wer more helpers then I desired.) for I perceyved that they had conspired to robb, & to cheat me of that mony: the cheif of those trechors was Wright the wyre-drawer,[1] & other his partners, & Hunt the yoman of the *Revells* were all in practise trecherously to bereaue me of the sayd mony beeing in-deed the k*e* mony. In the end wright closely gott the bagg of syluer vnder his cloak: but I thought I would soon vnfurnish him of it, & I willed Alex. Stafford the controuller to tak it from him, but he was cold in it. & indeed was secretly of the faction. when I went to tak boat I took both staffard, & Wright w\(^t\)h me: & Wright brought the bagg vnto the k*e* office where I lodg: but Al. stafford would need*e* land at the Temple & ther I left all my hope of him. & as soon as I was entred into my hous I went vp into my great chamber. & called to wright to follow, but so soon as I was out of his sight, he went back in hast & went out at the dore, & vnto certayn trecherous varlets, w\(^c\)h he had layd in wayt ther & to them he gaue the bagg, & they lik theues ran*n* away w\(^t\)h it w\(^t\)h all speed.

Buc protests that 'thos felonious wyerdrawers haue no reason to steale or to take violently & rapinously any mony fro*m* y\(^e\) M\(^r\) of the Revells,' though they claim the

1 By an amusing misreading this has become 'Wright the wynedrawer' in *Hist. MSS. Comm.*, IV, 316. For a petition by this Robert Wright see *ibid.*, p. 300, and for one by Peter Wright, wiredrawer, in 1597, see Feuillerat, *Materialien*, XXI, 417.

authority of Cranfield, for they have been paid for one year, '& this mony w^{c}h they haue stolen was due to my vnd^r offic^{rs} the Controler, ye clark the yoma*n* ye groo*m*,' still unpaid for the first of the seven years. He adds that he has already written Cranfield three letters on the affair; this one, which is dated from St. Peter's Hill, shows him still sane but evidently losing his authority. The situation was no better, however, under Astley, for on May 9, 1623, the artificers were still begging for £201 unpaid of the £701 due for 1615–17, to relieve 'there wives and Children wch in this deare and miserable time are readie to sterve for wante of foode,' and the next five years had not been accounted for. In one of the notes in *Tiberius E.* x Buc writes that the other officers 'murmur muc⟨h and ex⟩- clayme of me bycaus I com not dayly' to ask for the wages, and that they are 'out of hart, & allmost des⟨perate⟩'; in another note he and his fellows pray for their arrears, 'being not able any longer to forbear them.' [1] The financial tangle was not peculiar to the Revels but involved the whole Government through the reckless extravagance of the King and Court. It is no wonder that seven years of these troubles finally drove the Master of the Revels mad.

The last plays entered in the Stationers' Registers under Buc's hand are *Othello*, October 6, 1621, *The Virgin Martyr*, December 11, and *Herod and Antipater*, February 22, 1621–2. On December 21, 1621, a traveling license to Slatier and others was signed not by Buc but by the Lord Chamberlain.[2] On March 30, 1622, John Chamberlain (the two persons have been made one by several writers) mentions the news that 'Old Sir George Buck, master of the revels, has gone mad.'[3] A warrant had been issued the day

1 Marcham, pp. 36, 45.
2 Murray, *English Dramatic Companies*, II, 192.
3 *S. P. D. Jas.* 128/96.

before to swear in Sir John Astley as Master. Astley, who like Buc was a Gentleman of the Privy Chamber, had been granted the reversion on April 3, 1612.[1] Ben Jonson, who apparently was a rival of Buc for the place as early as 1601 (*Satiromastix*, IV, i, 244), had his hopes revived by Buc's decline and secured a secondary reversion on October 5, 1621. I think it likely that he asked for this gift instead of the knighthood James had wanted to give him the month before.[2] But Astley lived until 1640, and though in July 1623 he sold his life-estate in the office to a fellow Gentleman of the Privy Chamber, George Herbert's young brother Henry,[3] this did not affect Jonson's position.

A letter requiring the delivery of the Revels books and property was sent on May 16, 1622, to 'M[r] Buck.'[4] It has been assumed that the Chamberlain's office was corresponding with the lunatic, but 'M[r] Buck' was probably his nephew Stephen Buck, who had taken possession of his goods. Nothing more has been known of Buc until his death, which Malone dates September 20 and September 28, 1623, Chalmers and later writers September 22, and Greg September 29, all inadvertent errors except the first, which, as Adams thrice points out,[5] is the date given by Herbert in 1662. Its impossibility can be demonstrated from any one of half-a-dozen sources, such as the *List of Inquisitions in the Public Record Office*, the administrations at Somerset House, or the documents to which we shall now turn.

On March 4, 1622–3, Secretary Calvert wrote that the Spanish Ambassador had moved the King for Buck the priest, 'to whom (as the Ambassado[r] tells me) there is

1 Murray, II, 193; Malone, *Shakspeare* (1790), I, ii, 45.
2 Herford and Simpson, *Ben Jonson*, I, 87, 237.
3 Chalmers, *Apology*, p. 496; Cunningham, p. xlix.
4 Murray, II, 193.
5 *Dramatic Records of Sir Henry Herbert*, pp. 8, 67, 109.

some little Inheritance descended worth some 14. or 15. hundred pounds to be sold, or hardly so much. The man he saith yet is not discouered nor knowne.' The King had condescended and promised to 'grant him a generall Pardon, such a one as may make him capable of this Inheritance.' The Ambassador came from the King at Newmarket to London and urged the matter upon Calvert, to whom James had referred it, together with the granting of more liberty to the Jesuit Fisher, who the year before had converted Buckingham's mother and disputed with — or listened to a disputation by — the King. Father Buck was fortunate in having the question of his inheritance come up just at the time when the Court was willing to do everything the Spaniards wanted in exchange for the Infanta. In this first week of March Buckingham and Baby Charles were rushing toward Madrid, where Charles would swear to secure the repeal of all laws against the Catholics. The Jesuits in England claimed in this year 2,630 converts, and England was raised to a Province of their Society.[1] Calvert soon after announced himself a Catholic and as Lord Baltimore turned to the colonizing of Maryland. Accordingly, Robert Buck, clerk, at the instance of Carlo Coloma, the King of Spain's Ambassador, was pardoned for all treasons and felonies committed by his coming into England as a Jesuit and reconciling subjects to the Bishop of Rome, and order was given that he should not be molested in the future.[2]

The Guildhall jurors who officially declared Buc's lunacy on April 12, 1622, found his landed property in Lincolnshire to be worth £125 a year. His other property consisted of the lease of his house in St. Peter, Paul's Wharf,

---

1 Foley, VII, pt. ii, 1098.
2 *S. P. D. Jas.* 138/98; 139/10, 35, 87; 214, pp. 5, 6, 14. The signet bill for the pardon is dated April 23 (C 82/1961).

and of goods in the custody of Francis Heydon, clerk. As
to who might be his heir or coheirs, the jurors wisely declared themselves thoroughly ignorant.[1] For the same
reason, the inquisition post mortem was not held until
1625. It gives the date of Buc's death as October 31, 1622.[2]
These records show that Buc bought no further estates
with the profits of the Revels Office, as Herbert did. What
he could spare from keeping up the splendor necessary to
his position at Court he seems to have spent in buying
books and historical manuscripts.

Malone and Chalmers were not able to find any will or
administration for Buc; but letters of administration upon
the estate of Sir George Bucke, late of Broadwater, Sussex,
were issued to Francis Haydon of Broadwater on November 15, 1622.[3] The pitched battle that followed in Chancery has escaped the notice of writers on Buc, though a
Registrar of the Court called attention to its interest in
1847 and again in 1850.[4] It throws some curious light on
his last days; answers the riddle of the identity of George
Buck, who published Buc's works as his own; presents Sir
George in all the glory of his jewels and velvets, his 'fair
pictures' and other personal belongings; and even tells
something of the dispersion of his library of books and
manuscripts.

1 C 142/391/45. By an odd error this inquisition declares, 'Lunaticus est et
Lucidis gaudet interuallis Ita quod regimini . . . non sufficit,' *non* having been
omitted before *gaudet*.
2 C 142/566/17.
3 P. C. C. Act Book 1619–22, f. 205ᵛ.
4 Cecil Monro, *Acta Cancellariae* (London, 1847), p. 312; *N. and Q*. ii, 73.

VI. THE YOUNG PRETENDER

Briefly, the story is this. Buc made his last will on August 30, 1612, devising all his manors and lands, if he died without issue,

to his deare brother Roḇt Bucke Provided that he should be capable of his saide guifte & might safelye & lawfullye possesse & inioye those messuages & lands aforesaide wherof the saide Sʳ George was doubtfull because the saide Roḇt Bucke was a catholike preist & (as some saye) a Jesuite & lived beyond seas as on that had lost the benefitt of his Countrye & of his b(l)oud & parentage ffor that such men cominge into this land were reputed felons & beinge indicted were indicted of Treason. . . .

If the laws of England at that time should thus disable him, and unless he should conform himself and so be able to enjoy the land without forfeiting it, Sir George disinherited him in favor of Stephen Buck, son of their eldest sister Cecilia, 'the wife of William Buck of lincolnshire but originally of a Scotch race.' Or if the devise to Robert could take effect, then after his death the land was entailed in the same way on Stephen and on his son George, whose godfather declared that he thus disposed

by Gods especiall ordinance in regard it had plesed his divyne goodnes that that yonge boy & his nephewe meaninge the defdt George should Beare both his names as well the Cristian name George as the surname Buc or Bucke allsoe because it was his fortune to be borne & bred neare vnto his saide manoʳˢ of Skidbrooke & vnto his other lands & wherevnto the Children of his other Sisters weare meare strangers & of remote contries in the South. . . .[1]

The husband of Cecily Buck (the 'Scisseley' of Clarencieux in 1575) was evidently the William Buck who was

---

[1] Sussex. The men of this remote country (including Mr. Belloc) have been known to express a like misgiving as to 'foreigners from the shires.' The account of the will comes only from Stephen, who adds that Buc signed it again on August 14, 1620.

schoolmaster of Louth in 1580.[1] He was the elder son of
Stephen Buck of Louth, whose mysterious origin became
the theme of a suit against him as an unacknowledged
alien.[2] For thirty years Stephen had kept his shop and
paid his subsidies 'as a meere Englishman and not as a
straunger' (who would have to pay double), until a man
whom he had 'put from occupyinge' brought in revenge
an information against him. Robert Cooke testified that
in 1570 Stephen, meeting him, exclaimed:

> woe worth the(e) Cooke, thou haste vndonne me for m^r Porman
> sayth that thou sayst that I am a Scott and was borne of a Scotishe
> whore
> Naye Stephan said I, I said not so, I said thou was brought from
> Newcastle by Gilbert halliday to Hull and so to saltfletthaven,
> Nay sayth the sayd Stephan I was borne in Saltfleethaven,

Rumor declared that he was born in Legbourn Abbey,
and witnesses were asked what prioresses or nuns they
had known and whether any of these was his mother.
A nun who had lived there for sixteen years said that she
'did neuer knowe eny child borne w^thin that house' saving
that Ursula Taythwell had a son and a daughter, as a
scholar of Ursula's also testified, 'wth one Sr William
Holden a prest who flede the countrie for the same.'
Stephen had been a scholar in the abbey, but an old mar-
iner told of first seeing him fifty years since at Newcastle,
where Stephen 'beinge a litle boy came amonge other poore
people to the said shippe to crave almosse and relyf.'
Halliday, 'having good liking to him asked whether he
would go with him or no.' 'Willingly,' answered the boy.
'You have no need of him,' said the master, Captain

---

1 R. W. Goulding, *Louth Old Corporation Records*, p. 114; cf. p. 179 on Buck's
Charity, bequeathed by Stephen Buck.
2 Exchequer K. R. Depositions, Michaelmas 20–21 Eliz., no. 11, and Easter 21
Eliz., no. 13.

Orpyn. 'No matter,' Halliday replied, 'for I have no children, therefore I will do for him as for my own,' and being a tailor presently made for the boy (a four-year-old Joseph) 'a Coate of p*a*rtie colle*res* of such ould peces of clothe as were in the shippe.' The witness had received 'menassing*es* and thretnyng*es*' from Stephen to keep him from testifying.

The secret of Stephen's birth at last came to light when Margaret Sterne of Mablethorpe, aged fourscore, explained that he was the son of her father, Mr. John Fitzwilliam, by a Scottish woman 'in the tyme of ware.' His mother brought him to Newcastle and after inquiring amongst the shipmen wrote a letter to Fitzwilliam, who sent back word to send him the child, paid Halliday for keeping him, and set him to school until his wife heard of it and complained, 'thy faither careth for none but for the and younder bastarde Stephen.' But her father said to Margaret, 'make mouche of Stephen for he ys as nere vnto me as thou arte and it may be herafter y^t he may be thy frend and helpe the in th(y) nede.' Fitzwilliam's estate, by a curious chance, was the very manor of Skidbrooke which his great-grandson hoped to inherit from Buc, held earlier by his ancestor Sir Thomas Dymoke.[1] For all his blood of the King's Champions, Dymoke and Marmion, the boy Stephen 'did goe about w^{t}h a pittcher at that time for milke' and kept his father's sheep in a 'Conie warraunt' called 'straite gates'; but he learned 'to sowe in the sciens of' a tailor and made his own way in the world till he came to be a prosperous woolen-draper. The Crown inquires particularly into his wealth in Kendal and Manchester friezes, in Suffolk, Kentish, Yorkshire, and 'cotsale brodes,' in 'walsh,' 'yorshire,' 'hamshire,' and 'deaynshire carsses'

---

1 W. O. Massingberd, *History of Ormsby*, p. 261; cf. A. R. Maddison, *Lincolnshire Wills, 1500–1600*, p. 36.

(Devonshire kerseys). In a Chancery bill he calls himself 'yeoman,' but he died in 1590 a tenant-in-chief of the Queen and 'generosus.'[1] He left an annuity of ten pounds to his son William and most of his property to William's children, William and Stephen. The younger grandson became an attorney in the Prothonotary's office and described himself on September 9, 1622, as 'Stephen Buck of the parishe of St Botholphe wthout Aldgate London gent. aged 42 yeares.'[2] From this it is clear that his mother Cecily was older than her brother Sir George.

Since Robert stood indicted for a Jesuit in King's Bench, Stephen took possession of the lands at Buc's death. But the will was never proved; Heydon got in first by taking out letters of administration, which left the lands to be inherited by Robert. The Jesuit priest conveyed them in December to his brother-in-law the parson, who, for all that he was a country rector seventy years of age, was an excellent man of business, as he had shown when he testified for Buc in 1604. Francis Heydon and his wife, Buc's sister, brought a Chancery bill in February against Stephen, his wife Elizabeth, his son George, and his servant Robert Thomas, who had formerly attended on Sir George.[3] Stephen and his son retaliated the next week with a bill against the Heydons and others who were supposed to have shared Buc's personal property between them.[4] For the landed property Stephen brought suits against Robert Buck[5] and against the Lincolnshire tenants, appropriately named *Mudd et al.*[6] He also sued the

---

1 C 3/22/74; C 142/228/45; P. C. C., 76 Darcy.   2 C 24/482/18.
3 Bill, February 7, with answer, May 15, 1623 (C 2 Jas. I, H 25/62); replication, undated (C 2 Chas. I, H 117/88).
4 Bill, February 13, with answer of Sir Carew Reynell, February 20, of Francis and Susan Heydon, February 24 (C 2 Jas. I, B 9/57).
5 Bill, May 12 (C 2 Jas. I, B 2/74).
6 Bill, October 10, with answer of Leonard Beetsone of Boston, lessee of Greenpooles (C 2 Jas. I, B 23/4).

Heydons and others at common law; and he petitioned the ecclesiastical court to have the letters of administration revoked. Even before Buc died, Sir Walter Pye, Attorney of the Court of Wards, had sued in behalf of the lunatic to compel Stephen to account for rents which he had received under a letter of attorney from Sir George.[1]

The chief question at issue was whether Sir George had made over all his personal property to Stephen and George by deed of gift. Stephen produced such a deed, dated March 14, 1621-2, but was the signature genuine? and if so, was Buc sane when he made it? He remained sane until March 27, Stephen insisted; the Guildhall jurors found that he was lunatic by that date, but they knew not for how long before; according to Heydon it was in February that he became lunatic and utterly bereft of power to manage any business. Stephen told a circumstantial story of the signing: that Buc came and desired such a deed to be drawn up, in return for which he should live at Stephen's house and be maintained for life with convenient meat, drink, and apparel; that they repaired first to the house of Buc's friend Mr. Muskett, a counselor, who was from home; that a scrivener then penned the deed according to the instructions of Buc, who advisedly read and subscribed it and put Stephen in possession by the delivery of sixpence. Heydon, however, declared that Stephen drew the deed in the night time, by sinister means, and while Sir George was lunatic, not daring to come before on account of the many foul abuses and cosenage he had done Buc in receiving rents, for which there were divers lawsuits between them that were never ended. Heydon, 'be-

---

1 This, which bore date July 23, 1621, probably dates the sheet marked 'lre of attorney' in *Tiberius E.* x (Marcham, p. 18). Many further records could be found in the courts mentioned, though the fullest story is usually told in Chancery.

ing a preacher and desirous of peace,' told the court he would rest satisfied if the deed of gift were proved *bona fide* before Sir Eubule Thelwall, Master in Chancery. Thelwall reported in November that the deed was very suspicious; the only witnesses were the scrivener and a man who had kept Buc when he was distracted, and who in private examination could not deny that Buc 'when the saide deed was made, was scarce of sane memorie.' [1]

One who had served Sir George for sixteen or seventeen years testified in 1624 that he had always heard that his master intended to settle his lands on his Buc kinsmen, and that once when Heydon gave out that he intended to settle them on Heydon's son Edward, who had fallen in love with a knight's daughter in Sussex, the knight repaired to Buc to make sure, who answered that he had nearer kinsmen.[2] In his bill, however, Heydon offered to prove that Buc complained of Stephen's ill dealing in letters to his friends and in speeches, often in express words publicly revoking all wills so far as they concerned Stephen's family, whom he forbade the house, openly vowing and protesting 'that hee should never haue any penny worthe of his estate.' Stephen was equally confident of proving that Buc would not suffer the Heydons to come to his house, but ordered his servants to deny to them that he was within, 'allthoughe in truth he weare w[th]in.' Far from forbidding his visits, declared Stephen, Buc often importuned him and his wife to take a house in Holborn and let Buc live with them, paying £100 a year for diet and lodging, or else to take over the keeping of his house at

1 C 38/45.
2 C 24/506/5, deposition of Thomas Adams, aged 39. He had never seen Robert Buck. Henry Page of Garlickhithe, scrivener, testified to the deed of gift which he wrote and saw signed 'G Buc:' and to a copy of the will, of which he gave the heading, '*Deo O. M., patri, filio & Spiritui sancto Deo trino Q'rum sit omnis honor, Laus, & gloria in æternum.*'

St. Peter's Hill. The boy George, indeed, 'did serve the said Sr George & dwell in house wth him'; and Stephen afterwards claimed the house and paid the rent to Ambrose Randolph.

The boy George, however, was wakened one night in February, 1623, by Francis Heydon, clerk, 'Robert Buck a professed Jesuite Preiste Thomas Grafton of London Baker Richard Oakes of London yeoman together wth one John Raynbeard an Attorney of the Comon please & other lewd & dessolute fellowes' (in the eyes of Stephen), who between twelve and one o'clock did 'rioutuousely by force of armes vnlawfully enter into the house,' expelled George and two of his father's servants out of their beds and out of the house, and carried away goods and writings. Stephen may be including the clergymen on the principle of the more the merrier; but the visit formed a vigorous reply to his first Chancery bill, which demanded that the Heydons and seven others who possessed goods of Buc's should disclose the certain quantity and quality of every parcel. One of the defendants to this suit was 'John Selden gentleman.'

Another was Sir Carew Reynell, to whom 'His Matie was gratiouslie pleased to bestow the custodie' of Buc; in Heydon's plainer phrase, he had begged Sir George and his estate. He at once replied that, armed with an order from the Court of Wards, he had done his best to get Buc's personal goods into his hands, 'to his great charge and trauell,' but had got nothing, not even his expenses for keeping Buc. He was of opinion that Stephen ought to be punished for securing such a deed of gift from a lunatic, an absolute deed by which he 'might haue taken the very apparrell' from Sir George's back. Sir Carew had been a gentleman pensioner under Ralegh and cupbearer to Queen Elizabeth, and Drake had recommended him for first governor of Plymouth Fort (which went to Sir Ferdinando Gorges). The youngest of five brothers, he was the first of four to be knighted, by Essex in Ireland, and the employments he sought ranged from guarding Essex for the Queen to showing James how 'the King might take great advantage by the venom of this serpent' usury.[1] Of the other defendants, only the Heydons answered; but the last of them, Francis Fowler, came forward as chief witness for Stephen.[2]

Asked by whose authority Buc was carried to Heydon's house in the country, Fowler said that it was by means of Buc's sister and by warrant of Dr. Crooke, Governor of Bedlam house, for a night or two before the conveying away he heard the Governor and Mistress Heydon whispering together of such a business.[3] Fowler testified that Rainbeard had offered Sir Carew forty pounds a year to suffer him and the Heydons to have the keeping of Buc at Broadwater, but the agreement never went through. Since Buc died there, however, Reynell apparently never got possession of him. Rainbeard had married a daughter of the Heydons, and to her house in Chichester was sent a trunkful of apparel, containing doublets of cloth of silver and of white taffeta, a perfumed leather jerkin and black velvet breeches. To Broadwater went a bed with a 'val-

---

1 Prince, *Worthies of Devon*; *Hatfield MSS.*, III, 52; x, 43; *S. P. D. Jas.* 98/7 He was granted the office of Queen's printer for Latin, Greek, and Hebrew, but he sold this grammar monopoly in 1597 to a Plymouth merchant, John Battersby (*Cal. S. P. D. Eliz. 1595–97*, p. 378). This should be added to the entry under Battersby in McKerrow, *Dictionary of Printers and Booksellers, 1557–1640.*

2 Francis Fowler of St. Olave's, Southwark, baker, aged 28, April 22, 1623 (C 24/499/20). He had served Buc at the time of his death and for half-a-year before. Mrs. Heydon had given him two of Buc's old suits, but Stephen had evidently bid higher.

3 Dr. Helkiah Crooke, whose portrait by Droeshout may be seen before his *Description of the Body of Man* (ed. 1631), is said in Munk and the *D.N.B.* to have been the first medical man appointed Governor of Bedlam, in 1632; the date can now be placed at least ten years earlier.

ance, a silke Quilt, Blanquett*es*,' and other furniture, a 'window Cushion of red damaske, laced wth gold lace,' silver spoons, 'a payer of rich gold hangers,' 'a fine new wastcoate of Silke,' and a very fair gown of branched velvet, lined with shag velvet, 'being the ritchest Gowne that the *said* Sr George Buck then had.' All these Heydon sent down from London by carrier, and a dapple-grey gelding also went to Sussex. Sir George himself, apparently, ordered sent down his couch bed, money chest, 'Lady cupbord,' 'Cales table' and 'Cales Bedsted' — souvenirs, evidently, of his Cadiz excursion in 1596.

At St. Peter's Hill remained other goods, including 'diu*er*se & sundry faire pictures,' further evidence of the taste for painting shown in *The Third University*. The keys of the house were left with Thomas Grafton *alias* Crofton ¹ and his wife. A year later, when 'Raynbeard and such as he brought wth him' dispossessed Stephen of the house, he and Heydon carried away the household stuff 'by whole Cartloads at a tyme.' Fowler remembered that there was 'a cradle of yron to make charecoale ffyers in,' and, especially to be noted, 'a Glasse that ran fower howers togither.' Before this time, Stephen had entrusted to Grafton 'a Box of Wrytinge*s*, or other thing*es* therein, wth a padlock vpon yt,' which Fowler remembered carrying from Grafton's house 'vnto Mr Seldens chamber, at the Temple,' and later back again. He had likewise given into Grafton's keeping a trunk, which after a time was brought back to the house and thence conveyed by water to Camberwell to the house of one Mr. Dauson, the minister there. Fowler saw it opened both there and at the Temple, whither he and Heydon brought it not long after. In Selden's chamber the contents were spread out:

---

1 The Council in 1617 ordered Thomas Crofton arrested and sent to Newgate (*A. P. C. 1616-17*, p. 345).

three very rich black velvett Clokes, a payre of payned brooches richely broydered wth Gold, a very fayre silver Bason & Ewre, a fayre silver Sault wrought wth Pillars, two silver trencher plates, A stone Jugg flued & tipped about ye mowth wth silver . . . faire Ruff Band*es* & Cuff*es*, fine Holland shirt*es*, and other fine Lynen. . . .

For the value of the goods, 'They were so ritch as that it passeth his Skill, to sett any certeine Estimate vpon them'; but a rich hatband, all set with diamonds, was valued by some of the beholders at £100. All this was part of what Stephen spoke of as the 'rich apparell wch he vsed to wear fitt and necessary for his place and callinge.' Selden was left in possession of the whole.

As to Buc's books, Fowler deposed:

That all the Book*es* late of the said Sr Geo: Buck, after his death, came first to the hand*es* or posse*ss*ion of the def^t Grafton, vizt two Trunck*es* full, wherof one was a very great Trunck, one chist full & one deep Drawer full, And were there bestowed for a tyme. But after-ward*es* were dispersed abroade, some vnto the def^t Rainbeard, some vnto one m^r Thynn a Counsello^r of the Temple, (who had a cloke bag full,) and one other cloke bag full, vnto one Hinxon an Appothicarie in Pawles churchyard, And one fayre great Booke of Armes, iudged to be worthe a great Sum*m*e of money was sent by this dep^t vnto the *s*aid mr Selden, fro*m* the def^t Raynbeard. And moreover, one mr Bradburie as this dep^t now reme*m*breth his name, being a kinsman of the said def^t Heydon, had some parte of the *s*aid Sr Geo: Buck*es* Book*es*.

Heydon's pleadings are signed by his counselor, Egremont Thynne. 'Mr. Aegremont Thynne, eighth son' (really 'child') of Sir John, the builder of Longleat, entered the Middle Temple in 1597, and in 1610 succeeded to the chamber of Sir John Davys the poet, in Pump Court. In this year of 1623 the King made him a Serjeant.[1]

Not even this scattering to the winds accounts for all Buc's MSS. Heydon declared that Stephen during the

---

1 *Minutes of Parliament of the Middle Temple*, I, 373; II, 574, 676, 737, 749. For an epigram upon him see *MS. Rawlinson* D. 947, in the Bodleian.

time of Buc's distraction 'secretly imbesiled' ready money, plate, books, jewels and apparel to the value of £3000. One of these books must have been the manuscript *History of Richard III*. No doubt there were also Revels Office memoranda and waste papers that may have gone to the apothecary, but the Revels Books had been ordered sent to Astley, and as Professor Adams has pointed out, Herbert seems to quote from them after the Restoration.[1] Chalmers supposed that they had perished in a general fire of Buc's books, but the only evidence for such a fire is his paraphrase of an entry by Herbert, 'that he had licensed, without a fee, *Jugurth*, an old play, allowed by Sir George Bucke, and *burnt, with his other books*.'[2] Chambers suggests that it may have been burnt in the 1621 fire at the Fortune,[3] which is precisely where one would expect its loss to have occurred, since it belonged to the company there. Certainly Chalmers makes 'his' refer to Buc, but both his summaries of the entry are imperfect, and the beginning probably contained the proper antecedent, the name of the Fortune manager to whom it was licensed. The theory of a fire of Buc's books is hardly tenable now that we know how large a number remained at his death and to how many different owners they afterwards went. The fate of his office books, therefore, remains a mystery.

Selden, who acquired books that had belonged to Jonson, Donne, Spenser, and so many more, would probably take care to secure the most valuable of Buc's books and manuscripts, and these would then share all the vicissitudes of his own library. Part of this survives at the Bodleian, but another part was exposed for many years to robbers and borrowers, until it finally went up in smoke in 'the fire of

1 *Dramatic Records of Sir Henry Herbert*, pp. 10, 105, 112.
2 *Supplemental Apology*, p. 203; cf. p. 218.
3 *Review of English Studies*, I, 484.

the Temple,' with eight chests of manuscripts on English history.[1]

While Buc's personal goods were scattered about Sussex and London, the North Sea was invading his lands, until Stephen was allowed money to amend the sea-banks. He had got an injunction for their possession, through leaving a subpoena at Robert's usual lodging, 'where in truth he never came'; but they were later sequestered, and the tenants who had brought their rents up to London were ordered to pay them into the Court. Sir William Jones, in a report describing Buc's unusual will, asked that other opinions might be sought as well as his own, 'Because the Cause is newe and maie trench farre.'[2] Heydon's lessee of the lands, William Marshe, had assigned his lease, in June 1623, to Martha Blount, who also brought suit against Stephen. A year later, the Court ordered that Stephen should sue at common law and secure a speedy decision, or else lose the case.[3]

The final decree was issued on November 29, 1624. The Attorney General (Sir Thomas Coventrye), as counsel for Robert Buck, Heydon, and Martha Blount, informed the Court that his clients had good cause to suspect that the will was forged, since the deed of gift, as Thelwall had reported in January, was 'in all likeliehood forged.' 'And,' he continued,

there are many *lettres* & writing*es* shewing S*r* Geo: Buck*es* dislike of the sd Stephen whoe beeinge an Attorney at the Comon lawe hath beene ymprisoned for Counterfetting the Lo Hobart*es* hand, and sithence for divers other offences hath beene thrust owt of the Prothonotories office, and nowe latlie hee hath ioyned himselfe w*th* one Jo*n* Buck al*ias* Blount al*ias* Watson his Vncle to indict the sd deft Heydon & others, w*ch* sd John

1 Macray, *Annals of the Bodleian*, ed. 1890, p. 121.
2 C 38/45.
3 D. & O. 1623A, ff. 36, 177, 461, 713, 815, 883, 1036; 1623B, ff. 45, 210, 552, 874, 981, 1217.

Bucke for divers great offences & misdemeano^{r}s hath lost his eares & beene branded in the face w^{t}h the *lett*res C & S for counterfetting of a Statute by sentence in the Starrechamber, and hath allso beene comitted by the high Court of Parliam^t to p*er*petuall ymprisonm^t for Counterfetting a Peeres hand & Racked for high Treason & burnt in the hand for fellonye, And the sd Stephen beeing a man much hated by the sd Sr Geo: Buck it is not probable that the sd S^r: Geo: would make the sd Stepen [*sic*] his heire, But it is rather to bee presumed that the sd Will was forged.

Accordingly, since Stephen had not brought his common-law action against Robert, the Lord Chancellor dismissed his bill and established possession with Heydon's lessee, Martha Blount.^{1}

John Buck the forger was the second son of Stephen the elder, who left him 'my drap*er* shop in ye marketsted at Louth.' Star Chamber records show that he signed himself 'John Buck a̵l̵t̵ Blownt,' but being usually known as Blount forged signatures to a statute staple in two thousand pounds payable to himself as John Blount of Comberton, Worcs., esquire. The London haunts of himself and his friends, 'ill fellows that looked as if they were swaggerers,' included the Bankside, Bloomsbury, and the sign of the Bear, Smithfield.^{2} Henry Parrot in 1606 dedicated *The Mouse-Trap* 'To his no little respected friend *little Iohn Buck*,' addressing him familiarly as 'Sirrha *Iacke*,' but the name is too common to identify him or the

1 D. & O. 1624A, f. 414. The only Martha Blount before the time of Pope's friend to be be found in A. Croke, *History of the Croke Family, originally named Le Blount* (II, 334), was the wife of George, brother of Father Richard Blount, Robert Buck's superior as Provincial of the English Jesuits; but I do not know whether she was a widow and therefore capable of suing. Since Heydon lived in Sussex, his lessee is more likely to have been Martha, daughter of Richard Blount of Dedisham, Sussex (not mentioned by Croke). She is recorded as unmarried in the Visitation of 1623, elder sisters being married to Sir Lewis Lewknor and to Reginald Mohun of Cornwall: John Comber, *Sussex Genealogies* (Cambridge, 1931), p. 22. By an odd coincidence, Skidbrooke, thus acquired by Martha Blount, is one of the seven lordships recorded in Domesday Book as belonging to William le Blount.
2 Star Chamber 8, 281/7; *S. P. D. 1611–18*, p. 33.

John Bucke who in 1589 dedicated to Lady Hungerford *Instructions for the Use of the Beads*, printed at Louvain. A John Bucke, gent., of Croydon, died before 1627, when his son George entered Gray's Inn. Another notorious forger was the Robert Buck, of an Essex family, who manufactured as many licenses to go a-begging 'as would fill a hat,' and offered counterfeits of either the Great Seal or the Lord Admiral's for twenty shillings: 'this forginge companion,' the humorous Hunsdon called him 'that maketh so good cheape vagrants.' [1]

Robert Buck, esquire, was returned heir to the lands by inquisition taken at Boston June 8, 1625.[2] It is this document that gives the date of Buc's death as 'vltimo die Octobris,' 1622. The Heydons in their bill, followed by Stephen, spoke of it as 'in or about the Monethe of November'; but though they should have known, yet they may have been remembering the funeral,[3] and the precise date set down in the inquisition is perhaps more likely to be exact. Father Buck was stationed in the London district in 1621, and later in the Suffolk and Derbyshire districts. He became a Spiritual Coadjutor in 1626, and is named among the 'Veteran Missionaries' in a register confiscated in the 1628 raid on Jesuit headquarters known as the Clerkenwell Discovery. Nothing more is heard of him until his death on February 10, 1648.[4]

1 *Hist. MSS. Comm.*, VII, 541; *Egerton MS.* 2644, f. 82. The actor Benjamin Webster of the Haymarket claimed descent from Sir George Buc, according to the *D.N.B.*, citing a MS. autobiography; but in print he merely claimed that his father was 'the representative, by his mother's side, of the family of the Bucke's,' of Yorkshire (*Acting National Drama*, VI). The name was common enough in that county. A George Bucke, sheriff of the city of York, went out with a white rod to welcome James on his progress from Scotland in 1603 (Nichols, *Progresses of James*, I, 77, 79).
2 C 142/566/17.
3 This took place, the Rector of Broadwater courteously informs me, on an illegible day in November.
4 Foley, I, 132–133; VII, i, 101; G. Oliver, *Collections, S. J.*, p. 62.

The Chancery suits make clear for the first time the identity of 'Geo. Buck, Gent.' who published in 1635 *The Great Plantagenet*, a mere reworking of Buc's *Eclog*, and in 1646 the *History of Richard the Third*, 'By Geo: Buck Esquire.' Ritson naturally concluded that Buc's pastoral was changed and published by 'some fellow who assume'd his name,' while Malone on the other hand corrected the error that Buc wrote 'the celebrated *History of King Richard the Third*; which was written above twenty years after his death, by George Buck, Esq., who was, I suppose, his son.' [1] The editor was in fact his great-nephew, who, as we have seen, had secured a part of his papers. If we look for further evidence to confirm this, it can be found in verses before *The Great Plantagenet*, 'To his deserving Friend Maister *George Buc*,' by George Bradley. Bradley was of George's own town of Louth, of which he was Warden in the year he died, 1663. [2] Stephen Buck the elder had bequeathed to his grandson William 'ye markytstead wch I bought of Mr Bradley.'

Another friend who contributed laudatory verses was Robert Codrington, the translator of Ruggle's *Ignoramus*. To Codrington's works listed in the *D.N.B.* may be added his elegy in *Additional MS.* 37484, 'Teares on the Death of Edward, Lord Coke,' dedicated to Coke's daughter, Mrs. Anne Sadleir, and his autograph manuscript poems on the death of O'Brien, Earl of Thomond, in 1639. [3] Pride of place among the verses, however, went to those of '*O.Rovrke*,' 'To his noble Friend Maister *George Buck* upon his Poësie.' This was no less a person than The O'Rourke,

1 *Bibliotheca Poetica*, p. 146; *Variorum*, III, 59. Chalmers corrected Malone on this as on many other points which Boswell did not set right in the *Variorum*, pointing out that the authorship was proved by Buc's MS. (*Supplemental Apology*, p. 204).
2 *Harl. Soc.*, L, 170; Goulding, *Louth Old Corporation Records*, p. 21.
3 *MS. Rawlinson poet.* 96; cf. C. W. James, *Chief Justice Coke*, pp. 41–49.

who was well provided with noble friends if one may judge
by his verses 'To his noble friend Captaine Iohn Smith'
before *True Travels*, 1629.   Grandson of Sir Brian-na-
Murtha, 'the proudest man living on earth,' who was executed at Tyburn in 1591 (cf. *D.N.B.*), Brian O'Rourke was
brought up at Magdalen, Oxford, and at the Middle
Temple, where a 'brable' on St. Patrick's Day landed him
in the Gatehouse, and he spent most of the next ten years
either there (in a dungeon with his hands manacled to a
post) or in the Fleet, the King's Bench, the Marshalsea, or
the Tower, whence he wrote rhyming petitions to the King
for his freedom.   He was so unfortunate as to own most of
County Leitrim, which the Crown desired that it might
'plant it with civill men.'   Because his father had omitted
the slight formality of killing his wife's first husband before marrying her, Brian was declared a bastard.   Thus
passed the estates of his ancestors the Princes of Breffny.[1]

The career of George Buck offers a curious study in
literary dishonesty, for George, while following the bent
of his father and his great-uncle John the forgers, was more
delicate in his methods.   He plays hide-and-seek with his
conscience in the dedication of the poem to Chief Justice
Finch and of the *History* to Philip Earl of Pembroke (in
place of Arundel, who died in Padua a few days before the
book received its imprimatur).   In the first he says that he
is but like a young limner, copying an old painting, and to
Pembroke he writes of 'Having collected these papers out
of their dust'; yet after these casual phrases he speaks of
the works as though they were his own, calling the *History*
'the kindlings and scintillations of a modest Ambition.'
Careful not to assert his authorship, he manages to imply
it; and it is assumed in the verses of his friends.   If anyone

1 *S. P. Ir. 1615–25*, pp. 264–265, 401; *S. P. Ir. Add. 1625–60*, p. 99; *A. P. C.*
1616–17, pp. 66, 346.

found him out and objected to the title-pages, he could say that the printer had indeed forgot to give the author his knighthood, or that after all he had made a new work out of the old. He did add several stanzas to the poem, and throughout brought it up to date, as by stopping to shed a tear for Prince Henry, and of course making James give way to 'bright Charles his waine.' King Arthur yields to Neptune, and Richard III vanishes entirely. A few additions suggest Sir George rather than George, such as an excursus on the divers significations of 'gentle,' and a separate poem on Henry II, which George may have recast in couplets. His chief care in both books was to remove those personal references that might give him away: thus in the *History* he leaves out Buc's mention of having translated part of Ariosto before Haryngton, and where Buc says that for certain information he went to Sir William Dethick, principal King at Arms (until 1604), George changes 'Dethick' to 'Segar.'

The first name can still be read, though erased, in a manuscript of the *History* in George's hand with a signed dedication to Sir John Jacob, one of the farmers of the King's customs.[1] The dedication, which interweaves phrases from Buc's to Arundel, mentions that 'you pleased to receaue my poore translation of *Lipsius*.' This is now at Cambridge: 'Iustus Lipsius his two bookes de Constantia englished by George Bucke Esq.,' dated 1638.[2] The *Egerton MS.*, instead of being written for Sir George about 1619–20 (as Mr. Marcham supposed), was therefore written by George Buck and presented to Jacob after 1638 and probably before 1642, when Parliament confined him to Crosby House as a delinquent. Jacob was a rich East

1 *Egerton MS.* 2216, f. 86.
2 M. R. James, *Western MSS. in the Library of Trinity College, Cambridge*, III, 201.

India merchant who had the privilege of supplying the
King with spices, in succession to his father Abraham, and
served as commissioner for the Caribbee Isles and for the
Virginia tobacco-planters. It is he who appears in the
Lismore Papers, where Grosart has the frank note: 'Sir
John Jacob — Unknown to Editor.' [1]

Even before 1635 young George had succeeded in
marketing a manuscript of the *Eclog*, dedicated to Sir
John Borough, Garter, and therefore after Segar's death
in 1633.[2] Evidently he made what profit he could by
private copies before publishing either work, determined
to derive an income, if not from his godfather's land, then
from his literary estate. It is significant that in the *Egerton MS*. he has to clear himself from his shrewd customer-
patron's 'former doubt' by swearing deeply that 'but for
my rough papers there is no Copy saue this.' The fact that
at least three more of his copies of the *History* survive indicates that he considered a unique manuscript to be one
of those good things of which there can never be too many.
Additional MS. 27422, containing only the first two books,
'by Geo: Buck: esq^r.,' has no dedication. Mr. Marcham
quotes from another manuscript in private hands; but he
has overlooked one of the most interesting of Buck's trans-
scripts, *Malone MS*. 1 in the Bodleian. This is dedicated
'To the right hono:^{ble} and noblest Patron of Learning and
Arts Thomas vicounte Alesbourough Lo: Keeper of y^e
great Seale of England.' But Lord Aylesborough (he was
never a viscount) was the same Sir Thomas Coventrye who
in 1624 had denounced Stephen Buck as a forger and as an
ally of the felonious and earless John Buck. George was too
young to remember the incident, and in any case he felt con-

---

1 *S. P. D. Chas.* I, 492/45; *S. P. Colonial*; *Lismore Papers*, 2nd ser., II, 497;
  Harl. Soc., XVII, 4.
2 'Δαφνιϲ: or The Polyanthine Ghirland. by George Buc. gent.,' *MS. Rawlinson
  poet.* 105 (Madan, *Summary Catalogue of Western MSS. in the Bodleian*, III, 303).

fident that no one was likely to find out the secret of the *History*; besides, he was on the windy side of the law. Cleverer than the rest of a too clever family, he had thought up what Chicago would call a racket of his own, which had never been anticipated by the makers of statutes.

The manuscript of Δαφνις is signed in the dedication, as on the title-page, 'George Buc,' but when he published it in 1635 as *The Great Plantagenet* it was 'By Geo. Buck, Gent.,' though his friend Bradley still uses the form 'Buc.' It was evidently not until after exhausting this source of revenue that he turned to the more arduous task of copying out the five books of the *History*, in the manuscripts of which he has advanced himself to the rank of George Buck, Esquire. Lord Coventrye of Aylesborough had held that title since 1628, but the *Malone MS.* was probably presented within a few years before his death in 1639-40, just as the *Egerton MS.* must have been presented to Jacob not long after the Lipsius of 1638. By comparing the successive manuscript versions we are able to follow the descent of the text down to the edition of 1646, thrice reprinted, and to observe how young George gradually changed its complexion by his carefree rewriting and his haphazard efforts to conceal Buc's personal reminiscence.

George's impersonation seems to have been highly successful, and he moved in the best literary society. In the same year in which he published the *History*, he contributed verses to Shirley's *Poems*, resplendent with classical allusion, and calling the author 'dear James.' He has lines before *The Union of Honour* (1640) by James Yorke, a Lincolnshire blacksmith whom he speaks of as his 'countryman.' [1] In a poem prefixed to the Beaumont and Fletcher Folio of 1647 he places Fletcher's Muse beside '*Shakespeare, Chapman*, and applauded *Ben*.'

---

1 This was the basis for Anthony à Wood's statement that Sir George was a native of Lincolnshire (*Athenae Oxonienses*, ed. 1721, I, 38).

VII. QUIETUS EST

Sir George, who had read and criticized in manuscript plays of all these poets, had had his stormy moments with Chapman and no doubt with Jonson; but even Chapman's letter speaks of the many favors Buc has done him in the past. From what we know of his acts as Master, Buc seems to have been not at all a severe censor, but to have executed conscientiously and moderately, rather than with the zeal of Herbert, the duties of a difficult office. Lyly would also, I think, have made a good Master; but his reversion would never have taken effect, since he died in 1606, before Tyllney retired. Jonson was perhaps too independent to have held the office in peace, much as he would have enjoyed prescribing to his rival dramatists, as so good a critic could hardly have resisted doing. He has left us in no doubt as to what would have been his comment on Caliban or the seacoast of Bohemia.[1] If he had succeeded Tyllney in the prime of his career, he would probably never have written some of his best plays. On the whole perhaps it was as well that Elizabeth chose Buc, a gentleman poet and lover of plays, from the point of view of the Court rather than of the professional playwright, and one who had shown the diplomatic qualities necessary to mediate between the players and authority.

Buc expresses his enthusiasm for the theater in his chapter on poets in *The Third University*:[2]

That first and most ancient kind of Poesy the Dramatik, is so liuely expressed and represented vpon the publicke stages & Theaters of this citty, as *Rome* in the *Auge* of her pompe & glorie, neuer saw it better performed (I meane in respect of the action, and art, and not of the cost, and sumptuousnesse) for therein the *Romaynes* exceeded all the nations of the world.

---

1 *Induction to Bartholomew Fair*; *Conversations with Drummond*.
2 Sig. Oooo 1ᵛ.

At the end of his life he spoke scornfully of 'the ignorant, and never understandinge vulgare,' and of the writers of common ballads, pamphlets, and plays, who fed them with false history. This shaft, of course, was aimed at the uncritical acceptance of such popular entertainment as historical fact. His attitude here may be compared with the reason he gives for the censoring of *Barnavelt*. Both spring from his religious devotion to the scholar's guiding star: 'the great & strange power of Verity; & euer to be reverenced.' [1]

Buc, indeed, was born to be a scholar, as all his writings show. By profession, however, he was a courtier, and the conflict of circumstance and natural bent kept him from achievement. The manuscripts he has censored show curiously mingled his reverence for truth and for princes. He was of Bacon's generation, not of Selden's or Milton's. With all its errors, there is none the less something courageous about his loyalty to the memory of the last Plantagenet king, whom all men spoke ill of, and whose defence would never advance him in favor with the Court. His many friends, whose help in his works he took pleasure in acknowledging, were mainly scholars, such men as Selden and Camden, Coke and Lancelot Andrewes. It must have been another of his friends, one who had seen the *History* in manuscript, who in a copy of Ulpian Fulwell's *Flower of Fame* inserted a note on Buc's work, 'which hee hath (with special knowledge) written in King Richard's defence against all his malicious foes,' and spoke of him as 'the thrice noble and famous scoller S^r. G. Buc.' [2] In the proposal which Buckingham introduced into the House of Lords for the foundation of an English Academy, 'Sir George Buc, Master of the Revels' followed Sir Fulke

1 *Tiber. E.* x, f. 185.
2 Chalmers, *Supplemental Apology*, p. 206.

Greville in the first list of twenty-five 'living persons fit to
keep up and celebrate that Round Table.'¹   The last and
best witness is Camden, who in the *Britannia* wrote of
him as 'Georgius Buc non minus maioribus quam bonis
studijs clarus,' and again, 'vir literate doctus & qui (iuuat
enim profiteri per quos profeci) multa in historijs obser-
uauit, & me edocuit.' ²

1 Oldys at first attributed the project to Buc, but later manuscripts bear the
   pseudonym of Edmund Bolton (*Archaeologia*, I, xxii; XXXII, 135).
2 Ed. 1600, sigg. C 5, Aaa2ᵛ. In 1607 the last words become, '& candide im-
   pertijt'; in 1610, 'and gently imparted the same to mee.'

PEDIGREE

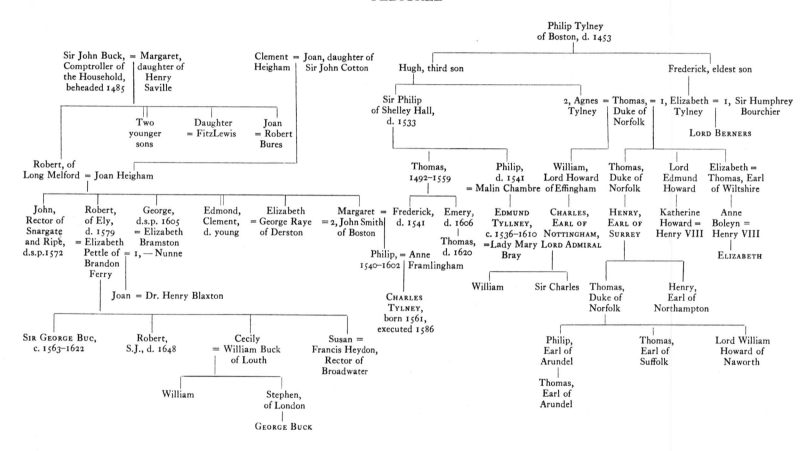

Philip Tylney
of Boston, d. 1453

Sir John Buck, = Margaret,
Comptroller of | daughter of
the Household, | Henry
beheaded 1485 | Saville

Clement = Joan, daughter of
Heigham | Sir John Cotton

Hugh, third son

Frederick, eldest son

Sir Philip
of Shelley Hall,
d. 1533

2, Agnes = Thomas, = 1, Elizabeth = 1, Sir Humphrey
Tylney | Duke of | Tylney | Bourchier
| Norfolk |

LORD BERNERS

Two
younger
sons

Daughter
= FitzLewis

Joan
= Robert
Bures

Robert, of
Long Melford = Joan Heigham

Thomas,
1492–1559
= Malin Chambre

Philip,
d. 1541

William,
Lord Howard
of Effingham

Thomas,
Duke of
Norfolk

Lord
Edmund
Howard

Elizabeth =
Thomas, Earl
of Wiltshire

John,
Rector of
Snargate
and Ripe,
d.s.p.1572

Robert,
of Ely,
d. 1579
= Elizabeth
Pettle of
Brandon
Ferry

George,
d.s.p. 1605
= Elizabeth
Bramston
= 1, — Nunne

Edmond,
Clement,
d. young

Elizabeth
= George Raye
of Derston

Margaret = Frederick,
= 2, John Smith | d. 1541
of Boston |

Emery,
d. 1606

EDMUND
TYLLNEY,
c. 1536–1610
= Lady Mary
Bray

CHARLES,
EARL OF
NOTTINGHAM,
LORD ADMIRAL

HENRY,
EARL OF
SURREY

Katherine
Howard =
Henry VIII

Anne
Boleyn =
Henry VIII

Thomas,
d. 1620

ELIZABETH

Philip, = Anne
1540–1602 | Framlingham

Joan = Dr. Henry Blaxton

CHARLES
TYLNEY,
born 1561,
executed 1586

William

Sir Charles

Thomas,
Duke of
Norfolk

Henry,
Earl of
Northampton

SIR GEORGE BUC,
c. 1563–1622

Robert,
S.J., d. 1648

Cecily
= William Buck
of Louth

Susan =
Francis Heydon,
Rector of
Broadwater

Philip,
Earl of
Arundel

Thomas,
Earl of
Suffolk

Lord William
Howard of
Naworth

William

Stephen,
of London

Thomas,
Earl of
Arundel

GEORGE BUCK

INDEX

INDEX

Academy, English, 506
Acolastus, 466 n.
Aconty, Jacobo, 293
Adams, George, 230
Adams, Thomas, 490 n.
Adderley, Ralph, 27
Adkyns, Francis, 401, 406
Admiral's Men, 479 n.
Africa, 16, 22
Albany, William, 276
Aldred, Joan, *see* Lodge, Joan
Aldred, Solomon, 146 f.
Alexander Neapolitanus, 466
Alfaro, Gregorio de, 466
Allen, George, 178
Allen, George, 'monyer,' 142
Allen, William, 385 f., 401, 406
Alleyn, Edward, 108, 131, 135
Allington, Jane, 99 f.
Allison, Henry, 52
Allison, Thomas, 52
Allthropp, George, 406
Aluori, 260
Alva, Duke of, 452
Amalteo, Giambattista, 247
America, 16, 232, 502
Ancre, Marquis d', 468
Andrewes, Lancelot, 505
Andrews, Mary, 369, 371 ff., 396 f.
Anne of Austria, 452 n.
Antelope in Holborn, 398
Antiquarian Society, 456
Antonio, 22, 103
Ardier, Henry, 342
Ariosto, *Orlando Furioso*, 234, 466, 501
Aristotle, 466
Art of English Poesy, 476
Arthur, 454, 501
Arundel, Earl of, *see* Howard
Arundell of Wardour, Thomas, Lord, 472
Ascham, Roger, *The Schoolmaster*, 427, 432; *Toxophilus*, 455

Asheley, Henry, 406
Ashley, Sir Anthony, 428
Astley, John, 46 f.
Astley, Sir John, 482, 495
Aston, Sir William, 27
Atkinson, Bridget, 274
Atkinson, Edward, Jr., 270, 274 ff., 307, 309, 324 f.
Atkinson, Edward, Sr., 274
Atkinson, Edward, III, 274 n.
Atkinson, Elizabeth, 274
Atkinson, James, 274
Atkinson, John, 274
Atkinson, John, grocer, 274 f.
Atkinson, Mary, 274; *see also* Bryskett, Mary
Atkinson, Vincent, 274
Aubigny, Lord, *see* Stewart
Audley, Lord, *see* Touchet
Aylmer family, 422
Aylmer, John, 421
Aylmer, Judith, 421
Aylmer, Samuel, 421
Ayloffe, Camilla, 356 f.
Ayloffe, Guicciardine, 350, 356 f.
Ayloffe, Jane, 356
Ayloffe, Lucrece, 356
Ayloffe, Mildred, 350, 356
Ayloffe, Sir Thomas, 315 f., 327, 346, 351 ff., 355–357
Ayloffe, Thomas, 357
Ayloffe, Sir William, 356 f.
Ayloffe, William, 55, 350, 356
Ayloffe, William, Justice, 355 f.

B., G., 422 f.; *The Famous History of St. George*, 420
Backhouse, Emma, 290 n., 291
Backhouse, Nicholas, 290 n., 291
Bacon family, 422
Bacon, Anthony, 219, 328
Bacon, Francis, 188 f., 292, 299, 301, 304 f., 412, 425, 441, 505

Bradley, George, 499, 503
Bradshawe, Ralph, 406
Bramston, Elizabeth, 418
Bramston, Sir John, 418
Branch, John, 36
Brasenose College, 224, 228
Breffny, Princes of, 500
Breton, Anne, 448
Breton, Nicholas, 448 .
Breton, William, 448
Brockett, Anthony, 273
Bromely, Elizabeth, 272
Brook, Ralph, 476
Browne, Sir Anthony, 351, 353, 355
Browne, Beatrice, see Lyly, Beatrice
Browne, Christopher, 214
Browne, John, 175 ff., 196 ff., 210 f.
Browne, Sir Richard, 183, 214 f.
Browne, Thomas, 351, 353
Browne, William, 247; *Britannia's Pastorals*, 451
Brownles, William, 201 ff., 206 f.
Brunker, Sir Henry, 141
Bruschetto, see Bryskett
Bryskett, Anthony, 254, 269 f., 273, 290 f.
Bryskett, Anthony, Governor of Montserrat, 280
Bryskett, Edward, 258 n.
Bryskett, Elizabeth, 254, 270
Bryskett, Elizabeth, daughter of Lodowick, 258 f.
Bryskett, Ellen, 255
Bryskett, Francis, 269
Bryskett, Henry, 254, 260, 273
Bryskett, Jane, 272
Bryskett, Joan, 270 f., 273, 294, 400
Bryskett, Lodowick, 243–273, 302, 314, 319, 338, 357 ff.; *Discourse of Civil Life* 245, 255 f.; *The Mourning Muse of Thestylis*, 245, 247–251; *Pastoral Aeglogue*, 245, 251–253
Bryskett, Lucrece, 179, 254, 257 f., 268, 270 f., 273 f., 290–327, 352
Bryskett, Mary, 270 f., 274, 300, 307, 309
Bryskett, Michael, 254, 256 n., 258, 260, 276 ff., 281–289, 300, 302 ff., 309 ff.

Bryskett, Philip, 258
Bryskett, Sebastian, 254, 257, 268, 271f., 302
Bryskett, Thomas, 254, 260, 278–281, 300, 322
Buc, Sir George, 411–506; *The Baron*, 412; *Commentaries*, 431; *Eclog*, 412, 438, 454 ff., 458, 474, 499, 502 f.; *The History of the Life and Reign of Richard III*, 412, 421, 430, 438, 454, 466, 474 ff., 495, 500 ff.; *Poetica*, 413; *The Third University of England*, 412, 420 f., 456, 465, 475, 504 f.
Buccleuch, see Scott
Buchanan, George, 247
Buck, Cecily, 485, 488
Buck, Clement, 417
Buck, Edmond, 417
Buck, Elizabeth, 417
Buck, Elizabeth, wife of Stephen, 488
Buck, George, Gentleman of the Chapel, 417 f., 420
Buck, George, son of Stephen, 474, 484 f., 488, 491, 499 ff.
Buck, Joan, 421
Buck, John, 417 f.
Buck, John, alias Blount, alias Watson, 496 ff.
Buck, Sir John, Comptroller of the Household, 415, 421, 453
Buck, Sir John, of Harthill, 415
Buck, Sir John, naval officer, 415
Buck, Sir John, Provost Marshal, 428
Buck, Joscelin de, 415
Buck, Laurence, 415
Buck, Margaret, 416 f., 440 f., 445, 447 f.
Buck, Robert, of Ely, 417 ff.
Buck, Robert, of Long Melford, 415 ff.
Buck, Robert, S. J., 419 f., 473, 483, 485, 488, 490 f., 496 ff.
Buck, Robert, forger, 498
Buck, Stephen, of London, 482, 485, 488 ff., 502
Buck, Stephen, of Louth, 486 ff., 497, 499
Buck, Walter de, 414 f., 454, 457
Buck, William, Sr., 485 f., 488
Buck, William, Jr., 488, 499

DATE DUE